The Ethnography of Communication

Language in Society

GENERAL EDITOR

Peter Trudgill, Chair of English Linguistics, University of Fribourg

ADVISORY EDITORS

J. K. Chambers, Professor of Linguistics, University of Toronto

Ralph Fasold, Professor of Linguistics, Georgetown University

William Labov, Professor of Linguistics, University of Pennsylvania

Lesley Milroy, Professor of Linguistics, University of Michigan, Ann Arbor

The Ethnography of Communication

AN INTRODUCTION

Third Edition

Muriel Saville-Troike

Blackwell Publishing

350 Main Street, Malden, MA 02148-5018, USA
108 Cowley Road, Oxford OX4 1JF, UK
550 Swanston Street, Carlton South, Melbourne, Victoria 3053, Australia
Kurfürstendamm 57, 10707 Berlin, Germany

First published 1982
Second edition published 1989
Third edition published 2003 by Blackwell Publishing Ltd

Library of Congress Cataloging-in-Publication Data

Saville-Troike, Muriel, 1936–
The ethnography of communication : an introduction / Muriel Saville-Troike. – 3rd ed.
p. cm. – (Language in society ; 3)
Includes bibliographical references and index. ISBN 0-631-22841-1 (alk. paper) –
ISBN 0-631-22842-X (pbk. : alk. paper)
1. Sociolinguistics. 2. Language and culture. I. Title. II. Language in
society (Oxford, England) ; 3.
P40 .S26 2003
306.44–dc21   2002006271

A catalogue record for this title is available from the British Library.

Set in 10½ on 12pt Ehrhardt
by Graphicraft Limited, Hong Kong
Printed and bound in the United Kingdom
by MPG Books Ltd, Bodmin, Cornwall

For further information on
Blackwell Publishing, visit our website:
http://www.blackwellpublishing.com

Contents

Preface

Any attempt such as this to present a synthesis of the growing field of the ethnography of communication is necessarily indebted to many people, as the bibliography will attest. Most of all I am indebted to Dell Hymes, who is truly the father of the field. While I have drawn heavily on the ideas of Hymes and others, responsibility for the formulation presented here must remain my own.

I would like to express my sincere appreciation to students at Georgetown University, the University of Illinois, and the University of Arizona who have served both as source and trial audience for much of this book. The names of those who have provided examples for the languages or countries indicated are listed at the beginning of the bibliography. In a few cases where the information might be politically sensitive, I have intentionally omitted the source; any other omissions are with my regrets and apologies.

Many scholars have made substantial contributions to the development and application of the ethnography of communication since the second edition of this book was published in 1989. These advances are reflected in this third edition by the addition of approximately 250 titles to the list of references, and by the addition of almost 40 languages to a comparative base for the analysis of patterns of communicative phenomena. The most extensive revisions have been made, first, in redefining the basic concepts of *communicative competence* and *speech community* to emphasize their dynamic nature and to give more consideration to multilingual individuals and groups, and second, in the addition of entirely new chapters on contrasts in patterns of communication (chapter 5) and on politeness, power, and politics (chapter 8).

The addition of chapter 5 extends methods of data collection and analysis to larger units of communication than those previously addressed, and to interaction which crosses traditional boundaries of community and culture. This extension results primarily from my application of the ethnography of communication to teaching and research in the domain of comparative rhetoric; it has been particularly enlightened by collaboration with my late colleague Donna M. Johnson and by input from many students with crosscultural knowledge and experience, as well as from other colleagues who have interdisciplinary interests which span linguistics, anthropology, sociology, psychology, and education.

The addition of chapter 8 acknowledges the ever-increasing influence and importance of critical approaches to sociolinguistic and ethnographic analyses, and reflects my own interests in the potential applications of this field to the delivery of social services, minority language education, and language planning. I feel strongly that scholars of language have an ethical responsibility both to the subjects and to the consumers of their research, and I have intended hereby to strengthen that message.

Preparing this edition 20 years after the first has highlighted for me how much progress has been made in integrating analyses of language with other aspects of social life, and in considering communication as praxis. In 1982 I concluded that "the effort to fulfill this task may barely be said to have begun." In 2002 I now conclude, "I am very pleased to be saying how much progress has been made, and to recognize the promise of future research."

1

Introduction

Ethnography is a field of study which is concerned primarily with the description and analysis of culture, and linguistics is a field concerned, among other things, with the description and analysis of language codes. In spite of long-standing awareness of the interrelationship of language and culture, the descriptive and analytic products of ethnographers and linguists traditionally failed to deal with this interrelationship. Even anthropological linguists and linguistic anthropologists until the 1960s typically gave little attention to the fact that the uses of language and speech in different societies have patterns of their own which are worthy of ethnographic description, comparable to – and intersecting with – patterns in social organization and other cultural domains. The realization of this omission led Dell Hymes to call for an approach which would deal with aspects of communication which were escaping both anthropology and linguistics.

With the publication of his essay "The ethnography of speaking" in 1962, Hymes launched a new synthesizing discipline which focuses on the patterning of communicative behavior as it constitutes one of the systems of culture, as it functions within the holistic context of culture, and as it relates to patterns in other component systems. The *ethnography of communication*, as the field has come to be known since the publication of a volume of the *American Anthropologist* with this title (Gumperz and Hymes 1964), has in its development drawn heavily upon (and mutually influenced) sociological concern with interactional analysis and role identity, the study of performance by anthropologically oriented folklorists, and the work of natural-language philosophers. In combining these various threads of interest and theoretical orientation, the ethnography of communication has become an emergent discipline, addressing a largely new order of information in the structuring of communicative behavior and its role in the conduct of social life.

As with any science, the ethnography of communication has two foci: particularistic and generalizing. On the one hand, it is directed at the description and understanding of communicative behavior in specific cultural settings, but it is also directed toward the formulation of concepts and theories upon which to build a global metatheory of human communication. Its basic approach does not involve a list of facts to be learned so much as questions to be asked, and means for finding out answers. In order to attain the goal of understanding both the particular and the general, a broad range of data from a large variety of communities is needed.

A major early contribution to the field included an outline of information to be collected in doing ethnographies of communication, by Dell Hymes, Joel Sherzer, Regna Darnell, and others (1967), and this served as a guide for the scope and organization of the first edition of this book in 1982. Other major contributors to the development of the field have included John Gumperz, Dan Slobin, Richard Bauman, Susan Philips, Susan Ervin-Tripp, Shirley Brice Heath, and Ben Blount. Hymes's influence has been so pervasive that it is impossible to specifically credit each of the concepts and visions for which he was initially responsible, and which inform this book and the work of others in various ways.

Scope and Focus

The subject matter of the ethnography of communication is best illustrated by one of its most general questions: what does a speaker need to know to communicate appropriately within a particular speech community, and how does he or she learn to do so? Such knowledge, together with whatever skills are needed to make use of it, is *communicative competence*. The requisite knowledge includes not only rules for communication (both linguistic and sociolinguistic) and shared rules for interaction, but also the cultural rules and knowledge that are the basis for the context and content of communicative events and interaction processes. Each of these components will be further delineated in the chapters which follow.

The focus of the ethnography of communication is the *speech community*, the way communication within it is patterned and organized as systems of communicative events, and the ways in which these interact with all other systems of culture. A primary aim of this approach is to guide the collection and analysis of descriptive data about the ways in which social meaning is conveyed: "If we ask of any form of communication the simple question what is being communicated? the answer is: information from the social system" (Douglas 1971: 389). This makes the ethnography of communication a mode of inquiry which carries with it substantial content.

Among the basic products of this approach are ethnographic descriptions of ways in which speech and other channels of communication are used in diverse communities, ranging from tribal groups in Africa and the Amazon regions, to nomadic herdsmen, to highly industrialized peoples in Europe, Asia, and North America. The priority which the ethnography of communication places on modes and functions of language is a clear point of departure from the priorities announced for linguistics by Chomsky: "if we hope to understand human language and the psychological capacities on which it rests, we must first ask what it is, not how, or for what purpose it is used" (1968: 62).

Hymes repeatedly emphasizes that what language is cannot be separated from how and why it is used, and that considerations of use are often prerequisite to recognition and understanding of much of linguistic form. While recognizing the necessity to analyze the code itself and the cognitive processes of its speakers and hearers, the ethnography of communication takes language first and foremost as a socially situated cultural form, which is indeed constitutive of much of culture itself. To accept a lesser scope for linguistic description is to risk reducing it to triviality, and to deny any possibility of understanding how language lives in the minds and on the tongues of its users.

Method

"Doing ethnography" in another culture involves first and foremost field work, including observing, asking questions, participating in group activities, and testing the validity of one's perceptions against the intuitions of natives. Research design must allow an openness to categories and modes of thought and behavior which may not have been anticipated by the investigator. The ethnographer of communication cannot even presuppose what a speech community other than his own may consider to be "language," or who or what may "speak" it: "language" for the Ojibwa includes thunder; dogs among the Navajo are said to understand Navajo; the Maori regard musical instruments as able to speak; and drums and shells are channels through which supernatural forces are believed to speak to members of the Afro-Cuban Lucumí religious cult.

Ethnography by no means requires investigating only "others": one's own speech community may be profitably studied as well. Here, however, discovering patterned behavior which operates largely unconsciously for the native investigator presents quite different problems for "objectivity." One of the best means by which to gain understanding of one's own "ways of speaking" is to compare and contrast these ways with others, a process that can reveal that many of the communicative practices assumed to be "natural" or "logical" are in fact as culturally unique and conventional as the language code itself. A valuable by-product which emerges from this process is an essential feature of all ethnography: a deeper understanding of cultural relativism.

Complete escape from subjectivity is never possible because of our very nature as cultural animals; however, the constraints and guidelines of the methodology are intended to minimize our perceptual and analytical biases. The tradition of participant-observation is still basic for all ethnography, but it may be augmented by a variety of other data collection and validation procedures depending on the focus of investigation and the relation of the investigator to the speech community being studied.

Historical Background

Ethnographic study has been at the core of anthropology virtually since its inception, both in Britain and America. The American tradition, begun by Franz Boas and Alfred Kroeber, tended toward a somewhat static presentation of cultural patterns and artifacts which was sometimes criticized as the "trait list approach." The British tradition, which came to be called "functionalist," was developed along two rather different orientations by A. R. Radcliffe-Brown and Bronislaw Malinowski, both of which strongly influenced American anthropology. The British tradition, especially following Malinowski, was much concerned with the social and cultural "meaning" of actions, events, objects, and laws as they functioned within the immediate or larger cultural context.

North American anthropologists, beginning with Boas, were primarily concerned with preparing ethnographic descriptions of Native American cultures before they were destroyed or assimilated by European settlers. Even before Boas, however, the Bureau of American Ethnology (BAE) under John Wesley Powell had placed a priority on describing Native American languages and collecting texts, which still serve as a major source of data for comparative studies of languages on the North American continent. Few of the linguistic descriptions from this period go beyond a sketch of the phonological system and grammatical structures (as outlined in Powell 1877; 1880; Boas 1911) and a list of vocabulary items collected according to a schedule distributed by the BAE (e.g., see Powell 1880), but accompanying reports often include observations which are relevant to understanding patterns of communication. In his *Introduction to the Study of Indian Languages*, Powell clearly states his intent to relate the description of language to other aspects of culture:

> It has been the effort of the author to connect the study of language with the
> other branches of anthropology, for a language is best understood when

the habits, customs, institutions, philosophy – the subject-matter of thought embodied in the language – are best known. The student of language should be a student of the people who speak the language; and to this end the book has been prepared, with many hints and suggestions relating to other branches of anthropology. (1880: vi)

One of the earliest sociolinguistic descriptions I can find within this tradition was prepared by a physician, J. B. White, who described Apache greeting behavior in an unpublished manuscript from the 1870s:

Kissing which seems to us natural [as] an expression of affection is never practised by the Apaches – and they seem to have no form of salute or of greeting – when meeting or of taking leave of each other. On one occasion the writer of this – being curious to know what kind of reception an Indian would give his wife and family after an absence from them of several months – placed himself in a position, where he could overlook (without himself being noticed) an Apache's entrance into his dwelling after a long absence. In this instance the Indian simply rode up to his little brush dwelling and dismounted. One of his wives took charge of the horse. [He] approached a fire along side of his hut where his family were collected without exchanging a word to any of them – not even to the wife who had taken the horse. There he stood motionless and speechless for some ten to fifteen minutes when at last he took a seat on the ground and engaged in ordinary conversation without having observed any form of greeting. (Cf. the more recent description of Apache greetings in Basso 1970.)

Occasionally, descriptions of traditional educational practices contained references to training in "speaking well," as in this brief mention of sociolinguistic constraints imposed on girls of the Carrier Indian tribe of Canada: "The stone labret worn by the noble maiden was a perpetual reminder to her that she should speak slowly and with deliberation" (Jenness 1929: 26). Most information on communication beyond the vocabulary lists and structural sketches of the language codes was limited to listings of kinship terms, reflecting social organization and role-relationships within the groups; ethnological dictionaries, indicating plants and animals in the environment and of importance to the culture; and accounts of language origins and attitudes toward language reflected in creation myths and other folkloristic texts.

The American tradition of descriptive linguistics in conjunction with anthropological fieldwork continued with such notable figures as Edward Sapir, and (in spite of the divergence of an "autonomous linguistics") more recently in the work of such Amerindian language scholars as Floyd Lounsbury, Mary Haas, Carl Voegelin, Paul Friedrich, and Dell Hymes.

Ethnography underwent a period of decline within anthropology during the middle years of the last century as values began to favor more "scientific" studies of social structure and issue-oriented research. There was a resurgence of interest, however, deriving from Goodenough's cognitive reformation of the concept of culture, and in the wave of growing disenchantment with behaviorism. Observed behavior was recognized as a manifestation of a deeper set of codes and rules, and the task of ethnography was seen as the discovery and explication of the rules for contextually appropriate behavior in a community or group; in other words, culture was conceived to be what the individual needs to know to be a functional member of the community.

Concurrent with this latter development in anthropology was the introduction of interactionist and cognitive orientations in sociology by Goffman and Cicourel, which focused attention on the processes by which members of a community negotiate relations, outcomes, and meanings, and construct new realities and meanings as they do so. Hymes reports that he and others who were advancing "a social approach to language" during this period were influenced by developments in European linguistics:

> Some of us with interest in the Prague School saw its attention to a range of functions and factors (e.g. Jakobson 1960) as healthy and desirable. That was a stimulus to me, in any case, seeming to provide a basis in linguistics itself for the study of language as organized as a part of social life. (2000: 313)

The convergent interest in sociology and linguistics, and the description of language use in a social context, raised serious questions about the autonomy of linguistics and the "ideal speaker-hearer" in the "completely homogeneous speech-community" (Chomsky 1965: 3), central concepts in the dominant theoretical model of American linguistics during the 1960s. By the end of that decade, merely accounting for *what* can (and cannot) be said in a language, but not *when*, *where*, *by whom*, *to whom*, *in what manner*, and *under what particular social circumstances* it can (or cannot) be said, came to be considered inadequate as a goal for linguistics by many linguists, and by all identifying themselves as "sociolinguists."

Significance

While the goals of ethnography are at least in the first instance descriptive, and information about diverse "ways of speaking" is a legitimate contribution to knowledge in its own right, the potential significance of the ethnography of communication goes far beyond a mere cataloging of facts about communicative behavior.

For anthropology, the ethnography of communication extends understandings of cultural systems to language, at the same time relating language to social organization, role-relationships, values and beliefs, and other shared patterns of knowledge and behavior which are transmitted from generation to generation in the process of socialization/enculturation. Further, it contributes to the study of cultural maintenance and change, including acculturation phenomena in contact situations, and may provide important clues to culture history.

For psycholinguistics, the ethnography of communication means that studies of language acquisition must now not only recognize the innate capacity of children to learn to speak, but must account for how particular ways of speaking are developed in particular societies in the process of social interaction. Experimental design can no longer presume that mothers are primary caregivers in all societies, for example, nor can a researcher assume that the presence of an observer (and a tape recorder) will distort data comparably in all settings among all groups. Any study of language pathologies outside of one's own speech community must include culture-specific information on what is considered "normal" and "aberrant" performance within the other group. Claims about universal strategies and processes need to be tested against descriptive data from other cultures, and such cross-cultural research requires the openness and relativism of ethnographic methods.

For sociolinguistic research, which generally involves recording naturalistic speech in various contexts, the potential contribution of this perspective was noted by Gumperz:

> Even after the material has been recorded, it is sometimes impossible to evaluate its social significance in the absence of ethnographic knowledge about social norms governing linguistic choice in the situation recorded. (1970: 9)

Again, the qualitative information which forms an essential part of ethnographies of communication should become an important prerequisite for sampling, data collection, and interpretation in quantitative studies. Experimental design which is based only on the researcher's own cultural presuppositions has no necessary validity in a different speech community.

For the field of applied linguistics, one of the most significant contributions made by the ethnography of communication is the identification of what a second language learner must know in order to communicate appropriately in various contexts in that language, and what the sanctions may be for any violations or omissions. There are also important applications for contrasting whole communicative systems in cross-cultural interaction and translation, and for recognizing and analyzing communicative misunderstandings.

For theoretical linguistics, the ethnography of communication can make a significant contribution to the study of universals in language form and use, as well as to language-specific and comparative fields of description and analysis. Its approach and findings are essential for the formulation of a truly adequate theory of language and linguistic competence.

Throughout this book, an attempt has been made to relate the methods and products of the ethnography of communication to the other disciplines which are concerned with the description, explanation, and application of various aspects of communication. Because the book is included in a series on sociolinguistics, particular emphasis is placed on the relationship of the ethnography of communication to other developments in this field. In particular, the position is taken here that qualitative and quantitative approaches to the study of culturally situated communication are not mutually exclusive, and that each can and should inform the other. While ethnography has tended to be identified exclusively with qualitative approaches, many practitioners today are recognizing the need to extend the boundary to include quantitative data in ethnographic descriptions. Gumperz and others have also stressed the need to look at the larger sociopolitical contexts within which culturally situated communication takes place, as these contexts may determine features of communication in ways that are not evident from a narrow focus on communicative patterns alone. An important development in ethnography and related fields has been emphasis on how sociopolitical contexts may be determined and reinforced by features of communication, as well as determinative of them.

Thus while the ethnography of communication has a unique contribution to make in terms of the questions it asks and its relativistic perspective, its contribution to the description and understanding of culturally constituted patterns of communication will be limited if its methods and findings are not integrated with other descriptive and analytical approaches. It is the nature of ethnography to be holistic in nature, and this should also characterize the disciplinary orientation of its practitioners.

A well-known fable tells of three blind men describing an elephant: to one (feeling the tail) it is like a rope; to one (feeling the side) it is flat and leathery; and to one (feeling the trunk) it is like a long rubber hose. While each perception is accurate so far as it goes individually, they fail to provide an accurate picture of the total animal because there is no holistic perspective. Such an integrative approach seems essential if we are to fulfill Hymes's call to develop an ethnographic model for the study of communication which will help us more fully to understand its role in human affairs.

Organization of the Book

Beyond this introduction, chapter 2 defines and discusses basic terms, concepts, and issues which are central to the ethnography of communication.

Chapter 3 surveys varieties of language which may constitute the communicative repertoire of a group, along with their relationship to social organization and practices, and considerations of selection and use. Chapters 4 and 5 emphasize methods for conducting research in the field: Chapter 4 focuses primarily on the description and analysis of recurrent, bounded units of communication within a single speech community, while chapter 5 extends application of descriptive and analytic procedures to longer stretches of discourse and to cross-cultural communication. Chapter 6 considers various aspects of attitudes toward communicative performance, including discussion of methods which may be used in this area of research and related considerations of language maintenance, shift, and spread. Chapter 7 on acquisition of communicative competence emphasizes the development of communicative knowledge by children and older learners in relation to socialization contexts, processes, and outcomes. Chapter 8 on politeness, power, and politics explores the interaction and reciprocal impact of these constructs with linguistic structure and use. Finally, chapter 9 provides a summary and projection.

2

Basic Terms, Concepts, and Issues

The principal concerns in the ethnography of communication, as these have been defined by Hymes and as they have emerged from the work of others, include the following topics: patterns and functions of communication, nature and definition of speech community, means of communicating, components of communicative competence, relationship of language to world view and social organization, and linguistic and social universals and inequalities.

Patterns of Communication

It has long been recognized that much of linguistic behavior is rule-governed: i.e., it follows regular patterns and constraints which can be formulated descriptively as rules (see Sapir 1994). Thus, sounds must be produced in language-specific but regular sequences if they are to be interpreted as a speaker intends; the possible order and form of words in a sentence is constrained by the rules of grammar; and even the definition of a well-formed discourse is determined by culture-specific rules of rhetoric. Hymes identifies concern for pattern as a key motivating factor in his establishment of this discipline: "My own purpose with the ethnography of speaking was . . . to show that there was patterned regularity where it had been taken to be absent, in the activity of speaking itself" (2000: 314).

Sociolinguists such as Labov (1963; 1966), Trudgill (1974), and Bailey (1976) have demonstrated that what earlier linguists had considered irregularity or "free variation" in linguistic behavior can be found to show regular and predictable statistical patterns. Sociolinguistics and the ethnography of communication are both concerned with discovering regularities in language use, but sociolinguists typically focus on variability in pronunciation and grammatical form, while ethnographers are concerned with how communicative units are organized and how they pattern in a much broader sense of "ways of speaking," as well as with how these patterns interrelate in a systematic way with and derive meaning from other aspects of culture. Indeed, for some, pattern *is* culture: "if we conceive culture as *pattern that gives meaning to social acts and entities* . . . we can start to see precisely *how* social actors enact culture through patterned speaking and patterned action" (Du Bois 2000: 94; italics in the original).

Patterning occurs at all levels of communication: societal, group, and individual (cf. Hymes 1961). At the societal level, communication usually patterns in terms of its functions, categories of talk, and attitudes and conceptions about language and speakers. Communication also patterns according to particular roles and groups within a society, such as sex, age, social status, and occupation: e.g., a teacher has different ways of speaking from a lawyer, a doctor, or an insurance salesman. Ways of speaking also pattern according to educational level, rural or urban residence, geographic region, and other features of social organization.

Some common patterns are so regular, so predictable, that a very low information load is carried even by a long utterance or interchange, though the social meaning involved can be significant. For instance, greetings in some languages (e.g. Korean) may carry crucial information identifying speaker relationships (or attitudes toward relationships). An unmarked greeting sequence such as "Hello, how are you today? Fine, how are you?" has virtually no referential content. However, silence in response to another's greeting in this sequence would be marked communicative behavior, and would carry a very high information load for speakers of English.

Greetings in many languages are far more elaborate than in English (e.g. Arabic, Indonesian, Igbo), but even a lengthy sequence may convey very little information as long as it is unmarked. In all cases, patterned variations can be related to aspects of the social structure or value and belief systems within the respective cultures.

The potential strength of a pattern may be illustrated by the opening sequence of a telephone conversation in English (Schegloff 1968). The ring of the telephone is a summons, and the person who answers must speak first even though the caller knows the receiver has been picked up. (Many people will not pick up the telephone in the middle of a ring because they feel it is an interruption of the summons.) Even an obscene telephone caller generally waits for the person who is answering to say something before the obscenities begin. If someone picks up the telephone and does not say anything, the caller cannot proceed. He or she can either say something like "Hello, hello, anybody there?" as a second summons, or else hang up. The caller may dial back again to repeat the sequence, but not continue if there has not been an appropriate response.

The relationship of form and function is an example of communicative patterning along a different dimension. Asking someone in English if he or she has a pen is readily recognized as a request rather than a truth-value question, for instance, because it is part of the regular structural pattern for requesting things in English; the person who answers "Yes, I do," without offering one is joking, rude, or a member of a different speech community.

Finally, communication patterns at the individual level, at the level of expression and interpretation of personality. To the extent that emotional factors such as nervousness have involuntary physiological effects on the vocal mechanism, these effects are not usually considered an intentional part of "communication" (though they may be if deliberately manipulated, as in acting). An example of a conventional expression of individual emotion (and thus part of patterned communication) is the increased use of volume in speech conveying "anger" in English. A Navajo expressing anger uses enclitics not recognized as emotion markers by speakers of other languages, and a friendly greeting on the street between Chinese speakers may have surface manifestations corresponding to anger for speakers of English. Similarly, American Indian students often interpret Anglo teachers' "normal" classroom projection level as anger and hostility, and teachers interpret students' softer level as shyness or unfriendliness. Perceptions of individuals as "voluble" or "taciturn" are also in terms of cultural norms, and even expressions of pain and stress are culturally patterned: people in an English speech community learn withdrawal or anger, in Japanese nervous laughter or giggling, and in Navajo silence.

Although I have listed societal, group, and individual levels of patterning separately, there is an invisible web of interrelationships among them, and indeed among all patterns of culture. There may very well be general themes that are related to a world view present in several aspects of culture, including language. There are societies that are more direct than others, for instance, and this will be manifested in ways of speaking as well as in belief and value systems. The notion of a hierarchy of control seems to be pervasive in several cultures, and must first be understood in order to explain certain language constraints as well as religious beliefs and social organization (see Witherspoon 1977; Thompson 1978; Watkins 1979).

The concern for pattern has always been basic in anthropology (cf. Benedict 1934; Kroeber 1935; 1944), with interpretations of underlying meaning dependent on the discovery and description of normative structure or design. More recent emphasis on processes of interactions in generating behavioral patterns extends this concern to explanation as well as description.

Communicative Functions

At a societal level, language serves many functions. Language selection often relates to political goals, functioning to create or reinforce boundaries in order to unify speakers as members of a single speech community and to exclude outsiders from intragroup communication. For example, establishing the official use of Hebrew in Israel functioned to unify at this level in building the new nation-state, while the refusal of early Spanish settlers in Mexico to teach the Castilian language to the indigenous population was exclusionary. Members of a community may also reinforce their boundaries by discouraging prospective second language learners, by holding and conveying the attitude that their language is too difficult – or inappropriate – for others to use.

Many languages are also made to serve a social identification function within a society by providing linguistic indicators which may be used to reinforce social stratification, or to maintain differential power relationships between groups. The functions which language differences in a society are assigned may also include the maintenance and manipulation of individual social relationships and networks, and various means of effecting social control. Linguistic features are often employed by people, consciously or unconsciously, to identify themselves and others, and thus serve to mark and maintain various social categories and divisions. The potential use of language to create and maintain power is part of a central topic among ethnographers of communication and other sociolinguists concerned with language-related inequities and inequalities.

At the level of individuals and groups interacting with one another, the functions of communication are directly related to the participants' purposes and needs (Hymes 1961; 1972c). These include such categories of functions as *expressive* (conveying feelings or emotions), *directive* (requesting or demanding), *referential* (true or false propositional content), *poetic* (aesthetic), *phatic* (empathy and solidarity), and *metalinguistic* (reference to language itself).

The list is similar to Searle's (1977a) classes of illocutionary acts (representatives, directives, commissives, expressives, declarations), but there are differences in perspective and scope which separate the fields of ethnography of communication and speech act theory. Among these are the latter's primary focus on form, with the speech act almost always coterminous with sentences in analysis; for ethnographers, the functional perspective has priority in description, and while function may coincide with a single grammatical sentence, it often does not, or a single sentence may serve several functions simultaneously. Further, while speech act theorists generally exclude the metaphorical and phatic uses of language from basic consideration, these constitute a major focus for ethnographic description. Phatic communication conveys a message, but has no referential meaning. The meaning is in the act of communication itself. Much of ritual interaction is included in this category, fully comprising most brief encounters, and at least serving to open and close most longer encounters (Goffman 1971). Not accounting for such functions of communication is ignoring much of language as it is actually used.

The distinction between *intent* and *effect* in function (Ervin-Tripp 1972) is comparable to the difference between *illocutionary* and *perlocutionary* acts in pragmatics (Searle 1969, 1977b). The difference between the functional intent of the speaker and the actual effect on the hearer is part of the notion of functional relativity (Hymes 1972c). Both are relevant to the description and analysis of a communicative event.

While many of the functions of language are universal, the ways in which communication operates in any one society to serve these functions is language specific. The same relative status of two speakers may be conveyed by their choice of pronominal forms in one language; in another, by the distance they stand apart or their body position while speaking; and between bilinguals, even by their choice of which language is used in addressing one another.

The social functions or practices of language provide the primary dimension for characterizing and organizing communicative processes and products in a society; without understanding why a language is being used as it is, and the consequences of such use, it is impossible to understand its meaning in the context of social interaction.

To claim primacy of function over form in analysis is not to deny or neglect the formal structures of communication; rather it is to require integration of function and form in analysis and description. Sentences and even longer strings of discourse are not to be dealt with as autonomous units, but rather as they are situated in communicative settings and patterns, and as they function in society.

Speech Community

Since the focus of the ethnography of communication is typically on the speech community, and on the way communication is patterned and organized within that unit, clearly its definition is of central importance. Many definitions have been proposed (e.g. Hudson 1980: 25–30), including such criteria as shared language use (Lyons 1970), shared rules of speaking and interpretation of speech performance (Hymes 1972c), shared attitudes and values regarding language forms and use (Labov 1972), and shared sociocultural understandings and presuppositions with regard to speech (Sherzer 1975).

Linguists are generally in agreement that a speech community cannot be exactly equated with a group of people who speak the same language, for Spanish speakers in Texas and Argentina are members of different speech communities although they share a language code, and husbands and wives within some speech communities in the South Pacific use quite distinct languages in speaking to one another. Speakers of mutually unintelligible dialects of Chinese identify themselves as members of the same larger speech community (they do indeed share a written code, as well as many rules for appropriate use), while speakers of Spanish, Italian and Portuguese are not members of the same speech community although their languages are to some degree mutually intelligible. Questions arise in deciding if speakers of English from England and the United States (or Canada and Australia, or India and Nigeria) are members of the same speech community. How different must rules of speaking be to be significantly different? Are deaf signers and hearing interpreters members of the same speech community? Answers to such questions are based on history, politics, and group identification, rather than on purely linguistic factors. It is thus useful to distinguish between participating in a speech community and being a member of it; speaking the same language is sufficient (yet not necessary) for some degree of participation, but membership cannot be based on knowledge and skills alone.

All definitions of *community* used in the social sciences include the dimension of shared knowledge, possessions, or behaviors, derived from Latin *communitae* 'held in common,' just as the sociolinguistic criteria for speech community enumerated above all include the word 'shared.' A key question is whether our focus in initially defining communities for study should be on features of shared language form and use, shared geographical and political boundaries, shared contexts of interaction, shared attitudes and values regarding language forms, shared sociocultural understandings and presuppositions, or even shared physical characteristics (e.g., a particular skin color may be considered a requirement for membership in some communities, a hearing impairment for others). The essential criterion for "community" is that some significant dimension of experience be shared, and for "speech community" that the shared dimension be related to ways in which members of the group use, value, or interpret language.

While sociolinguistic research has often focused on the patterning of language practice within a single school, a neighborhood, a factory, or other limited segment of a population, an integrated ethnographic approach would require relating such subgroups to the social and cultural whole. There is no necessary expectation that a speech community will be linguistically homogeneous, nor that it will be a static entity which necessarily encompasses the same membership over time or situations – although degree of fluidity will depend on the nature of bounding features and attitudes concerning their permeability.

At any level of speech community selected for study, the societal functions of language will include the functions served by such bounding features, of *separating*, *unifying*, and *stratifying*. The interactional functions which are present will be dependent on the level of community studied, with a full complement of language functions and domains present only at the level defined as including a range of role opportunities. At this more inclusive level, a speech community need not share a single language, and indeed it will not where roles are differentially assigned to monolingual speakers of different languages in a single multilingual society (e.g. speakers of Spanish and Guaraní in Paraguay, discussed in chapter 3).

An informal typology of speech communities as "soft-shelled" versus "hard-shelled" may be distinguished on the basis of the strength of the boundary that is maintained by language: the "hard-shelled" community has of course the stronger boundary, allowing minimal interaction between members and those outside, and providing maximum maintenance of language and culture.

Speech communities which primarily use one of the world languages are more likely to be "soft-shelled," because it will be known as a second language by many others, and interaction across the boundary will be relatively easy in both directions. A speech community speaking a language with more limited distribution would more likely be "hard-shelled," because relatively few outside the community learn to use it. Educated speakers learn a world language for interaction across the boundary, but this is unidirectional, with outsiders still very restricted in their internal linguistic participation. The most extreme form of a "hard-shelled" community would be one like Mongolia, where members speak a language outsiders do not know, yet few learn a world language for wider communication; another would be the Tewa-speaking San Juan pueblo in New Mexico, where outsiders are forbidden even to hear the language, and only a few insiders traditionally learn either English or Spanish.

Language often serves to maintain the separate identity of speech communities within larger communities, of which their speakers may also be members. Within the United States, for instance, Armenian continues to function in some areas as the language of home, religion, and social interaction among members of the group. Because the Armenians are bilingual and also speak English, they participate fully in the larger speech community, but because outsiders seldom learn Armenian, the language is a barrier which keeps others from participating in their internal social and religious events. A similar situation exists in Syria, where Armenians bilingual in their native language and Arabic participate in two speech communities; these remain separate entities because of the one-way boundary function the Armenian language serves. In cases where individuals and groups belong to more than one speech community, it is useful to distinguish between primary and secondary membership.

On the other hand, there is no necessary reason for a speech community to be geographically contiguous. Armenians in California and Syria may be considered members of the same speech community even if they have little interaction with one another, and (especially with widespread access to telephones and e-mail) individuals and groups who are dispersed may maintain intensive networks of interaction. Largely because of the internet, "virtual" communities of interest have been established world-wide. Even with no face-to-face contact, patterned rules for communication have emerged and become codified.

Individuals, particularly in complex societies, may thus participate in a number of discrete or overlapping speech communities, just as they participate in a variety of social settings. Which one or ones a person orients himself or herself to at any moment – which set of rules he or she uses – is part of the strategy of communication. To understand this phenomenon, it is necessary to recognize that each member of a community has a repertoire of social identities, and each identity in a given context is associated with a number of appropriate verbal and nonverbal forms of expression. It is therefore essential to identify the social categories recognized in a community in order to determine how these are reflected linguistically, and how they define and constrain interpersonal interaction in communicative situations.

The use of the speech community as a basic social unit for study has been criticized by some because of its implicit acceptance of existing social/political boundaries and categories as legitimate entities. One alternative is a more complex model of "nested" speech communities reflecting expanding fields of individuals' interactions and networks (Kerswill 1994; Santa Ana and Parodi 1998). Another is the *discourse community*, which is a flexible grouping of individuals who share rules for "discursive practice." This construct (based on notions from Foucault, e.g. 1972)

> creates a group of compelling unspoken historic rules, which in turn determine in a certain social, economic, geographic or linguistic area what can be said, how it can be expressed, who may speak, where, and under which dominant predictions. A discursive practice oversees the distribution of knowledge and arranges certain ways of speaking into a hierarchy. (Lehtonen 2000: 41–2)

Yet another alternative is the *community of practice*, defined as "a group whose joint engagement in some activity or enterprise is sufficiently intensive to give rise over time to a repertoire of shared practices" (Eckert and McConnell-Ginet 1999: 185; see also Holmes and Meyerhoff 1999). This latter construct seems especially appropriate for the study of processes in the development of norms of interaction within dynamic groups, involving either enculturation or acculturation and sometimes lengthy periods of apprenticeship.

Of particular interest in relation to all of these constructs is how membership involves learning how to use language – the acquisition and extension of communicative competence.

Communicative Competence

Hymes (1966a) observed that speakers who could produce any and all of the grammatical sentences of a language (per Chomsky's 1965 definition of *linguistic competence*) would be institutionalized if they indiscriminately went about trying to do so without consideration of the appropriate contexts of use. *Communicative competence* involves knowing not only the language code but also what to say to whom, and how to say it appropriately in any given situation. Further, it involves the social and cultural knowledge speakers are presumed to have which enables them to use and interpret linguistic forms. Hymes (1974, 1987) augmented Chomsky's notion of linguistic competence (knowledge of systematic potential, or whether or not an utterance is a possible grammatical structure in a language) with knowledge of appropriateness (whether and to what extent something is suitable), occurrence (whether and to what extent something is done), and feasibility (whether and to what extent something is possible under particular circumstances). The concept of communicative competence (and its encompassing congener, social competence) is one of the most powerful organizing tools to emerge in the social sciences in recent years.

Communicative competence extends to both knowledge and expectation of who may or may not speak in certain settings, when to speak and when to remain silent, to whom one may speak, how one may talk to persons of different statuses and roles, what nonverbal behaviors are appropriate in various contexts, what the routines for turn-taking are in conversation, how to ask for and give information, how to request, how to offer or decline assistance or cooperation, how to give commands, how to enforce discipline, and the like – in short, everything involving the use of language and other communicative modalities in particular social settings.

Clear cross-cultural differences can and do produce conflicts or inhibit communication. For example, certain American Indian groups are accustomed to waiting several minutes in silence before responding to a question or taking a turn in conversation, while the native English speakers they may be talking to have very short time frames for responses or conversational turn-taking, and find long silences embarrassing. Conversely, Abrahams (1973) has pointed out that among African Americans conversations may involve several persons talking at the same time, a practice which would violate White middle-class rules of interaction. And as mentioned earlier, even such matters as voice level differ cross-culturally, and speaker intent may be misconstrued because of different expectation patterns for interpretation.

The concept of communicative competence must be embedded in the notion of cultural competence, or the total set of knowledge and skills which speakers bring into a situation. This view is consonant with a semiotic approach which defines culture as meaning, and views all ethnographers (not just ethnographers of communication) as dealing with symbols (e.g. Douglas 1970; Geertz 1973). The systems of culture are patterns of symbols, and language is only one of the symbolic systems in this network. Interpreting the meaning of linguistic behavior requires knowing the meaning in which it is embedded.

Ultimately all aspects of culture are relevant to communication, but those that have the most direct bearing on communicative forms and processes are the social and institutional structure, the values and attitudes held about language and ways of speaking, the network of conceptual categories which results from experiences, and the ways knowledge and skills (including language) are transmitted from one generation to the next and to new members of the group. Shared cultural knowledge is essential to explain the shared presuppositions and judgments of truth value which are the essential undergirdings of language structures, as well as of contextually appropriate usage and interpretation.

While referential meaning may be ascribed to many of the elements in the linguistic code in a static manner, situated meaning must be accounted for as an emergent and dynamic process. Interaction requires the perception, selection, and interpretation of salient features of the code used in actual communicative situations, integrating these with other cultural knowledge and skills, and implementing appropriate strategies for achieving communicative goals.

The phonology, grammar, and lexicon which are the target of traditional linguistic description constitute only a part of the elements in the code used for communication. Also included are the paralinguistic and nonverbal phenomena which have conventional meaning in each speech community, and knowledge of the full range of variants in all elements which are available for transmitting social, as well as referential, information. Ability to discriminate between those variants which serve as markers of social categories or carry other meaning and those which are insignificant, and knowledge of what the meaning of a variant is in a particular situation, are all components of communicative competence.

The verbal code may be transmitted on oral, written, or manual (signed) channels. The relative load carried on each channel depends on its functional distribution in a particular speech community, and thus they are of differential importance in the linguistic repertoire of any individual or society. Full participation in a deaf speech community requires ability to interpret language on the manual channel but not the oral, for instance; a speech community with a primarily oral tradition may not require interpretation of writing; and a speech community which relegates much information flow to the written channel will require literacy skills for full participation. Thus, the traditional linguistic description which focuses only on the oral channel will be too narrow to account for communicative competence in most societies. Although it may cause some terminological confusion, references to *ways of speaking* and *ethnography of speaking* should be understood as usually including a much broader range of communicative behavior than merely speech.

The typical descriptive focus on oral production has tended to treat language as a unidirectional phenomenon. In considering the nature and scope of communicative competence, it is useful to distinguish between *receptive* and *productive* dimensions (Troike 1970); only shared receptive competence is necessary for successful communication. Knowledge of rules for appropriate communicative behavior entails understanding a wide range of language forms, for instance, but not necessarily the ability to produce them. Members of the same community may understand varieties of a language which differ according to the social class, region, sex, age, and occupation of the speaker, but only a few talented mimics will be able to speak them all. In multilingual speech communities, members often share receptive competence in more than one language but vary greatly in their relative ability to speak one or the other.

The following outline summarizes the broad range of shared knowledge that is involved in appropriate communication. From the ethnographer's perspective, this inventory also indicates the range of linguistic, interactional, and cultural phenomena which must ultimately be accounted for in an adequate description and explanation of communicative competence (see also Gumperz 1984; Hymes 1987; Duranti 1988).

1   Linguistic knowledge
    (a)   Verbal elements
    (b)   Nonverbal elements
    (c)   Patterns of elements in particular speech events
    (d)   Range of possible variants (in all elements and their organization)
    (e)   Meaning of variants in particular situations
2   Interaction skills
    (a)   Perception of salient features in communicative situations
    (b)   Selection and interpretation of forms appropriate to specific situations, roles, and relationships (rules for the use of speech)
    (c)   Discourse organization and processes
    (d)   Norms of interaction and interpretation
    (e)   Strategies for achieving goals
3   Cultural knowledge
    (a)   Social structure (status, power, speaking rights)
    (b)   Values and attitudes
    (c)   Cognitive maps/schemata
    (d)   Enculturation processes (transmission of knowledge and skills)

Communicative competence within the ethnography of communication usually refers to the communicative knowledge and skills shared by a speech community, but these (like all aspects of culture) reside variably in its individual members. The shared yet individual nature of competence reflects the nature of language itself, as expressed by von Humboldt (1836):

> While languages are in the ambiguous sense of the word . . . creations of nations, they still remain personal and individual creations of individuals. This follows because they can be produced in each individual, yet only in such a manner that each individual assumes a priori the comprehension of all people and that all people, furthermore, satisfy such expectation.

Considering communicative competence at an individual level, we must additionally recognize that any one speaker is not infrequently a member of more than one speech community – often to different degrees. For individuals who are members of multiple speech communities, which one or ones they orient themselves to at any given moment – which set of social and communicative rules they use – is reflected not only in which segment of their linguistic knowledge they select, but which interaction skills they utilize, and which aspects of their cultural knowledge they activate. The competence of non-native speakers of a language usually differs significantly from the competence of native speakers; the specific content of what an individual needs to know and the skills he or she needs to have depend on the social context in which he or she is or will be using the language and the purposes he or she will have for doing so.

This further emphasizes why the notion of an "ideal speaker-listener, in a completely homogeneous speech-community" (Chomsky 1965: 3) is inadequate for ethnographic purposes. Also, multilingual speakers' communicative competence includes knowledge of rules for the appropriate choice of language and for switching between languages, given a particular social context and communicative intent, as well as for the intralingual shifting among styles and registers which is common to the competence of all speakers. An extension has been made to "intercultural communicative competence," which requires an additional level of metacompetence involving explicit awareness of differential usages and ability to adapt communicative strategies to a variety of cultural situations (Kim 1991). Liu (2001) further extends the construct to "adaptive cultural competence" as a goal for second language learners, which also encompasses social identity negotiation skills and culture-sensitivity knowledge. He argues that such a higher level competence is needed for appropriate and effective social participation of non-native speakers who are in roles of international students or immigrées.

Accounting for the nature of communicative competence ultimately "requires going beyond a concern with Language (capital L) or a language.

It requires a focus on the ways in which people do use language..."
(Hymes 1993: 13). Problems arise when individual competence is judged in
relation to a presumed "ideal" monolingual speech community, or assessed
with tests given in a limited subset of situations which do not represent the
true range of an individual's verbal ability (Hymes 1979b). The problems
are particularly serious ones when such invalid judgments result in some
form of social or economic discrimination against the individuals, such as
unequal or inappropriate educational treatment or job placement. Awareness of the complex nature of communicative competence and the potential
negative consequences of misjudgments is leading to major changes in procedures and instruments for language assessment, but no simple solutions
are forthcoming (see Philips 1983a; Milroy 1987a; Byram 1997).

The Competence of Incompetence

Part of communicative competence is being able to sound appropriately
"incompetent" in a language when the situation dictates. This may be done
to signal deference when interacting with someone of high rank: e.g., in
Burundi, lower ranking persons are expected to speak in a bumbling and
hesitating manner to those of higher rank, but the same individuals speak flu-
ently with peers or others of lower rank than they (Albert 1972). Similarly,
members of a subordinate group in the community may adopt a "powerless
speech style" with members of the dominant group, including women
with men, ethnic minorities with majorities, and children with adults (Giles,
Scherer, and Taylor 1979). Conversely, in Wolof "for the highest of the
nobles incorrectness in certain aspects of speech is considered appropriate,
since high-ranking persons are not supposed to be very skilled at speaking,
at least in terms of superficial elaboration" (Irvine 1973: 40–1).

On some occasions, faking "incompetence" may have practical benefits.
Actors or actresses may cultivate a "sexy" foreign accent to increase box
office receipts, and applicants to at least one federally funded training project
for which limited English proficiency was an entry criterion were caught
cheating downward on the language test used for admission.

In a religious context, such as "speaking in tongues" among charismatic
Christian groups, inarticulateness may be taken as evidence of divine inspiration, proof that the speaker is not in conscious control of what is being
said (Douglas 1970: 109–10). Paradoxically, saying "I don't know what to
say" to someone who is bereaved may be interpreted as the most sincere
expression of deep sympathy.

Speakers of a second language are often well advised not to try to sound
too much like a native. A foreign accent will often allow as yet imperfectly

learned rules of etiquette to be excused as such, while a speaker who has mastered the phonology of a language is assumed to have also mastered all other aspects of its use, and violations are more likely to be interpreted as rudeness or worse. Additional consequences of perfecting pronunciation in a second language may be suspicion or resentment from native speakers if they do not welcome new members, or feelings from the primary speech community that one is being disloyal to it.

Units of Analysis

In order to describe and analyze communication it is necessary to deal with discrete units of some kind, with communicative activities that have recognizable boundaries. The three units suggested by Hymes (1972) are *situation*, *event*, and *act*.

The *communicative situation* is the context within which communication occurs. Examples include a religious service, a court trial, a holiday party, an auction, a train ride, or a class in school. The situation may remain the same even with a change of location, as when a committee meeting or court trial reconvenes in different settings, or it may change in the same location if very different activities go on there at different times. The same room in a university building may successively serve as the site of a lecture, a committee meeting, or a play practice, and a family dwelling may provide the venue for a holiday party. A single situation maintains a consistent general configuration of activities, the same overall ecology within which communication takes place, although there may be great diversity in the kinds of interaction which occur there.

The *communicative event* is the basic unit for descriptive purposes. A single event is defined by a unified set of components throughout, beginning with the same general purpose of communication, the same general topic, and involving the same participants, generally using the same language variety, maintaining the same tone or key and the same rules for interaction, in the same setting. An event terminates whenever there is a change in the major participants, their role-relationships, or the focus of attention. If there is no change in major participants and setting, the boundary between events is often marked by a period of silence and perhaps a change in body position.

Discontinuous events are possible, if one is interrupted and then resumes without change in major components. A conversation between student and professor in an office may be interrupted by a telephone call, for instance. The professor then participates in a different event with the caller, leaving the student "on hold." They may say "Now where were we?" before resuming the first event, but participants can usually continue from the point of interruption. In this case the student has not been an active participant in the intervening event, generally looks elsewhere, and at least pretends not to listen. He or she has essentially left the situation, although physically still present.

Discovering what constitutes a communicative event and what classes of events are recognized within a speech community are a fundamental part of doing ethnography of communication. The designation of some events may be inferred from the fact they are given different labels in the language, and may be identified as categories of talk, but some are not neatly differentiated. However, an important first step in research is determining the existing inventory of labels in the language for such events.

The *communicative ac*t is generally coterminous with a single interactional function, such as a referential statement, a request, or a command, and may be either verbal or nonverbal. For example, not only may a request take several verbal forms (*I'd like a pen* and *Do you have a pen?* as well as *May I please have a pen?*), but it may be expressed by raised eyebrows and a "questioning" look, or by a longing sigh. In the context of a communicative event, even silence may be an intentional and conventional communicative act, and used to question, promise, deny, warn, insult, request, or command (Saville-Troike 1985). The same observable behavior may or may not constitute a communicative act in different speech communities. A belch at the end of a meal is not a communicative act if it is merely a sign of indigestion, but it is a communicative act in societies where one burps to symbolize appreciation and thanks for the meal; the ways stones, shells, or bones configurate when thrown are considered communicative in many parts of the world, but they are not considered potential elements of communication in others.

The study of speech acts within linguistic theory is the basis for this level of analysis, but must be extended to account for a broader range of phenomena within the ethnography of communication, and to allow for possible differences with regard to what segments of language are considered basic functional units by members of different speech communities.

The following examples illustrate the three different units of analysis.

I observed and videotaped a group of limited-English-speaking elementary school students each week over the course of an entire school year in a *communicative situation* that occurred when these children left their regular English-medium classrooms for 30 minutes each day for a common class in English as a Second Language (ESL) (Saville-Troike 1984; Saville-Troike, McClure, and Fritz 1984). Although the composition of the group changed as the result of student illness or family trips and the appointment of a new teacher at midyear, and the specific activities changed with seasonal interests and the students' developing English language proficiency, the overall structure and purpose of the sessions remained the same. Selecting a simple communicative situation such as this in longitudinal and/or comparative research provides a consistent frame wherein the effects of minimal variation in components of communication (e.g. setting, participants, goal) can be observed and interpreted. (These components are discussed in chapter 4.)

Within the ESL situation, the class periods were found to divide into a regular sequence of recurring *communicative events*:

1 Unstructured play
2 Claiming a seat at the large table where the lesson was conducted
3 Opening routines (e.g., *What day is it today?*)
4 Teacher-directed lesson on a targeted language form
5 Follow-up activity (usually involving arts and crafts or a game)
6 Closing routines (e.g., *Time to clean up, See you tomorrow*, etc.)

The event as a unit for analysis is important in part so that observations made at different times will be comparable, and so that generalizations can be made about patterns of communication within a constant context. In the ESL situation I studied, for instance, patterns and forms for communication varied greatly from event to event, and yet they stayed relatively constant for each type of event throughout the year. It was possible, therefore, to analyze the development of students' competence in English and the strategies that they used to achieve different communicative functions within each event; any comparison of student or teacher language forms and rules for language use at different points of the lesson (or in other situations) would have been quite misleading without taking this unit into account.

For example, the word *is* in such sentences as "Today is Monday" or "This is a table," which was used consistently in the ESL opening routines and teacher-directed lessons beginning during the first week of school, was still absent in the speech of several students in all other events (and in the other situations) after weeks and even months of English instruction. Without reference to different event structures, it might appear that this grammatical form occurred randomly, rather than as part of memorized patterns that were used only during teacher – student interaction when the focus was on the form, and not on the content, of communication. Students and teachers also (unconsciously) recognized that organizational rules, such as raising hands and talking one at a time, operated only during certain segments (events) of the class.

In this research, analysis at the level of the *communicative act* made it possible to determine the relative frequency of different communicative functions for students in different events and across time (e.g., warnings and threats to other students declined significantly, and requests for clarification increased) and to compare the linguistic form that was selected within events across time for each type of act (e.g. from gestures and nonspeech sounds used for warnings and threats at the beginning of the year, to holistic routines, to increasing syntactic complexity in English).

A second communication situation I have regularly observed is a Christian religious service. It typically includes these communicative events:

1　Call to worship
2　Reading of scriptures
3　Prayer
4　Announcements
5　Sermon
6　Benediction

Even though a single set of participants is involved (perhaps even a single speaker), and the setting and general purpose remain the same, the change between events is clearly marked by different ways of speaking, different body position for both leader and congregation, and periods of silence or musical interludes. Within the event labelled "prayer," the sequence of communicative acts predictably includes the summons, praise, supplication, thanks, and closing formula.

Robbins describes the clear boundaries of this event as it is enacted in a Papua New Guinea Society:

> Urapmin prayers have discrete beginnings. To begin a prayer, one first asks all of those present to close their eyes. Once people have closed their eyes and thus marked a discrete break with the flow of social life up to that point, the person praying will use one of several formulae to call out to God and mark the formal beginning of the prayer . . . Along with these openings, prayers also have patterned closings, wherein the person praying intones that "I have spoken (or asked) sufficiently and what I have said is true". . . With this ending, eyes open, marking the return to life outside of prayer. (2001: 906)

Categories of Talk

As with the identification of communicative events, labels used by a speech community for categories of talk provide a useful clue to what categories it recognizes and considers salient. The elicitation of labels is one aspect of *ethnosemantics* (also called *ethnolinguistics, ethnoscience, ethnographic semantics,* and *new ethnography*). These may be coterminus with some notions of genre, in that they may serve "as a nexus of interrelationships among the constituents of the speech event and as a formal vantage point on speaking practices" (Bauman 2000: 84).

As a procedure to discover categories of talk, on various occasions when verbal interaction is observed, the ethnographer may ask an informant the equivalent of "What are they doing?" Frake (1969) provides an excellent example in his study of the Philippine Yakan. Their native categories of talk elicited in this manner include *mitin* 'discussion,' *qisun* 'conference,' *mawpakkat* 'negotiation,' and *kukum* 'litigation.' Frake then analyzes each of these categories in terms of their distinctive communicative features, which in this case contrast on the dimensions of focus, purpose, roles, and integrity (the extent to which the activity is perceived as an integral unit).

In a collection of studies on categories in the domain of political oratory (Bloch 1975), ethnographers have elicited labels as part of their procedure for segmenting and organizing political activities into meaningful units for analysis. A listing of some of these illustrates the diverse dimensions along which such units occur: the Melpa speakers in Mt. Hagan, New Guinea, reportedly categorize types of oratory as *el–ik* 'arrow talk' or 'war talk' (the most formal), *ik ek* 'veiled speech' or 'talk which is bent over or folded,' and *ik kwun* 'talk which is straight' (Strathern 1975); communicative event labels for the Maori of New Zealand include *mihimihi* 'greeting speeches,' *whai koorero* 'exchange of speeches,' and *take* or *marae* 'discussion of serious matters' (Salmond 1975); and labels for speech acts in Balinese include *mebetènin ngeraos* 'self-abasement,' *nyelasang* 'statement of common knowledge,' *ngèdèngang pemineh pedidi* 'statement of current speaker's opinion,' and *nyerahand tekèn banjar* 'commitment to follow what the assembly decides' (Hobart 1975). Listings of category labels in English include *conversation, lecture, oratory, gossip, joking, story-telling,* and *preaching.*

Categories of talk in each language have different functional distributions, and most are limited to a particular situation, or involve constraints on who may speak them, or what topic may be addressed. Their description is thus of interest not only because of the linguistic phenomena which distinguish one from another, but also because these categories may provide clues to how other dimensions of the society are segmented and organized.

Since we cannot expect any language to have a perfect metalanguage, the elicitation of labels for categories of talk is clearly not adequate to assure a full inventory and must be supplemented by other discovery procedures, but it is basic to ethnography that the units used for segmenting, ordering, and describing data should begin with the categories of the group which uses them, and may include, but should not be limited to, the a priori categories of the investigator (see Wierzbicka 1985).

Language and Culture

The intrinsic relationship of language and culture is widely recognized, but the ways in which the patterning of communicative behavior interrelates with that of other cultural systems are of interest both to the development of general theories of communication, and to the description and analysis of communication within specific speech communities. Virtually any ethnographic model must take language into account, although many relegate it to a separate section and do not adequately consider its extensive role in a society. The very concept of the evolution of culture is dependent on the capacity of humans to use language for purposes of organizing social cooperation.

There are still questions regarding the extent to which language is shaping and controlling the thinking of its speakers by the perceptual requirements it makes of them, or the extent to which it is merely reflecting their world view, and whether the relationship (whatever it is) is universal or language-specific. There is no doubt, however, that there is a correlation between the form and content of a language and the beliefs, values, and needs present in the culture of its speakers. The vocabulary of a language provides us with a catalogue of things considered important to the society, an index to the way speakers categorize experience, and often a record of past contacts and cultural borrowings; the grammar may reveal the way time is segmented and organized, beliefs about animacy and the relative power of beings, and salient social categories in the culture (e.g., see Whorf 1940; Hill and Mannheim 1992; Gumperz and Levinson 1996).

Hymes suggests a second type of linguistic relativity which sees in grammar evidence not only of static social categories, but also of speakers' social assumptions about the dynamics of role-relationships, and about what rights and responsibilities are perceived in society. While the first type of linguistic relativity claims that cultural reality in part results from linguistic factors, Hymes contends that

> people who enact different cultures do to some extent experience distinct communicative systems, not merely the same natural communicative condition with different customs affixed. Cultural values and benefits are in part constitutive of linguistic relativity. (1966b: 116)

The interrelationship of patterns in various aspects of culture is pervasive enough in many cases for us to call them *themes*, or central organizing principles which control behavior. Opler (1941) exemplifies this concept with the Apache theme of male superiority, which is realized in patterns of communication as well as in religious and political domains. At tribal meetings, for instance, only a few older women may speak before all of the men have been heard, and it is very unusual for a woman to pray out loud in public. The Manus of New Guinea have been characterized in part as having an anti-sex theme in their culture: there are no purely social dances, no love songs, no romantic myths – and no word for 'love' in their language (Mead 1930).

Where directness or indirectness are cultural themes, they are always language-related. As defined in speech act theory, *direct acts* are those where surface form matches interactional function, as "Be quiet!" used as a command, versus an *indirect* "It's getting noisy in here" or "I can't hear myself think," but other units of communication must also be considered.

Indirectness may be reflected in routines for offering and refusing or accepting gifts or food, for instance. A *yes* or *no* intended to be taken literally is more direct than an initial *no* intended to mean "Ask me again." Visitors from the Middle East and Asia have reported going hungry in England and the United States because of a misunderstanding of this message; when offered food, many have politely refused rather than accept directly, and it was not offered again. English speakers have the reverse problem in other countries when their literal no is not accepted as such, and they are forced to eat food they really do not want.

An indirect apology is illustrated by Mead (1930), who reports a situation where a Manus woman fled to her aunt's home after being beaten by her husband. His relatives, coming to retrieve her, engaged her relatives for an hour of desultory chatter about such topics as market conditions and fishing before one made a metaphorical reference to men's strength and women's bones. Still without saying a word, the wife joined the husband's relatives in their boat, and returned with them.

The use of metaphors and proverbs is a common communicative strategy for depersonalizing what is said and allowing more indirectness. Criticism is often couched in this form, as when chiefs of the San Blas Cuna Indian tribe of Panama express opinions in metaphoric songs (Sherzer 1974, 1983), or when an English speaker reproves another with "People who live in glass houses shouldn't cast stones."

Joking is also a common way of mitigating criticism that might not be acceptable if given directly. This has reached the level of art in Trinidad, where ritual verbal protests culminate in the song-form of the calypso. "It is a means of disclaiming responsibility for one's words. It is only because the norms of the event are shared by members of the community – political leaders included – that many a calypsonian does not end up with a law suit filed against him" (Sealey).

At the level of the grammatical code, using passive rather than active voice, or using impersonal pronouns are yet other common means of indirectness. Talmy (1976) illustrates the difference this may make in directness with his example of a Yiddish story in which a boy invites a girl to the woods. In English, she would have to respond with embarrassingly direct pronouns, "I can't go with you. You'll have to kiss me." In Yiddish this is avoided with a nonspecific pronoun, *Me tor ništ geyn ahin. Me vet zix vein kušn.* 'One mustn't go there. One will want to kiss another.'

While it may be easier to be indirect in some languages than others, communicative patterns are not necessarily tied directly to language forms. The native speaker of Arabic, Yiddish, Farsi, Indonesian, or Japanese often uses English more indirectly than does a native speaker of English, for instance. There is no intrinsic reason that the structures and vocabulary for one language cannot be used in many domains of communication within other speech communities to express the cultures of those communities, and in ways in keeping with their rules of appropriate behavior. As it is developed and used creatively as an auxiliary language in Nigeria, India, and elsewhere in the world, English becomes "Englishes" (Kachru 1980; 1986) in the enactment of different cultural values and beliefs.

Although language is unquestionably an integral part of culture, to assume that specific cultural experiences and rules of behavior will invariably correlate with specific linguistic skills is a naive oversimplification of the relationship of language and culture. The issue of their relationship is one which pervades the whole of the ethnography of communication.

Social Structure and Ideology

The role of language is not the same in all societies, but it often includes the identification or marking of social categories, the embodiment of sociopolitical ideologies, the maintenance and manipulation of individual social relationships and networks, and various means of effecting social control.

The relationship is not a static one, but varying and constitutive in nature. Social categories are primarily part of the social system, but also become embedded in the language system as it is used to mark them; the use and valuation of the linguistic markers in turn may affect the nature and persistence of the categories themselves.

Societies vary in the extent to which communicative behavior is bound up with the definition of social roles. In some, such as that of the Cuna Indians of San Blas, Panama, speaking ability is an integral and necessary part of role achievement and validation (Sherzer 1974; 1983). In others, communicative ability may have little or no significance in terms of roles, although certain social categories (such as age and sex) may be marked by characteristic communicative behavior. Also, societies may recognize distinctive role types, such as Abrahams' (1983) "man of words" in African American culture, which are defined primarily in terms of communicative behavior.

There are many who feel that language markers help perpetuate inequalities in the social system, and that language can be changed to eliminate the inequality. It is felt, for instance, that using generic terms like *policeman* rather than *law enforcement officer*, or calling all doctors *he* and all nurses *she* perpetuates occupational inequality between men and women by influencing thought and perception. Some feel that the way to break down social categories is to break down the language distinctions that mark them; others feel that the symbols would only be replaced by new ones unless the underlying social structure is itself changed in some more basic way. Still others believe that changing labels may have little effect on present beliefs and values, but will prevent their being transmitted as readily to the next generation.

Similarly, there is widespread belief in both the United States and England that speaking nonstandard English is a causal factor in the low economic status of large segments of minority group populations, and that learning "good" English will automatically erase class boundaries and prejudice. This view is epitomized in Shaw's *Pygmalion*, where Henry Higgins succeeds in changing Eliza Doolittle's social class status by changing her speech patterns. However, working-class members may value the group-identificational features of their speech, and actively resist or subvert efforts to change it. This may explain the perduring survival of *ain't* despite massive institutional attempts to eradicate it.

Major changes in categories in the social structure, as in social revolutions, usually entail change in communicative patterns as well. Movement to the political left may be accompanied by changing terms of address or titles and pronominal forms to symbolize class leveling (e.g., see Brown and Gilman 1960; Paulston 1976; Fang and Heng 1983). Since the Communist revolution in Cuba, a rural, once nonstandard variety of Spanish has become prestigious, and the variety once considered an educated standard has been disparaged and devalued, although to be sure, differential pronominal distinctions are creeping back into Hungarian, and the Indonesian language, originally adopted as more democratic than Javanese, has developed the capacity to make most of the same social distinctions.

Change in language use caused by changing ideologies is illustrated by the decline in Cuba of such exclamatory terms as *Jesús* and *Dios mío*, which are now used almost exclusively by the older generation. This change is attributed to the influence of Marxist attitudes toward religion. Another illustration of this relationship is the banning of the Bavarian greeting *Grüss Gott* during Hitler's reign in Germany.

The effect of social change on language use is clearly evident when we contrast a sociolinguistic domain such as address terminology among Mandarin Chinese speakers in Mainland China and in Taiwan. On the basis of interviews with students in the US from both locations in the 1980s, Jin found two significant differences in patterns of address. During the Cultural Revolution in Mainland China (1966–78), the use of *tongzhi* 'comrade' largely replaced professional titles. The usage has diminished with subsequent social change, however, and *tongzhi* is now used only with (1) strangers, (2) those whose occupations are unknown, and (3) those whose occupations carry no title and with whom the speaker is not familiar. It is also noteworthy that while the introduction of *tongzhi* served to neutralize male-female distinctions (in accordance with political ideology), the gender distinction has been reintroduced with the invention of *nu tongzhi* 'female comrade' and *nan tongzhi* 'male comrade.' More recently, Yang reports that without that modification, *tongzhi* has taken on the connotation of 'gay' or 'gay rights,' especially in internet messages. Use of simple *tongzhi* unmarked for gender does continue in official Communist Party meetings, but private usage (as by employer to employee) implies that a negative message is coming. Another recent change is in the use of *shifu* 'master' as a general title in Mainland China, contrasted with a narrower use of the term in Taiwan to refer to individuals who actually teach skills (such as a locksmith or a Kungfu instructor). *Shifu* is apparently beginning to replace *tongzhi* when addressing members of the working-class in Mainland China, in order to signal their higher position.

The differences found in norms of address terms between Mainland China and Taiwan thus reflect differing social organization and political values, while the far more extensive similarities suggest there is still more shared culture. The changes within Mainland China in recent years are evidence of the responsiveness of language use to the dynamics of social development, even within a relatively short time span. This is also reflected in reports that

> Terms such as nouveau riche and "middle-class" now abound in the non-government media. This class rhetoric represents the myths of the right and the exaggerated image of urban consumption spreading throughout Chinese society. (Hsu 2002)

The wider acceptance in US society of male-female cohabitation without marriage, and increased recognition of the validity of homosexual relationships, has been accompanied by pressure for change in the English language. A major etiquette problem of our day, judging from letters for advice submitted to such syndicated newspaper columnists as Ann Landers and Miss Manners, may well be what term of reference to use for the person with whom someone lives, but is not married to. *Mistress* is considered condescending, *boy friend* or *girl friend* childish, *partner* too businesslike, and *roommate* confusing. *Consort* makes Miss Manners "think of Prince Philip walking three paces behind," and *coviviant* of someone "who will only cook on copper pots," and so the problem continues. The response that it should not be necessary for people to declare their sexual affiliation is sociolinguistically naive; if the relationship does not have a label, others cannot be sure of how to interact appropriately.

Social change may impact whole genres, as Taminian reports in contemporary Yemen, where "poetry constitutes an integral part of the sociopolitical realm and practices, [and] is employed to stimulate local and national debates" about "the polemical relation between modernity and authenticity" (2001: 50). On another dimension, the type of orthography or print used may be significant: e.g., Ataturk mandated a shift from Arabic to Roman script in 1928 as part of a policy of turning Turkey ideologically toward the West; for some former republics of the USSR, abandonment of the Cyrillic alphabet has accompanied dissociation from Russia; and connotations currently associated with Gothic type in Finland would possibly be "German," even "Fascism" (Lehtonen 2000: 52). The use of Cyrillic to write Romanian spoken in Moldova when this republic was part of the Soviet Union has impeded efforts to reunify the province with Romania.

The pervasiveness of connections between orthography and politics is illustrated in the history of writing reform in China: the first emperor who unified China (Qin Dynasty 221–207 BC) decreed a standard way of writing characters as one means to consolidate centralized power; movement toward modernization and the end of imperialism essentially involved *bai hua* 'plain speech' style of writing to make written language more accessible to the people; and the ideological struggle between the Communists and the Nationalist government during the 1930s and 1940s was symbolized in part by the former's promotion of simplified characters and the latter's resistance "in order to strengthen unity under its leadership" (Gao 2000: 40). The continued division between the People's Republic of China and Taiwan is still reflected in simplified versus traditional writing, although recent economic influence from Hong Kong and Taiwan has made it popular for mainland Chinese businessmen to write advertisements and brand names in traditional characters. (The National Language Committee of the PRC issued directives in the 1990s for provisional and municipal language committees to be watchful for such orthographic ideological incursions; see Gao 2000: 29–51.) Another example of language practice linked to economic change is the renaming of Russian businesses for their owners as a public symbol of privatization since 1991 (Yurchak 2000).

One of the most obvious indications of the relationship of language and social organization is in the renumeration or reclassification of languages which may accompany political change. For example, the demise of Yugoslavia as a political entity led to the official distinction of Bosnian and Montenegrin, which had been categorized within former Serbo-Croation. That region is also facing issues of orthography and standardization in Macedonian and Albanian, and debates concerning the use of Albanian, Roma, and other languages in the media and in education.

At an interactional level, the maintenance and manipulation of social relationships are importantly served by greeting events in many communities, which for first encounters may include questions about family, income, occupation, place of origin, or where one went to school. This is usually interpreted as "friendly" behavior, but it also provides information for assignment of the new acquaintance to a social category. What is considered "appropriate" interactional behavior is largely determined by such categorization.

Language most obviously serves a role in social control by providing a medium for telling people directly what to do, but it also allows for such indirect control forms as threats, curses, teasing, and gossip. One of the strongest control forms in many societies is silence, or "shunning," which is also part of the communicative system.

Stories told to children are often intended to control their behavior: Aesop's fables in Western tradition, Anancie tales of Africa and the Caribbean, Monkey tales of Japan, Coyote stories of North American Indians, and Brer Rabbit stories of African Americans all serve this function, as the Trickster's antisocial behavior focuses attention on the social norms, and allows for the verbalization of morals and collective group wisdom.

Rights and responsibilities involved in such systems as law, medicine, and religion cannot be fulfilled without language. Its importance is perhaps most clearly seen in situations where the social systems are thwarted because of a breakdown in communication. A man who was jailed in the state of Illinois, for instance, could not be tried because he could not hear or speak. He had to be taught sign language first so that he could defend himself. More problematic are people on trial in a speech community other than their own, or through the medium of a language in which they lack fluency, who may be equally unable to defend themselves.

Language also serves in social control by the way it is used in politics. Much attention has been given to the thought control potential of "Newspeak" in George Orwell's *Nineteen Eighty-Four*, and a standing committee of the National Council of Teachers of English in the US is devoted to "Doublespeak." It gives annual awards for particularly flagrant euphemistic or evasive language use by government agencies or representatives seeking to justify or minimize the impression of negatively-perceived actions, such as "terminate with extreme prejudice" (meaning 'to kill') and "collateral damage" (meaning 'civilian casualties during war') (Shearer 1988). During the Nazi regime, the Office of the Press in Germany issued "Language Regulations" stipulating the terms to be used or abandoned in newspaper reporting, or redefining them: e.g., on January14, 1937, "According to the new government, the term 'propaganda' is a legally protected one, so to speak, and cannot be used in a derogatory sense . . . In short, 'propaganda' only if it serves us; 'agitation' for those who are against us" (Mueller 1973: 31).

A different dimension of the effect of patterns of communication on political thought and activity has been explored extensively by Maurice Bloch (1974), whose general thesis is that political language should be studied as a preliminary to studying politics, since the intentions of speakers may be inferred from the implications of the type of speech they use.

Bloch distinguishes between formal language and informal language, or formal speech situations and everyday speech situations, and their relative degree of social control. When a speech event is formalized, there are fewer options for participants; thus, as language becomes more formalized, more social control is exerted on participants. In formalizing a situation, the propositional content, the logic, is essentially removed. What is said is accepted because it is the right thing to say, and not because it is true or false. Bloch and others claim that in societies where there is more emphasis on ritual events, there is less freedom and more direct control than in societies where there is less emphasis on ritual. The control may be in both directions, controlling those in authority as well as those being governed: i.e., the speaker also gives up some freedom in ritual, even if he or she has power.

Ritual events are much more likely to be important to closed social groups than to those that are open. In making this point, Douglas (1970) contrasts the lack of ritual among the mobile Ituri pygmies of Africa (Turnbull 1961) and the Basseri nomads of Persia (Barth 1964b) with the pervasive ritual activity among the Navajo, which demands exact ordering in fixed ceremonial events (Aberle 1966).

Both Bloch and Douglas relate the formal-informal communicative situations to the ritual and anti-ritual in types of religion, and to Bernstein's (1971) distinction between positional and personal family structures and their relation to strong boundary maintenance and weak boundary maintenance in education. According to them, Bernstein's restricted code is appropriate in a ritualized situation where the context is highly coded, roles are rigidly delineated, meanings are local and particular, and there is a small range of alternative forms. An elaborated code is appropriate in a less structured context where meanings must be made more explicit, and speakers have a wide range of choice. The restricted code serves the social function of control as well as communication, and creates solidarity. Bloch and Douglas interpret Bernstein's general distinction as essentially one of context, with the structural characteristics of the two types of code in any one speech community a matter for investigation: "the distinction between restricted and elaborated codes must be relative within a given culture or within the speech forms of a given group" (Douglas 1970: 77). (Additional issues of language and power are discussed in chapter 8.)

Routines and Rituals

Linguists are very interested in humans' ability to be creative with language as part of defining competence, but also in how, when, and why humans choose not to be creative, to repeat what has been heard and said many times before, often in exactly the same form. The relation of ritual to social control has already been discussed, but the general nature of routines and rituals requires further consideration.

Linguistic routines are fixed or relatively fixed utterances or sequences of utterances which must be considered as single units, because meaning cannot be derived from consideration of any segment apart from the whole. In form, they often constitute a sentence "stem" (Aijmer 1996), a core which may be expanded in conversational contexts but is often frozen in ritual ones. The routine itself fulfills the communicative function, and in this respect is performative in nature. Such communication essentially defines the situation.

Routines must be learned, as well as analyzed, as single units, although they may vary in length from single syllables (*Hi*) to phrases (*How do you do*, *April fool*, and *Have a nice day*) to a sequence of sentences (the well-rehearsed pitch of a door-to-door salesman or telemarketer). They may be uttered by an individual, or may require cooperation between two or more persons, as in a greeting sequence or in minister/congregation alternation in the reading of scriptures.

Non-native speakers of English often complain that native speakers do not really care about the state of their health when they ask *How are you?* The non-natives are not recognizing that this question is part of a greeting routine, which by nature has no meaning apart from its phatic function in communication. If English speakers *really* want to know how someone is feeling, they repeat the question after the routine is completed, or they mark the question with contrastive intonation to indicate it is for information, and not part of the routine.

Understanding routines requires shared cultural knowledge because they are generally metaphoric in nature, and must be interpreted at a non-literal level. They include greetings, leave takings, curses, jokes, condolences, prayers, compliments, and other formulaic language. Sneezes, hiccoughs, or other involuntary noises may require routines to repair the situation, as may simultaneous talking or spontaneous silence in a group. In Japan or Korea, a sneeze means someone is talking about you, and many English speakers say *Bless you* to a sneezer because of traditional beliefs that it is the soul or spirit escaping, or a sign of illness; Turkish speakers wish the person a long life. Someone who hiccoughs in Germany makes a wish, and in Puerto Rico, a common response is "Did you steal something?"

Speech communities place differential value on knowledge of routines versus creativity on the part of individual speakers, with oral versus literate traditions a significant factor (cf. Tannen 1979a), along with degree of formalization and ritualization of other aspects of culture. English speakers are often quite opposed to routines and rituals at a conscious level, because they are "meaningless" and depersonalize the ideas expressed. One occasion where a prescribed routine is considered too impersonal is the bereavement of a friend; condolence therefore often takes the form of *I don't know what to say*, which has itself become a routine. This contrasts sharply with other speech communities where fixed condoling routines are considered an essential component of funerary ritual.

Ritual is made up of routines, but these are given far greater cultural significance for being part of a ritual context, rather than everyday encounters. Its context-bound nature was noted by Malinowski (1935), who found in studying ritual that the meaning of symbols could not be interpreted in isolation, but only in the context of the meaning of the ritual situation. This observation creates serious problems for any discipline of autonomous semantics, which requires individual units of meaning to carry a semantic load in themselves. On the other hand, because the total meaning is already known to the group from the context, we can explain why it is the case that even though "the receiver of a ritual message is picking up information through a variety of different sensory channels simultaneously (and these over a period of time), all these different sensations add up to just one 'message'" (Leach 1976: 41).

Magical incantations provide one example of ritual: the language is fixed, and the linguistic formulae themselves are expected to exert some control over the supernatural. Parts of a spell have no meaning uttered by themselves; the whole must always be recited in full to have effect. Paralinguistic features of production are clearly differentiated from "normal" language, with spells often recited in a sing-song manner, and with distinctive rhythm and pitch.

Comparable to the sing-song of magical incantation, intoned speech (or "wailing") is common for expressing grief, and both intoned speech and chanting are often used in religious rituals. These varieties of language are on a speech-song continuum, with the song end of the continuum used in more formal contexts (Bloch 1974).

As routines often mark the boundaries of speech events by opening and closing them, rituals serve as boundary markers for major changes in social status: puberty rites, weddings, funerals, and graduation ceremonies. Perhaps the most important characteristic of routines and rituals is that truth value is largely irrelevant. Their meaning is dependent on shared beliefs and values of the speech community coded into communicative patterns, and they cannot be interpreted apart from social and cultural context.

To return to considerations of routines in social control, this irrelevance of truth value in routines is an obviously important factor. So, too, is the potential of slogans and chants to organize and control mass energy, whether the *Sieg Heil* of Hitler's rallies, the *Go, team, go* of athletic contests, or the *We shall overcome* of US civil rights demonstrations.

Universals and Inequalities

It is precisely because the ritual use of language encodes cultural beliefs and reflects community social organization that it has been of primary interest to ethnographers, but this has led to the criticism that the field has focused on the ceremonial or "special" uses of language to the neglect of more everyday communication.

Bloch (1976) asserts that nonritual communication has much more in common cross-culturally, while ritual communication reflects "strange other ways of thinking," which may explain why such researchers as Levi-Strauss, Geertz, and Douglas stress differences in systems of classification which link systems of cognition to social structure, while such researchers as Berlin and Kay find universal criteria for classification. The former concentrate almost exclusively on ritual communication, the latter on nonritual. "Only concentrating on the picture of the world apparent in ritual communication obscures the fact of the universal nature of a part of the cognitive system available in all cultures" (Bloch 1976: 285).

The nature of language cannot be described or explained without both perspectives. Hymes considers the type of explanatory adequacy proposed by Chomsky and that of a socially constituted linguistics to have complementary goals:

> Chomsky's type of explanatory adequacy leads away from speech, and from languages, to relationships possibly universal to all languages, and possibly inherent in human nature. The complementary type of explanatory adequacy leads from what is common to all human beings and all languages toward what particular communities and persons have made of their means of speech. (1974: 203)

To be sure, the ethnographer is interested in such constructs as a proposed universal framework of conversational maxims (e.g., see Grice 1975), but as working hypotheses against which conversational patterns in different speech communities may be tested and compared rather than as facts or as a given framework for analysis. Keenan (1976) has reported that speakers of Malagasy regularly violate the maxim to "be informative," for instance, as do Kaingáng speakers in Brazil (Kindell), and undoubtedly speakers of many other languages. In fact, in many communities (including the most technologically advanced societies) ". . . it may be one's obligation to lie, successfully, or avoid giving pertinent information" (Hymes 1987: 222). The degree to which Grice's maxims hold in a particular community, and in relation to what particular sociocultural conditions, is important for the ultimate understanding of all human communication as well as for descriptions of conversational patterns in particular communities.

Similarly, while there is a finite general set of functions which language may serve in a society, and it is indeed universal that language serves a plurality of functions in each community, it is fundamental to the ethnography of communication that research begin from the perspective *that functions are problematic rather than given*. Hymes contends

> that the role of language may differ from community to community; that in general the functions of language in society are a problem for investigation, not postulation. . . . If this is so, then the cognitive significance of a language depends not only on structure, but also on patterns of use. (1967: 116)

It is quite probable that some aspects of language function will prove to be universal, although perhaps in a hierarchy of importance which is relative to particular communities, but this remains a topic for empirical investigation. Clearly in multilingual societies, different languages often serve differential functions, and a single a priori assumption regarding Language might obscure enlightening sociolinguistic data.

A related issue which this raises is that of the inequality of languages: not all languages are equally capable of serving the same functions in a society. This assertion violates most pronouncements of linguists made during the last half century that all languages are adequate as communicative systems for members of a social group, but it will be accepted by most administrators concerned with education and economics in developing countries. While all languages are inherently capable of expressing all concepts and fulfilling all functions, they have evolved differently through processes of variation, adaptation, and selection. The fact that each language may retain the *potential* to serve all functions does not alter this conclusion.

> The official preference is to stress the potentiality of a language and to ignore the circumstances and consequences of its limitations. Yet every language is an instrument shaped by its history and patterns of use, such that for a given speaker and setting it can do some things well, some clumsily, and others not intelligibly at all. The cost, as between expressing things easily and concisely, and expressing them with difficulty and at great length, is a real cost, commonly operating, and a constraint on the theoretical potentiality of language in daily life. (Hymes 1973: 73)

Hymes enumerates "the sources and consequences of linguistic inequality" as differences in adaptive resources, patterning of agents and personalities (e.g. male and female roles) developments in relation to a community's institutions (e.g. styles associated with science, religion, and politics), and in values and beliefs (1996: 57–8).

It therefore remains central to our concerns to describe what a community has made of its language, and why, and how – not only as part of our scientific inquiry, but because one of the responsibilities and motivations of a socially constituted study of language is the welfare of its human speakers. Ethnographers, who by the nature of their perspective reach beyond the "facts" of observable behavior to interpret meaning/culture, have an ethical responsibility to the "subjects" of investigation.

The question of inequality is also raised with respect to the degree to which individual speakers are competent in the language(s) of their group. The concept of possible "semilingualism" (cf. Cummins 1979) in some language contact situations is rejected by many on philosophical grounds, yet it may be one of the social problems to which findings from ethnography of communication may be applied. From this perspective, Hymes suggests that the term *competence*, rather than be defined as ideal knowledge, "should retain its normal sense of actual ability."

> As a term for ideal knowledge, competence may overcome inequality conceptually, but only as a term for actual abilities, assessed in relation to contexts of use, can it help to overcome inequality practically. (1996: 59)

Bloomfield, in a study of the North American Menomini, noted:

> White-Thunder, a man around forty, speaks less English than Menomini, and that is a strong indictment, for his Menomini is atrocious. His vocabulary is small; his inflections are often barbarous; he constructs sentences of a few threadbare models. He may be said to speak no language tolerably. His case is not unknown among younger men, even when they speak but little English. (1927: 437)

We are thus concerned with the obsolescence and loss of ways of speaking as well as with their development and maintenance. Of central interest will be the community's attitudes toward these phenomena, and ultimately the potential applications of our findings in furtherance of its goals.

3

Varieties of Language

Within each community or complex of overlapping and interacting communities there exist a number of different language codes and ways of speaking available to its members, which constitute its *communicative repertoire*. This includes "all varieties, dialects or styles used in a particular socially-defined population, and the constraints which govern the choice among them" (Gumperz 1977). Any one speaker also has a variety of codes and styles from which to choose, but it is very unlikely that any individual is able to produce the full range; different subgroups of the community may understand and use different subsets of its available codes.

The means of communication used in a community thus may include different languages, different regional and social varieties of one or more of the languages, different registers (generally varying on a formal-informal dimension which cross-cuts regional and social dimensions), and different channels of communication (e.g. oral, written, manual). The nature and extent of this diversity is related to the social organization of the group, which is likely to include differences in age, sex, and social status, as well as differences in the relationship between speakers, their goals of interaction, and the settings in which communication takes place. The communicative repertoire may also include different occupational codes, specialized religious language, secret codes of various kinds, imitative speech, whistle or drum language, and varieties used for talking to foreigners, young children, and pets.

Identification of the varieties which occur in any community requires observation and description of actual differences in pronunciation, grammar, lexicon, styles of speaking, and other communicative behaviors which are potentially available for differentiation, but it must ultimately depend on the discovery of which differences are recognized by members of the group as conveying social meaning of some kind. In addition, the communicative repertoire of a group includes the variety of possible interaction strategies available to it. These are most commonly used to establish, maintain, or manipulate role-relationships. Speakers' choices of interaction strategies provide a dynamic connection between the language code, speakers' goals, and the participant structure in specific situations.

Language Choice

Given the multiple varieties of language available within the communicative repertoire of a community or complex, and the subset of varieties available to its subgroups and individuals, speakers must select the code and interaction strategy to be used in any specific context. Knowing the alternatives and the rules for appropriate choice are part of speakers' communicative competence. Accounting for the rules or system for such decision-making is part of the task of describing communication within any group, and of explaining communication more generally.

The concept of *domain* developed by Fishman (1964, 1966, 1971, 1972) remains useful for both description and explanation of the distribution of means of communication. He defines it as:

> ... a socio-cultural construct abstracted from topics of communication, relationships between communicators, and locales of communication, in accord with the institutions of a society and the spheres of activity of a speech community. (1971: 587)

Factors determining domains may thus include the general subject area under discussion (e.g. religion, family, work), the role-relationships between the participants (e.g. priest–parishioner, mother–daughter, boss–secretary), and the setting of the interaction (e.g. church, home, office).

No fixed set of domains can be posited a priori for all speech communities, since the set of activities which will constitute a cluster of purpose, role-relations, and setting will be culture-specific. Different levels of *focus* have also proved to be salient in different communities: e.g. societal–institutional (family, school, church, government) versus social–psychological (intimate, informal, formal, intergroup). These levels tend to coincide (family with intimate, for instance, and religious institution with formal), but may provide an interesting additional dimension for investigation (Fishman 1971).

Topic is often a primary determinant of language choice in multilingual contexts; bilinguals have often learned about some topics through the medium of one language and other topics through the medium of the second, and thus only know the vocabulary to discuss a topic in one of their languages, or feel it is more "natural" to use one language for a particular topic.

Linguists from non-English speaking countries who were trained in an English-medium university provide a good example: they sometimes continue to discuss, lecture, and publish about linguistics in English, often even when their students are not fluent in that language. This may be because they do not know the necessary terminology in their national language, or because they have come to believe it is more appropriate to use English to talk about such subjects as grammatical analysis, and even to use English examples rather than their own Chinese, Arabic, or Japanese. This may also be due in part to the "power" of English, as discussed in chapter 8.

In bilingual education programs in the United States, native speakers of other languages frequently find it easier to teach in English if they themselves are products of English-only education. For this reason, university training programs are recognizing the need to teach methods and content area courses in the language the teachers will be using to teach the subject. Some teachers have asserted it is impossible to teach a subject like American History in languages other than English because "only English can be used to express American concepts." A similar belief is held even more strongly by many Navajo teachers, that Navajo history and culture cannot be taught adequately in English. In this case, the Navajo language is believed to be so integrally related to the culture that religious beliefs must be understood in order to know how to use the language correctly, and the beliefs can be fully expressed only in Navajo.

In addition to topic, appropriate language choice may depend on *setting* (including locale and time of day) and *participants* (including their age, sex, and social status). A bilingual child may regularly use English at school with a grandmother if she has come to observe the class, and English at home with the teacher if he or she has come to visit. Language choice is also importantly influenced by social and political *identity* (discussed further in chapter 6), especially in areas of the world where regional or ethnic languages have become symbols for emerging nationalism (e.g., see Woolard 1987 on factors in speaker choice of Catalan versus Castilian in Spain).

Choice of varieties within a single language is governed by the same factors. Speakers may select from among regional varieties in their repertoire depending on which geographic area and subgroup of the population they wish to express identity with, or as they travel from one area to another. On a paralinguistic dimension, whispering is likely to be chosen for conversation in a church, or when the topic is one that should not be overheard by others, while shouting may be chosen for greeting out of doors, and from a distance. Shouting may be an appropriate choice even in this setting only for males under a certain age, and only when greeting other males of the same or lower age and status, or with other restrictions (including perhaps time of day). *Choice of channel* may depend on environmental conditions: drums may be used in jungle regions, signal fires where there are barren bluffs, and whistle languages or horns where there is low humidity. Choosing oral or written channels is usually dependent on distance, or the need for a permanent record.

Choice of register depends on the topic and setting, and also on the social distance between speakers. The possible complexity of levels of formality may be illustrated by different forms which would be chosen in a single speech event, in this case a Japanese woman offering tea in her home. According to Harumi Williams, the act of offering a cup of tea in upper- and middle-class homes demonstrates how Japanese place each other in society, and so requires careful choice of language forms and manner of speaking. The hierarchy of forms used with addressees of lower to higher status is usually as follows:

1   *Ocha?* (to own children) [tea]
2   *Ocha dō?* (to own children, friends who are younger than self, own younger brothers and sisters) [tea how–about]
3   *Ocha ikaga?* (to friends who are the same age, own older brothers and sisters) [tea how–about (polite)]
4   *Ocha ikaga desu ka?* (to husband, own parents, own aunts and uncles, husband's younger brothers and sisters) [tea how–about (polite) is Q]
5   *Ocha wa ikaga desu ka?* (to own grandparents) [tea topic how–about (polite) is Q]
6   *Ocha ikaga deshō ka?* (to husband's elder brothers and sisters) [tea how–about (polite) is (polite) Q]
7   *Ocha wa ikaga deshō ka?* (to teachers, husband's parents, husband's boss, husband's grandparents) [tea topic how–about (polite) is (polite) Q]

Williams reports that ranking varies with such factors as how often she sees the people, and the level of respect form used for her husband would be different if the marriage were *miai* 'arranged marriage' rather than *renai* 'love marriage.'

Nonverbal alternatives are also important in this event: when tea is offered in a Japanese *tatami* room it should not be offered standing, but standing is appropriate if the room is Western style. If there is a picture on the tea cup, the picture side should face the receiver; the cup should be held with the right hand on the body of the cup and the left supporting the base. When offering tea to people ranking higher than her own husband, a woman should bow slightly. Vocally, increased formality not only involves choice of higher level respect forms, but a higher pitched voice. In general, the longer the sentence, the more polite; but the most honorific expression is silence, which would be the appropriate choice when offering tea to a guest of a very high position in the society.

The choice of appropriate language forms is not only dependent on static categories, but on what precedes and follows in the communicative sequence, and on information which emerges within the event which may alter the relationship of participants.

Rules for language choice are usually not consciously formulated by native speakers, as they are in the Japanese example above, and must be inferred by the ethnographer from a variety of observation and interview techniques (which will be discussed in chapter 4). Essentially, the questions of language choice we are seeking answers to are: who uses what (variety of) language; with whom; about what; in what setting; for what purpose; and in what relationship to other communicative acts and events. Relating patterns of language choice within a speech community to these dimensions of context is discovering and describing the rules of communication.

Diglossia and Dinomia

The clearest example of language choice according to domain is *diglossia*, a situation in which two or more languages (or varieties of the same language) in a speech community are allocated to different social functions and contexts. When Latin was the language of education and religious services in England, for example, English and Latin were in a diglossic relationship.

The term was coined by Charles Ferguson (1959), who used it initially to refer only to the use of two or more varieties of the same language by speakers under different conditions. He exemplified it in the use of classical and colloquial varieties of Arabic, Katharevousa and Demotike varieties of Greek, Haitian Standard French and Creole, and Standard German and Swiss German. In each case, there is a high (H) and low (L) variety of a language used in the same society, and they have the following relationship:

1 There is a specialization of function for H and L.
2 H has a higher level of prestige than L, and is considered superior.
3 There is a literary heritage in H, but not in L.
4 There are different circumstances of acquisition; children learn L at home, and H in school.
5 The H variety is standardized, with a tradition of grammatical study and established norms and orthography.
6 The grammar of the H variety is more complex, more highly inflected.
7 H and L varieties share the bulk of their vocabularies, but there is some complementary distribution of terms.
8 The phonology of H and L is a single complex system.

Diglossia was extended by Fishman (1972) to include the use of more than one language, such as the situation in Paraguay where Spanish is the H language of school and government, and Guaraní is the L language of home (cf. Rubin 1968). Since the term diglossia refers to language distribution in the whole society and not in the usage of individuals, the fact that only a relatively small percentage of the population of Paraguay speaks both H and L does not affect the designation; only those who speak Spanish have traditionally participated in education and government, although this situation may be changing with the advent of bilingual education. To distinguish societal and individual language distribution, Fishman suggests a four-way designation: both bilingualism and diglossia, diglossia without bilingualism, bilingualism without diglossia, and neither bilingualism nor diglossia.

Regional distribution is not a determining factor in identifying a diglossic society. French and Flemish are in complementary regional distribution in Belgium, but each is used for a full range of functions in each part of the country; this is characterized as bilingualism without diglossia. The situation in Paraguay is characterized as diglossia without bilingualism.

Most (but not all) of the features by which Ferguson characterized monolingual diglossia are also true of multilingual situations. There is a comparable specialization of function for H and L languages; the H language generally has more prestige; and L is learned at home and H at school. Also, although the L language in a multilingual society may well have a literary heritage, tradition of grammatical study and established norms and orthography, these often are not known to its speakers in a diglossic situation. The only clear differences between monolingual and multilingual diglossia are those that relate to the structures of the codes themselves: i.e. the relationship of their grammars, vocabularies, and phonological systems.

Because our interest in communicative behavior includes not only language structures, but also the social and cultural systems which govern how they are used, I have added the concept of *dinomia* (Saville-Troike 1978), which translates roughly from Greek as 'two systems of laws.' There are clear analogies between language domains and choice, and cultural domains and choice, and obvious parallels with language in the appropriate use of cultural rules, and in switching between alternative cultural systems. The minority culture first learned by many Spanish speakers in the United States, for instance, is comparable to the L variety of a language in a diglossic situation, and the dominant US "mainstream" culture is analogous to the H variety of a national language. Just as with L and H language varieties, the L culture is generally learned by children at home, and H at school; the H culture has more prestige in the society than the L; and there is a specialization of function for H and L. Dinomia may thus be defined as *the coexistence and complementary use within the same society of two cultural systems*, one of which is the dominant culture of the larger society and the other a subordinate and less prestigious subculture from within that same society. The relationship of these terms is shown in figure 3.1. As with diglossia, dinomia may apply to situations where there is an indigenous tradition of differences in sociocultural strata (often associated with urban/rural or

	LANGUAGE CODE	CULTURE
SOCIETY	diglossia	dinomia
INDIVIDUAL	bilingualism	biculturalism

Figure 1

social or occupational class distinctions) and to situations which result from migration or conquest.

Dinomia, like diglossia, is a societal state of affairs; biculturalism, like bilingualism, refers to individual distribution. A society in which an entirely different set of cultural norms governs behavior in home and school, for example, is considered dinomic. This is the case in many African and Asian communities where Western educational systems (often including Western teaching and administrative personnel, as well as curriculum and instructional material) have been incorporated without adaptation into the indigenous cultures. This is also the case in the Navajo community, where the dominant US culture governs behaviors in most educational contexts, but a different culture governs behaviors at home (even though one language – either English or Navajo – may be used in both domains). Individual Navajos who are both bilingual and bicultural and travel off the reservation may change ways of speaking as well as language codes, including greeting forms, nonverbal behavior, and timing between questions and responses. A complete switch of rules for appropriate communicative behavior involves more than language; otherwise, the switch is only a partial one which identifies speakers as bilingual, but not bicultural.

Nonverbal aspects of communication are likely to prove more closely associated with dinomia and biculturalism than with bilingualism, since most individuals who can switch language codes with ease still use the gestures and proxemics of their native language, as well as its interactional strategies.

Part of my intent in coining the term dinomia is to separate language code from patterns of use of the language code (and other means of communication) at the societal level; it is quite possible for language codes and rules of communicative behavior (as part of culture) to be distributed differently in the society. Fishman (1980) has accepted the analogy of *diglossia/ bilingualism: dinomia/biculturalism* given here, but suggests a narrower concept would be more useful, which he terms *di-ethnia*. However, a concept relating to ethnicity is not coordinate with the *language:culture* distinction envisioned here. To adapt his suggestion in turn, one may find cases of biculturalism with or without dinomia, as well as dinomia with and without either bilingualism or diglossia.

Code-Switching and Style-Shifting

Because of the proliferation of terms and inconsistent usage in the field, it is necessary to begin any discussion of this topic with definitions. I have been intentionally vague in using *varieties* to indicate any patterned or systematic differences in language forms and use which are recognized by native speakers as being distinct linguistic entities, or "different" from one another in some significant way. More precise distinctions must be made about types of varieties within any one speech community, but their nature cannot be presumed for all languages prior to investigation.

We first require a definition of *codes*, by which I will mean different languages, or quite different varieties of the same language (comparable to classical versus colloquial Arabic, or Katharevousa versus Demotike Greek). *Code-alternation* (Gumperz 1976) refers to change in language according to domain, or at other major communication boundaries, and *code-switching* to change in languages within a single speech event. *Style-shifting* will refer to change in language varieties which involves changing only the *code-markers*; these are variable features which are associated with such social and cultural dimensions as age, sex, social class, and relationship between speakers (discussed in the next section).

The distinction among these three types of code-variation is illustrated in the following sequence of speech acts (reported by Silverio-Borges) at the Cuban interest section office in an embassy in Washington, DC prior to official political recognition of the Castro government and full embassy status. To begin with, the receptionist is talking to a visitor in Spanish when the telephone rings. This *summons* marks a major boundary point, a change in events, and the receptionist changes to English (an example of *code-alternation*). The conversation begins:

1 Receptionist (R): *Cuban Interest Section.*
2 Caller (C): *¿Es la embajada de Cuba?* (Is this the Cuban embassy?)
→3 R: *Sí. Dígame.* (Yes, may I help you?)

This is an example of the receptionist *code-switching* (→) from English to Spanish, changing languages within the same speech event, because she had identified the caller as a Spanish speaker.

4 C: *Es Rosa.* (This is Rosa.)
↓ 5 R: *¡Ah, Rosa! ¿Cóma anda eso?* (Oh, Rosa! How is it going?)

This is downward *style-shifting* (↓) from formal to informal Spanish as the receptionist identifies the caller as a friend, still in the same event. There is a shift to more marked intonation and faster speed, as well as use of the informal *¿Cóma anda eso?* rather than formal *¿Cómo le va?* or *¿Cómo está usted?* There is also a change to louder voice volume because the call is recognized as long distance, which may also be considered a kind of style-shifting. (I am introducing here an "arrow convention" to distinguish between code-switching (→) and style-shifting (↑) or (↓), indicating shifts to higher or lower level, respectively.)

On another dimension, we may distinguish between *situational code-switching* and *metaphorical code-switching* (Blom and Gumperz 1972), a distinction which applies to style-shifting as well.

Situational code-switching occurs when a language change accompanies a change of topics or participants, or any time the communicative situation is redefined. Within a single conversation, Navajo teachers usually speak English to one another when discussing matters related to school, for instance, but may switch to Navajo to discuss their families, or rodeos and other community activities. They may also situationally switch into English if non-Navajo speakers join the conversation, so the new arrivals will not be excluded. Nishimura (1997) describes switching among three codes by second-generation Japanese-English bilinguals (Niseis) in Canada depending on their addressees: a basically Japanese code to Japanese-dominant speakers, a basically English code to other Niseis, and a combination of the two when a group being addressed includes both. Code-switching within a conversation may be used to create a new *participation framework*, or shift in "footing" (Goffman 1979). Cromdal and Aronsson describe this phenomenon in the context of children's interaction in an English-Swedish setting as "important rhetorical and dramaturgic play devices, e.g. when contextualizing changes of addressee and shifts of frame (e.g. serious, nonserious)" (2000: 435).

Style may also shift situationally within a conversation, perhaps as the addressee shifts from female to male, or adult to child, or with a shift in topic from personal to work-related: e.g., D. H. Lawrence employs style-shifting as a literary device to redefine situations in *Lady Chatterley's Lover* as Mellors shifts from standard English to a "broad Derbyshire dialect" with changes in topic and addressee (Shuy 1975). Similarly, N. Scott Momaday makes conscious and effective artistic use of style alternation in *On the Way to Rainy Mountain* to cyclically tell stories in three different voices: the ancestral voice of Kiowa tradition, the voice of historical commentary, and the voice of personal reminiscence.

Metaphorical code-switching occurs within a single situation, but adds meaning to such components as the role-relationships which are being expressed. Since speaking different languages is an obvious marker of differential group membership, by switching languages bilinguals often have the option of choosing which group to identify with in a particular situation, and thus can convey the metaphorical meaning which goes along with such choice as well as whatever denotative meaning is conveyed by the code itself.

An example of such metaphorical switching was reported by Tuladhar, who described an event which occurred at a border checkpost between India and Nepal. A woman was stopped by the guard, accused of carrying too much tea, and threatened with a heavy fine. The woman first used Nepali (the official language) to make an appeal to the law, and to argue on legal grounds that she was within her limits of legitimate allowances. From the guard's accent in Nepali she inferred he was also a native speaker of Newari and switched into that language to make an entreaty on the grounds of common ethnic identity, an appeal to solidarity. She finally switched into English "for formulation of thought above the system," which was both an implicit attack on the corruption of the system, and an assertion that she belonged to an educated class in society which had no intent or need of "smuggling" across a few packages of tea. She consciously used code-switching as a verbal strategy in this instance, and was successful.

A third type is *discourse contextualization switching*, defined by Bailey as switches which "do not co-occur with external changes in the context or significant shifts in sociocultural framework" (2000: 242). These function to frame components such as quotations, to mark them off from surrounding verbal context.

Yet another dimension to be distinguished is the scope of switching, or the nature of the juncture at which language change takes place. The basic distinction in scope is usually between *intersentential switching*, or change which occurs between sentences or speech acts, and *intrasentential switching*, or change which occurs within a single sentence. Some sociolinguists refer to the latter type as "code-mixing," but I avoid that term because of the pejorative connotation it carries that intrasentential switching involves a random or unprincipled combination of languages.

I recorded the following examples of intrasentential switching by Navajo-English (1)–(3) and Chinese-English (4)–(6) bilingual children. These are the most common type, which involves the incorporation of a single noun, noun phrase, or "routine" (i.e. memorized chunk) from one language into the other.

1   *The boy* → *łéécha'í biłanné.*
               [dog with-him-playing]
    'The dog is playing with the boy.'
2   *Table* → *yaa sidá.*
               [under-it seated]
    '[He] is seated under the table.'
3   *Table* → *tł'ááhi* → *dollie* → *dóó* → *drum* → *sinił.*
               [under]   [and]   [are (in position)]
    'The doll and drum are under the table.'

4   *Neige → fox → yao chi ta.*
    [that]   [want eat him]
    'That fox wants to eat him.' (Telling a story)
5   *Ta yong yige → picture of a fox.*
    [he use a]
    'He used a picture of a fox.' (Another child telling the same story)
6   *Clean up time → le.*
                     [aspect marker]
    'It's already clean up time.'

Switches at other constituent boundaries occur, but with much less frequency (e.g. example 7 in Navajo and English):

7   *Boy is → łéécha'i yiłaané.*
                [dog with-it-playing]
    'The boy is playing with the dog.'

Gunarwan recorded informal conversation among Bahasa Indonesian (I), Dutch (D), and English (E) trilinguals, including the following sentences:

1   (I) *Akan ada rapat* → (D) *van avond.*
    [will be meeting]   [this evening]
    'There will be a meeting this evening.'
2   (D) *Samengaan,* → (I) *yok?*
    [go-together]   [let's]
    'Shall we go together?'
3   (I) *Berapa panjangnya* → (E) *this side?*
    [how-many length-the]
    'How long is this side?'
4   (I) *Jam berapa* → (E) *New Year's Eve's party* → (I) *-nya?*
    [clock how-many]   [the]
    'What time is the New Year's Eve party?'

The greatest number of his examples are also of switching for a noun phrase, but some are at other constituent boundaries (e.g. the tag in 2), and some even within words (e.g. the article in 4, which is a suffix). Gunarwan reports some utterances in which all three languages were used by the same speakers within a single turn:

5   (I) *Ini, ini.* → (D) *Tien* → (E) *centimeter.*
    [this this]   [ten]
    'This, this. Ten centimeters.'

6   (I) *Ee,* → (D) *Tante, je hebt verkeerd gedaan.* →
    [hey]   [aunt you have mistake made]
    (I) *Kan harus begini.* → (E) *You see?*
    [must like-this]
    'Hey, Aunt, you have made a mistake. It should be like this. You
    see?'

When the two languages used in intrasentential switching do not
share the same word order, an additional distinction is needed between
guest and *host* languages in an utterance (e.g. Sridhar and Sridhar 1980),
or between *matrix* and *embedded* languages in Myers-Scotton's (1993) model.
The host or matrix language is the one to which the basic grammatical
structure is assigned; elements of the guest or embedded language are
switched into it following systematic rules and constraints. In the following
sentence, for instance, a child inserted an English noun while maintaining
Korean Subject-Object-Verb word order (Korean-English examples from
Oh 1988):

Na → *toy* → *chueyo.*
[me]   [give]
'Give me a toy.'

Korean is also considered the host or matrix language in the following
example, where a Korean inflection (s.m. = subject marker) is attached to an
English noun:

Bird → *-ga wasseyo.*
        [s.m. came]
'The bird came.'

The guest language or embedded component may maintain its own integrity of word order, as in the following sentence (in this case, Korean is
embedded in an English structure):

I'm → *palli wa* → *-ing.*
        [quick come]
'I'm coming quickly.'

The integrity of embedded structures is further illustrated in the following
utterance by an adult Arabic speaker from Jordan, who was receiving technical training in electronics in the US (Al-Rusan):

Es → *circuit* → *lat ṭandhīm,* → *but you can bypass it* →
[the]   [this regulator]
bidūn mushkileh idha kān el → *voltage* → *9adi.*
[without problem if was the]   [normal]
'This is a regulator circuit, but you can bypass it without any problem if
the voltage is normal.'

There is need to distinguish further between code-switching and borrowing, in which lexical items from one language are adapted phonologically to
the sound system of the other, and are frequently subject to its morphological inflections. If someone says *I'm going to <u>Los Angeles</u>* (pronounced as
Anglicized [las ænjɪləs]), the place name is a borrowing from Spanish. If
someone says *I'm going to* → *[los ánxeles]*, using Spanish pronunciation,
they are code-switching. Similarly, *He's going to work on one of the kibbutzes
next year* includes a lexical borrowing from Hebrew because the term
kibbutz has been used with an English plural inflection. *He's going to work on
one of the* → *kibbutzim* → *next year* is code-switching for some, because the
Hebrew plural inflection is used along with the lexical item.

This is not an absolute distinction, because there are lexical borrowings in
English such as *datum*, *data*, *alumnus*, and *alumni* where these have included
the morphological inflection and they have been incorporated as exceptions in
English grammar; this does not mean they involve code-switching into Latin.
Kibbutzim is a borrowing in English for those who are not consciously using
a Hebrew inflection. Speakers' attitudes about how "native" a word is must
be taken into account, as well as formal criteria. It is possible that a word which
is a borrowing for the person speaking may be perceived as code-switching
by the listener, or vice versa, depending on subgroup membership within
the speech community. A New Yorker may use Yiddish words like *schlemiel*
and *schlok* quite natively, but the initial consonant sequence is considered
non-English in most other parts of the country, and thus code-switching.

Intrasentential style-shifting occurs when the variety of language being
used changes within a sentence, as in *Hi,* ↑ *Mr. President*, where an informal
greeting is followed by a formal term of address. A more extreme example is
Hey, ↑ *Professor Smith,* ↓ *ain't ya'* ↑ *promulgating* ↓ *a gob of* ↑ *unwarranted
presuppositions?*, which involves not only a shift in level of formality between
greeting and term of address, but also in grammar and lexicon.

Unless it is being intentionally used for humorous purposes, such shifting
is likely to be viewed negatively as "style-slipping" by school teachers,
particularly if it occurs in a written mode. In other languages, however,
such intrasentential style-shifting may be quite appropriate. In Javanese
(prior to World War II), for instance, there were at least three levels of "status
styles" encoded in both grammar and lexicon: *Krama*, the most formal and
polite (H); *Madya*, intermediate (M); and *Ngoko*, informal (L). Since the

choice of levels to be used depended not only on the relationship and relative status of speaker and hearer, but also on that of persons being referred to, a single sentence often contained words from different levels. If a speaker was using an H style to speak to a person of superior rank and said:

> *Dalem bade ↓ kesah ↑ dateng ↓ gryanipun katja ↑ dalem.*
> H   H   M   H   M   M   H
> 'I am going to my friend's house.'

the forms referring to 'I go' and 'friend's house' would be shifted down to M. If he was using M style speaking to a friend and said:

> *Kula adjeng kesah teng ↑ daleme pak guru.*
> M   M   M   M   H   H   H
> 'I am going to my teacher's house.'

he would shift the forms referring to 'teacher's house' up to H (examples from Retmono 1967).

The sociolinguistic resources on the island expanded with the addition of the Bahasa Indonesia language; switching became more complex, illustrating the analogous functions of alternating styles and languages. Errington (1998) reports that *Ngoko* and *Básá* styles of Javanese are used for lower and higher references, respectively, with Indonesian serving a more objectifying, referential function.

Some languages, such as Japanese, mark foreign words as such visually in their written form (using katakana rather than the usual hiragana symbols for Western borrowings, and kanji for Sino-Japanese), which adds another dimension to code-switching. Studies of code-switching have been limited almost entirely to the spoken channel of communication, but consideration should be given to written and nonverbal channels as well.

A number of linguists have suggested universal constraints on where within a sentence switching may occur, and interest in this topic continues (e.g., see Muysken 2000). Our emphasis here is rather on the variety of functions that code-switching and style-shifting may have within or between speech communities: group identification, solidarity, distancing, and redefinition of a situation have already been mentioned. Additionally, switching languages may serve either to soften or strengthen a request or command, and saying something twice in different languages may serve either to intensify or to eliminate ambiguity. Jong A. Kiem reports that a superlative seems more powerful in Sranan than Dutch, for instance, and that a bilingual reduplication is used if something is really "out of this world." Morray provides the following examples for degrees of intensification in Sranan: *pikin* 'small'; *pikin-pikin* 'very small'; *pikin-tjoti* 'very, very small' ('small' in Sranan + 'small' in Hindi).

Even young children make use of the choices in their linguistic repertoire for a variety of communicative purposes. They commonly use intrasentential code-switching, for instance, to give additional force to part of an utterance, such as highlighting the object of a claim or the thrust of an insult. The following insults were uttered by two four-year-old boys, the first Korean and the second Chinese, each in talking to his younger brother:

1   *He is a* → *baba.*
          [idiot]
    'He is an idiot.' (Referring to a third Korean child they were playing with)
2   *Ni shi* → *rug.*
    [you are]
    'You are a rug.'

In both of these cases, the child also knew the switched lexical item in the other language.

This strategy is in contrast to the intersentential code-switching that children often use to speak disparagingly about speakers of other languages who are within hearing when they do not wish them to understand. For example, a four-year-old Chinese girl spoke disrespectfully of two nearby nursery school teachers, knowing they did not understand Chinese:

3   *Tamen hao taoyan ei. Taoyande laoshi.*
    'They are very disgusting. Disgusting teachers.'

A final example of this strategy involved a twelve-year-old Korean boy who was speaking to his brother disapprovingly about an Icelandic girl who was trying to talk to him:

4   *Zigo mueonde?*
    'Who is she [to tell me]?'

Code-switching may be quite unconscious, and the fact of switching itself may be as meaningful in expressing a closer or more informal relationship as the referential content or specific language forms used. Blom and Gumperz (1972) report that speakers in Norway could not accurately recall their own switches between Ranamål, the local dialect, and Bokmål, the standard, and census takers in India have reported individuals who are not even aware of being bilingual although they can converse in more than one language, depending on the addressee (Kachru 1977).

Metaphorical style-shifting occurs in such situations as faculty meetings, where professors may address each other formally by title when making motions and conducting other official business, but shift to a first name level when trying to win the support of a colleague for their point of view. In some universities a ritual shift occurs at the end of a successful dissertation defense, when professors address the (former) student as *Doctor* and may invite first names in return.

Mohammed Abdulaziz (personal communication) reports policemen in Kenya switch from Swahili to Pidgin English to establish authority in a confrontation situation, and professors may switch into English if someone comes to their office at an inconvenient time. They may say in English, "Oh, did we have an appointment at this time?" but different rules would be in operation if they used Swahili, and a referentially comparable expression would be considered rude. (If the visitor dropped by their house instead of their office, the professors would be constrained from switching into English, and would have no choice but to take time to visit.)

Switching may also be used for a humorous effect, or to indicate that a referentially derogatory comment is not to be taken seriously. It is also used for direct quotations, which may range from stereotypical imitative speech in joking to learned citations in Latin or Greek.

Switching may occur because of real lexical need, sometimes because formulaic expressions in one language cannot be satisfactorily translated into the second, sometimes because the speaker knows the desired expression only in one language, and sometime because access to one of the languages is diminished (perhaps in the process of language attrition). The first of these reasons explains why native speakers of English who have learned some French, German, or Arabic continue to use such expressions as *savoir faire*, *macht's nichts*, and *inshallah*, respectively, in otherwise English sentences, and why speakers of many other languages insert English *OK*.

The following examples illustrate the second and third types of lexical need (from Saville-Troike, Pan, and Dutkova 1995). These utterances were produced by children living in an English-dominant social setting. The first three show children inserting English lexical items for terms they do not know in their first language:

1 *Birthday cake* → *deedąą*.
          [it-we-ate]
   'We ate a birthday cake.' (Navajo child, at 3 years 7 months)
2 *Wo gang gang cai* → *butter pecan*.
   [I just to]
   'I'm just now up to butter pecan.' (Chinese child, at 4 years 4 months, referring to a flavor of ice cream)
3 *Tohle je mu:j* → *summer sandwich*.
   [this is my]
   'This is my summer sandwich.' (Czech child, at 7 years 10 months)

The next three examples are utterances by children from the same first language groups who are more strongly influenced by English, due to longer periods of residence in the US (in the case of the Czech and Chinese speakers) or to stronger English dominance at home (in the case of the Navajo). These illustrate progressive incorporation from single words to longer segments, which we found to be a common pattern for children who seem to have decreasing access to their first language in processing:

4   *Shima* → *house clean* → *iilee.*
     [my-mother]   [it-do]
     'My mother is cleaning house.' (Navajo child, at 4 years 0 months)
5   *Wo* → *wish* → *women* → *could build a house just for ourselves.*
     [I]   [we]
     'I wish we could build a house just for ourselves.' (Chinese child, at 6 years 1 month)
6   *Homework* → *ya: ma:m kazhdey den* → *except Friday, Saturday, and Sunday.*
                   [I have every day]
     'Homework I have every day except Friday, Saturday, and Sunday.' (Czech child, at 8 years 2 months)

Yet another social function of code-switching is to exclude other people within hearing if a comment is intended for only a limited audience, such as some of the children's insults I reported earlier. This may be considered rude, but it is not necessarily so. A Tanzanian professor residing in the United States, for instance, says that in the presence of guests in their home a husband and wife would employ code-switching for discussion concerning the comfort and needs of their guests. The exclusionary function was used by US President and Mrs. Herbert Hoover around the White House; they reportedly switched into Chinese when they did not wish to be understood by others. My husband made similar use of this strategy when we were hosting friends for dinner in a restaurant and he asked me in Chinese, *You qian ma?* 'Do you have any money?' In such situations, the other language functions as a "secret" language, as may artificial creations.

Indeed, the use of secret codes is apparently very common. In one study of the phenomenon, Gaudart (1995) reported that 94percent of her Malaysian informants who are speakers of English consciously used a code that they knew some listeners in the group would not understand. In addition to the exclusionary and "face-saving" functions noted above, many mentioned inclusion (group identity and group cohesiveness) and some "playing with language." Secret codes reported in Malaysia included "F Language," which involves the insertion of /f/ after every vowel. The secret languages of my own teen years were "Op Talk" and "Circus Language," which used insertion of /ap/ or /iyəz/, respectively, in each syllable to make the words uninterpretable to listeners who didn't know the rule. Fluent speakers of these codes who were members of my church youth group could even perform recitation of Bible scriptures in the "languages," exemplifying both inclusive and playful motivation.

Most phonological changes intended to obscure various languages are quite simple. Of the secret varieties of Welsh which have been described, for instance, two involved merely inserting a vowel plus consonant in each syllable (Awbery 1984). (This process is essentially the same as the one I described for the creation of "Op Talk" and "Circus Language" in English.) These two Welsh varieties appear to have been quite widely used, while the distribution of another with a more complex structure seems to have been much more limited.

Code-switching is also used as an avoidance strategy, either if certain forms are incompletely learned in one of the languages, or if one language requires (usually because of pronominal selection or verb inflection) a social status distinction one does not wish to make. For this latter reason, a speaker of a status-marking language such as Korean or Thai may switch to English with another speaker of that language when he or she prefers not to be deferential.

In some cases code-switching functions as a repair strategy, when the speakers realize they have been using an inappropriate code. This was a relatively frequent occurrence in Greece, during the period when liberal politicians trained in a rhetorical tradition which ranked Katharevousa over Demotike for formal speaking realized they were (ironically) using Katharevousa to advocate democratization of the national language. Shifting for repair is necessary when speakers realize they have begun an event, such as a telephone conversation, at an inappropriate stylistic level. The unitary nature of the telephone calling/answering routine is evident in the fact that such repair usually requires backing up to start over with a different greeting form, rather than switching or shifting in the middle of the routine.

Switching may be used to make an ideological statement, as in the case of Mexican Americans referring to New Mexico as *Nuevo Mexico* [méxiko], or Texas as [téxas], in an otherwise English sentence. Not infrequently, such switching is employed even by monolingual speakers of English or English-dominant bilinguals who wish to assert their Hispanic ancestry. A contrasting function was observed in Barcelona during a period of considerable tension between speakers of Castilian and Catalan (Woolard 1987). Code-switching by a popular entertainer there helped to ease group boundaries, serving for boundary-leveling rather than for maintenance. Also involved in the Barcelona events was *bivalency*, or "the use by a bilingual of words or segments that could 'belong' equally . . . to both codes" (Woolard 1999: 7). Similar integration of ethnic identities has often been served by code-switching in literature: for instance, Jean Giraudoux's *Ondine*, written in 1939, alternates lines in French and German to convey dual allegiances as war was breaking out between the two countries; and T. S. Eliot's *The Waste Land*, written at the end of World War I, alternates lines written by Wagner in German with lines written in English in order to convey a juxtaposition of emotions in a manner that a single language could not have achieved. In analyzing this poem, Kramsch says:

> The pain evoked by one language (the fear of death in the memory of a war that pitted English speakers against German) is soothed by the other (in Tristan and Isolde's longing for love and death). The combination of the two codes expresses a tragic mixture of sweetness and sadness. (1997: 367)

Using strategies of linguistic integration, entirely new identities may be created:

> By appropriating the language of others, multilingual speakers create new discourse communities whose areal existence monolingual speakers hardly suspect. (Kramsch 1997: 365)

Attitudes toward language switching and shifting are of interest for ethnographic description. These appear to be changing rapidly among English-speaking bilinguals in the United States, with the ability to code-switch now widely accepted as a symbol of ethnic viability and integrity. This is evident in the fact that in the American Southwest poetry is being written, songs sung, plays performed, and formal speeches delivered in an alternating Spanish-English mode (e.g., see Valdés 1977; Lipski 1982). Radio and television stations also utilize code-switching in commentaries and commercials. There are still conflicting attitudes about the phenomenon, however, based on both age and political sentiment.

Whatever specific functions are served by code-switching within and across communities, it adds to the verbal strategies that speakers have at their command, and is to be recognized as a dimension of communicative competence.

Code-Markers

The concept of code-markers is based on the distinction between *marked* and *unmarked* language forms which was first developed within the Prague School of linguistics. This distinction may be applied to all aspects of communicative behavior, and indeed has been adopted for more general descriptive and explanatory purposes, including language choice (e.g., see Myers-Scotton 1998). The basic assumption is that behavior can be distinguished as marked or unmarked according to certain component features, and that the unmarked is more neutral, more normal, or more expected.

In explaining the recognition and interpretation of different varieties of language within a speech community, it is necessary to assume that speakers have a concept of naturalness both for their language in general and in any specific context. Markedness on the more general level identifies language forms as belonging to a particular variety, such as a regional dialect, register, or social category. Markedness in a specific context refers to usage which calls attention to itself, like an Australian variety of English being spoken in Canada, a formal register being used in an intimate relationship, feminine gestures and interaction strategies being used by a male, or adult language structures being used by a young child.

Language forms must be perceptibly different in some systematic way to be recognized as distinct varieties. Variability in any aspect of a language may potentially serve a marking function, including vocabulary, pronunciation, grammar, paralinguistic elements, and visual appearance (in the case of written and manual forms). Variation in interactional strategies may also pattern along these dimensions. Different variables will be considered significant in each speech community, so no single set may be posited, and different aspects of language may mark different kinds of varieties within a single community. In American English, for instance, regional varieties are most marked by vocabulary and pronunciation features, but seldom by grammar; social class is most marked by grammatical features; ethnicity, sex, age, and personality most by pronunciation, paralinguistic features, and discourse strategies; and register most by vocabulary, grammatical complexity, and rhetorical organization.

It is possible that some kinds of linguistic features are inherently more suitable for signaling particular kinds of social meaning, but it remains a topic for empirical investigation. The lexical, syntactic, and rhetorical features marking register in English are more likely to be under conscious control than the phonological and paralinguistic features marking ethnicity, sex, age, and personality, and thus more likely to be available for manipulation. Since relative level of consciousness is related to both circumstances of acquisition and neurological factors, it is a possible universal.

Although some neurological factors are also involved in determining how much of a difference in language productions will be perceived by humans, no single degree of variability can be established as significant in all languages; very small differences in an absolute sense may carry a heavy load of social information, while major absolute differences may be socially meaningless. The difference between [s] and [š] is the shibboleth of Biblical days (Judges 12: 4–6), which served a password function with mortal consequences, yet the same variation in Tonkawa (once indigenous to Texas) apparently carried no social weight, and may not have even been noticed, e.g. as in [maslak] versus [mašlak] 'white.'

The term *code-marker* as I am using it includes all variable features which are available to members of a speech community for distinguishing among the varieties of a language in their communicative repertoire. It includes social markers (which mark such characteristics as social and educational status, occupation, and regional affiliation), physical markers (which mark such characteristics as age, sex, and physical condition), and psychological markers (which mark personality characteristics and affective states) (cf. Laver and Trudgill 1979).

In identifying and defining what a linguistic variable is, Labov (1972) distinguishes among three levels of these features, which he calls *indicator*, *marker* (with a different meaning than that used here), and *stereotype*. An indicator is a variable which is not perceived at a highly conscious level in the speech community, although it does serve to mark varieties of language. The pronunciation of *caught* with the same vowel as *cot*, for instance, is one regional marker in American English, but it does not carry much social significance. A marker for Labov is a variable which has taken on social valuation, and is perceived at a conscious level. Voicing of the medial consonant in *greasy* is also a regional distinction in English, but one that has more social significance: the voiced variant [z] generally carries a pejorative connotation toward the object being described for users of the [s]; the pronunciation is quite consciously perceived, and regional identity of the speaker inferred. The New York [r]-less variable described by Labov (1966) is also at this level, as is calling the evening meal *dinner* versus *supper*. Because this marker level is conscious, such variables may be used for intentional metaphorical switching, while indicators may not.

A stereotype for Labov is the highest level of code-marking. It is likely to be commented on, and is used in characterizing groups when joking about them, but it need not conform to actual usage. Someone from Brooklyn (New York) may be characterized as saying *Toidy Toid (33rd) Street*, but that pronunciation is disappearing from actual use because of being heavily stigmatized. Similarly, French speakers when speaking English are stereotyped as saying *I sink (think)*, Texans as greeting everyone with *Howdy, pardner*, and Britishers as calling all men *chap*. Others in the speech community will recognize the group being referred to by such marking since this, too, is part of communicative competence, but it does not necessarily conform to linguistic reality.

Some code-markers are absolute, or *categorical* in their distribution, occurring only and always in a particular variety of language, but most are *gradient phenomena* which occur more or less in one variety than in another. It is not clear exactly how and to what extent native speakers interpret relative frequencies of marked occurrence, but perception is undoubtedly conditioned by the relative importance of the social information its use conveys.

Determining the social meaning of code-markers is an important contribution of qualitative ethnographic research to variation theory, since "Quantitative techniques can only sensibly be applied after a prior examination of the dependencies that a linguistic variable's significance has on other aspects of interaction structure and process" (Brown and Levinson 1979: 333). An illustration of the contrastive meaning which may be conveyed by alternating variables is found in Huspek's (1986) analysis of *-ing* versus *-in* in workers' speech. Huspek found that *He went jogging* conveyed an attitude of either respect or resentment toward the individual being referred to, while *He went joggin'* conveyed lower social status, but also in-group identification. On the other hand, the same linguistic variable may have different social meaning depending on other features in the interaction situation, and on other code-markers which may be present. The same intonational variables which mark "baby talk" signal warmth and affection toward a young child, but may be interpreted as mocking and demeaning if used with an older child or adult, for instance, and the [r]-less variant which has negative valuation when used by a working-class native of New York is a marker of social prestige when it (along with the different variants in vowel quality and lexicon) indicates the speaker is an upper-class native of Boston.

Statistical analysis of frequencies and correlations may help to verify or define certain tentatively identified relationships, but in general the identification of hypotheses to be tested regarding possible relationships should precede the application of statistical techniques. Occasionally, however, quantitative analysis will reveal previously unrecognized associations, or will demonstrate regular patterns in data which seemed amorphous.

The following sections of this chapter illustrate a number of the social and cultural dimensions with which varieties of language might be associated in a speech community, and the range of communicative phenomena which might be marked.

Varieties Associated with Setting

Varieties of language which are more closely associated with the setting or scene in which they are used than with the people who are using them are usually included in the concept of *register*, and distinguished from one another primarily on the dimension of relative formality.

The physical setting of an event may call for the use of a different variety of language even when the same general purpose is being served, and when the same participants are involved. English greeting forms may differ inside a building versus outside, for instance, or inside an office versus inside a church, as well as between participants at differing distances from one another. In this case, primary markers are voice level and nonverbal behaviors, but often also involve a choice of lexical and grammatical structures along a polite-casual, impersonal-personal, sacred-secular, or public-private dimension; all of these may be generally subsumed under formal-informal (Brown and Fraser 1979).

In question-and-answer exchanges between professor and students, appropriate language use is determined in large part by the setting, including the size of the room and the seating arrangement (e.g. chairs in fixed rows, in a circle, or around a conference table). In this case, different levels of formality are signaled primarily by whether or not students are expected to raise their hands and be formally recognized before speaking, and by whether or not strict turn-taking applies. Relative level of formality as determined by the setting will also affect how questions and answers are phrased, and what topics may be queried.

A formal greeting in a locker room would be considered a highly marked communicative event (especially if the participants were not fully clothed), as would informal questions and interruptions by students in a large lecture hall. In these cases where level of formality in language use does not coincide with level of formality in the setting, language may serve to increase or decrease the distance between speakers. When physical distance cannot be maintained for some reason, such as in a crowded Japanese household where all four grandparents sometimes live with children and grandchildren, very polite language (the highest form of *Keigo*) may be used to maintain social distance, even though a less formal variety of Japanese would normally be appropriate.

In some communities a particular setting is required for an event to take place: e.g., there may be a particular place in which it is appropriate to pray, or teach, or to tell stories, and these events are often concomitant with choice of different language varieties. Language restrictions or taboos are also often related to setting, such as constraints against talking about certain topics at the dining table, whistling in the house, or cursing in a place of worship.

Varieties Associated with Activity Domain

Included in this category are languages or varieties of language which serve the wide-ranging purposes of groups that are organized along lines of shared beliefs, skills or training, and interests, and which are used in the conduct of their affairs. For illustrative purposes, we will consider the diverse domains of religion, secret societies, governmental agencies, occupations, and hobbies or special interests. With the exception of some religious sects into which children may be enculturated from infancy, these languages and varieties share the trait of being no one's "native" language code; their addition may thus be conceived of as extended acquisition of communicative competence (discussed in chapter 7).

Language codes used primarily for religious purposes include Geez by Christians in Ethiopia, Latin by Catholics, Classical Arabic by Muslims, and Pali by Buddhists.

> When a Japanese Buddhist priest in a California Buddhist church recites a sutra in Pali with his English-speaking congregation, this is a fine example of the spread of a particular language variety over enormous distances in space and time. When accounts of the Buddha and his sayings were collected and came to be accepted as the canon of Buddhist scripture, they were in a Middle Indo-Aryan language, Pali, whose exact provenience is not clear. When the Pali scriptures were used in worship in India and Ceylon, the language functioned as a special religious register in many speech communities where related Indo-Aryan languages were the worshippers' mother tongues. When Buddhism spread to areas such as Burma, Thailand, China, and Japan, the sacred scripture went along. Buddhist missionaries and scholars translated Pali and Sanskrit texts into other languages, but just about everywhere at least some uses of Pali were kept. In these new areas, the Pali language, still functioning as a religious register, was no longer related at all to the language of the worshippers, but retained its aura of sacredness. (Ferguson 1978: 3)

The use of glossolalia, or 'speaking in tongues,' by certain charismatic Christian groups also exemplifies language choice for religious purposes, although much of its meaning is conveyed through features other than verbal code (Goodman 1969). Certain language forms themselves are believed in some communities to be prescribed by a supernatural being and the only ones mortals may use for communication with that force, or they may be considered the medium through which the supernatural may speak to humans. In other cases the language forms themselves are considered imbued with power, and they may be used to control the forces of nature. Harding (2000) adds the level of narrative framework for consideration, including fundamentalist Christian preacher Jerry Falwell's adaptation of biblical forms to contemporary themes and self-presentation, and to performance in contexts of modern media and political power.

When the same language is used in a community for both secular and religious purposes, the religious variety is often marked by more conservative forms: e.g. second person *thou*, *thee*, and *thy* in English. Other common markers are lexical (such as the use of different terms of address, or words used with unique meanings), morphological (often involving more deferential forms), paralinguistic (intoned speech, or different patterns of pitch, stress, and rhythm), and kinesic (head, hand, and body position and movement). Different channels of communication are often utilized, including bones, shells, horns, and drums, and receptive senses may be heightened or otherwise altered by drugs and trance states. Organization of discourse in religious events is frequently marked, including prescribed ritual openings and closings and the genre-specific "one-many dialog, in which a speaker addresses the whole group and receives a unison response" (Ferguson 1986: 209).

Some opponents of modernization of the English Bible believe that modernization ignores speakers' feelings that sacred beliefs are more appropriately expressed in a "special" code rather than an everyday one, and that modernization thus reduces the capacity of English to serve aesthetic and religious purposes. Those who disagree often support Biblical language modernization on the grounds that religion should be accessible to each person without need for interpretation by others, and thus that its concepts are more appropriately expressed in the vernacular. Because the religious functions of language are not the same in all speech communities, any resolution of this controversy cannot necessarily be generalized to other societies.

A comparable issue in dispute is whether language used for such specialized purposes as curing, legal briefs, or contracts should be a "special" variety, or "plain" language. Specialized forms are required in many communities for curing rituals, including among the Rosebud Sioux, where a formal style of Lakota is used for such purposes.

> Labels for herbs, medicines and powers as well as prayers are uttered in the formal style because proper ritual prescriptions must be observed if the spirits are to respond as desired. Prayer is almost always spoken in formal speech, as supplication must be in the ritually prescribed form to be received. (Grobsmith 1979: 357–8)

Sociolinguists studying doctor–patient communication in English (e.g. Shuy 1974; Skopek 1975; Pliskin 1987) document the misunderstanding which can result when technical medical terms are used, but many patients do not have faith in a doctor who "doesn't talk like one."

Specialized varieties of language are often used when the purpose is to be secretive, or to deceive, although this function sometimes merely involves change in vocal quality (whispering). Argots have been created by criminals for secret communication among themselves since the days of the Roman underworld (Maurer 1940), and adolescents in many societies use a secret code comparable to Pig Latin in English, which involves permutation and addition of phonological segments. In a bar district of Addis Ababa, for instance, an Amharic argot which was created by schoolboys has reportedly been adopted by unattached young women for such purposes as "concealing conversations and planning tricks at the customers' expense" (Demisse and Bender 1983: 340). The pattern also primarily involves phonological substitution and duplication, but in this case there is in addition grammatical change, with occurrence of compound verbs in a form that does not occur in "normal" Amharic.

Franklin (1977) describes three types of secret speech among the Kewa of New Guinea. *Ramula agaa* 'pandanus language' is used to protect people who travel in swamp forest areas where ghosts and wild dogs are present. People are instructed by their ancestors not to speak their "normal" language, and to use a secret variety marked by special vocabulary. *Mumu n agaa* 'whispering talk' is used whenever others within hearing of speech produced at normal volume are not supposed to know what is going on, as when the topic is trading, bespelling, or stealing something. *Kudiri ne agaa* refers to 'secret talk,' or talk limited to insiders, such as cult initiates. The first of these types is for external secrecy, known by all in the speech community and directed toward outsiders; the latter two are for internal secrecy, or inhibition of information flow within the community.

Brandt (1977) describes these phenomena in Pueblo societies, where internal secrecy assures that no single member possesses all necessary information for the performance of rituals, and preserves the interdependence of subgroups in the social organization. Pueblo strategies for secrecy include: barring outsiders from performance of ceremonies in ritual spaces, such as kivas; constructing false and misleading information; evasion of questions; purging the language of Spanish and English loanwords in the presence of those who might understand them (sometimes requiring elaborate circumlocutions); use of special ritual varieties which contain archaic words, borrowings from other languages, and different semantic systems (i.e. different referents); and special styles of speaking, such as "talking backwards."

Specialized language for governmental purposes in most Western societies includes the extensive use of acronyms (often deliberately chosen for pronounceability) to designate administrative units: e.g. US *OBEMLA* 'Office of Bilingual Educational and Minority Language Affairs,' British *CILT* 'Centre for Information on Language Teaching,' Belgian *AIMAV* 'Association Internationale pour la Recherche et la Diffusion des Méthodes Audio-visuelles et Structuros Globales,' Mexican *INI* 'Instituto Nacional Indigenista,' Peruvian *CILA* 'Centro de Investigación en Linguística Applicada.' This pattern is generally tied to an alphabetic writing system; Chinese, in contrast, regularly selects elements for combination that are no smaller than what is represented by a single character, as in *Bei Da* for *Bejing Daxue* 'Peking University.' In part, however, patterns are also related to political orientation. Since the communist revolution, the Russian pattern has been to use the first syllable of words rather than the initial letters; this pattern was used metaphorically by Orwell in *Nineteen Eighty-Four* for designating administrative units. The association of this linguistic pattern with a particular kind of political system is further illustrated by Cuba's change from an acronym to *Min Ed* 'Ministerio de Educación' with the rise of Castro to power. Further study of comparable patterns in other speech communities would be of interest, especially as they are related both to typological features of language structures and orthographic systems, and to sociocultural features of the society. Specialized vocabulary and phrases must also be mastered in order to communicate about governmental functions and processes, as in US "federalese": *zero-based budgeting, inhouse capabilities, RFP* (request for proposal), and *regs* (regulations).

Lexical requirements are also quite specific to many occupational areas (including linguistics), which is one reason why training received through the medium of one language cannot be easily discussed in others. It is probably safe to estimate that no more than three percent of the English lexicon can be considered immediately relevant to all of its speakers.

Very large corpuses of texts in different genres and registers are now being used in computerized linguistic analyses to determine differential frequency patterns in vocabulary and grammar (e.g., see Biber 1995). These are proving to be highly relevant for development of programs and materials targeting second language learners who need to function immediately within a single occupational domain (e.g., see Conrad 1999), as well as for application to machine translation and artificial intelligence.

Beyond patterns of lexical selection and grammatical structure, sociolinguists have documented occupation-specific discourse structures, formulaic elements, and prosody. These are particularly notable in occupations which involve public performance, such as auctioneering, weather forecasting, sports commentary, DJ patter, and pitching sales on TV for a used car lot. Further, within a single general category such as auctioneering or sports commentary, there is systematic variation in forms for auctioning tobacco versus fine art, and for horse racing versus other venues (Kuiper 1996).

We may find many similar discrete varieties of language among avocational special-interest groups which participate in structured interactional events. Serious players of Bridge, for instance, have highly codified rules for usage: strict turn-taking for bidding is observed, starting with the dealer and progressing clockwise; a "maxim of quantity" is enforced, with the amount of information bidders may impart about their cards explicitly regulated; and some bids have a conventional meaning that is shared only by other members of the group (e.g., a bid of *four no trump* is never taken literally, but interpreted as a directive for the partner to declare how many aces he or she has – a response of *five clubs* means 'no aces,' *five diamonds* means 'one ace,' etc.). Any violation of language usage in tournament play may result in penalties or disqualification.

A special-interest group which has a very different membership base is that of the pop group 'N Sync's fans, but it also has highly codified rules for language use. As reported to me by one of the fans, the content of intragroup communications is often mocking or derogatory toward members of 'N Sync, but the tone is affectionate and teasing; much of the discourse is based on recreating conversations used by 'N Sync in television appearances, in which phrases are co-opted and used to create new utterances; and commonly used phrases have meaning only to members of the group. This interest group may interact via e-mail as well as face-to-face.

Because the languages or varieties associated with activity domain are normally no one's "native" language code, but are usually acquired in relation to training and social practices which are not uniformly accessible to members of a community, this is one dimension of its linguistic repertoire which clearly illustrates the unequal distribution of competence which was discussed in chapter 2.

Varieties Associated with Region

Regional varieties of language develop as different norms arise in the usage of groups who are separated by some kind of geographic boundary. This is commonly in vocabulary, as when English speakers in New England carry water in a *pail* and those in Texas in a *bucket*, and in pronunciation, as when Navajo speakers call 'snow' *yas* versus *zas* on different sides of the Lukachukai mountain range. Grammatical markers associated with region are less common, but they do develop: e.g., English speakers in the south and southeastern regions of the United States use such double modal constructions as *might could* and *might will*, which are rare or nonexistent elsewhere in the country.

As geographic boundaries increase in strength, so generally do the degrees of difference between speakers of the "same" language. The very rugged terrain of the state of Oaxaca, Mexico, for instance, and the resultant difficulty in traveling from one village to another, is in large part responsible for the maintenance of 25 distinct languages in an area no larger than the US state of Indiana (ca. 36,000 square miles). The major distinction in the colloquial Arabic spoken in Algeria is between sedentary and nomadic dialects, which although not a strict regional division, similarly reflects ecological influences in limiting interaction between subgroups.

Regional phonological and lexical markers have been studied in many languages as the result of research on dialect geography, but little attention has been paid to regional patterning in other aspects of communication. One notable difference which has been studied in the United States is in naming practices, with southerners using double names (e.g. *Billy Joe*, *Billy Gene*, *Larry Leroy*, *Mary Fred*) and nicknames or diminutives, even in formal contexts (e.g. former First Lady *Lady Bird Johnson*, *Dr. Billy Graham*, *President Jimmy Carter*); also *Bobby*, *Johnny*, and *Jimmy* are bisexual only in southern usage (Pyles 1959). Another regional difference is in terms of address: e.g., a southern man may call his wife or a female friend *ma'am* with no negative connotation intended, while a northern interpretation would be one of distancing, or implications that the woman is of a more advanced age. It has also been more common in southern deferential address to use title plus first name, rather than last. Well-known examples are "Mister Sam" (Rayburn) for the former Speaker of the US House of Representatives, and "Miss Scarlet" (O'Hara) for the main character is Mitchell's *Gone with the Wind*. The pattern also occurs in more general usage, as with "Judge Judy" and "Dr. Laura" on popular TV.

Nonverbal behavior may also differ regionally, including facial expressions and the scope of body movements, but these patterns have received little attention as markers associated with regional varieties. Some nonverbal behaviors pattern regionally even across unrelated languages. The emblem for "no" is a vertical head movement in Greece, Turkey, the Arabian Peninsula, and most of North Africa, for instance; Israel seems to be the one regional exception, using the horizontal head movement of the Northern European area. Other gestures which exhibit areal over genetic influence are those of greeting and farewell.

Although the development of mass communication and rapid transportation has done much to retard the forces of regional differentiation, local forces remain most powerful during the early years of language acquisition and hence are unlikely to be entirely offset. Furthermore, since these markers themselves serve a boundary function between a local group and "outsiders," or provide a means of identifying people from "home" when in another area, the differences may be accentuated (cf. Labov's 1963 report of linguistic change in Martha's Vineyard, which illustrates this process). The importance of this function differs from community to community, and is related to the value placed on being different or unique.

Prestige factors contribute to this process, which supports Baugh's argument that linguistic standards in the US may be considered from both national and regional perspectives:

> The national standard . . . may be reinforced through broadcast speech, whereas regional standards can be traced to the old upper-class families who still speak with strong regional dialects. Many of our senators and congressional representatives reflect these regional standards in their speech. (2000: 35)

When several members of a group migrate to another area where the group is identified with higher or lower than average status, markers associated with their regional variety may become associated with social class. The stigmatized [r]-less variety of English used by lower-class African Americans in New York City as reported by Labov (1966), for instance, represents a subgroup immigration from the south, where that is a non-stigmatized regional pronunciation.

Varieties Associated with Ethnicity

A multiethnic speech community may pattern in several different ways with respect to language use: (1) subgroups in the community may use only their minority ethnic language(s); (2) minority group members may be bilingual in their ethnic language(s) and the dominant language; or (3) minority group members may be monolingual in the dominant language. In conditions (2) and (3), members of minority groups who identify themselves as such often speak a distinctive variety of the dominant language. These "accents" are usually interpreted simply as arising from the influence of the ethnic language(s), and features indeed may be attributed to substratum varieties or to the mother tongue, but they may be maintained and cultivated (consciously or unconsciously) as linguistic markers of ethnic identity (Giles 1979).

Ethnicity code-markers occur at levels of phonology, vocabulary, morphosyntax, and overall style, although in English grammatical markers are more likely to be associated with social class and educational level on a standard–nonstandard dimension. One notable exception is the "invariant *be*" of African American Vernacular English (AAVE), which is generally recognized as an ethnic marker (except by teachers in the schools, who misinterpret it as "ungrammatical"); the use of a "double negative" in English, on the other hand, is not considered a marker of Hispanic or French ethnicity (although it is a grammatical feature in both mother tongues), but rather as nonstandard and uneducated usage.

African American English in the United States has been the best described ethnically marked speech, although linguists' attention has generally been limited to nonstandard varieties, and has rarely focused on the range of social levels within identifiably African American usage (Wright 1975; a notable exception is Baugh 1983). Most attention has been given to AAVE phonology and morphosyntax (e.g. Rickford 1999), with some significant additional contributions made to understanding differences in discourse patterns and ways of speaking (e.g. Kochman 1972; Folb 1980; Gumperz 1982; Heath 1983; Morgan 1998).

African American standard varieties differ from White standard varieties primarily in intonational features, and in the marked pronunciation of a few lexical items (including *particularly*, in which the penultimate syllable has secondary stress and an unreduced vowel). Other descriptions of ethnically marked speech include Indian English (Kachru 1976; 1983; Gumperz 1977), Gästarbeiterdeutsch (Dittmar 1977), American Indian English (Leap 1993), Puerto Rican English (Wolfram 1973), and Chicano English (Ornstein-Galicia 1984). Ethnic markers also occur in American Sign Language, where African American signers in the south have developed some characteristics which are different from the signs used by Whites in the same region (Woodward 1976). Differences in signs are both lexical and phonological: African American signing has not shared with White signing the same changes with respect to centralization, symmetry, and morphological preservation.

Markers associated with ethnicity may include nonverbal features as well, including the side-to-side head movement of some speakers of Indian English, and the different eye contact patterns of several ethnic groups (cf. Harper, Wiens, and Matarazzo 1978).

Tannen (1981) discusses ethnic markers in conversational style, including differences in the use of questions, methods for getting and keeping the floor, topic cohesion, and the use of irony and humor. Dimensions of differences between New York Jewish and Los Angeles non-Jewish style in her study include relevant personal focus of topic; paralinguistic features of pitch, loudness, voice quality, and tone; pacing and timing with respect to other utterances; rate of speech; and choice of lexical items and syntactic forms. Analysis of narratives collected from different groups (e.g. Tannen 1980) provides additional interesting information on ethnic markers in patterns of language use.

Ethnic differences in style may be modified in accordance with the situation, of course, as may other variables. Baugh reports the perceptions of one of his African American constituents about an event which required consistent style-shifting when he addressed different participants:

> I'm in the middle cause I know them both. They are both my friends. . . . I have to talk to them [the whites] one way and then I have to turn back around and talk to them [the black girls] another way . . . and try to keep him [the white man] from feeling left out of this conversation, and the girls from feeling left out in the other conversation . . . so . . . it's kind of hard to sit in the middle of a situation like that. (1983: 28)

Unlike using a foreign language, using an ethnically marked variety of a language generally requires being born into group membership, unless the intent is to ridicule or joke (which indeed is often the case). One of the best sources of data on which ethnic markers are stigmatized and stereotyped is the imitative language markers used in telling ethnic jokes.

On the other hand, individual speakers born into the ethnic group – or the entire group membership – can generally succeed in eliminating all ethnic markers in their speech if they desire to fully assimilate to the dominant group, or they can develop both marked and unmarked varieties and shift between them depending on desired group identification in specific situations. However, because ethnic varieties of speech are often salient and evaluated dimensions of ethnicity, adopting the linguistic norms of another group may be viewed with suspicion and hostility.

Changes which are occurring in AAVE provide good evidence for the types of social factors that may be involved in ethnic marking. The usage of young speakers appears to be diverging further from White norms than does the speech of adults. Bailey and Maynor (1987) attribute this increasing divergence to such social developments as migration to inner cities, economic stagnation, and residential segregation. African American youth appear to be cultivating linguistic divergence as a vehicle for identification and solidarity, as well as covert prestige. Folb (1980) additionally reports secrecy and identification of non-group members as motivation among the teens for ethnically marked language use, along with peer-group pressure in contexts where those prevail.

Varieties Associated with Social Class, Status, and Role

When describing patterns of language use in a complex and heterogeneous speech community, determining what subgroups are accorded differential status and prestige, and understanding what criteria are used within the community for defining subgroup membership, must precede discovery of how the rights and means of communication within the total linguistic repertoire may be differentially allocated according to social class, status, and role.

Social class may be defined primarily by wealth, or by circumstances of birth, or by occupation, or by other criteria specific to the group under investigation. If wealth is a criterion, this may be calculated in terms of money, or in terms of how many pigs, sheep, or blankets an individual or family possesses, or how much land they claim. *Status* is often largely determined by social class membership, but age or education may be more salient, or whether a person is married and has children. *Role* refers to the position(s) an individual holds which entails particular expectations, rights, and responsibilities vis-á-vis others in the society: e.g. chief, minister of education, head of family, friend.

In rigidly stratified communities social class membership is clearly defined, roles strictly compartmentalized, and associated varieties of language clearly differentiated. In such communities members of the lower strata have little opportunity to acquire "higher" language forms. In more democratic communities individuals have a wider range of roles potentially open to them, and generally command a wider range of socially marked speech. Studies in the United States and Canada have shown that those who are upwardly mobile tend to adopt the variety of language spoken by the group just above them, often to the point of hypercorrection, although a social revolution may include the overthrow of prestige language forms as well as people who speak them.

The wider range of language available to higher social classes is exemplified by speakers of the East Godavari (India) dialect of Telugu (Sjoberg 1962). In this group only members of the upper class can use both formal and informal varieties, which are marked by two distinctive phonemic systems. This range relates directly to patterns of education, since the formal variety is learned only by those who attend school. For the same reason, written means of communication in many societies are available only to the upper class.

Most research on social class markers in language have focused on phonology and grammar, but other aspects of language may also be involved. There appears to be a social stratification in the use of color terms for women's fashion in English, for instance, with advertisements of clothes targeted for lower income groups using a limited set of color terms such as *blue*, *red*, *green*, *yellow*, and *purple*, perhaps together with the modifiers *light* and *dark*. Expensive clothes are advertised using a much greater variety of basic color terms: e.g., an advertisement from Saks Fifth Avenue included *rust*, *russet*, *camel*, *plum*, *wine*, *fuchsia*, *teal*, *sapphire*, *turquoise*, *emerald*, *seafoam*, *bone*, and *taupe*. A similar observation has been reported to me by native speakers of German, Spanish, and Arabic, although there is some disagreement over whether the diversity of color terms carries connotations of higher prestige or merely reflects the greater range of hues available in more expensive fabrics.

Status is often marked in forms of address, and in different levels of formality corresponding to different levels of prestige or deference. These include differential naming patterns for married versus unmarried women in many societies, and the Iranian practice of shaking hands with an unveiled woman, but not with one wearing a *chadour*. Change in status may be signaled linguistically, as with the change in name at marriage.

Roles are also often marked by different pronouns or terms of address. English-speaking rulers may refer to themselves with the "imperial" *we*, for instance, and a French businessman was fined for addressing a policeman as *tu*. This was judged to be a "rude" form of address to someone in that role (Eliason 1980). Such linguistic marking of a particular social role is to be distinguished from markers of the dyadic role-relationship of speakers, which will be discussed below.

Another linguistic characteristic of the rights and responsibilities inherent in some roles is the type of performative that can be uttered, and how others must respond. For example, *You're out* is felicitous only if spoken by someone in the role of baseball umpire, and *I hereby sentence you to . . .* only if spoken by someone in the role of judge (cf. Searle 1969). The function of clothing in signaling role or status is illustrated by all uniforms, whether nurse, police, or soldier (with auxiliary markings indicating exact rank). Complaints about nuns and priests abandoning religious garb generally reflect the uncertainty caused by the loss of signals of identity, which in turn help to structure appropriate interaction with them.

The comprehensive description of royal communication in Akan by Yankah (1995) gives an integrative view of how forms of speech, participant structure, rhetorical strategies, discourse organization, dress and props, and other contextual and cultural features contribute to the construction and fulfillment of political roles in that society.

Change in role may also be signaled linguistically by a change in the term of reference for the individuals after they assume the position and again after they step down. Soon after Haile Selassie was deposed as emperor of Ethiopia, for instance, official references changed from "king of kings" to merely "king" (used to distinguish him from other people with the same name). The choice of ways to refer to him constituted a conscious political statement at that time, as conservatives continued to refer to him with a respectful pronoun and the imperial title *janhoi*, radicals used an informal pronoun, and extremists used his former name *Teferi*.

Individuals being trained to fill particular roles in a society may learn varieties that others do not: e.g., a Samoan "talking chief" learns to use rhetorical forms limited to speakers in that role, and a boy who is expected to assume his father's role as curer, chief, or judge often learns the appropriate language forms in the process of informal observation, an opportunity which is not open to other children.

The use of "role-playing" techniques often allows a researcher to elicit informants' perceptions of the speech of people who are in the particular roles they pretend to assume. Children playing "school" or "house" often adopt the language markers they consider typical of teacher or parent roles, while adults asked to take the role of children use high voices and their perception of "baby talk."

A number of questions have been raised about the accuracy of judgments on social class which are based on linguistic markers alone, but several studies suggest they may in fact be quite reliable. Ellis (1967) for English found a correlation of 0.80 between the actual social class of speakers and the estimation of judges merely hearing them count from one to ten, and Shuy, Baratz, and Wolfram (1969) found considerable accuracy in social class identification of their Detroit sample based only on 30-second speech samples. Reviews of these and similar studies are available in Brown, Strong, and Rencher (1975) and in Robinson (1979); cross-cultural research is quite limited. Of interest is not only what markers are being perceived, but also beliefs people have in different speech communities about the relationship of language markers and social class and how these may affect both social organization and patterns of language use.

Varieties Associated with Role-Relationships

While many aspects of language use consistently mark a particular role, the roles which individual speakers assume and the status they are accorded is generally dependent on their relationship to other participants in the communicative event. While the French court declared it "rude" to call a man *tu* while he was in the role of a policeman, for instance, it would be equally inappropriate for the same man to be addressed as *vous* if he were in the role of husband or friend. The relativity is clearly illustrated in Japanese, Javanese, Korean, Thai, Tibetan, and other languages which make extensive use of status-marking honorifics; the same speakers use different forms when speaking to someone in a superior versus someone in an inferior social position, even within the same conversation. These forms are not static markers of social class, but markers of the relative status of speakers in dyadic role-relationships. Further, other contextual dimensions influence choice of indexing elements in the constructive and creative processes of communication, even when addressee and relative status remain the same (e.g., see Agha 1993 for Lhasa Tibetan; Morford 1997 for French; Keating 1998 for Pohnpeian (Micronesia); and Cook 1999 for Japanese).

In addition to the choice of pronouns and use of honorific particles, the relative status of speakers and their role-relationship may be marked in a variety of ways. These include other linguistic elements such as grammatical particles and address terms, paralinguistic features such as voice pitch or volume, nonverbal behaviors, discourse and event ordering, selection of pragmatic strategies, and avoidance or taboo. The wide-ranging occurrence of these phenomena is suggested in the following references:

1 Tyler's (1972) description of kinship terminology used by Koya speakers in India illustrates how choice of terms relates in a systematic way to both expectations and differences in contextual features; and Nahuatl (Aztec) speakers in central Mexico use reflexive prefixes with causatives to imply respect for the person addressed or spoken of: e.g., "he sleeps" is more politely expressed as "he causes himself to sleep" (Sapir 1915).

2 Tzeltal speakers in Chiapas, Mexico use a sustained falsetto to express deference to the addressee (Brown and Levinson 1979). Among the Sierra Popoluca (Mexico), women whisper to their husbands as a mark of deference, and children are expected to whisper when they are first learning

to talk. This is an example of the "powerless speech style" which women may adopt with men, children with adults, or ethnic minorities with majorities, and it marks a power relationship rather than the social categories of sex, age, or ethnicity (Giles, Scherer, and Taylor 1979). (Markers of politeness and power are discussed more fully in chapter 8.)

3   An example of nonverbal relative status-marking is reported by Goffman (1967), who notes that doctors touch other (lower) ranks as a means of showing support and comfort, but others consider it presumptuous to even return (let alone initiate) such contact with a doctor. Nonverbal relative status marking in body attitude is also common, including inclination of the head, bowing or prostration, and hand position (e.g., see Keating 1998 for Pohnpeian).

4   In conversation, subordinates more often pursue topics raised by those with superior status than the other way around, and superiors interrupt more frequently (Zimmerman and West 1975). In a cyclic or interaction event with several people in sequence, such as greetings, introductions, or thanks, the order of address may mark relative deference or closeness. A subordinate or younger individual may be expected to initiate greetings with a superior or elder, for instance, as in Yoruba, Ogori, and Nigerian English (Adegbija 1989). The cycle of Iranian families exchanging traditional New Year Greeting visits always begins with an early call of the youngest on the eldest relative, then the closest relative or friend, and then acquaintances, with the ordering considered an important sign of relative love and respect for each. The eldest in the family does not pay return visits until the third day or later in the celebration (Jafapur).

5   The strategic selection of different linguistic forms for such functions as requesting or directing also indicates the nature of the role-relationship between speaker and addressee: i.e., pragmatic strategies are potential markers of social relationships (Brown and Levinson 1979). Various markers of indirectness are most general in conveying deference, including hesitancy, hedging, and circumlocution. The form of reply for subordinates in age as well as social status is not uncommonly complete silence, with perhaps a nod of the head.

6   In some speech communities particular role-relationships require that clearly distinct varieties of language be used, often involving avoidance or taboo in some respect. An aboriginal Guugu Yimidhirr man in Australia must use only a specialized vocabulary with his brother-in-law (Haviland 1979), for instance, and a Navajo man traditionally cannot speak directly to his mother-in-law, or even be in her presence. Furthermore, he cannot refer to her with the usual third person pronoun form, but employs a more remote fourth person to indicate deference and respect. Avoidance of personal names in some role-relationships is also found in several languages, for direct address and/or in reference. For example, Subrahamian (1978)

reports this taboo is observed in Indian villages where women cannot mention their husband's name; this must be circumvented in census taking by asking neighbors.

Relative status in particular role-relationships involves complex consideration of situational factors, and the relative importance of such features as age, sex, occupation, kinship, and social class in the determination differs in different speech communities. Their relative salience is interesting not only for discovering patterns of language use in interaction, but as potential indicators of the communities' social organization and cultural values. Such complexities are likely to be magnified at stages when dyadic relationships become more ambiguous: e.g. a child is reaching adulthood, a parent is becoming aged or infirm, a student is becoming a professional colleague, or close friends or lovers are severing ties.

Varieties Associated with Sex

The label for this category is in dispute, between advocates of *gender* versus *sex*. Those who advocate "gender" consider it a socially-constructed category, versus "sex," which is biologically determined. I use "sex" (including sexual orientation) because "gender"-marking in linguistics relates to noun class and includes such phenomena as object shape (e.g. round versus straight and rigid in Navajo) and such arbitrary grammatical assignment as the German article *der* (masculine gender) to males, *die* (feminine gender) to married women, but *das* (neuter gender) to young females. I mean to refer to a socially-constructed category, but one that is delimited to a male-female dimension.

A differential distribution of language resources by this definition of sex in a complex community is often associated with differential patterns of education and distribution of labor, including trade versus childrearing responsibilities. Males are more likely to be educated, and thus to control the formal and written varieties of a language. They are also more likely to be bilingual, both because of educational level, and because of mobility and contact in military encounters and trade. In Algeria, for instance, the only remaining monolingual speakers of Berber are women. Exceptions to this pattern occur in societies where women have equal opportunities for education, and possibilities for mobility without dependence on indigenous social structures (e.g. where there are no preferred cross-cousin marriages or other family-arranged alliances), or in communities where women assume a primary marketing role (e.g. in Guatemala, where women take products to market and are most likely to be bilingual in Spanish and their native Mayan language).

In some communities, participation in certain kinds of events is restricted to a single sex, as where it is considered appropriate only for men to tell stories or preach; in others a particular mode of communication is restricted, as where only men whistle, or only women wail. The "tuneful weeping" mode of northern India is used only by women, for instance (Tiwary 1975). Educated, urban women in that area have refused to accept this communicative role as one aspect of change in their social role in the community. A comparable shift among women in eastern Austria from German-Hungarian bilingualism to German-only is reported by Gal (1978, 1979) as a correlate of social change, including women's rejection of peasant life (and peasant husbands).

Some type of sexual differentiation in patterns of speech is likely, perhaps universal, whenever there is social differentiation between male and female roles. Linguistic markers associated with sex often include phonology: e.g., English-speaking women tend to use more socially prestigious speech forms than men (Labov 1966; Trudgill 1975), as well as higher pitch and more variable intonation patterns (Smith 1979); Boas (1911) found that female speakers of some Eskimo dialects used voiced nasals in final position, which corresponded to male stops; and Sapir (1915) found Yana women devoicing final vowels.

Morphological markers include different first person inflections used by men and women in the North American language Koasati (Haas 1944; cf. Saville-Troike 1988), reduplication for emphasis of a verb by Thai women versus the addition of *mak* by Thai men, and the sentence-final particle *ne* in Japanese used almost exclusively by female speakers (Smith 1979). Morphology may also be marked for the sex of the addressee, as with the second person inflections of Hebrew, or the different terms for "they" in the North American language Tunica depending on whether a man or woman is being addressed (Haas 1941). Based on data collected for the Linguistic Atlases of the Upper Midwest and the North Central States, Van Riper (1979) reports that women at all levels of education use significantly more of the past tense forms prescribed as "correct" in English usage handbooks than do men, although there is less difference between male and female speakers who have more formal education. Grammatical markers associated with sex in Japanese include affirmative and nonaffirmative usage of the copula, and differential use of interjections at the beginning and end of utterances; syntactically, women are more likely to use subject inversion and topic-comment constructions.

Lexical markers may also be associated with the sex of either speaker or listener: e.g., a Hopi woman would use a different term if expressing the concept "That's a beautiful area" to a man than she would to a woman, and swear words in many languages differ not only with the sex of the speaker, but also with whether a member of the opposite sex is within hearing. Some English words, such as *adorable* and *lovely*, are associated more with female speakers, and *beautiful* and *handsome* are more appropriately used in reference to females and males respectively.

Topics considered appropriate for discussion may also differ for men and women, as may form or content of insults or other speech acts. In a study of the topics of teachers' conversations in a US faculty room, for instance, Kipers (1987) found females most likely to talk about social issues such as child abuse and women's rights, and males about recreational and work-related activities. At the University of Illinois, in one department female graduate students lodged a formal protest that they were excluded from the opportunity for interaction with male faculty equal to that accorded male graduate students because the principal topic of conversation was usually sports, with which they were less familiar than the males. Tiwary (1975) reports males in Northern India may insult each other by threatening the chastity of mother, sister, or daughter, while women assert the other's sexual activities with father, brother, or son, and curse each other with barrenness or widowhood. In English, a man is traditionally congratulated on the occasion of engagement or marriage, while a woman is offered "best wishes."

Nonverbal marking associated with sex traditionally included male hat-doffing and handshaking in English, although handshaking between women or between men and women has become increasingly common, providing another example of sex differentiation in communicative patterns declining with the lessening of division in social roles. In Mali, where role distinctions are more strictly maintained, Bambara men also shake hands in greeting, but women never do; a female may kneel down when greeting a man, which is never done by males, and she may use only limited eye contact. Clothing markers associated with sex may be relevant to interpreting patterns of communication, including whether or not one or more participants are veiled. (Although this is usually associated with women, men are also veiled in the nomadic Atobak tribe of southern Algeria, and can show their faces to no one except their wives.) Whether women wear dresses or trousers may also be significant, as may whether members of a non-Western society wear traditional or Western garb. (A type of "code-switching" may be observed on flights from Western Europe into some Islamic countries as women depart their seats for the lavatory facilities in Paris fashions and return in traditional dress.)

The maintenance of clearly distinct male/female roles is also illustrated by the rules of speech such as those followed by Tamil couples, at least in rural areas of central Tamil Nadu: the husband can address his wife by her name, but the wife is expected to use a non-specific respect term; the husband uses a familiar verb inflection with his wife, while the wife uses the more respectful second person plural ending in return; and the wife is expected to give the "right of way" to her husband in conversation with other adults (Britto).

Either men or women are often considered to be more polite or indirect than the other in their style of speech. For example, Keenan (1975) reports only men in Malagasy possess the valued skills of using metaphor and proverb, with women perceived as informal and direct, and Strathern (1975) finds Melpa women excluded from taking part in public verbal display because they cannot use "veiled talk" and are always direct; on the other hand Laver and Trudgill (1979) report men use a higher percentage of direct imperative constructions in English when "giving suggestions," while women use a higher percentage of more indirect interrogatives and tag questions. Some of the stylistic differences attributed to men versus women have not been corroborated in observational studies of actual usage, or yield contradictory evidence (e.g. Tannen 1993b; Freed and Greenwood 1996; see also Holmes 1995).

The potential of sex-related differences in English to contribute to sexism and sexist discrimination against women has been hotly debated, and has resulted in some change in usage. Targets include obligatory sex-marking in third person singular pronouns *he* and *she*, pairs of terms such as *actor/actress*, and titles with *man* such as *chairman* and *policeman*. Change (including official style guidelines from publishers) includes rewording to plural *they* or indefinite pronouns *everyone* and *anybody*, use of an unmarked term for both sexes (e.g., the Screen Actors Guild winner is now called *Outstanding Female Actor*), and retitling positions as *chairperson* and *police officer*. Specific changes are especially noticeable in the revision of scripts for long-running TV shows: in *Star Trek*, for instance, the opening routine ". . . where no man has gone before" has changed to ". . . where no one . . . ," and female officers are addressed as *sir*.

The attitudes and expectations revealed even by unsupported stereotypes within a community are of considerable ethnographic interest, as are their social implications. Also of interest are perceptions and attitudes regarding apparent violations in sex-differentiated usage, such as female markers used by males and vice versa. A Japanese female who uses less polite forms is considered "rough," for instance, while a Japanese male who is too polite is "effeminate," as is a Tunisian male who speaks a Parisian variety of French. Male speech considered imitative of women's is called "sweet-talking" by African Americans, on the other hand, and is quite appropriate for use in a courting situation without threatening male identity (Abrahams 1973). Part of the distinction between male and female speech may be because many societies seem to expect women to adhere more strictly to social norms than they do men (Trudgill 2000).

Switching to a style of speech in which stereotyped features considered characteristic of the opposite sex are exaggerated may function as a marker of homosexual identity, or may be used in teasing or mocking the addressee by suggesting sexual deviance. The mocking signs used to refer to deaf homosexuals are touching the middle finger to the nose and flinging it back with a limp wrist, for instance, or by touching it to the tongue and then flattening the eyebrow (Rudner and Butowsky 1980). A general characteristic of American Sign Language which may also be interpreted as reflecting sex stereotypes is that signs associated with males are made on the forehead (as are those referring to intellect and decision-making), while those associated with females are made near the mouth (as are those for words of emotion and feeling, or for personal appearance).

Description and analysis of varieties of language actually used in gay and lesbian communities has received increasing attention, with a range of identifiable patterns found in phonology, morphosyntax, lexicon, and ways of speaking comparable to other socially constructed groups. The topic of study is commonly known as "queer speech," or "lavender linguistics"; a Lavender Language Conference has been held annually since 1993, with presentations generally focusing on these phenomena. Usage specific to sexual orientation includes the lesbian spelling of "women" as *womyn* and the addition of *ze* as a transgender third person singular pronoun. (Important contributions to the sociolinguistics literature include Leap 1995, 1996; Livia and Hall 1997; Moonwomon-Baird 2000.)

Sex differences in language forms and patterns of interaction cannot be understood apart from situation and social factors. In all speech communities they are interrelated with setting, age, social class, education, occupation, and (perhaps most importantly) with the role-relationship of participants in the communicative event, as well as the activities in which they are engaged.

Varieties Associated with Age

In most speech communities, age is a major dimension for social categorization. Three kinds of markers associated with age should be distinguished: those which yield information about the speaker, those which yield information about the receiver, and those which yield information about the role-relationships between the two which are influenced by their relative age. Markers associated with young children as speakers, for instance, generally relate to developmental stages and processes in language acquisition. "Baby talk" is associated with young children as receivers; it is characterized by the linguistic modifications which adults make when addressing young children, rather than direct imitation of child language forms. The use of baby talk is often associated with a caretaker role-relationship, and marks this relationship even if participants are not adult and young child: e.g., a young child who does not speak baby talk with adults or peers may use baby talk with a doll or infant sibling, or an adult may use baby talk with a small pet. Use of baby talk between adults may mark an affectionate relationship or be interpreted as insulting, depending on the context.

Baby talk is not part of the linguistic repertoire in all speech communities, but where it is, similar modification of adult language forms are to be found. In his characterization of baby talk in 15 languages, Ferguson (1964) lists these shared features: processes of reduction (especially in phonology), substitution, assimilation, and generalization; repetition of words, phrases, and sentences; exaggerated intonational contours and deliberate articulations; diminutive affixes; and high pitch. A few alternative modifications have been reported for other languages, including using a relatively fixed word order and whispering in Quiché, a Mayan language of Guatemala (Pye 1986).

The actual effect of such modifications on child language development is not clear, although there is some evidence children may attend better to baby talk (Snow 1972), and that its prosodic features may facilitate the acquisition of segmentation (Garnica 1977).

Beliefs about the appropriateness of baby talk and its relation to child language acquisition are of considerable interest. Among English speakers, baby talk is generally considered appropriate for females to use with children from birth to age three or four. The use of baby talk with a child approaching school age is considered potentially damaging to his or her emotional and linguistic development, both by parents and teachers. Children who use baby talk when they enroll in kindergarten or first grade are the subject of peer ridicule, and they almost immediately switch to more mature linguistic forms. Some English-speaking males use baby talk with young children, but father's language does not usually indicate the same caretaking relationship as does "motherese" (cf. Gleason 1975; Gleason et al. 1977; Gleason and Weintraub 1978). This difference may be diminishing with the middle-class trend to share childrearing responsibilities; Gleason (1976), for instance, does not find significant differences in the speech of male and female day care attendants, although she reports that English-speaking children taking the role of father when playing with dolls typically do not use baby talk, but use a "gruffer" voice quality and a greater percentage of threats and imperatives than when they play "mother." In addition to linguistic forms, communicative phenomena associated with young children include beliefs about the appropriateness of children listening to or participating in conversations among adults, beliefs about what topics should be discussed by them or in front of them, different terms of address used by them and for them, and expectations regarding their nonverbal behavior.

Other age-specific ethnographic research has focused primarily on how forms and patterns of communication relate to group identity. These include studies of adolescents (e.g. Mendoza-Denton 1997; Eckert 1999; Cheshire 2000) and elderly women (e.g. Paoletti 1998).

The elderly in a society may be accorded higher status and greater deference, or they may be considered less competent. General ways in which deference for age may be marked are listed by Silverman and Maxwell (1978): spatial (special seats), victual (given choice foods), linguistic (addressed in honorifics), presentational (special posture assumed in their presence), service (housekeeping performed for them), presentative (given gifts, or having the right to sing certain songs), and celebrative (ceremonies held in their honor).

The view that they are less competent may be conveyed by others talking to old people in a loud voice and at a very slow rate, assuming they are hard of hearing and losing mental faculties (Helfrich 1979), or the elderly may be recipients of demeaning caretaker behavior similar to that used with children: e.g., a son or daughter may order meals for them in a restaurant, or speak about them in the third person when they are present. Infantilizing intonation is viewed as the most patronizing characteristic of this variety by non-institutionalized elders (Whitbourne, Krauss, Culgin, and Cassidy 1995).

Some of the speech markers associated with age relate to physiological change, but many more are stylistic in nature, or reflect the different status or rules of speakers which relate to age. Some markers may also be the result of language and culture change, but we cannot assume that age-grade differences in a speech community indicate diachronic processes until their relation to the life cycle has been explored. An American's age may be marked by saying *ice box* rather than *refrigerator*, for instance, or *Negro* rather than *Black* or *African American*, reflecting actual shifts in usage. However, in some languages it may be the case that a different term is appropriate for an older person to use, and that the young person who uses one term today will change to the other at age 50 or so.

One very interesting age marker has been reported by Gardner, who says the Paliyans of south India "communicate very little at all times and become almost silent by the age of 40" (1966: 398). There has been speculation that elderly speakers of English employ different strategies for topic switching than younger speakers, and that they pause longer in narratives or conversations without giving up the floor. Helfrich (1979) reports age differences in a speaker's preference for action-oriented style (verbs dominating) or qualitative style (adjectives and nouns dominating), but few studies have yet been done which identify markers associated with speaker age other than those dealing with child language development.

Varieties Associated with Personality States and "Abnormal" Speech

Markers associated with personality states include some that are physiological in nature, as well as some that are socially determined. Even among the former, however, there may be culture-specific constraints and interpretations that are of interest for the ethnography of communication.

The most extreme examples are probably markers associated with psychotic states, such as schizophrenia. Language is considered by some psychologists to be such a reliable indicator of this disease that purely verbal measures have been said to prove valid in diagnosis and judgments of severity (Gottschalk and Gleser 1969). The content of a doctor–patient interview is analyzed in terms of (1) theme (unfriendly, hostile, avoidance), (2) inaudible or unintelligible remarks or words, (3) illogical or bizarre statements, (4) repetition of phrases or clauses, and (5) questions directed to the interviewer. Linguistic analysis can also be used to distinguish false and genuine suicide notes. Gottschalk and Gleser report that in genuine notes, the percentage of references to others is less than 14 percent, and the percentage of references to inanimate objects is greater than 1 percent. This procedure predicts 94 percent of the genuine notes and misidentifies only 15 percent of the false ones, as judged by whether the writer of the note actually attempts suicide. Other themes are also related to personality disorders. We consider depressed people laconic; they talk about self-deprecatory and morose topics. Manic people are verbose, and talk about achievements and frequent superficial contacts with people.

Research is now being conducted to discover deceptive patterns in electronic transmissions, with potential application for improved national security. One such project is developing software to search for words or phrases in e-mail or cell phone transmissions which are likely to be used by terrorists (Swedlund 2002).

Although comparable features may be found across languages, cross-cultural diagnosis/interpretation cannot necessarily be generalized. Mental illness and deception are culturally defined, and behavior a person may be institutionalized or imprisoned for in one society may be considered "normal" in a second, and valued as supernaturally determined in a third.

Several studies show that the same features of speech are interpreted as markers of different personality characteristics in males and females within the same speech community, but few have compared perceptions and interpretations in different cultures. Scherer (1979) reports correlations between certainty-uncertainty markers in American speech with self-rating of aggressiveness and dominance, and with ratings by American judges, but not by German-speaking judges. Scherer also suggests there are subcultural differences, such as loudness of voice indicating friendliness and sociability for lower-class people, and boorishness and aggressiveness for upper-class.

Speakers of English have stereotypic perceptions of personality differences between Americans, British, and Australians, and it would be interesting to know what specific differences are serving as markers for the groups, and how and why the personality attributions are derived. Similar studies might be conducted across languages to determine what markers are associated with personality traits considered "typical" of particular ethnic groups, and the extent to which similar markers are used by members of one speech community to type all "others." Such verbal behavior as repeated interruptions and dominating a conversation may be characteristic of a particular personality type, but these may also be strategies which have been learned in a particular speech community as conversational rules for asserting power or solidarity, and thus may be markers of role-relationship more than of personality.

Finally, speech may be intentionally marked to indicate personality traits or emotions in someone else. Sapir (1915) reported that in Nootka, "Cowards may be satirized by 'making one's voice small' in referring to or addressing them, in other words by speaking in a thin piping voice that suggests timidity." Hymes (1979a) analyzes [s] and [ł] prefixes inserted in the speech of bear and coyote in Takelma folklore as having a similar metaphorical function: the [s] conveys "diminutive meanings that have to do with condescension, sympathy, even affection on the part of an audience, and closeness between actors," while the [ł] conveys greater emotional distance, "depreciation, disdain for coarseness and stupidity, and . . . distance between actors."

Speech markers may also be used to imply physical characteristics, In Nootka this speech-mockery was done by suffixed participles and by inserting or altering consonants:

> The physical classes indicated by these methods are children, unusually fat or heavy people, unusually short adults, those suffering from some defect of the eye, hunchbacks, those that are lame, left-handed persons, and circumcised males. (Sapir 1915: 180–1)

Sapir reported that speech-mockery in Nootka was also used in reference to or address with people who have speech defects. Those recognized in the community are: (1) involuntary nasalization of all vowels and continuants (a "nasal twang"), (2) "hole in palate" (cleft palate?), (3) palatalization of all [s] and [ts] to [š] (speakers are thought to be keeping their teeth open), (4) "to talk as one with missing teeth" (lisping), and (5) stuttering. Speech-mockery takes the form of imitation of the defect.

Like mental illness, what is considered pathological speech is culturally determined. Discovering what is considered "abnormal" provides an enlightening dimension in revealing the perceptions and attitudes of a group, and in defining "normal"; it deserves more attention than it has thus far been accorded in sociolinguistics.

Non-Native Varieties

Three very different types of language varieties are included in this category: (1) the marked forms and patterns used by speakers in a foreign or second language; (2) the lingua francas or international language codes; and (3) the languages which have developed with official or auxiliary but "transplanted" status in societies where there are no indigenous speakers.

Within the first category there is a major distinction to be made between foreign and second languages in terms of function and the relationship of their speakers to a speech community. The former are generally used for learning about another culture or for intercultural communication, and may enable speakers to participate more or less successfully in that speech community without becoming members of it; sometimes they are used for one-way knowledge transfer, and many are content to acquire only reading skills, and do not become "speakers." Second languages are used within a speech community for many of the same functions they serve for native speakers, and their speakers must usually be considered members of the community in its sociological/anthropological sense even when the linguistic forms and rules are as yet quite imperfectly acquired. Both kinds of varieties are most commonly marked by an "accent" which identifies speakers' native language identity, intralingual developmental phenomena, and ways of speaking and writing which are inappropriately translated into the target language.

English has replaced French as the most common international language, and the variety generally used for international communication is characterized by minimal use of metaphorical or idiomatic expressions, and neutralization of regional differences. Suprapto calls this "Standard English for Foreigners," and reports from her observation:

> Even the native speakers of English strive to minimize their type of English
> in pronunciation and syntax. Thus, for example, an Englishman would try
> not to sound too British, nor an American too American.

This variety functions as a lingua franca at the World Bank and many other international agencies, and at meetings and conferences where there is a forum for the exchange of information in various academic or political domains. It is an elaborated code which makes minimal assumptions about shared cultural experiences among its speakers, other than that they all have a high level of formal education.

The essential difference in the nature and functions of non-native official/ auxiliary languages from those of the other varieties has been argued most extensively with respect to "Indian English" by Kachru (e.g. 1976; 1980; 1983), who extends the distinctions to the Englishes of the Philippines, the Caribbean, and West Africa as well. He is primarily concerned with a situation

> in which *Indian* English is used as a language of interaction, for maintaining *Indian* patterns of administration, education, and legal system, and also for creating a pan-Indian (Indian English) literature which forms part of the world writing in English. (1976: 223, emphasis his)

In other words, "The medium is non-native, the message is not" (Kachru 1986: 12).

It is interesting that this role for English has developed while efforts to promote a more artificial international language, such as Esperanto, Novial, Occidental, Interlingua, and Volapük have had only limited success. This may be because of language attitudes, or because a natural language is more adequate as a medium for communication.

The range of varieties used for auxiliary national purposes even within a single country, such as India, runs from pidginized English on the one extreme, through regionally marked varieties (e.g. Punjabi English, Kashmiri English), to "educated Indian English," and finally to varieties which very closely approximate British or American norms.

Such varieties are part of the communicative repertoire in India, West Africa, South Asia, and the West Indies, with important functions in each of the national contexts. Kachru (1983) lists these as: (1) instrumental, especially for education; (2) regulative, in legal systems and administration; (3) interpersonal, as a "link language" between speakers of different languages and a symbol of prestige and modernity; and (4) imaginative/innovative. The use of a non-native language in creative contexts, as a medium for literature and drama, indicates that it is being more deeply embedded in the culture of its speakers and undergoing nativization. Subvarieties develop as part of this process, as variables in the transplanted language begin to serve as markers in the society.

The development and creative use of non-native varieties of language provides further evidence for the point made earlier that there is no intrinsic reason that the structures and vocabulary of one language cannot be used in many domains of communication within other speech communities to express the cultures of those communities, and in ways in keeping with their rules of appropriate behavior.

4

The Analysis of Communicative Events

In undertaking an ethnography of communication in a particular locale, the first task is to define at least tentatively the speech community to be studied, attempt to gain some understanding of its social organization and other salient aspects of the culture, and formulate possible hypotheses concerning the diverse ways these sociocultural phenomena might relate to patterns of communication (as discussed in chapters 2 and 3). It is crucial that the ethnographic description of other groups be approached not in terms of preconceived categories and processes, but with openness to discovery of the way native speakers perceive and structure their communicative experiences; in the case of ethnographers working in their own speech communities, the development of objectivity and relativity is essential, and at the same time difficult. Some early steps in description and analysis of patterns of communication include identifying recurrent events, recognizing their salient components, and discovering the relationship among components and between the event and other aspects of society.

The ultimate criterion for descriptive adequacy is whether someone not acquainted with the speech community might understand how to communicate appropriately in a particular situation; beyond that, we wish to know why those behaviors are more appropriate than alternative possibilities. Observed behavior is recognized as a manifestation of a deeper set of codes and rules, and a major goal of ethnography is the discovery and explication of the rules for contextually appropriate behavior in a community or group; in other words, accounting for what the individual needs to know to be a functional member of the community.

Relationship of Ethnographer and Speech Community

In part because anthropology until relatively recently has been concerned primarily with non-Western cultures, and has relegated the study of Western cultures to sociology, psychology and the other social sciences, the techniques of ethnography were little applied in our own society except occasionally in caricature. It has been observed that this division of effort was not accidental, and that anthropology traditionally reflected Western ethnocentric distinctions between conquered colonial (or internal neo-colonial) groups and their conquerors. The outside observer, foreign to the society and unfamiliar with the culture, could innocently collect and report any information, confident that the group would allow indulgence for breaches of etiquette, and that protection would be provided by the fact that involvement in the society could be terminated at any point by returning home.

In recent decades awareness has grown that the researcher can develop a deeper understanding of the culture under study by adopting a functional role and becoming a participant. This may in fact be necessary at times if the lack of a defined status and role would cause problems of acceptance by the community. Some kind of rationale may be required for the observer's presence, particularly in studies within his or her own society. When the observer knows the rules of the culture, and the members of the community know that he or she knows the rules of the culture, they expect the observer to behave like a member of the society. Thus, they are likely to find it aberrant for observers to inquire about or record behavior which they are assumed to know, and little tolerance will be shown for violations of rules. There is considerable awkwardness, severe constraints are involved, and problems of ethics emerge. In addition, observers, taking for granted large aspects of the culture because they are already known "out of awareness," may find it difficult and less intellectually rewarding to attempt to discover and explicate the seemingly obvious, the "unmarked" case.

Nevertheless ethnographers, precisely because of this knowledge of a broad range of the world's cultures, are able to bring a comparative perspective to work even within their own society. And by keeping a mental distance from the objects of observation, and by treating subcultures such as that of the school or the factory as "exotic," they can maintain some of the detached objectivity for which anthropology is noted.

One of the advantages of studying one's own culture, and attempting to make explicit the systems of understanding which are implicit, is that ethnographers are able to use themselves as sources of information and interpretation. Chomsky's view of the native speaker of a language as knowing the grammar of the language opened the way to introspection by native speakers as an analytical procedure, and recognized that the vastness of this knowledge extended far beyond what had been revealed in most linguistic descriptions by non-native speakers. The extension of this perspective to the study of culture acknowledges the member of the society as the repository of cultural knowledge, and recognizes that the ethnographer who already possesses this knowledge can tap it introspectively to validate, enrich, and expedite the task of ethnographic description.

A further advantage to ethnographers working within their own culture is that some of the major questions regarding validity and reliability raised by the quantitatively oriented social sciences can be at least partially resolved. While there may be no one to gainsay claims concerning cultural practices in a remote New Guinea village, any description of activities in the observer's own society becomes essentially self-correcting, both through feedback from the community described and through reactions by readers who are themselves members of the same society.

At the same time, the emphasis in ethnographic work on an existential/ phenomenological explication of cultural meaning further justifies the value of ethnographers working within their own culture. Combining observation and self-knowledge, the ethnographer can plumb the depths and explore the subtle interconnections of meaning in ways that the outsider could attain only with great difficulty, if at all. In the same way then, with the ethnographer able to function as both observer and informant, some of the problems of verification can be overcome, and a corrective to unbridled speculation provided.

When ethnographers choose to work in other cultures, the need for extensive background study of the community is critical, and a variety of field methods must be employed to minimize imposition of their own cultural categories and perceptions on recording the interpretation of another system. In some cases "outsiders" may notice behaviors that are not readily apparent to natives of the community, for whom they may be unconscious, but conversely no outsider can really understand the meaning of interaction of various types within the community without eliciting the intuitions of its members. Garfinkel notes:

> The discovery of common culture consists of the discovery *from within* the society by social scientists of the existence of common sense knowledge of social structures. (1967: 76–7, emphasis his)

It is likely that only a researcher who shares, or comes to share, the intuitions of the speech community under study will be able to accurately describe the socially shared base which accounts in large part for the dynamics of communicative interaction.

A second issue is that of community access. Milroy provides good illustrations of how this may be negotiated in her discussion of the methodology used by Blom and Gumperz in Norway and of her own in Belfast:

> I introduced myself initially in each community not in my formal capacity as a researcher, but as a "friend of a friend". . . so that I acquired some of the rights as well as some of the obligations of an insider. (1987b: 66)

Obtaining access to minority communities which may have a history of exploitation poses ethical as well as practical problems. In the United States, most research on minority communities has traditionally been conducted by members of the majority group or by foreigners (e.g. the work of Madsen, Rubel, and Holtzman and Diaz-Guerrero on Mexican Americans, or Hannerz and Ogbu on African Americans). A member of the group under study who is also a researcher will already have personal contacts which should contribute to assuring acceptance, although taking such a role can result in the (sometimes justified) perception that a group member has "sold out" to the dominant establishment.

Often access can be negotiated to the benefit of all by including relevant feedback into the community in a form it may use for its own purposes. Positive examples can be found in the work of a number of anthropological linguists working with Indian groups in the United States. These include Ossie Werner (Northwestern University), whose research on Navajo anatomical terminology and their beliefs about the causes and cures of disease provided input to improvements in the delivery of health care, and William Leap (American University), whose research on Isletan Tiwa yielded a written form of the language and bilingual reading materials. These materials were developed in response to community fears that the language was in a state of decline, and to their desire to maintain it.

There are some data that should go unreported if they are likely to be damaging to individuals or the group. Whenever the subjects of research are human beings, there are ethical limits on scientific responsibility for completeness and objectivity which are not only justified but mandated. Furthermore, information which is given confidentially must be kept in confidence. The two linguists whose work with communities was cited above also provide positive examples of this dimension of professional integrity: some of the information about Navajo health beliefs and practices should be disseminated only within the Navajo community, and although the complete data base was reported by Werner, this portion will remain untranslated into English. Leap made no attempt even to elicit stories which had religious significance for the Tiwa (and thus were secret in nature), and his selection of content for the bilingual readers was submitted to a Parents' Advisory Board for approval prior to publication. Leap and Mesthrie (2000: 373–6) describe similar sensitivities in a bilingual program on the northern Ute reservation, where the community had strong beliefs that the Ute language could not and should not be written, as well as the procedures that were used with and within Tribal groups to achieve acceptable compromises which enhanced educational outcomes.

A third issue, partly contained within the second, is that of interviewer race or ethnicity. In the past, when studies were carried out in foreign environments or in minority communities by members of the majority group, the myth of the observer as a detached, neutral figure obscured the social fact that whether a conscious participant or not, the observer was inescapably part of the social setting and affected the behavior of other participants, as well as being influenced and sometimes even manipulated by them. The lack of familiarity of researchers with the culture, the language, and the community often made them vulnerable to such influence, the more so since it was unperceived.

The effect of the observer's presence on other participants – the *observer's paradox*, so called because the observer cannot observe what would have happened if he or she had not been present – has been studied in certain situations, and appears to be variable. In a classic case, Labov (1970) discovered that replicating the interview procedures of Bereiter and Engelmann (1966), using a White interviewer with African American children in a threatening environment, produced a very low amount of verbalization compared with using an African American interviewer in a familiar (home) environment. However, Galvan and Smith (Smith 1973), both White, were successful in eliciting fluent speech from African American children in Texas schools, suggesting that ethnicity is not necessarily a critical inhibitor to communication. The bilingual situation is perhaps even more complex, at least as it affects the study of language behavior, but the effect on the study of other cultural features is less certain. We may be quite sure, however, that at the outset researchers must know the general framework, institutions, and values which guide cultural behavior in the community and be able to behave appropriately, both linguistically and culturally, within any given situation, if their participation is to be genuinely accepted. Similarly, researchers must be able to establish a common basis of shared understandings and rules for behavior if interviews or interactions are to be productive. (For discussion of network analysis theory and procedures in sociolinguistic research, see especially Milroy 1992; Milroy and Milroy 1997.)

Types of Data

While not all types of data are necessarily relevant for every study conducted, at least the following should be considered for any ethnographic research on communication:

1 Background information

Any attempt to understand communication patterns in a community must begin with data on the historical background of the community, including settlement history, sources of population, history of contact with other groups, and notable events affecting language issues or ethnic relations. A general description is also generally relevant, including topographical features, location of important landmarks, population distribution and density, patterns of movement, sources and places of employment, patterns of religious affiliation, and enrollment in educational institutions. Published sources of information should be utilized as background preparation wherever they are available, and a search should be made of MA and PhD theses to avoid duplication of research effort. Relatively current data may be available from national, state, regional, or local levels of government, or through embassy representatives.

2 Material artifacts

Many of the physical objects which are present in a community are also relevant to understanding patterns of communication, including architecture, signs, and such instruments of communication as telephones, radios, books, television sets, computers, and drums. Data collection begins with observation and may include interviewing with such questions as "What is that used for?" and "What do you use to . . . ?" The classification and labeling of objects using ethnosemantic procedures is an early stage in discovering how a speech community organizes experience in relation to language.

3 Social organization

Relevant data may include a listing of community institutions, identities of leaders and office holders, and composition of the business and professional sectors, sources of power and influence, formal and informal organizations, ethnic and class relations, social stratification, and residential and association patterns. Information may be available in newspapers and official records of various types, and collected through systematic observation in a sample of settings and interviews conducted with a cross section of people in the community. A network analysis may also be conducted, determining which people interact with which others, in what role-relationships, and for what purposes. The procedure may also be used to identify subgroup boundaries within a heterogeneous community and discover their relative strength.

4 Legal information

Laws and court decisions which make reference to language are also relevant: e.g. what constitutes "slander," what "obscenity," and what is the nature and value of "freedom of speech," or how is it restricted. Laws may also prescribe language choice in official contexts, as those enacted in Quebec and Belgium, or as in bills passed in most US states intended to prohibit use of languages other than English for governmental functions. In communities where such information is formally codified, much is available in law books, court records, and on web sites, and in all communities it is accessible through interviews with participants in "legal" events of various kinds, and observation of their procedures and outcomes.

5 *Artistic data*

Literary sources (written or oral) may be valuable for the descriptions they contain, as well as for the attitudes and values about language they reveal. Additionally, the communicative patterns which occur in literature presumably embody some kind of normative idealization, and portray types of people (e.g. according to social class) in terms of stereotypic use of language. Relevant artistic data also include song lyrics, drama and other genres of verbal performance, and calligraphy.

6 *Common knowledge*

Assumptions which underlie the use and interpretation of language are difficult to identify when they are in the form of unstated presuppositions, but some of them surface after such formulas as "Everyone knows . . . ," and "As they say . . . ," or in the form of proverbs and aphorisms. These are "facts" for which evidence is not considered necessary, the "rules of thumb," and the maxims which govern various kinds of communicative behavior. Some of the data can be elicited with questions about why something is said the way it is in a particular situation instead of in an alternative way, and even more by studying the formal and informal processes in children's acquisition of communicative competence (discussed in chapter 7). Ethnoscience and ethnomethodology are most directly concerned with discovery of this type of data (discussed under Data Collection Procedures below).

7 *Beliefs about language use*

This type of data has long been of interest to ethnographers, and includes taboos and their consequences. Also included are beliefs about who or what is capable of speech, and who or what may be communicated with (e.g. God, animals, plants, the dead). Closely related are data on attitudes and values with respect to language, including the positive or negative value assigned to volubility versus taciturnity.

8 Data on the linguistic code

Although it is a basic tenet in this field that a perspective which views language only as static units of lexicon, phonology, and grammar is totally inadequate, these do constitute a very important type of data within the broader domain. These, along with paralinguistic and nonverbal features in communication, are included in the model for the analysis of speech events as part of the message form component (discussed under Components of Communication below). Preparation to work within any speech community, particularly if the language used is not native to the ethnographer, should include study of existing dictionaries and grammars. Skills in ethnography of communication are probably best added to skills in linguistic analysis in its narrower sense in order to assure that this component is not neglected or misinterpreted.

Survey of Data Collection and Analytic Procedures

There is no single best method of collecting information on the patterns of language use within a speech community. Appropriate procedures depend on the relationship of the ethnographer and the speech community, the type of data being collected, and the particular situation in which fieldwork is being conducted. The essential defining characteristics of ethnographic field procedures are that they are designed to get around the recorders' biased perceptions, and that they are grounded in the investigation of communication in natural contexts.

Ethnographers should thus command a repertoire of field methods from which to select according to the occasion. Although an ethnographic approach is quite different from an experimental one, quantitative methods may prove useful (even essential) in some aspects of data collection, especially when variable features of language use are being explored. Quantitative methods are essentially techniques for measuring degree of consistency in behavior, and the amount and nature of variation under different circumstances. The ethnographer may profitably collaborate with the sociologist, psychologist, or sociolinguist interested in quantitative analysis, but if quantitative methods are to be used, they must first be developed and validated by qualitative procedures. Quantitative procedures may in turn serve to determine the reliability of qualitative observation, which is apt to be casual and uncontrolled, and to further test the validity of generalizations which may be made on the basis of a very limited sample.

The criterion for descriptive adequacy which will be kept in mind is that enough information should be provided to enable someone from outside the speech community under investigation to fully understand the event, and to participate appropriately in it.

1 Introspection

Introspection is a means for data collection only about one's own speech community, but it is an important skill to develop for that purpose. This is important not only for data collection per se, but for establishing the fact that everyone has a culture, and that questions about various aspects of language and culture require answers from the perspective of researchers' own speech communities as well as those of their subjects. Ethnographers who are themselves bicultural need to differentiate between beliefs, values, and behaviors which were part of their enculturation (first culture learning) and acculturation (second culture learning or adaptation), and this exercise in itself will provide valuable information and insights on the group and on individuals.

The most productive means for developing this skill in a training program is to ask individuals to formulate very specific answers from their own experience to various questions about communication, such as those listed in the section below on Components of Communication. A second step is to recognize the significance of differences between answers which reflect the cultural *ideal* or norm, and the *real*, or what actually occurs. This distinction between the "ideal" and the "real" – long familiar to anthropologists – is not a matter of truth and falsehood, and should not be put in a negative light. Rather it is a recognition of specific behaviors. A useful analogy may be drawn with the question of what drivers do when they encounter a stop sign: the "ideal" answer is that they always stop; the "real" specific behaviors show that slowing (but not completely stopping) is a common response, and sometimes drivers fail to slow at all. Distinguishing between "ideal" and "real" behaviors is an important stage in viewing culture objectively. Responses to questions about language and culture will usually be in categorical "ideal" terms, and learning the "ideal" answers is an important part of the formal education of group members. "Real" behaviors, which exist on a continuum, are more often acquired by informal modeling, and are more likely to occur "out of awareness" where they may be difficult for individuals to consciously recognize. Thus there is no inherent contradiction if someone asserts that he or she never fails to stop at a stop sign, and then proceeds to do so. The actual behavior may be quite honestly denied even if it is pointed out, or dismissed as an aberration which does not affect the validity of the general categorical statement.

Thus, even when researchers are sure they "know" about patterns of language use in their own speech community, it is important to check hypotheses developed on the basis of their own perceptions with the perceptions of others, and against objective data collected in systematic observation.

2 Participant-observation

The most common method of collecting ethnographic data in any domain of culture is participant-observation. The researcher who is a member of the speech community was born into that role, and anthropologists have found it possible to perceive and understand patterned cultural behaviors in another society if they are immersed in the community for a year or more. The key to successful participant-observation is freeing oneself as much as humanly possible from the filter of one's own cultural experience. This requires cultural relativism, knowledge about possible cultural differences, and sensitivity and objectivity in perceiving others.

Malinowski was responsible for leading a revolution in fieldwork about 1920, and is credited with the establishment of this approach. Prior to that date, ethnographers described other cultures on the basis of travelers' reports, or at best lived apart from the group under investigation (often in the more comfortable housing of colonial administrators), merely visiting on a regular basis to observe and take notes.

One of the most important benefits of participation is being able to test hypotheses about rules for communication, sometimes by breaking them and observing or eliciting reactions. Participation in group activities over a period of time is often necessary for much important information to emerge, and for necessary trusting relationships to develop. The role of the outside ethnographer in a community remains problematic, but if at all possible it should be one which contributes to the welfare of the host group in a way they recognize and desire. Whether this is as teacher or construction worker cannot be determined out of context, but the ethnographer should not be "taking" data without returning something of immediate usefulness to the community.

Potential problems for "outsider" ethnographers include not only what role to assume, but what information to provide about themselves before knowing the meaning of such information in the community. Furthermore, it is very difficult to behave "appropriately" (even when one knows what to do) when one is ill, or when appropriate behaviors violate one's own values and mores. Ethnographers must first of all understand their own culture, and the effects it has on their own behavior, if they are to succeed in participant-observation in another.

It should be clear that for a participant-observation approach, a high level of linguistic as well as cultural competence is a *sine qua non* for successful fieldwork, particularly if it is to take place within a delimited time frame. The investigator, to be able to enter into various speech events relatively unobtrusively as a participant-observer, and one with whom other participants can feel comfortable, should share as closely as possible the same linguistic background and competence as the members of the community under observation. Nevertheless, some naturalistic experimental variation of conditions or interaction will be desirable in order to evoke or test for the occurrence of different response patterns.

Collecting data in situations in which they themselves are taking part requires ethnographers to include data on their own behaviors in relation to others, and an analysis of their role in the interaction as well as those of others.

3 Observation

Observation without participation is seldom adequate, but there are times when it is appropriate data collection procedure. Some sites are explicitly constructed to allow unobtrusive observation, such as laboratory classrooms with one-way mirrors, or others which allow the researcher to be visible but observe quite passively without being disruptive to the situation. Also, in observing group dynamics in a meeting or other gathering, it is generally better for a marginally accepted observer to refrain from taking active part in the proceedings. Observation from a balcony or porch is usually less disruptive to the patterns of children's interaction when their play is under observation than any attempt at participation.

Observation of communicative behavior which has been videotaped is a potentially useful adjunct to the participant-observation and interview, particularly because of the convenience of replaying for microanalysis, but it is always limited in focus and scope to the camera's perception, and can only be adequately understood in a more holistic context. Furthermore, ethnographers should always remember that the acceptability of taping, photographing, and even note-taking depends on the community and situations being observed. When filming or videotaping is feasible in a relatively fixed context, it is best to use a stationary wide-angle studio camera for "contextual" footage as well as a mobile camera to focus on particular aspects of the situation. To obtain a visual record of interactional events in which participants are more mobile (such as children playing together out-of-doors, or scenes in a hunting or fishing expedition), a hand-held and battery-operated video camera is most suitable. In such situations a small radio microphone may be attached to a single focal participant, with a receiver on the camera which records the sound directly on film. Most radio microphones will pick up not only what the focal participant says, but anything said by a speaker within at least three or four feet. When a wider range of audio coverage is needed, a second radio microphone and receiver tuned to a different frequency can provide input to an auxiliary tape recorder. Multiple input from different frequencies directly to the camera audio track requires additional equipment which greatly reduces portability. Microphones which record sound from the full scope of video input are most appropriate in some cases, but they often pick up sounds extraneous to the focal communicative event which make decipherment of speech more difficult. (For a discussion of electronic recording in linguistic fieldwork, see Troike and Saville-Troike 1988; Duranti 1997a.)

Since the potential range of settings for observation is enormous, priority must be determined by the focus or primary purpose of investigation. If the focus is on children in an educational situation, for instance, these include most obviously school itself, but also the playground, home, and the social environs most frequented by the child or which appear to have the greatest affective and linguistic effect on the child, such as perhaps the church. The work plan should be sufficiently flexible and open ended so that important settings which emerge in the course of ethnographic and linguistic research can be added or substituted, as appropriate. It would not be adequate in this education example to limit observation to the classroom setting without taking into account the larger social context of communication.

Persons first developing skill in this method should just report observable behaviors without imposing value judgments or drawing conclusions; more advanced steps involve making inferences about such unobservable aspects of culture as beliefs and values from the behaviors or things which are observed. The key to successful observation and inference is, again, freeing oneself from one's own cultural filter.

4 Interviewing

Interviewing may contribute a wide range of cultural information, and may include collection of kinship schedules, information on important religious and community events, and elicitation of folktales, historical narratives, songs, exposition of "how to" in relation to various aspects of technical knowledge, and descriptions of encounters among members of the community in different contexts. While an interview setting is often formal and contrived, it need not be, and the procedure is an efficient – perhaps necessary – supplement to observation and participation. Types of questions and interviewing styles may be so different that few overall generalizations can be made.

The most common ethnographic interview is composed of questions which do not have predetermined response alternatives. These are appropriate for collecting data on virtually every aspect of communication: what regional varieties are recognized, and what features distinguish them from one another (e.g., Do the people who live on Red Mountain/in Green Valley, etc., talk in a different way from you? Can you understand them? What are some examples?); attitudes toward varieties of language (e.g., Who talks the "best"? Who talks "funny"? Why do you think they talk that way?); identification of different kinds of speech events (e.g., What are they doing [with reference to people interacting in various ways]? What kind of talk is that?); social markers in speech (e.g., How do you greet someone who is older than you? Younger? A man? A woman? A servant? Your employer?).

Where possible, it is probably best to impose as little structure as possible on an interview, and to insert questions at natural points in the flow rather than having a rigid schedule of questions to follow.

The essence of the ethnographic interview is that it is open ended, and carries as few preconceptions with it as possible, or at least constantly attempts to discover possible sources of bias and minimize their effect. The ethnographer must be open to new ideas, information, and patterns which may emerge in the course of interviewing, and to differences between "ideal" and "real" culture as reflected in statements of belief or values and in actions, respectively.

Closed-ended questions which are precoded for statistical analysis may also be used, but only after the probable range of answers and possible interpretations have been established. Even so, in precoding there is danger of violating the principle of being open to new meanings and unforeseen patterns of behavior, and continuous qualitative validation is required.

Answers to the "simplest" of survey questions are culture specific. Responses regarding age and number of children, for instance, cannot be interpreted without first knowing on what basis age is calculated within a particular speech community, or if "how many children" means only living children, or only male children, or only children of the same sex as the respondent. In interviewing Tanzanian nationals living in the United States, Jalbert discovered it is inappropriate to ask how many children are in a family because, he was told, "We don't count children." The desired information can be elicited by asking "How many of your children were born in Tanzania and how many were born here?" Especially when interviewing members of a minority group in a society, family membership and house occupants may be considered sensitive topics if dominant marriage customs are not being followed, and they may be very threatening if undocumented aliens are present in the home.

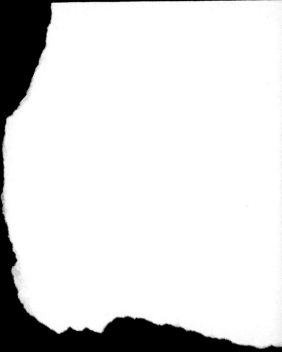

The meaning of terms typically used in the closed-ended survey questions must often be explained, even when administered to native speakers of the same language. When I have asked about "marital status," for instance, a common answer has been "yes," and questions on the "ordinal rank" of a child have often been answered with identification of religious affiliation.

Questions which utilize scaled responses, such as a semantic differential, may also be used in some situations, but only if they are preceded and followed with open-ended questions to allow valid interpretation. The importance of probing scaled responses was illustrated when I asked students from several different countries to rate characteristics like ambitious, competitive, dominating, sympathetic, and tactful according to whether they are more typical of men or women in their own speech community. Responses were then used as a basis for elicitation of how these characteristics are reflected differentially in the ways males and females speak. While almost all students rated men as more "dominating," some said this was reflected in their talking more, while others said the same characteristic was reflected in their greater taciturnity. Similarly, when students rated members of speech communities other than their own on such traits as friendliness, subsequent discussion on what constitutes "friendly" verbal behavior revealed substantial differences: the same questions about school and family background which Japanese perceived as "friendly," for instance, were considered "unfriendly" by Americans, who thought they were an attempt to rank addressees socially; and the quantity of small talk considered "friendly" by speakers of Spanish was considered "unfriendly" by Japanese, who in general feel a great quantity of talk indicates social distance rather than friendliness. As one Japanese student exclaimed, "If you are friends with someone you know them, and thus have no need to talk much."

Such group interviews of members of several different speech communities can be very useful for developing concepts of relativity during the training process; while all of the students participating in this discussion agreed that "friendly" behavior is a good thing, it became clear that communicative behaviors that will be interpreted as being "friendly" are language and culture specific. The ethnographer can never assume that the same labels used in close-ended or scaled responses refer to similar patterns of language use, even if they have been translated into the respondents' language; that remains to be determined by open-ended interview and observation-participation procedures.

Possible effects of interviewer ethnicity have been discussed above, but sex and age are factors which must also be considered. Females are considered less threatening than males in many communities, and are thus more readily accepted as interviewers, but in other communities it is considered entirely inappropriate for women to behave in such a manner.

Further, there are often limitations on what kinds of questions an interviewer of one sex may ask an interviewee of the other.

Eliciting information from child informants involves additional considerations, both because their perspective on the world is different from adults' (even within the same speech community), and because an adult–child interview is likely to embody an unequal power relationship in which children cannot communicate freely. Special precautions must be taken to avoid "adult-centrism" in interpreting responses (Tammivaara and Enright 1986), and to convey complete openness to a child's knowledge and point of view. When children's responses are carefully probed, it becomes apparent that they have their own well-developed notions about the world around them, including the language(s) they hear and speak, and how people learn them.

Among the critical issues in any kind of interviewing are:

(a) Selecting reliable informants. Often the people who make themselves most readily available to an outsider are those who are marginal to the community, and may thus convey inaccurate or incomplete information and interfere with the acceptance of the researcher by other members of the group.

(b) Formulating culturally appropriate questions. This includes knowing what is appropriate or inappropriate to ask about, why, and in what way.

(c) Developing sensitivity to signs of acceptance, discomfort, resentment, or sarcasm. Such sensitivity relates to the first two issues by contributing information on informant reliability and the appropriateness of questions, and on when an interview should be terminated.

(d) Procedures for data transcription, arrangement, and analysis. These will differ to some extent with the kind of information that is being collected and often with the theoretical orientation of the researcher; whenever the interview is conducted in a language not native to the researcher, however, transcription requires skill in using another orthographic system or a phonetic alphabet (even if a tape recorder is in use).

These issues are discussed at length in Briggs (1986) and Spradley (1979), while Brislin, Lonner, and Thorndike (1973) provide a useful list of potential communication problems between interviewer and respondent which may affect the validity of the findings. The potential biases they describe include cultural differences in respondents' feelings of ability to answer questions. People in the US, for instance, often feel they must answer any question that is put to them, but this may or may not reflect real knowledge of the subject. Some respondents will answer questions in the way they feel will most please the interviewer (the "courtesy bias"), while others consider it great sport to "put on" outsiders (the "sucker bias"). In some speech communities, respondents are concerned about possible "after effects" of talking (either social or supernatural), and these must be given particularly serious consideration. It must also be remembered that an interview itself is a communicative event which will have culture-specific rules for conduct and interpretation. Indeed, an "interview" may not be an appropriate mode at all for getting information. Briggs (1984; 1986) discusses how metacommunicative competence in native events which function to elicit information may increase the "cooperativeness" of collaborators, and similar insights are reported by Stoller (1986) regarding his work among the Songhay. The following exchange was with an elder in the community who was willing to advise Stoller after he found out that he had not been getting truthful responses to his questionnaire:

> "You will never learn about us," he told me, "if you go into people's compounds, ask personal questions, and write down the answers. Even if you remain here one year or two years and ask us questions in this manner, we would still lie to you."
> "Then what am I to do?"
> "You must learn to sit with people," he told me. "You must learn to sit and listen. As we say in Songhay: 'One kills something thin only to discover that it is fat'." (Stoller 1986: 53)

Many problems can be avoided by doing a pretest before attempting a large-scale data collection, including an exploration of who can be interviewed, how people within the community exchange information, and what forms of questions are appropriate (Hymes 1970).

The reliability of information can best be judged by asking similar questions of several people in the community and comparing their answers, and by relating information collected through interviews to observations. These should be required steps in all interview procedures.

5 Ethnosemantics (Ethnoscience)

Ethnosemantics is concerned primarily with discovering how experience is categorized by eliciting terms in the informants' language at various levels of abstraction and analyzing their semantic organization, usually in the form of a taxonomy or componential analysis. Because an adequate ethnography of communication must include the categories and contexts which are culturally significant within the speech community under investigation, including how they group language use into kinds of communicative events (as described in chapter 2), the perspective and methods of ethnosemantics are highly relevant.

A possible initial step in data collection is selecting a domain or genre, and then asking (recursively), "What kind of insults are there?" for instance; if the response was "Friendly insults and unfriendly insults," the next question would be "What kind of friendly insults are there?" in order to elicit subcategories and examples, and then "What kind of unfriendly insults are there?" etc. This step is usually followed by questions which elicit the dimensions which the speaker is using for comparison and contrast: e.g., "In what way are these two things/acts/events different?" "How are they the same?" "Of these three, which two are more alike and in what way?" "How does the third differ from them?" The first type of questioning strategy yields information primarily about hierarchically structured categories, and the latter primarily about feature sets.

An extension of this method might be called *ethnopragmatics*, or the discovery of why members of a speech community say they do things as opposed to why ethnographers say they do them: e.g., why people say what they do when someone sneezes.

The ultimate goal of ethnographic description is an *emic* account of the data, in terms of the categories which are meaningful to members of the speech community under study; an *etic* account in terms of a priori categories is a useful preliminary grid for reference and for comparison purposes, but is usually not the ultimate goal of description.

6 Ethnomethodology and conversation analysis

As developed by Harold Garfinkel (1967; 1972), ethnomethodology is concerned primarily with discovering the underlying processes which speakers of a language utilize to produce and interpret communicative experiences, including the unstated assumptions which are shared cultural knowledge and understandings. According to Gumperz (1977; 1984), this is the first tradition to deal with conversations as cooperative endeavors, and to focus on sociological analysis of verbal interaction. To Garfinkel, social knowledge is revealed in the process of interaction itself, and the format required for description of communication is dynamic rather than static.

There are general (perhaps universal) processes through which meaning is conveyed in the process of conversational interaction (Gumperz 1977):

(a) Meaning and intelligibility of ways of speaking are at least partially determined by the situation, and the prior experience of speakers.
(b) Meaning is negotiated during the process of interaction, and is dependent on the intent and interpretation of previous utterances.
(c) A participant in conversation is always committed to some kind of interpretation.

(d) An interpretation of what happens now is always reversible in the light of what happens later.

A clearly emerging concept is that of the extent to which speakers must share experience to successfully develop conversational exchanges of any depth and duration.

Gumperz builds on this in proposing the outline of a theory of conversational inference, of how social knowledge is acquired through communicative experience, stored in the mind, retrieved from memory, used in formulating expectations of what is to follow, and integrated with grammatical knowledge in the act of conversing (Gumperz 2000).

A similar tradition in Conversation Analysis (CA) follows from the work of Harvey Sacks in the 1960s (see Sacks 1992). The basic theme is summarized by Pomerantz and Fehr:

> The organization of talk or conversation (whether "informal" or "formal") was never the central defining focus in CA. Rather it is the organization of the meaningful conduct of people in society, that is, how people in society produce their activities and make sense of the world about them. (1997: 65)

Because of its cultural base, the "meaning" that emerges in a conversation is likely to be different for different participants if they are not members of the same speech community. Examples of cross-cultural (mis)communicative events serve to highlight the importance of such factors as the information or presuppositions the communicants bring to the task, the extralinguistic context, and the nonverbal cues. For example, I observed the following exchange in a kindergarten classroom on the Navajo Reservation:

> A Navajo man opened the door to the classroom and stood silently, looking at the floor. The Anglo-American teacher said, "Good morning" and waited expectantly, but the man did not respond. The teacher then said "My name is Mrs. Jones," and again waited for a response. There was none.
>
> In the meantime, a child in the room put away his crayons and got his coat from the rack. The teacher, noting this, said to the man, "Oh, are you taking Billy now?" He said, "Yes."
>
> The teacher continued to talk to the man while Billy got ready to leave, saying, "Billy is such a good boy," "I'm so happy to have him in class," etc.
>
> Billy walked toward the man (his father), stopping to turn around and wave at the teacher on his way out and saying, "Bye-bye." The teacher responded, "Bye-bye." The man remained silent as he left.

From a Navajo perspective, the man's silence was appropriate and respectful. The teacher, on the other hand, expected not only to have the man return her greeting, but to have him identify himself and state his reason for being there. Although such an expectation is quite reasonable and appropriate from an Anglo-American perspective, it would have required the man to break not only Navajo rules of politeness but also a traditional religious taboo that prohibits individuals from saying their own name. The teacher interpreted the contextual cues correctly in answer to her own question ("Are you taking Billy?") and then engaged in small talk in an attempt to be friendly and to cover her own discomfort in the situation. The man continued to maintain appropriate silence. Billy, who was more acculturated than his father to Anglo-American ways, broke the Navajo rule to follow the Anglo-American one in leavetaking.

This encounter undoubtedly reinforced the teacher's stereotype that Navajos are "impolite" and "unresponsive," and the man's stereotype that Anglo-Americans are "impolite" and "talk too much."

Describing and analyzing the negotiation of meaning requires discovering what aspects of speech signal role and status relations, and serve as a meta-language for transmitting information about them. The researcher then infers changes in assumptions about the relationships as a conversation progresses. Potential problems arise in applying these methods to research in other speech communities because speakers' inferences must usually in turn be inferred by the researchers, and this secondary level of inference may be based on quite different assumptions.

While the foci and procedures of traditional ethnography and various models of interaction analysis differ, they are in a necessary complementary relationship to one another if an understanding of communication is to be reached. Ethnographic models of observation and interview are most useful for a macro-description of community structure, and for determining the nature and significance of contextual features and the patterns and functions of language in the society; interactional microanalyses build on this input information, and feed back into an ethnography of communication clearer understandings of the processes by which members of a speech community actually use and interpret language, especially in everyday interaction – a vital aspect of their communicative competence. (See Watson and Seiler 1992; Schiffrin 1994; Titscher, Meyer, Wodak, and Vetter 2000 for descriptions and comparisons of methods.)

An ethnographic perspective on data collection and analysis is summarized by Duranti:

> to be an ethnographer of language means to have the instruments to first hear and then listen carefully to what people are saying when they get together. It means to learn to understand what the participants in the interactions we study are up to, what counts as meaningful *for them*, what they are paying attention to, and for what purposes. (1997a: 8)

7 Philology

The interpretation and explanation of texts, or *hermeneutics*, has traditionally been a science or art applied to writing, rather than speech, and especially to Biblical texts. (The Greek term for "to interpret" derives from *Hermes*, the messenger of the gods.) In addition to the referential meaning of the texts themselves, a variety of written sources may yield information on patterns of use in the language, and on the culture of the people who read and write it. According to Lehtonen:

> Hermeneuticians particularly concern themselves with such questions as producing certain meanings from a text, the role of the author's intentions in the formation of meanings, historical variability and the reader's part in the creation of textual meanings. (2000: 123)

As discussed under Types of Data above, much of the necessary background information on a community may be found in written sources, including theses and dissertations, governmental publications, old diaries and correspondence, and archival sources. Newspapers and census records may also be used as clues to the social organization of the community, law books and court records to language-related legal information, and literature to idealized patterns of language use, and to attitudes and values about language.

For information on contemporary language usage, one good source is the advice columns published in most US newspapers (e.g. "Ann Landers," "Miss Manners," and "Dear Abby"). These contain letters from people asking advice or giving opinions, with replies from the columnists. They regularly include questions and comments on appropriate forms of address, appropriate responses to compliments, etc. These might be compared with the older advice columns and books written by Emily Post, in order to document changing ideals of usage. An example of the use of this type of data source comes from Kempf (1985), who demonstrates how use of pronouns and terms of address in a newspaper, *Neues Deutschland*, can be used to study language variation in relation to social class, political party membership, and other social factors. Although generalization from written text to other channels must be used with caution, direct investigation of spoken usage in this case would have been subject to severe political and practical limitations.

Obituary notices in newspapers may provide information on social organization and values by allowing inferences as to who is given special treatment when they die (e.g., is the notice on the front page or near the classified section, and of what length), what accomplishments are mentioned (e.g., for women, the husband's occupation is frequently mentioned; the reverse is almost never the case), and what is taboo or requires euphemisms. Classified advertising sections are an index to goods and occupations that are available, and their organization indicates salient categories and labels in the community.

For communities with a literate tradition, written sources may be used to document language shifts over time: e.g., historical reconstruction for English speech communities has long included contrasting the forms used in letters versus plays, and secular versus religious writings, and has been used to document changes in such aspects of the language as the use of second person pronouns, and the relation of such changes to the sociocultural context of time. Changes in the status and functions of languages can be inferred in the shift of language choice for the same genre: e.g. Latin versus English, English versus French.

Old travelers' accounts, texts, dictionaries, and grammars are the only evidence now available from which we may reconstruct cultural information about many communities which have been exterminated or have fully assimilated to another culture, including many American Indian groups. A combination of techniques from ethnomethodology and literary analysis has been applied by Hymes (1980; 1981) and others to the oral texts recorded as prose by linguists and anthropologists, uncovering internal poetic structure and coherence, verbal patterns of openings, closings, and transitions, and assumptions about characters and their appropriate behaviors and fates – the "common knowledge" we seek to understand.

Identification of Communicative Events

Communication in societies tends to be categorized into different kinds of events rather than an undifferentiated string of discourse, with more or less well defined boundaries between each, and different behavioral norms (often including different varieties of language) appropriate for each kind. Descriptive tasks include enumerating the kinds of events which are recognized or can be inferred in a community, the nature of boundary markers which signal their beginning and end, and the features which distinguish one type from another.

Since a communicative event is a bounded entity of some kind, recognizing what the boundaries are is essential for their identification. A telephone conversation is a communicative event bounded by a ring of the telephone as a "summons" and hanging up the receiver as a "close." Event boundaries may be signaled by ritual phrases, such as *Did you hear this one?* and then laughter to bound a joke; *Once upon a time* and *They lived happily ever after* to bound a story; or *Let us pray* and *Amen* to bound a prayer. Instead of these, or in addition, there may be changes in facial expression, tone of voice, or bodily position between one communicative event and the next, or a period of silence. Perhaps the surest sign of a change of events is code-alternation, or the change from relatively consistent use of one language or variety to another. Boundaries are also likely to coincide with change of participants, change in topical focus, or change in the general purpose of communication. Major junctures in communication are signaled by a combination of verbal and nonverbal cues.

Consecutive events may be distinguished in a single situation. In a trial, for instance, the opening event begins when the bailiff cries *Hear ye, hear ye* and ends when the judge enters the courtroom and sits down on the bench, and all others are seated. Within the same situation, direct and cross examination of witnesses or the defendant may be identified as separate events because participants are in a different role-relationship, and there is a change in manner of questioning and responding: i.e. different rules for interaction. These events may be bounded by a change in participants, and perhaps by a verbal routine such as *I call – to the stand* to open and *You may stand down* or *Your witness* to close. If a recess is called before a boundary is reached, the interaction can be considered a single discontinuous speech event, even if continued on another day.

Formal ritual events in a speech community have more clearly defined boundaries than informal ones because there is a high degree of predictability in both verbal and nonverbal content of routines on each occasion, and they are frequently set off from events which precede and follow by changes in vocal rhythm, pitch, and intonation. Brief interactions between people almost always consist of routines, such as greetings and leavetakings, and the boundaries of longer and most informal communicative events, such as conversations, can be determined because they are preceded and followed by them (Goffman 1971).

Since the discovery of communicative norms is often most obvious in their breach, examples of boundary violations may highlight what the appropriate boundary behavior is. Some people are annoyed with what they consider to be premature applause by others at the end of an opera, for instance, which indicates differences in what "the end" of the event is perceived to be: the end of the singing or the end of all music. Still others may whisper through the overture, since for them the event has not yet begun. Christina Paulston (personal communication) reports the occurrence of a serious misunderstanding between Jewish and Christian parents attending an ecumenical service because the Jewish parents continued conversing after entering the place of worship, while the Christians considered this inappropriate behavior once the physical boundary into the sanctuary was crossed.

Microanalysis of boundary signals in less formal situations commonly requires filming a communicative situation, and then asking participants to view the film themselves and to indicate when "something new is happening." The researcher then elicits characterizations of the event, and expectations of what may happen next (and what may *not* happen next), in order to determine the nature of the boundary signals, and how the context has changed from the point of view of the participants.

The communicative events selected initially for description and analysis by one learning to use this approach should be brief self-contained sequences which have readily identifiable beginnings and endings. Further, they should be events which recur in similar form and with some frequency, so that regular patterns will be more easily discernible: e.g. greetings, leavetakings, prayers, condolences, jokes, insults, compliments, ordering meals in restaurants. More complex and less regular events yield themselves to analysis more readily after patterns of use and norms of interpretation have already been discovered in relation to simpler and more regular communicative events.

Components of Communication

Analysis of a communicative event begins with a description of the components which are likely to be salient (cf. Hymes 1967, 1972c):

1 The *genre*, or type of event (e.g. joke, story, lecture, greeting, conversation)
2 The *topic*, or referential focus
3 The *purpose* or *function*, both of the event in general and in terms of the interaction goals of individual participants
4 The *setting*, including location, time of day, season of year, and physical aspects of the situation (e.g. size of room, arrangement of furniture)
5 The *key*, or emotional tone of the event (e.g. serious, sarcastic, jocular)
6 The *participants*, including their age, sex, ethnicity, social status, or other relevant categories, and their relationship to one another
7 The *message form*, including both vocal and nonvocal channels, and the nature of the code which is used (e.g. which language, and which variety)
8 The *message content*, or surface level denotative references; what is communicated about
9 The *act sequence*, or ordering of communicative/speech acts, including turn-taking and overlap phenomena
10 The *rules for interaction*, or what proprieties should be observed
11 The *norms of interpretation*, including the common knowledge, the relevant cultural presuppositions, or shared understandings, which allow

particular inferences to be drawn about what is to be taken literally, what discounted, etc.

All of these will be discussed in turn below.

Scene (genre, topic, purpose/function, setting)

The first four components comprise the *scene*, or extra-personal *context* of the event. Identification of the *genre*, or category of communication, requires procedures which elicit perceptions from within the speech community under study (as discussed in chapter 2 and in the section on Ethnosemantics above). Its importance as an organizing principle in communication is summarized by Bauman, who defines genre as

> a constellation of systematically related, co-occurrent formal features and structures that serves as a conventionalized orienting framework for the production and reception of discourse. . . . a speech style oriented to the production and reception of a particular kind of text. (2000: 84)

Topic also requires culture-specific inferencing, since it is frequently not overtly identified.

Determination of *purpose* involves the potential for multiple levels which need to be taken into account. The genre of greeting, for instance, may simultaneously function to reinforce solidarity and to display (or manipulate) relative status. In an exploration of its universal versus culture-specific functions, Duranti (1997b) also identifies greeting functions as searching for new information and sanctioning social behavior.

Indeed, the *setting* is the only component of the scene which may be directly observed, although even for this component researchers might not notice an aspect of the setting which is not salient in their own culture: e.g. the relative elevation of chairs (as in Japanese) or seatings at the front, back, or side of a space (as for Polynesians), which may be very important for understanding the meaning of the event; and whether chairs in a classroom are arranged in straight rows or a circle, which may signal the appropriate level of formality (as for Americans).

The time of day, day of the week, or season of the year often affects choice of language form. This may include whole genres of events designated only for particular times; e.g., in Navajo one cannot talk about hibernating animals except during winter months, so that traditional stories about them may only be told at certain times of the year, and Orthodox Jews are constrained from discussing secular topics on the Sabbath. Routines such as *Merry Christmas, Happy New Year,* and *April Fool,* when spoken out of their appropriate temporal or physical context, can only be interpreted as joking or sarcastic.

Place and time may affect the meaning of greetings. It is not appropriate for a speaker of the Abbey language to greet everyone in just any location, for instance. Hepié reports on his own usage:

> Suppose I go back to my country [Côte d'Ivoire] and run into a relative in the street. I won't greet him, but quickly let him know that I am on my way to his home to greet him. [This is because] the greeting in such cases shows you care about such people. Therefore it has to be at home, where the relative can at his ease get the news from you.

Nwoye reports that for Igbo, morning greetings are the most significant,

> since the morning is the beginning of the day and it is believed that the sort of person you first encounter in the morning determines your fortune for that day. . . . Therefore people consciously refrain from speaking to those who they know or suspect can bring ill luck and ruin their entire day.

Descriptive questions to be answered regarding the scene are:

- What kind of communicative event is it?
- What is it about?
- Why is it happening?
- Where and when does it occur?
- What does the setting look like?

Additional questions which may prove relevant to understanding the significance of a setting include:

- How do individuals organize themselves spatially in groups for various purposes (e.g. in rows, circles, around tables, on the floor, in the middle of the room, around its circumference)?
- What geospatial concepts, understandings, and beliefs exist in the group or are known to individuals?
- What is the knowledge and significance of cardinal directions (north, south, east, west)?
- What significance is associated with different directions or places (e.g. heaven is up, people are buried with heads to the west, the host at a meal should sit facing the door)?
- What beliefs or values are associated with concepts of time of day or season, and are there particular behavioral prescriptions or taboos

associated with them (e.g. not singing certain songs in the summertime lest a snake bite, not telling stories until the sun has set)?

The organization of time and space is of enormous significance in most cultures, and one of the most frequent areas for cross-cultural conflict or misunderstanding, in large part because it is so often unconscious. In particular, ethnographers cannot assume that many of the concepts and attitudes regarding time and space (including personal space) which are held in their culture will hold for others.

Key

According to Hymes, "Key is introduced to provide for the tone, manner, or spirit in which the act is done" (1972c: 62). In labeling this component in English, we may think in terms of contrasts: e.g. teasing versus serious, sincere versus sarcastic, friendly versus hostile, sympathetic versus threatening, perfunctory versus painstaking. Key is often redundantly ascribed to genre (e.g., jokes are jocular, condolences are sympathetic), but this is not a necessary relationship. In some cases jokes may be made in a sarcastic key, or condolences may be threatening. A particular key may also be associated primarily with a particular function of language use, role-relationship between participants, or message form and content.

The importance of this component in the description and analysis of communicative events lies in the fact that while redundancy is common, key may be independently variable with respect to any other component of a communicative event. When there is an apparent conflict between components, the key generally overrides other elements. For example, if a compliment is made in a sarcastic key, the sarcasm overrides the form and literal content of the message, and signals a different relationship between participants than would be the case if the compliment were sincere.

Key may be signaled by choice of language or variety, by nonverbal signals (e.g. wink or posture), by paralinguistic features (e.g. degree of aspiration), or by a combination of elements. In the sample analyses later in this chapter, for instance, the sorrowful key of the formal condoling event among the Abbey is dependent on men's not standing fully erect during the ceremony, and the friendly and casual key of the Chinese dinner invitation event is signaled primarily by the frequency of interjections used in the message form and the extent of rising and falling intonation.

As with other components of communication, interpretation of key is culture-specific and must be determined according to indigenous perceptions. Because of its overriding importance to the meaning of an event, accounting for key is a crucial aspect of analysis.

Participants

The basic descriptive questions to answer about *participants* are:

- Who is taking part in the event?
- How are they organized?

This category includes not only speakers, but also hearers and overhearers (or writers and readers, signers and interpreters, etc., in other modalities).

An adequate description of the participants includes not only observable traits, but background information on the composition and role-relationships within the family and other social institutions, distinguishing features in the life cycle, and differentiation within the group according to sex and social status. An analysis of how participants are organized in an event is essential to understanding what roles they are taking in relation to one another, and how they are actively involved in the construction and performance of communication (cf. *participant structures*, Philips 1983b).

Answers to such questions as the following may prove relevant:

- Who is in a "family"? Who among these (or others) lives in one house?
- What is the hierarchy of authority in the family?
- What are the rights and responsibilities of each family member?
- What are the functions and obligations of the family in the larger social unit?
- What are criteria for the definition of stages, periods, or transitions in life?
- What are attitudes, expectations, and behaviors toward individuals at different stages in the life cycle? What stage of life is most valued? What stage of life is most "difficult"?
- Who has authority over whom? To what extent can one person's will be imposed on another? By what means?
- Do means of social control vary with recognized stages in the life cycle, membership in various social categories, or according to setting or offense?
- What roles within the group are available to whom, and how are they acquired?
- Do particular roles have positive or malevolent characteristics?

Among the questions relating participants to language and culture which will be answered in the process of ethnographic description and analysis are:

- How is language related to the life cycle?
- Is language use important in the definition or social marking of roles?

- What forms of address are used between people in various role-relationships?
- How is deference shown? How are insults expressed?
- Who may disagree with whom? Under what circumstances?
- How do the characteristics of "speaking well" relate to age, sex, or other social factors?
- How does speaking ability, literacy, or writing ability relate to achievement of status in the society?
- What roles, attitudes, or personality traits are associated with particular ways of speaking?
- Who may talk to whom? When? Where? About what?
- What is the role of language in social control? What variety is used? In multilingual contexts, what is the significance of using one versus the other language?

The dress of participants may also be relevant to the interpretation of their communicative behavior, and thus require description: e.g., Arab males may stand closer to females when talking if the woman is wearing a veil, and the Akan of Ghana assign communicative significance to the type of staff which is carried by royalty or the particular costume which is worn (Yankah 1995).

Belief about who may participate in communicative events is culture-specific, and is often not limited to humans. In the sample analyses below, for instance, Abbey speakers consider the drum and the invisible people who are invoked by the drum to be participants in condoling events, and the spirit of the deceased is an important participant for Igbo speakers; speakers of English and other European languages often believe they can communicate with pets.

Message form

In studying the various social, cultural, and situation constraints on communicative behavior, both verbal and nonverbal codes are significant in the *message form, message content,* and *act sequence* components of communicative events, and each type of code as transmitted by both vocal and nonvocal channels. This four-way distinction on the dimensions of verbal-nonverbal and vocal-nonvocal is shown in figure 2. Where there are varieties recognized on any dimension (e.g. register or regional dialect), this is also considered part of message form.

Each of these cells may be further subdivided by channel. Patterns in spoken language differ significantly, for instance, if the channel of transmission is face-to-face communication, telephone, or a tape recording which

CHANNEL

		Vocal	Nonvocal
CODE	Verbal	Spoken language	Written language (Deaf) Sign language Whistle/drum languages Morse code
	Nonverbal	Paralinguistic and prosodic features Laughter	Silence Kinesics Proxemics Eye behavior Pictures and cartoons

Figure 2

will be played by the addressee at a later time. Patterns in written communication differ if the channel of transmission is hard copy or electronic, with e-mail typically exhibiting many characteristics of vocal communication, perhaps in part because it also involves little preplanning or post-editing. E-mail has even developed nonverbal visual symbols to represent affective states which are conveyed by intonation in speech: e.g. : -) 'happy,' : -('sad,' etc. Written electronic communication has become even more spontaneous with the development of two-way pagers that buzz with instant messages.

Descriptions of verbal codes are generally limited to spoken and written language, but other modes of verbal communication are quite widespread. Communicative systems based on instrumental sounds (such as whistles and drum beats) are found in several parts of the world, for instance, and codes have been developed for electronic and telegraphic transmission, communication between ships, and other specialized purposes. Whistle or drum codes may involve a signal mode where short texts are repeated over and over, or they may involve a "speech" mode in which a much wider range of texts is transmitted.

A more common example of verbal/nonvocal communication is the occurrence of well developed systems of manual sign language in communities which include individuals who are deaf or hearing impaired. Even though sign language may not be accompanied by any vocalization, it shares all other features of verbal communication with speech. In signing, a range of visual behaviors in addition to hand movements (which would be considered nonverbal in speech) operate on the verbal dimension. These include some facial expressions, which may even function at a syntactic level in this code. The nonverbal dimension of sign language includes the silence deliberately induced by closing the eyes or averting eye gaze.

Within linguistics, silence has traditionally been ignored except for its boundary-marking function, delimiting the beginning and end of utterances. The tradition has been to define it negatively – as merely the absence of speech. I will focus on it here in the discussion of message form to emphasize that adequate description and interpretation of communication requires that we understand the role of such phenomena as silence, as well as of speech.

In considering silence, a basic distinction must be made between silences which carry meaning, but not propositional content, and silent communicative acts which are entirely dependent on adjacent vocalizations for interpretation, and which carry their own illocutionary force. The former include the pauses and hesitations that occur within and between turns of talking – the prosodic dimension of silence. Such nonpropositional silences may be volitional or nonvolitional, and may convey a wide variety of meanings. Their meanings are nonetheless symbolic and conventional, as is seen in the various patterns of use and norms of interpretation in different speech communities (see examples in Tannen and Saville-Troike 1985).

Silent communicative acts conveying propositional content may include gestures, but may also consist of silence unaccompanied by any visual cues. Even in a telephone conversation where no visual signals are possible, silence in response to a greeting, query, or request which anticipates verbal response is fraught with propositional meaning in its own right. Just as "One can utter words without saying anything" (Searle 1969: 24), one can say something without uttering words. Silence as part of communicative interaction can be one of the forms a "speech" act may take – filling many of the same functions and discourse slots – and should be considered along with the production of sentence tokens as a basic formational unit of linguistic communication.

Analyzing the structure of silent communication might best be approached by considering how silence which carries grammatical and lexical meaning may replace different elements within discourse. One form of the WH- question typically used by teachers, for instance, is a fill-in-the-blank structure, e.g., "This is a –?" (often said with lengthened or tensed *a* and nonterminal intonation), meaning "What is this?" This form may also occur in conversational contexts when one speaker asks someone he or she has just met, "And your name is –?" Utterances are also commonly completed in silence when the topic is a particularly delicate one or the word which would be used is taboo, or when the situation is emotionally loaded and the speaker is "at a loss" for words. The Japanese term *haragei* "wordless communication" captures the essence of this latter type of silence. There is a belief in Japanese that as soon as an experience is expressed in words (oral or written), the real essence disappears.

Complete "utterances" may also be composed of silence, as illustrated in the following conversational exchange:

P1 We've received word that four Tanzanian acquaintances from out of town will be arriving tomorrow. But, with our large family, we have no room to accommodate them. (Implied request: "Would you help us out?")

P2 [Silence; not accompanied by any distinctive gesture or facial expression] (Denial: "I don't want to" or "I don't have any room either.")

P1 What do you think?

P2 Yes, that is a problem. Were you able to finish that report we were working on this morning?

The negative response by the second participant (P2) in the cultural milieu in which this took place violated P1's expectation that guests would be welcomed, and frustrated his goal in initiating the conversation (reported by Jalbert). Communicative events which include silent "utterances" are also included in the sample analyses below.

Silence is often used over even longer segments of communication to convey a more generalized meaning, as in the "stylized sulking" by young African Americans that Gilmore observed in classrooms. This was intended to call attention to the "speaker" and express disapproval of others' behavior. The following excerpts are from her description of this phenomenon:

> Girls will frequently pose with their chins up, closing their eyelids for elongated periods and casting downward side glances, and often markedly turning their heads sidewards as well as upwards. . . . Striking or getting into the pose is usually with an abrupt movement that will sometimes be marked with a sound like the elbow striking the desk or a verbal marker like "humpf."
>
> Boys usually display somewhat differently. Their "stylized sulking" is usually characterized by head downward, arms crossed on the chest, legs spread wide and usually desk pushed away. Often they will mark the silence by knocking over a chair or pushing loudly on their desk, assuring that others hear and see the performance. (1985: 149)

Entire communicative events without sound are also common. Especially in ritual contexts, silence may be conventionally mandated as the only form which could achieve the event's communicative goals. Thus the invocation in Christian ritual: "The Lord is in His holy temple; let all the earth keep silence before Him."

Methodologically, in the description of an unfamiliar (or even a familiar) culture, silence is often not documented because it does not attract attention in the same way that audible or visible behavior does. Because linguists typically define silence negatively as the *absence* of other features, Whorf's ghost stalks the pages of field notes and tape transcripts which omit potentially meaningful occurrences of silence. A special meta-awareness is needed to attend to the range of possible silences, and particular care is required in seeking their proper interpretation.

A similar case might be made for the importance of including occurrences of backchannel signals and laughter in the description of communicative events. The *backchannel* in an interaction is composed of the responses of participants who are being addressed. In English conversations, for instance, these include such nonverbal vocalizations as *mm hm* and *uh huh*, verbal *yeah* and *I see*, or nonvocal head nods and postural shifts. These may function merely as passive acknowledgment, actively encourage continuation, or indicate that change of topic or speaker turn is called for. Similar phenomena in other genres include responses of *Amen* by Christian congregation members during a preacher's sermon, or audience feedback to performers during an entertainment event. Although laughter is seldom even transcribed, it too is socially organized and thus patterns in relation to type of event, topic, key, and other components of communication.

One problem which must be faced in recording communicative behavior other than spoken and written language codes is the complexity it adds to transcription. In describing such nonverbal/nonvocal behavior as kinesics and facial expression, for instance, it is important to identify: (1) the part of the body (i.e. what is moving or in a marked position), (2) the directionality of the movement, or how it differs from an unmarked state, and (3) the scope of movement, if any. Several systems for transcribing nonverbal behaviors have been developed (e.g. Birdwhistell 1952; Hall 1963; Ekman, Friesen, and Tomkins 1971) especially for use when this channel is the primary focus of analysis. It is particularly important to correlate verbal and nonverbal behavior with an indication of their relationship to the verbal act sequence.

In most communicative events the message is carried by both verbal and nonverbal codes simultaneously, albeit only one or the other may be involved. Although such forms are universal, the specific value and meanings of each are relevant only in terms of individuals or particular groups.

Selection rules govern the use of particular message forms when a choice is made between possible alternatives. An example is provided by the selection of kinship terminology: while ethnographers may collect a single set of static reference terms for people in a particular genealogical relationship, in actual use speakers may select from a great variety of alternatives for the same individual in order to express nuances of feeling, or because of differences in other components in the event.

Once a selection has been made there are restrictions on what other alternative forms may co-occur. The usual distinction is between *paradigmatic constraints* and *syntagmatic constraints*: paradigmatic constraints govern selection of a form from among a possible set of items which might fill the same slot, and syntagmatic constraints govern the sequential selection within the same speech act.

Message content

Message form and message content are closely interrelated, and the two components often cannot be separated in description and analysis. Message content refers to what communicative acts are about, and to what meaning is being conveyed. Hymes (1972c: 60) suggests that one context for distinguishing form and content would be: "He prayed, saying '. . .'" (quoting message form (which also includes content)) versus "He prayed that he would get well" (reporting content only). In the conversational exchange reported in the previous section, both the direct quotation of speech and the silent response exemplify message form, while their interpretation as a request for help in providing room for guests and a denial of help, respectively, exemplify message content which is not included in what was actually said.

In face-to-face communication meaning is derived not only from verbal and nonverbal message form and its content, but also from extralinguistic context, and from the information and expectations which participants bring to the communicative event. Because the various elements are processed simultaneously, it is difficult in most instances to isolate any subset for analysis. In order to examine the role of nonlinguistic factors in communication, I have chosen to study interaction between speakers of mutually unintelligible languages who lack knowledge of the language being spoken by the other participant – a phenomenon I call *dilingual discourse* (Saville-Troike 1987).

The following examples illustrate the extent to which negotiation of meaning can be successful even without the availability of a common linguistic code. These exchanges involved a young Chinese-speaking child (P1) who had just arrived in the US and an English-speaking nursery school teacher (P2) who did not understand any Chinese:

1   P1   *Wode xie dai diao le.*
          'My shoelace is loose.'
     P2   *Here you go.* [She ties it.]
2   [P1 holds up a broken balloon.]
     P1   *Kan. Kan. Wo zhei mei le. Kan. Kan.*
          'Look. Look. Mine is gone. Look. Look.'
     P2   *Oh, it popped, didn't it? All gone.*

3   [P1 is looking at water standing in the sink.]
   P1   *Zemme zheige shui dou bu hui liu a?*
        'How come the water doesn't drain out?'
   P2   *It fills up, uh huh. It doesn't drain out very fast, does it?*

In each of these examples, agreement on the topic of interaction is achieved because there was an object or an unusual condition upon which mutual attention could be focused, and which was needing repair or was otherwise worthy of mention. P2 responded appropriately to what P1 had said both because of the physical context, and because her experience had given her the skill to anticipate what a child would likely comment on in that context (an inexperienced teacher whom I observed was far less successful at this).

The importance of expectations is highlighted in the next example, where semantic coherence was not achieved. In this dialogue, the teacher had just shown some children a picture of a dog, and she expected that any comments they made would be about a dog in their own experience. She thus interpreted P1's Chinese utterances to be about a dog he had, and his gestures to be indicating the dog's size. Instead, P1 was informing her about dinosaurs, and his horizontal hand movements were illustrating geological formations. The teacher could not infer the message content in this case because it was outside of her *structures of expectations*, or *interpretive frames* (Tannen 1993a), for what a child in nursery school would be talking about, as well as for the setting.

4   P1   *Konglong hao jiu hao jiu. Konglong xian zai dou yi jing bian cheng mei huang le.*
        'Dinosaurs long time ago, long time ago. Dinosaurs now all already become coal mine.'
   P2   *Do you have a dog with you?*
   P1   *Hen shen o. Yi bo yi bo yi bo. Benlai di zai zhe bian. Di shi zhe yang chi lai. Gao dao zhe bian.*
        'Very deep. One layer after another. Originally it was on the ground. The ground rose up like this. The ground is here.'
   [P1 uses his hands in horizontal gestures to show what the ground looked like.]
   P1   *Konglong zai zhe bian.*
        'Dinosaurs are here.'
   P2   *Oh. Growing big.*

Correctly conveying and interpreting message content is central to the establishment of even a minimal level of what is to be considered "successful communication," although that concept may best be dealt with in terms of degree rather than absolutes. The first three examples of dilingual discourse related above can be considered successful at least to the extent that there was a shared topic for reference and understanding of speaker intent. While these illustrate that message content can be conveyed in some (highly predictable) situations even in the absence of a common linguistic code, abundant examples could also be cited of misunderstandings of message content when participants are speaking the same language, but do not share the same intralinguistic knowledge and expectations. To ignore any of these elements in the analysis of communicative interaction is to limit understanding of the processes involved.

Act sequence

The *act sequence* component includes information about the ordering of communicative acts within an event.

> We deal with the sequencing of action in which the move of one participant is followed by that of another, the first move establishing the environment for the second and the second confirming the meaning of the first. (Goffman 1971: 149)

Ordering is usually very rigid in ritual events, such as greeting, leavetaking, complimenting, and condoling, and less so in conversation.

In describing a sequence, communicative acts may be characterized in terms of their function, with a typical example of the message form and content often also listed. Although description is usually at a level of abstraction which accounts for regular patterns in recording events, verbatim examples are useful as illustrations. In analyzing opening sequences in Japanese door-to-door sales encounters, for instance, Tsuda (1984) bases her generalizations on 23 which she observed and recorded, but includes a verbatim transcript of only one which she considers "typical." Her data might be arranged in the following manner:

> P1   (Salesperson): Greeting
> *Gomen kudasai.*
> 'Excuse me.'
> P2   (Housewife): Acknowledgment
> *Hai.*
> 'Yes.'
> P1: Identification
> *Shitsurei shimasu. J degozai masu. Hai, J de gozaismasu.*
> 'Excuse me, I'm from J [company's name]. Yes, J [company].'
> P2: Question about purpose
> *Nande shō?*
> 'What do you want of me?'

P1: Information about purpose

Anō, Okusan terebi de senden shite orimasu de shō? Anō, atsumono demo usumono demo nuero to yū.

'Do you know, *Okusan* [meaning housewife] about television commercial? The one we can sew even very thick ones or even very thin ones. . . .'

P2: Expression of disinterest/interest

Un, anō, mishin uchi ni aru wa.

'Well, a sewing machine. We have one at home.'

This level of abstraction not only allows regular patterns to be displayed, but cross-cultural comparisons to be made. In this case, the act sequence is found to be the same in openings of "typical" door-to-door sales encounters in the United States, although there are significant differences in the form and content: e.g., American salespeople usually identify themselves first by name rather than by company affiliation, as in Japan.

Rules for interaction

The *rules for interaction* component includes an explanation of the rules for the use of speech which are applicable to the communicative event. By *rules* in this context, I am referring to prescriptive statements of behavior, of how people "should" act, which are tied to the shared values of the speech community. They may additionally be descriptive of typical behavior, but this is not a necessary criterion for inclusion in this component. How, and the degree to which, this ideal is indeed real is part of the information to be collected and analyzed, along with positive and negative sanctions which are applied to their observance or violation.

The rules may already be codified in the form of aphorisms, proverbs, or even laws, or they may be held unconsciously and require more indirect elicitation and identification. Rules for interaction are often discoverable in reactions to their violation by others, and feelings that contrary behavior is "impolite" or "odd" in some respect. Because of such reactions, violation of accepted rules is a common strategy in the construction of comedy.

One example of rules for interaction is turn-taking rules in conversation: in English, if one speaker utters a compliment, request, or invitation, politeness usually requires the addressee to make an appropriate response on the next turn; in describing communicative patterns of speakers who live on the Warm Springs Indian reservation, Philips (1976) reports politeness would not require any response, or the response might be given at a later date.

In the sample analyses below, rules for interaction in a Bambara village meeting require turn-taking based on order of influence or importance in the group, and that each prospective speaker first request permission to speak from the chief. Rules may also prescribe nonverbal behavior, as in the examples of Abbey condolences, a Japanese marriage proposal, and a Newari prospective bride interview. They may even prescribe silence, as in the Igbo condolence when there had been a "premature" death.

Norms of interpretation

The *norms of interpretation* component should provide all of the other information about the speech community and its culture which is needed to understand the communicative event. Even the most detailed surface level description is inadequate to allow interpretation of the meaning conveyed. In the sample analyses below, for instance, a Bambara speaker in a village meeting must know that direct speech is used to defend a point, while riddles or parables are to be interpreted as opposition; an Igbo speaker condoling family members must know that an early death cannot be by natural causes, and that someone who causes another's death cannot stand before the spirit of the deceased without incurring immediate retaliation.

I am calling these *norms* of interpretation because they constitute a standard shared by members of the speech community. They may also be related to rules of use in the prescriptive sense (cf. Shimanoff 1980), but the positive or negative valuation and sanctions on use which characterize rules are not a necessary condition for inclusion in this component.

Relationship among Components

In addition to identifying the components of a communicative event, it is important to ask questions which relate each component to all of the others. For instance:

- *How do the genre and topic influence one another?* There is probably a limited range of subjects which can be prayed about, joked about, or gossiped about. Conversely, it may be appropriate to mention a particular topic only in a religious genre, or perhaps only in a joke.
- *What is the relationship between genre and purpose?* The primary purpose of myths might be to entertain, to transmit cultural knowledge, or to influence the supernatural; jokes might serve primarily to entertain, or might be a means of social control, or a testing ground for determining hierarchical relationships between speakers in the social structure.
- *How are genre or topic and setting related?* Prayers might be said in a particular place, perhaps with altar and specified religious paraphernalia,

and at certain holidays or seasons. Topics for stories might be limited by location, with different ones appropriate at the dinner table or in a classroom from those appropriate in a clubroom or a camp in the woods. Often topics are limited by season, as illustrated above.

- *What is the relationship between genre, topic, setting, participants, and message form?* Some genres will require a more formal variety of language than others, or a different language entirely. In two events of the same genre, such as a greeting, the form might differ depending on season, time of day, whether indoors or outside, or other features in the setting. A lecture on the same topic might be more or less formal depending on the size of the room, the arrangement of furniture, and the number (or identity) of persons in the audience. The genre may also influence word order: Kululi speakers prefer Object-Subject-Verb for requests and teasing, for instance, but Subject-Object-Verb for narratives and stories (Duranti 1985).

The interrelationships of components may be very complex, as when the message form of a greeting is influenced not only by the season, time of day, and physical location, but the age, sex, and role-relationship of the participants, and the purpose of the encounter. While not all components will be salient in each event, nor even necessarily in each speech community, they provide one type of *frame* (Bateson 1955) within which meaningful differences can be discovered and described. The interpretation by the addressee of the utterance "It's cold in here" as an informative statement, complaint, request, or command depends on the scene, participant role-relationships, what precedes and follows in the sequence of communicative acts, and such paralinguistic and prosodic features of speech as pitch, intonation, rhythm, and amplitude. These signal what kind of speech event participants are engaged in: i.e. their metacommunicative frame.

Elicitation within a Frame

Part of the task of analysis is discovering which components are relevant within the particular speech community under investigation. At an early stage in description it is generally useful to consider the *frame*, a somewhat static entity which may be manipulated in the data collection process to allow elicitation of what differences in and among the components are meaningful from the perspective of native speakers.

In its simplest form the use of the frame is not unlike the minimal pair technique of structural linguistics. In investigating possible differences in a greeting event, for instance, the ethnographer may observe and record several greetings, noting any differences in message form, content, participant, key, and scene. Participants may then be interviewed to discover if they perceive any difference in meaning among varieties of greeting which have been observed. The ethnographer may probe further by holding the frame constant except for minimal changes and elicit information about what differences these would make in communicative behavior or its interpretation. Questions might include: What if one participant were older than the other? What if one were male and one female? Would it make a difference whether or not the woman wore a veil? What if it were evening instead of morning, or on the street instead of in a building? And so on.

A more complex discovery procedure discussed earlier calls for role-playing on the part of informants, where they are asked to pretend to be in a particular situation so the ethnographer can observe what they believe appropriate behavior would be. Role-playing often yields idealized or stereotypic behavior which cannot be accepted as actual usage unless validated by more naturalistic observation, but in itself provides interesting insights into the perceptions of native speakers in the event.

A creative extension of this technique of elicitation within a frame was used by Laughlin to collect data on communicative situations in the Zinacantán (Mayan) community in Chiapas, Mexico, which he was not permitted to directly observe.

> Amorous intrigues and daredevil elopements are the spice of daily gossip; but so vigilant is the watch upon the trails and waterholes that it has always seemed to me a nearly superhuman feat to exchange a word with a girl without the knowledge and chastisement of the town. Piqued by curiosity, but despairing over the prospects of ever becoming a participant observer, I finally handed Romin Teratol [his informant] three titles and asked him to provide the scenarios and script for the melodramas that follow. These fictional accounts present what Romin believes to be typical exchanges of conversations between a man and his prospective girlfriend. (1980: 140)

Laughlin is thus able to include in his ethnographic texts "Fictitious Seduction of Girl," "Fictitious Seduction of Widow by a Married Man," and "Fictitious Seduction of Girl by a Drunk."

Analysis of Interaction

Adequate analysis must go beyond a static concept of frame to the consideration of frame in an interactive model, as dynamic *schemata* or *structures of expectation* (as discussed under message content above). This approach requires us to recognize that:

people approach the world not as naive, blank-slate receptacles who take in stimuli as they exist in some independent and objective way, but rather as experienced and sophisticated veterans of perception who have stored their prior experiences as "an organized mass," and who see events and objects in the world in relation to each other and in relation to their prior experience. This prior experience or organized knowledge then takes the form of expectations about the world, and in the vast majority of cases, the world, being a systematic place, confirms these expectations, saving the individual the trouble of figuring things out anew all the time. (Tannen 1979b: 144)

Understanding what the speakers' frames are, what processes they are using to relate these expectations to the production and interpretation of language, and how the schemata and interaction processes relate to their shared cultural experiences, is the ultimate goal in explaining communicative competence; but developing methods for collecting and analyzing such information is a formidable challenge.

A project directed by Wallace Chafe has involved showing a film to subjects in ten different countries, and then eliciting narratives describing its content (the *Pear Stories*). Speakers' culturally determined structures of expectation were then inferred from the way objects and events were organized and changed in the retelling (Chafe 1980; Tannen 1981). Films (or even still photos) of various communicative situations within the community may also be used in eliciting subsequent explanations from participants about what was going on at the time the picture was taken, from their own perspective. Since the film maker must select and focus on particular features in the total context, another potentially useful technique in collecting ethnographic data is to have one or more members of the group being studied control the camera themselves, collecting examples of different types of speech events. Where culturally appropriate and acceptable, this is likely to yield data not only on the classification of events and their salient components, but also on their temporal and spatial boundaries, and on the "point" of the interaction.

Another model for dynamic analysis is provided by the work of Gumperz in the analysis of cross-cultural conversation events. In one interview session between a British counselor and a Pakistani mathematics teacher, for instance, Gumperz (1979) illustrates how the different sociocultural rules for appropriate language use each participant brings to the encounter yield different interpretive frames. The types of rules highlighted there include those in the "structures of expectation" as they emerge in the process of *conversational inferencing* (Gumperz 1977), as discussed in the section on ethnomethodology and conversation analysis above. This analytic procedure makes an important contribution to the description of speech events by yielding not only abstract communicative frames, but by accounting for the dynamic interaction processes which occur within those frames – the construction and negotiation of meaning.

Other methods which have proved useful in inferring the principles being used by speakers in their dynamic use of language include *playback* (Fanshel and Moss 1971; Labov and Fanshel 1977), in which participants are interviewed in depth about the meaning of their own utterances in the process of microanalysis, and the study of institutionalized speakers who are judged by psychiatrists to exhibit communicative behavior which is "inappropriate in the situation" (Goffman 1963). Such procedures may be profitably integrated with more traditional ethnographic methods to assist in discovering patterns of communication.

Sample Analyses of Communicative Events

The following are examples of communicative events based on descriptions by former graduate students at Georgetown University and the University of Illinois who are native speakers of the languages involved: Bambara, Abbey, Japanese, Thai, Igbo, Cebuano (Bukadon/Philippines), Newari, and Chinese. In these events the message form, content, and act sequence are generalized as "typical," and are reported here without verbatim examples. They are intended to illustrate the type of information perceived as relevant in the components that are identified by these speakers, and one possible model for the arrangement of data.

(1)   Issiaka Ly describes a traditional village meeting among Bambara speakers in Mali.

TOPIC: How animals should be kept away from farms

FUNCTION/PURPOSE: Making a decision that will regulate the village
   life

SETTING:
   If mid-afternoon with a hot sun overhead, under trees
   If in the late afternoon or during evening hours, in the village
      common place

KEY: Serious

PARTICIPANTS:
   All of the male inhabitants of the village
   P1 – Chief
   P2 – Herald

P3 – Active inhabitants (age 45+)
P4 – Semi-active inhabitants (age 21–45)
P5 – Passive inhabitants (age 14–20)

MESSAGE FORM:

Spoken Bambara
P2 uses loud voice; others use soft voices

ACT SEQUENCE:

P1 recites agenda
P2 transmits agenda to assembly
P3 (one) asks for floor
P2 transmits request to P1
P1 grants consent or rejects request
P2 transmits consent or rejection to speaker P3
P3 gives opinion (if P1 consents)
P2 transmits opinion to P1 and assembly
[Acts 3–8 are repeated as active members (P3s) take turns giving
      their opinions]
P1 summarizes the debate and makes a proposal
P2 transmits the summary and proposal to the assembly

RULES FOR INTERACTION:

Only active members (age 45+) may ask to speak.
Semi-active members (21–45) may be asked their opinion, but not
      volunteer it.
Each speaker must request permission to speak from the chief.
The chief and other participants should not talk directly to one
      another; the herald always transmits speech from the chief
      to the assembly, or from any individual speaker to chief
      and assembly.
Active inhabitants should take turns speaking in order of influence
      or importance.

NORMS OF INTERPRETATION:

Direct speech (laconic and clear) means the speaker is defending a
      point.
Indirect speech (e.g. riddles and parables) means the speaker is
      opposing a point.
The people in the assembly are serious.
The Herald is not necessarily being serious.

(2) Marcellen Hepié describes a greeting event between Abbey speakers
in the Côte d'Ivoire to illustrate the concept of "variation in a frame"
with respect to the sex and age of participants. His focus is on differences

this makes in the act sequence. The setting of the greeting also makes a difference in the content and sequence, but that component is held constant in this example.

FUNCTION/PURPOSE: Reaffirming the good relationship between participants at the beginning of a visit

SETTING: A private home

KEY: Friendly

PARTICIPANTS:
P1 – Resident of home
P2 – Visitor
Variable conditions
A P1 and P2 are both adult males, or P1 is male and P2 female
B P1 is female, P2 male
C P1 is child, P2 adult
D More than one visitor comes at the same time

ACT SEQUENCE:
Condition A
Phase One – "Greeting and response"
P2 Greeting
P1 Acceptance of greeting
P1 looks for chair for P2 (if none is immediately available, this may involve a long pause in the greeting sequence)
Phase Two – "Having a seat"
P1 offers P2 a seat
P2 returns greeting
Phase Three – "Asking the news"
P1 and P2 sit down
P1 asks P2 of the news
P2 gives standard, formulaic response
Condition B
Phase One and Phase Two are the same
P2 then rushes to seek nearest man to complete greeting sequence
If she does not find any, she breaks the rules, apologizes, and completes the greeting herself by "Asking the news"
Condition C
If P1 is a young child, no greeting takes place
P2 asks P1 to call parents
If P1 is older child, Phase One and Phase Two may be completed before seeking an adult

Condition D

> The youngest visitor who is considered an adult is the one who carries out the news
>
> For Phase Three, P1 talks directly to the one who has been appointed by the group to give the news; the person must consult the group before responding

RULES FOR INTERACTION:

> A child beyond age ten has a "right" to be greeted.
>
> Between friends, the order of greeting may be relaxed, but "a woman who always greets first would not be well-judged."

NORMS OF INTERPRETATION:

> If Phase Two or Phase Three is omitted, or there is any change in order, it indicates there is something amiss in the relationship between P1 and P2.
>
> "Asking the news" is part of the greeting and not considered the point of the visit.
>
> After conventional responses regarding the "news," P2 will bring up the actual reason for the visit (beginning another speech event).

(3)   Hepié illustrates variation within another genre of Abbey communication as he contrasts formal (A) and informal (B) condoling events.

PURPOSE/FUNCTION:

A   The goal of formal condolence is more than simple sympathy to the family of the deceased. It is a proof of solidarity and unity within a village, and between villages, because outsiders come to condole the afflicted village.

B   The goal of informal condolence is to provide moral support for the bereaved, plus material assistance.

SETTING:

A   Takes place on a street nearest to the bereaved family's residence

> The time is in the evening after dark, within 24 hours of death; it is prior to the burial ceremony
>
> Two lines of seats are up – one for receivers (on the right side), the one facing it for visitors

B   Takes place at the bereaved's home, usually under a shelter in the courtyard (A shelter is normally built for any dead person, except perhaps a baby.)

> It may take place a week or more after death, and after burial

KEY: Sorrowful

PARTICIPANTS:
A P1 – Males from the village which receives condolences
   P2 – Principals who come to condole, both male and female
   P3 – Spectators, including women, children, and men who are not directly involved (and will not occupy seats)
   P4 – The drum, a sacred instrument only used in formal situations for communicating with the invisible world and transmitting bad news to neighboring villages
   P5 – Invisible people invoked by the drum
B P1 – Men and women in two separate groups, usually members of the family (children are normally kept away from a place where a dead body is exposed)
   P2 – Outsiders, men and women who come to condole, whether they are from the same village or not

MESSAGE FORM AND SEQUENCE; RULES FOR
INTERACTION:
A Condolences are nonverbal. Participants offering condolence gesture with their right hand, one after another. A participant in such an event is expected to walk appropriately. A condoling person should not be standing fully erect during the ceremony. Also, he should bow when he arrives in front of an important person. Women in the condoling visitors line do not make any gesture, but just walk normally and usually go to the end of the line.
   P4 transmits the bad news.
   P2 arrive, announced by three guns firing.
   P4 spreads the news of the arrival of P2.
   P1 are already in place, seated in chairs, are waiting to be condoled.
   P3 get closer to the scene to watch.
   P2 are joined by some people in the host village who guide them to act appropriately.
   P2 condole P1 in a line, from right to left – nonverbal, as described above.
   P1 watch condoling gestures seriously.
B P2 can cry loudly while approaching the scene. Crying is the women's duty. Men, whether P1 or P2, are not expected to cry except for a very short time (less than one minute).
   P2 women are crying.
   P2 men walk straight and verbally condole P1 men.
   P1 women then take a seat among the P1 men.
   P2 women keep on crying until P1 women demand that they stop, then P2 women verbally condole P1 men.
   P2 women take seats among P1 women.
   (Men usually sit in chairs, women on the ground.)

NORMS OF INTERPRETATION:

Formal condoling is required in situations such as where a woman from one village marries a man in another. If she dies, she will be buried in her village of origin (except where there is strong opposition). People from her village of origin go to the village of residence to condole not only her relatives there, but the whole village as well; i.e., those being condoled include affinal kin, those condoling include consanguinal kin.

(4) Harumi Williams describes a Japanese marriage proposal, a communicative event which consists of only one verbal utterance.

FUNCTION/PURPOSE:

To declare intention to marry
To establish or develop an appropriate role-relationship

KEY: Serious

PARTICIPANTS:

P1 – Male; young adult
P2 – Female; young adult
(Their occupation and status is not relevant)

MESSAGE FORM:

Verbal – spoken Japanese; silence
Nonverbal – kinesics; eye gaze

MESSAGE CONTENT AND SEQUENCE:

P1   Holds P2's hand (optional)
     Looks at P2
     Says "Please marry me"
P2   Stands with head down
     Silence

RULES FOR INTERACTION:

A man must propose to a woman.
At an emotional climax, there should be silence.
The woman's head should hang down, and the direction of her eye gaze should be lower than the man's.

NORMS OF INTERPRETATION:

The head of the household is to be the man, and therefore he has to take the initiative in the decision of marriage. This custom has its roots in an early Japanese myth when Ezanami (female god) and Izanagi (male got) married. First Ezanami proposed marriage to Izanagi and they married, but they could produce only evil creatures like worms, so they had to have the marriage ceremony again. This time Izanagi proposed, and the marriage was a success, producing a country called "Japan." This custom continues until the present day and the commonly held view is that the rule should not be violated.

There is also a belief that as soon as an experience is expressed in words (oral or written), the real essence disappears. When parents die, when the son passes the entrance examination to a university, and when we see something extremely beautiful, there should be silence. There is a well-known poem which starts "Oh, Matsushima (name of an island in Japan) . . . ," but because the poet was so impressed by its beauty he could not continue; this poem is considered one of his masterpieces.

Marriage is a climax in a girl's life, its main goal. The proposal is therefore such an important event, the only appropriate response can be silence. The hanging head and lowered gaze imply modesty, a highly prized virtue in a girl.

This response is what the young man expects, and it confirms that this is indeed the girl he wants for his wife; their future life will be quiet, and one with him as head of the household. He was not really asking her a question and expecting an answer, but declaring his decision to marry her.

(5) Suphatcharee Ekasingh describes an introduction among Thai speakers.

PURPOSE/FUNCTION:
To establish participants' relationship

SETTING:
An informal social gathering

KEY: Friendly and polite

PARTICIPANTS:
P1 – Thai female in early 40s
P2 – Thai male student in mid 20s
P3 – Thai female in late 40s
P1 and P2 know each other very well; P1 is a very close friend of P2's parents and she considers P2 to be a relative
P1 and P3 are acquaintances; both have lived in the same neighborhood for more than ten years

MESSAGE FORM:
> Spoken Thai, central dialect, polite register
>> The polite register includes the tone of the utterances and the use of appropriate pronouns according to age, sex, and social status
>
> Hand gestures and body position
>> The *wai* is a gesture made by putting the palms of the hands together and then raising them in front of the face while bending down the head and bowing the body

MESSAGE CONTENT AND SEQUENCE:
> P1   introduces P2 to P3, using their first names
> P2   greets P3, using male polite particle; simultaneously performs the *wai*
> P3   accepts greeting, using female polite particle; simultaneously performs the *wai*
> P1   provides P3 with more information about P2
> P3   then continues conversation with P2, asking primarily about his studies

RULES FOR INTERACTION:
> In an informal setting like this where differences in social status are not salient, P2 and P3 should be introduced by first name. Once the relationship has been established, nicknames may be used.
>
> The younger P should be introduced to the older P.
>
> The polite register must be used.

NORMS OF INTERPRETATION:
> Age plays a significant role in this genre; it is believed that if the older does the *wai* first, they will have short lives.
>
> The height of the *wai* indicates the degree of respect.
>
> Asking personal questions is part of getting to know another and not considered impolite, although questions about income or age may be offensive.

(6) A communicative event may take place with no speech at all, as illustrated by Gregory Nwoye in this description of a condoling event among Igbo speakers in Nigeria on the occasion of a "premature" death.

PURPOSE/FUNCTION:
> To express sympathy, and to prove innocence of being responsible for the death

SETTING:
   Inside the home of the bereaved family
   Approximately four days following the death
   Seats are around the room for mourners

KEY: Sympathetic

PARTICIPANTS:
   P1 – Sympathizer/mourner; adult male
   P2 – Family members
   P3 – Spirit of the deceased
   P4 – Other mourners; adult males

MESSAGE FORM:
   Silence and proxemics

ACT SEQUENCE:
   P2 are standing inside the house
   P3 is hovering nearby
   P1 a) enters
       b) stands before P2 and P3
       c) sits silently among P4
       d) again presents himself to P2 and P3
       e) leaves

RULES FOR INTERACTION:
   The bereaved family should be avoided for several days after the
       death.
   Mourners should present themselves in the home of the bereaved
       while the spirit of the deceased is still present (before
       final burial rites).
   Mourners should not speak.

NORMS OF INTERPRETATION:
   Death is a normal part of the life cycle and should occur only at a
       ripe age; premature death causes profound grief, and must
       have been caused by malevolent forces.
   Verbal reference to death increases grief.
   Physical presence indicates sympathy with the bereaved.
   Someone who causes another's death cannot stand before the spirit
       of the deceased without incurring immediate retaliation.

(7)   Genoveva M. Ablanque describes a ritual response to lightning
among the Bukidons of the southern Philippines.

FUNCTION/PURPOSE:
   To avoid punishment for doing something unnatural

SETTING:
> Inside a house during a severe thunderstorm, usually in afternoon
> Lightning and thunder often accompanied by impending rain and
> > strong wind
> Air sometimes dark and heavy

KEY: Foreboding

PARTICIPANTS:
> P1 – Evil spirits
> P2 – All persons in the house
> P3 – Member of household who accepts responsibility for ritual acts

MESSAGE FORM:
> Silence
> Cutting and burning of locks of hair

ACT SEQUENCE:
> P1   arrival signalled by lightning and thunder
> P2   cease speech and all other activity
> P3   builds a fire, if there is not one; gets scissors and cuts a lock of
>   hair from each P2 (including self); carries locks to stove and
>   burns them

RULES FOR INTERACTION:
> The individual who performs the ritual cutting and burning of hair
> > (P3) self-selects, but it should be a mature adult (usually
> > the mother).
> There must be absolute silence during the ritual.
> The smell of burning hair should be strong enough to dominate the
> > air.

NORMS OF INTERPRETATION:
> After someone does something unnatural, evil spirits are present.
> "Unnatural" acts include marrying a relative, causing animals of
> > some different species to fight, talking to an animal, and
> > laughing while playing with worms, picking lice, or watch-
> > ing dogs copulate.
> Lightning is sent as punishment from the spirit who presides over
> > destiny; if a person is struck by lightning, it would be
> > presumed that the individual was guilty.
> The belief is traced to a legend that a girl and her suitor were struck
> > by lightning after she talked to her pet dog; the rain fell so
> > hard that the place became Pinamaloy ('punishment') Lake.
> Children are most likely to be guilty since they may not know how
> > to discern what is considered "unnatural," but they are
> > still vulnerable to the punishment.

(8)   Jyoti Tuladhar describes a typical event among Newari speakers in Nepal in which a prospective bride is being interviewed by a member of the suitor's family.

PURPOSE/FUNCTION:
>   To determine the suitability of the bride by initial superficial examination

SETTING:
>   The prospective bride's home, in the evening
>   The participants are seated close to one another

KEY: Judgmental

PARTICIPANTS:
>   P1 – Suitor's aunt
>   P2 – Prospective bride's aunt
>   P3 – Prospective bride

MESSAGE FORM:
>   The Kaltimandu dialect of the Newari language as used in traditional households, interspersed with no foreign loan words except *school* and *college*
>   The women's bodies are relaxed, but still

CONTENT AND SEQUENCE:
>   P1   Such a pretty girl, your niece. Where do you go to school, child?
>   P3   At Kirtipur.
>   P2   She'll be graduating in April.
>   P1   Wonderful! I hear you're very smart?
>   P3   (Smile) (Silence)
>   P2   She's never stood second in her class.
>   P1   My nephew broke the record in his college, too. Did you hear about that?
>   P3   (Nod) (Silence)

RULES FOR INTERACTION:
>   Genteel women do not make "gross" hand gestures. The position of the body should be relaxed and still.
>   Young girls should be shy, silent, and accept compliments with a smile.
>   Direct remarks like "such a pretty girl" in the presence of the subject can be made only by an elderly person to a young girl, and only in such situations as this interview. It is not the general practice among Newars to compliment someone on her beauty directly in social interchanges. A

girl may even be offended by such a remark on other occasions.

Genteel young girls stay silent in the presence of unfamiliar elderly women (even more so with men), unless addressed with direct questions. Their replies should be short or even monosyllabic. If they choose not to reply at all, this is not considered rude or impolite.

A verbal response to the final question might have been considered arrogant; its intent was to place her in a difficult situation as a test of her manners.

NORMS OF INTERPRETATION:

In a situation such as this, the girl's family already have decided that the suitor was a suitable match for their daughter, and would have agreed to the encounter so that his family could decide if she was appropriate for him. The girl would generally be unaware of the purpose of the visit.

Even though the suitor's aunt asks the girl a number of questions she is not interested in the answers so much as the manner of response. She had obtained all necessary information from the girl's aunt prior to this meeting. The girl's performance in this case would be considered quite satisfactory.

(9) As a final example, Hong-Gang Jin describes an informal dinner invitation between Chinese graduate students who are temporarily residing in the US.

FUNCTION/PURPOSE:

To enhance personal relationships

To express gratitude for help which others have offered

SETTING:

P2's office at a US university, 5 p.m.

KEY: Friendly and casual

PARTICIPANTS:

P1 – Chinese graduate student, male

P2 – Chinese graduate student, male

P1 and P2 are from the same city in China, and got to know one another through relatives there

P2 recently returned to China for a short visit, and brought back some things for P1 from P1's parents

MESSAGE FORM:
> Spoken standard Chinese, Beijing dialect
>> Casual register, including many interjections during discourse; rising and dropping intonation
>
> Head movement (nodding, shaking); facial expression

CONTENT AND SEQUENCE (organized into phases):
> Phase One: Opening
>> P1   Greeting
>>
>> P2   Accepts greeting
>>
>> Offers a seat
>>
>> Returns greeting
>
> Phase Two: Invitation
>> P1   hints that he will ask P2 to do something; pauses to look for P2's reaction (observes facial expression); offers the invitation to dinner at his home
>>
>> P2   refuses the invitation (surprised expression, then frown)
>>
>> P1   insists on acceptance
>>
>> P2   accepts indirectly (facial expression indicates he has no alternative)
>>
>> P1   reassures P2 of sincerity of invitation; sets definite time
>>
>> P2   agrees on time; expresses thanks
>>
>> P1   reassures P2 it will be informal
>
> Phase Three: Closing
>> P1   confirms the time; makes an excuse for leavetaking
>>
>> P2   thanks P1 again
>>
>> Closing salutation
>>
>> P1   Closing salutation

RULES FOR INTERACTION:
> The host should insist at least two or three times, but control his insistence according to the reaction of the person being invited.
>
> The invitation should be refused two or three times before it can be accepted:
>> First decline modestly, then accept indirectly.
>>
>> Show through facial expressions that one is reluctant to accept the invitation, and accepts it because there is no other alternative.

NORMS OF INTERPRETATION:
> In China, inviting someone to a dinner is seen as an important social activity which fulfills basically two functions: (a) to enhance social relationships, and (b) to express appreciation for

something another has done for the host, or sometimes to
express a need for someone to offer help.

The host's degree of insistence varies according to his reading
of the guest's face and the wording and tone of his
answer.

If the guest's face shows hesitance or indifference, or if the answer
is directly "no" or a good excuse, the host will not insist
further.

The way of accepting an invitation reflects a person's manners and
self-discipline: modestly declining and then accepting
indirectly and with thoughtfulness is considered courteous,
good-mannered, and considerate; the opposite will be considered discourteous or ill-mannered.

Further Illustrations of Ethnographic Analysis

The ethnography of communication, like the blend of scientific and
humanistic approaches which it is, seeks always to discover the general from
the particular, and to understand the particular in terms of the general, to
see the unique event and the recurrent pattern both from the perspective of
their native participants and the vantage point afforded by cross-cultural
knowledge and comparison. There are a number of published studies which
provide excellent models of procedures for data collection and analysis. The
few listed here as exemplary differ greatly from one another in focus and
scope, but all involve extensive and intensive observation and attention to
participants' points of view, as well as interpretation which is grounded in
the social and cultural situations of performance.

General ethnographies on ways of speaking are still very limited in number
despite the general recognition of their theoretical and methodological
importance. One of the notable exceptions remains the work of Ethel Albert
with the Burundi of Central Africa from 1955 to 1957, which was conducted
before the concept of the ethnography of communication was enunciated by
Hymes (Albert 1972). She relates situation-specific "rules for speaking" to
Burundi cultural views and social structure, relates both to personal strategies,
and discusses some of the problems encountered in cross-cultural communication and fieldwork.

Other important holistic models are provided by such work as that of
Blom and Gumperz (e.g. 1972), who account for the interrelationship of
social constraints, cultural values, and language rules in Norway; Barth's
([1964a] 1972) study of social processes and language boundaries in Pakistan;
Abrahams' (1983) analysis of African American speaking behavior; the

Scollons' (1979a) analysis of linguistic convergence at Fort Chipewyan, Alberta; Philips' (1983b) description of the Warm Strings Indian Reservation in Oregon; Sherzer's (1983) extensive study of the ways of speaking among the Kuna population of San Blas, Panama; Duranti's (1994) situated linguistic analysis of a Samoan village, and Graham's (1995) community study of the Xavante of central Brazil.

Most other holistic research has focused on a single subculture within a society, such as those defined by religion (Bauman 1974; 1983; Enninger and Raith 1982; Schiffrin 1984), by age (Eckert and McConnell-Ginet 1999 on adolescents and others mentioned in chapter 3 and chapter 7), or by ethnicity (e.g. Blacks in a neighborhood in Washington, DC (Hannerz 1969) or a bar in Philadelphia (Bell 1983), immigrants from Mexico near El Paso, Texas (Valdés 1996), or a Puerto Rican neighborhood in New York City (Attinasi et al. 1982; Torres 1997; Zentella 1997). Other research has focused on a particular social function or setting, such as medical encounters (Treichler et al. 1984; Ainsworth-Vaughn 1998), law (Conley and O'Barr 1990; Goldman 1993; Gibbons 1994), occupation (Kuiper 1996), and the marketplace (Lindenfield 1990).

Many exemplary descriptions and analyses of single genres or individual communicative events in diverse communities have appeared. Most of these focus on ritual events rather than on everyday encounters, in part because such events by their nature are most likely to recur in regularized form, and in part because their meaning is most clearly dependent on shared beliefs and values of the speech community. Some of these are book-length (e.g. Maskarinec 1995 on Nepalese shamanic texts; Yankah 1995 on Akan (Ghana) royal oratory; Wilce 1998 on complaints in Bangladesh), and many shorter works appear in the journals *Anthropological Linguistics, Journal of Sociolinguistics, Language in Society*, and *Linguistic Anthropology*. A number of these are referenced in relation to other topics in this book.

The wedding of the ethnography of communication with research on folklore has yielded a productive model which is performance-centered and analyzes folkloric events as they involve setting, performer, audience, and the other components of communication. Particularly noteworthy contributions include Hymes' (1981) development of *ethnopoetics* and Clements' (1995) wide-ranging survey of issues and methods in the field, as well as earlier work by Paredes and Bauman (1972) and Bauman (1977). The potential significance of such analysis for sociolinguistic study in general is noted by Hymes, who says in part:

> In its analysis of performance, folklore recognizes the differentiation of knowledge and competence within a community with regard to speaking; it recognizes the structure that obtains beyond the individual in the norms

of interaction of communicative events; and it recognizes the emergent properties of such interactions, both normally and as specific to particular performances . . . . (1972a: 48)

A final caveat is in order in this discussion of methodology. Even as we attempt to be faithful to the realities of behavior as it is enacted, we must not ignore the broader context within which the actions we observe are situated. We must constantly seek for both the antecedents and the contingencies which give meaning to the scenes we witness. At the same time, we must continually test our perceptions and understandings against those of the participants, if our "objective" account of their communicative competence is to adequately reflect the experienced reality of their own subjective world.

5

Contrasts in Patterns of Communication

Ethnography inherently involves a comparative approach to description and analysis: indeed, without comparing forms and functions in diverse languages and social settings, the difference between culture-specific and universal communicative phenomena could hardly be recognized and understood as such. The components which are likely to be salient in speech events (genre, topic, function, setting, etc.) were introduced in the previous chapter as one type of framework for purposes of comparative analysis. Emphasis in the methods of research presented in chapter 4 was on identifying patterns and interpreting meaning from the perspective of the speech community to which the participants belong, with the assumption that all participants in a single event essentially share rules for use and norms of interpretation. The same general constructs and methods are also appropriate for studying contrasts in patterns of communication as they occur in different communities, and as they are used by participants with differing linguistic and social backgrounds interacting with one another. In this chapter, these constructs and methods will be applied to two domains of research: *comparative rhetoric* and *cross-cultural communication*. For the first domain, I will present a number of examples (many from former students) involving different languages and cultures; for the second, I will focus in more depth on methods and findings from a single communicative situation to illustrate data collection and analytic procedures which may be used.

Comparative Rhetoric

The literature in comparative rhetoric is fraught with widely-differing definitions of terms and foci for analysis, which reflect differences in the purposes of study and the disciplinary perspectives of the researchers. Many of these differences are non-trivial, beginning with the definition of *rhetoric* itself. Traditional rhetorical analysis defines rhetoric as the artful and skilled use of language, and often further limits it as a field of study to language which is used for persuasive purposes. More recent rhetorical analysis is often related to the teaching of composition and typically also includes the developmental study of novice and relatively ineffectual language use, as well as language which is used for virtually all communicative functions. The comparative analysis of rhetoric from the perspective of applied linguists who are primarily interested in teaching composition in a second language has typically focused on the influence which conventions of writing in a first language have on writing in a second, and has been mostly concerned with expository and argumentative functions within academic genres.

The dimensions of contrast which have been used for study are similarly diverse. Traditional rhetorical analysis is not essentially comparative in nature, but focuses on the rhetorical strategies of native speakers in relation to an audience with the same language and culture. The extensions which may be made for comparative analysis are in contrasting a rhetor in one speech community with a rhetor in another within an otherwise similar context of performance (e.g. a community leader making a speech in the US versus Samoa) and to contrasting rhetors within the same society who represent different social subgroups or different styles (e.g. male versus female politicians making campaign speeches in the US, or ministers delivering sermons in conservative versus liberal churches). Comparing stylistic patterns has long been used as a major technique in literary analysis and related scholarly research (e.g. comparison of style in the novels of Hemingway versus Faulkner, or determining the authorship of anonymous texts). A further extension can be made to comparing the performances of rhetors diachronically (e.g. editorials published in the same newspapers before and after a major social change, or speeches of politicians addressing large audiences before and after the advent of television cameras and teleprompters).

The dimensions of contrast chosen for study by researchers in the field of composition instruction are typically ones which are located within the same *discourse community*, defined as a group with similar social characteristics and/or academic or professional orientations, as well as a shared set of rhetorical norms and conventions. Analysis often focuses on different styles for the pedagogical purpose of raising students' awareness of effective strategies, or compares usage across genres and academic disciplines for the purpose of teaching situation-specific appropriateness of different writing conventions. The concept of discourse community is used in part

To point out the highly convention-bound nature of writing and learning to write, and to urge that the business of teaching and learning this conventional activity be made more transparent by considering openly the costs and benefits of conforming to conventions. (Rafoth 1990: 142)

Research on developmental features in student composition may include qualitative in-depth and longitudinal investigation of learners' and teachers' perceptions and experiences, as well as the more common sampling and quantitative rating of texts.

The purposes of many applied linguists are also pedagogical, but their focus has been primarily on language learners' performance in their second language (L2), often within a speech community where they as yet have only limited participation and marginal membership. The initial interest from this perspective was primarily in academic writing, but this has broadened across channels and functions of communication. Ideally, comparative analysis for novice second language writers involves triangulation with multiple sources of data which include learners' performance in the L2, performance of comparable events in the learners' dominant language (L1), and performance of the target L2 events by a native or highly proficient speaker of that language.

A much less common focus of applied linguists is on the skilled speaker and writer of multiple languages, although questions of multilingual competence are of steadily increasing interest, as are issues of the nature and function of non-native varieties of world languages.

Historical Development

Rhetorical analysis has roots in the classical work of Plato and Aristotle. The traditional analytical focus has not been on the learner of language, but upon its master; and (in its classical origins, at least) not on the writer, but on the orator. Etymologically, the term *rhetoric* was the adjective form of *rhetor*, or 'speaker.'

Another characteristic of the work of traditional rhetoricians is that considerable attention is given to the effects of particular rhetorical strategies on audiences: i.e., analysis focuses not only on the production strategies of the speaker, but also on the interpretation and response of the listener (which in turn provide feedback for production), and on the joint construction of contexts and meanings. The modern concept of discourse community extends the older notion of audience to consider broader social and political contexts of communication, analogous in many respects to the concept of speech community discussed in chapter 2, although it is generally considered to be much more homogeneous than is the construct of speech community used in ethnographic analyses.

Most work on comparative rhetoric from the perspective of second language acquisition and teaching traces its roots to Kaplan's (1966) publication which defined *contrastive rhetoric* as a field. Kaplan extended the notion of "contrastive" from the theory and practice of *contrastive analysis*, which was widely used at that time (e.g. Fries 1945; Lado 1957). This theory/ practice called for the comparison of learners' native language and target language, with the expectation that such contrast would predict and explain errors that would be likely to occur in the process of second language learning. Kaplan's model involved the application of error analysis procedures to rhetorical forms or structures in the learners' production of second language text, as perceived and interpreted by native speakers of the second language. The assumption of contrastive analysis that comparison of the target language and native language would predict learners' errors was transformed into the assumption that learners' errors would reflect transfer from the native language. Another transformation involved a shift from an almost exclusive focus on oral production in contrastive analysis, to an almost exclusive focus in early contrastive rhetoric on the production of written text. This shift was motivated largely by concerns for improving the academic writing skills of international students who were entering US universities, but also as a reaction against the commonly held view within linguistics at that time that speech is primary and writing is but a secondary representation (Kaplan 1988: 289).

More recently, second language acquisition and teaching approaches have been heavily influenced by interlanguage (IL) theory (as formulated by Selinker 1972), which argues that deviations in second language structures often cannot be explained solely by transfer from the native language. One of the first systematic studies to use the triangulation procedure called for above was by Indrasuta (1987), who conducted a comparative analysis of writing by Thai students in Thai (L1), Thai students in English (L2), and American students in English (L1), and showed quite conclusively that inferring native language rhetorical structures from IL production is overly simplistic: patterns occur in second language writing which are different from those which are produced by native writers of either the source or target language (in Indrasuta's study, Thai and English, respectively). Interpretation of the sources of IL rhetorical production is also complicated by the fact that many learners are multilingual and multiliterate, and that they are often using the second language in contexts of cross-cultural communication. Also, their anticipated audience is often speakers of additional languages, with English (or another second language) serving as a lingua franca.

Another disciplinary perspective which is concerned with comparative rhetoric is that of *text linguistics*. Both at its inception and after some decades of evolution, most who have worked on contrastive rhetoric have considered their field to be part of "the basic tradition of text analysis" (Kaplan 1988: 278), making a clear distinction between text and context and claiming text (not context) as its domain. While there has been mention of factors such as audience considerations and rhetorical context features from a second language acquisition and teaching perspective, these generally have not been integrated into analyses of text production.

While we can find exceptions, the major limitations of comparative analysis within the framework/approach of contrastive rhetoric which has focused on structural differences between learners' L2 production and native language "norms" have been (1) that it generally has neglected pragmatic considerations of "the interaction between communicative codes and the contexts of their use" (Duranti and Schieffelin 1987: i), and (2) that it typically has failed to establish validity of interpretation or explanation for claims of transfer of linguistic or cultural patterns. The major limitation of traditional rhetorical analysis has been its general assumption that participants in a communicative event are members of an idealized homogeneous discourse community, and to this extent most sociolinguists would consider it inappropriate for study of language production in socially complex groups and in multilingual contexts. A number of efforts have been made to overcome these limitations (e.g., see Connor 1996). Incorporating an ethnography of communication perspective appears to be especially promising for comparative analysis of rhetoric which gives critical attention to pragmatics and situational context, and which involves procedures for establishing validity of interpretation or explanation from both external and internal points of view. Other important possible directions are on examining how rhetorical forms and strategies may interactively become constitutive of a discourse community, and how and why rhetorical forms and content, and responses to them, may change over time.

Ethnographic Perspective

The pragmatic factors and issues which are often neglected in product-oriented approaches are addressed by giving priority to the *functions* of language, by emphasizing that what language *is* cannot be separated from *how* and *why* it is used. From this perspective, putting primary emphasis on structural differences between texts may be likened to focusing attention on the tip of an iceberg: what can be most easily observed is often not what is most important. As discussed in chapter 2, the situational context within which texts must be interpreted includes cultural, social, and political settings, as well as physical ones.

This concept of *situational context* goes well beyond the concept of *rhetorical context* as it is usually applied in rhetorical analysis. Situational context includes much richer specification of participants in a communicative event than does the traditional rhetor/audience notion, for instance, particularly in terms of their role-relationships, and their respective rights and responsibilities. The relationship of rhetor and audience must be viewed as dynamic involvement, and rhetorical strategies must be considered in terms of their role in shaping and changing that relationship. These issues add further requirements for adequate analysis. Even when the text under consideration is a printed product which cannot change in physical form, constructivist views stress the audience's changing perception of text and author as part of a dynamic communicative process (Duranti and Goodwin 1992).

An example of what is involved in specifying and interpreting situational context may be found in a comparison of advertisements seen on television in the US and Japan. One salient pragmatic contrast between US and Japanese persuasive strategies is the common American imperative to "buy this" versus the Japanese strategy of developing pleasant sensory images within a scene which is subsequently associated with the product (reported by Takano). Another salient difference is the explicit comparison of one product with another in US advertisements, and the absence of this strategy in the Japanese (reported by Suzuki). Text analysis alone could not account for either difference. Interpretation of the lack of explicit comparison needs to be situated in an understanding of the different level of responsibility Japanese television stations accept for the content of advertising which they broadcast, the degree of loyalty which is expected of them by their customers, and how such loyalty is defined. Particularly because the same television station is likely to air commercials for competing products (or at least might wish to be able to accept advertising from the other company in the future), to explicitly criticize one customer in favor of another would be unwise business practice in Japan. We will return to the difference in persuasive strategies in the discussion of validity below.

Some other aspects of situational context which are likely to be relevant for comparative rhetorical analysis may be suggested by the following questions:

- What medium is utilized in different cultures for dissemination or broadcasting of different rhetorical genres?

Many features of performance may be influenced by the quality and availability of radios, television sets, and computers, as well as by printed media. There have been dramatic changes in political speaking styles in the US, for instance, with a shift from large public gatherings (originally without electronic amplification) and radio to the medium of television, and interactive web sites accessible by computer have essentially changed the scope and nature of audience response. Contrasts in patterns of communication across speech communities, as well as in the same society across time, must take such contextual factors into account.

• What social roles in each culture require particular rhetorical skills?

In many societies, highly developed (and systematically different) speaking skills are expected of religious leaders and politicians, for instance, but do not constitute an expectation for college professors or engineers. Religious leaders must sound inspirational and self-effacing, and politicians must project sincerity and solidarity according to societal norms of interpretation. Although professors are usually not required to develop specific speaking skills, they are expected to have mastered the technical writing conventions of academic publication, and students may respond differentially to their particular presentational styles. These attitudes and values (along with the performance factors they relate to) are likely to be culture-specific, and should be determined as part of the task of comparative analysis. Again, such contextual factors must be taken into account in contrasts across cultures, or across domains in any one society.

• How does distribution of differing rhetorical styles and skills relate to the access to power and distribution of prestige in a society?

Some styles require special interpretive skills, a fact which preserves limited access to certain domains. Philips (1982) claims that this is the case for legal cant, for instance, and Prelli claims that scientists have cultivated language differences in order to

> draw sharp contrasts between themselves and "nonscientists" to enhance their intellectual status and authority vis-à-vis the "out groups," to secure professional resources and career opportunities, to deny these resources and opportunities to "pseudo-scientists," and to insulate scientific research from political interference. (1989: 52)

Another example comes from China, where for generations writers learned established conventions for writing eight-legged essays as a prerequisite for obtaining prestigious positions in the civil service. Which domains in a society involve limits on access in this respect must again be determined as part of comparative analysis.

Interest in the relation of rhetorical strategies to social organization in different cultures does not merely reflect relatively recent developments in sociolinguistics; the Aristotelian conception of rhetoric was also essentially social in nature. Halloran described the "cultural ideal" in the classical tradition as the orator and civic leader "who understood all the values of this culture and used artful speech to make those values effective in the area of public affairs" (1982: 246), and many contemporary rhetoricians would still hold that this is a core characteristic.

Current interests in discourse analysis and applied linguistics take the comparative analysis of contrasts in patterns of communication well beyond the restricted definition of rhetoric which limited attention largely to public speech/writing for persuasive purposes. Similar methodological concerns for adequate description of function and situational context, and for establishing both external and internal validity, are equally important for comparing how to persuade the seller in the market place to give one a lower price, how to negotiate for a needed service, or how to establish and maintain everyday networks of social support.

Establishing Validity

The issue of establishing validity of interpretation or explanation applies to both structure and cultural context. With respect to validating claims of transfer of structural elements of language code and organization from L1 to L2 for multilingual speakers and writers, it is essential to include native or near-native samples of L1 and L2 production in comparative analysis, and not make assumptions that all differences between non-native and native production can be attributed to transfer from the non-native's L1. With respect to validating the interpretation of contrasting patterns as reflecting cultural differences, it is basic to any ethnographic approach that the perspective of "insiders" be determined and represented. For comparative analysis, this entails including the perspective of both cultures involved, and usually requires cross-cultural collaboration of researchers and/or the use of methods which elicit perceptions and interpretations of events from multiple points of view. Even researchers who consider themselves fully competent in both languages and cultures should check their interpretations with others who are dominant in each, since perceptions can be (and often are) influenced by prolonged cultural contact.

A major problem with establishing validity in interpretation is that cultural differences in rhetorical style are likely to be plotted onto dimensions which imply value judgments and implicitly privilege the researcher's point of view. Most US analysts taking a contrastive rhetoric approach would compare the American and Japanese strategies of advertisements in the example cited above on a dimension of "directness-indirectness," with the American "buy this" strategy described as more "direct." This very labeling is ethnocentric; the notion that an imperative form in syntax is more direct in pragmatic intent and effect than evocation of satisfying sensory experiences is itself a cultural artifact. From a different cultural point of view, there may be reasons to consider appeals to sensory experiences as more "direct" than those which require verbal mediation. We must also consider the possibility that the US analysts' valued notions of directness are even considered offensive in certain cultures or are not viewed as important categories/ dimensions of analysis or evaluation.

It is important that such a relativistic perspective be incorporated into comparative rhetorical analysis. The methodology and terminology of contrastive rhetoric (including the application of error analysis to L2 texts) has given us a deficit model in which it is difficult to be objective. For instance, even some Japanese and Chinese researchers, in order to relate to the existing US-dominated literature in contrastive rhetoric, adopt the language and concepts of that discourse community, and use the negative terms that Americans have employed to describe "what's wrong" with their rhetorical styles from the viewpoint of the American audience and analyst: "nonlinear," "circular," "slow to get to the point," "indirect," "lacking cohesive ties," "digressive," etc. To take a somewhat Whorfian view, they are being forced into a colonialist deficit perspective rather than a multiculturalist difference perspective. There is a clear need for ethnosemantic research in this field, to determine how different rhetorical structures and strategies are perceived and labeled by their users.

We should be especially aware of the hazards of dichotomized categories applied across languages and cultures. In addition to "direct" versus "indirect," some commonly used dichotomous terms in contrastive rhetoric are "group-oriented" versus "individual-oriented," "linear" versus "nonlinear," and "reader-responsible" versus "writer-responsible." As noted above, part of the problem such polarities present is that they imply culturally biased value judgments. An additional problem is that analysts tend to write about these constructs in quantitative rather than qualitative ways. The notion of "reader versus writer responsibility" provides a good example, since this is a widely accepted dichotomy first posited by Hinds (1987) to characterize differences between Japanese and English. There is a danger of ethnocentric bias or stereotyping and oversimplification in the claim that the reader in Japan makes *more* inferences than the reader in the US. Rather, because all human communication involves inferencing, description should focus on contrasts in the *kinds* of inferences that one is expected to make in the two speech communities, not just in written texts, and how this might relate to issues of "face" (discussed below) and social relations.

The comparative view I am taking focuses on the speech community as a basic unit for analysis, on the way structures and strategies are organized, realized, and situated within that unit, and it takes as its primary analytic task describing and accounting for similarities and differences in patterning within different speech communities. Unlike the definition of discourse community for mainstream rhetorical analysis, there is no expectation from an ethnography of communication perspective that a speech community will be linguistically homogeneous. Still, when comparative analysis includes subjects who are in the process of acquiring a second language, or includes multilingual populations, the construct remains problematic.

Situated Event Analysis

Comparative analysis of patterns of communication may focus on many different levels or aspects of performance (e.g. macrostructure, pragmatic or rhetorical strategies, discourse development, content, linguistic structure), but the clearly bounded, recurring communicative event remains a useful construct when beginning comparative study. Contrasts at the level of macrostructure involve the organizing principles for texts and their inter-pretation, including the bases for coherence and what is considered relevant. At the level of pragmatic or rhetorical strategies, differences in such factors as bases for argumentation, seats of authority, and what constitutes "proof" are frequently salient. Also in this general category are contrasts in the pre-sentation of "face," interpersonal metadiscourse features (expressing atti-tudes, attribution, etc.), and uses of rhetorical questions, analogies, anecdotes, literary allusions, and proverbs. Discourse development differs in the logical relation among sentences and in what yields cohesion; content differs in topic and vocabulary/symbol selection as well as what is said versus what is left unstated. Linguistic structure is perhaps the most difficult level to compare across languages, but contrasts can be made in the patterns of choice that speakers/writers make from their available repertoires of codes and conventions, such as those which signal focus or relative formality.

Control of research design, by which the components of comparable events are as similar as possible across language groups, is important in order to assure a grid within which contrasts are most likely to be salient and interpretable.

The telephone conversation as a unit for analysis provides a good example from everyday communication of the control which using recurring events may make possible, since it has the same recognized boundaries (the ringing as "summons" and hanging up as "close") wherever telephones are used for vocal interaction. An exemplary research design for the contrastive study of this event was adapted by Hao Sun (1998), who analyzed Chinese and American conversations and examined the possible influence of Chinese patterns in English conversations by Chinese speakers. Her design follows the procedures for triangulation recommended above by including three groups of subjects as callers:

1   Chinese L1 speakers in Chinese, in China
2   Chinese L1 speakers in Chinese, in the US, and in English, in the US
3   English L1 speakers in English, in the US

All of her subjects were females within the same age range to limit the variables to L1 (Chinese or English), native or second language use of English, and geographical/political setting (China or the US). All groups placed calls for both transactional and interactional functions (based on Brown and Yule 1983), but these types were kept separate for analysis.

Sun focused on contrasts in patterns of opening, closing, and presentation of purpose in the telephone conversation, and she was able to distinguish them on the following dimensions:

Setting – China versus the US (L1, language of use, and function kept constant)

Language – Chinese versus English L1 (setting [US] and function kept constant)

L1/L2 – English L1 versus English L2 (setting and function kept constant)

L1/L2 – Chinese L1 versus English L2 (caller identity, setting, and function kept constant)

Because hers is a "situated analysis," Sun's discussion includes contextual information which relates to multiple dimensions of contrast. To explain the significant difference which geographical/political setting makes in patterns of transactional calls, for instance, she found that it is important to understand the differences in the social role of service people answering the calls, and differences in business practices between the US and China; relevant contextual factors include the degree to which callers are experienced with telephone use, clarity of electronic connections, and whether local calls are charged by the minute; further, relative scarcity of goods in China is more likely to place callers to business establishments in the position of asking for favors or making a potential imposition, and may account for service people who answer the calls being less "polite" by some criteria. Sun further validates her interpretation with follow-up interviews and questionnaires with American and Chinese collaborators.

In another example, Syahdan compares patterns in advertisements in English and Indonesian. For maximum comparability in analysis, the two events he selected are both advertisements for the same product (a Toshiba notebook computer) which appeared in popular magazines in the US and Indonesia. The purpose of both is to inform potential customers about a new computer product and to persuade them to buy it. Syahdan finds the most salient contrast to be in the persuasive strategies which are used. The English text uses the word *buy* explicitly, and presents the advantages of the product by comparing it with other products and stating technical specifications. The Indonesian text does not include the word 'buy.' It justifies the value of the product by prominently portraying the image of a *keris* above the computer in the advertisement; the *keris* is a sacred object (resembling a staff) which has power and charisma and is considered a symbol of power and achievement for its owners. The *empu* (a sacred person who makes *keris*) dedicates it only to special persons. Syahdan concludes that the technical capabilities of the computer are less important for potential Indonesian customers than the prestige it would give to the owner. His "insider" interpretation is that the message is, "there is an exclusive gift for a successful business figure like you that is the Toshiba Notebook," and that the power it possesses gives charisma to the owner.

Greetings, as commonly occurring bounded events, also provide a good communicational unit for situated comparative analysis when other components can be held constant. Rodney Tyson, for instance, contrasts the situations of a couple returning from a long trip greeting their parents and parents-in-law in the US and in Korea. In his analysis, the young couple doing the greeting are the same in both cases, the husband being of Anglo-American and the wife of Korean ethnicity. There is also constancy in the warmth and sincerity of tone, and in the content of parents' questions about the couple's health and travels. Patterns of contrast are most salient in the setting and message form. The greeting in the US setting takes place immediately upon reunion, no matter where that occurs (inside or outside a home, in an airport, etc.). The initial exchange (outside in this case) in Korea is quite superficial, with the "real" greeting postponed until the participants are in the *anpang* (the central room of a Korean house) and positioned appropriately to indicate they are ready for the greeting. The parents sit side-by-side facing the door, and the couple stands facing them until the initial phase of greeting is complete. The message form differs not only in language code (English versus Korean), but also in nonverbal behaviors and the style or register which is considered appropriate. In the US greeting, all four participants hug and kiss in turn, and all are expected to smile enthusiastically and speak in an excited and somewhat louder-than-normal tone of voice. There are no strong restrictions on styles or register, though language is expected to be informal on the part of all participants. In the Korean greeting, the couple place their hands against their foreheads with elbows extended, kneel on the floor, and bow very deeply – usually a man actually touches his hands to the floor; a woman bends only about halfway. Then they slowly stand up straight and bow again, this time from the waist. The parents encourage the couple to dispense with tradition and skip the bow, but they are expected to bow anyway. The number and type of bows (in this case, one deep bow followed by a bow from the waist) is significant; ceremonies performed at ancestors' graves involve two deep bows followed by a bow from the waist.

It is important for the American son-in-law to use the formal/polite style of speech during the greeting sequence in Korean, while the wife uses the informal/polite style (used most often by women). After the greeting, the son-in-law may alternate between the formal and informal polite styles, and the daughter may use a mixture of the informal/polite and more intimate styles with her parents. The Korean parents use an informal style when addressing their son-in-law, but never the *panmal* (the most intimate style) they use with their daughter. They would use *panmal* when speaking to a daughter-in-law, however.

Another example of comparative analysis of greetings is provided by Akmaral Mukanova, who focuses on contrasts in the content and form of questions asked by Americans and Kazakhs in this event. The Kazakh asks not only about the health and welfare of the addressees (common with Americans), but how their animals, family, relatives (both close and distant), and neighbors are doing. Mukanova provides the following translations from Kazakh, along with cultural interpretation:

> *Are livestock-souls healthy and secure?*
> *Mal-zhan* 'livestock-souls' is a compound word in Kazakh which includes in its scope both domestic animals and family members. For Kazakhs the well-being of livestock (camels, horses, sheep, cows, and goats) is vital. This is because: (1) they provide meat, which is the basis of all Kazakh meals and the most worthy food in their eyes; (2) they provide milk, including fermented horse and camel milk and hundreds of milk products; (3) they provide clothing; (4) they constitute precious gifts on a special occasion; (5) they provide entertainment, with many traditional Kazakh traditional sports and games (e.g. "Chase the girl," "Kokpar," "Fighting for a goat's carcass," and "Wrestling on horseback") played on horseback; and (6) they represent beauty. Girls who have eyes like those of a baby camel are considered the most beautiful. The most frequently used female name in Kazakh is *Botakoz* 'baby camel's eye.' Men who have a face the form of which is like a horse's are considered handsome.
> *Are relatives and distant relatives healthy?*
> Both close and distant relatives (even very distant descendants of the same tribe) play an important role in the life of every Kazakh.
> *Are your neighbors healthy?*
> Kazakhs tend to have a close relationship with their neighbors. Neighbors support each other morally and materially, and their welfare is thus important to note.

Phosy Chanhming provides an example in which he compares two narrative texts, both in Lao and both relating a well-known story of the legendary figure Xieng Mieng. Primary variable components are time of writing (1968 versus 1996) and message form (poetry versus prose). Chanhming describes structural differences which characterize the different forms, but of particular ethnographic interest is his discussion of contrasts in the social context of story-telling in Laos between times of the productions of the texts, and how they relate to contrasts in form.

Chanhming reports that stories have been transmitted orally for centuries from elders to children for didactic purposes, but that recent cultural changes (including the spread of literacy and developments of media and other entertainment sources) have radically influenced the nature of the story-telling event. For example, he says:

> In the sixties, from my own perspective in growing up in the countryside of Laos, not many Lao were able to read or write; therefore, most of the written materials had to be read to the people by a few literate individuals [such as] monks or teachers.

Story-telling events in Laos through the 1960s were addressed to a relatively large audience, and the accepted form was categorized as a "general reading poem, whose purpose is to entertain readers or listeners by means of reading." (This is one of ten types of poetic forms for reading in Lao.) Since the spread of literacy and competing entertainment sources, transmission of stories is most frequently from writer to individual reader. Texts must be shorter and be "very clear" to capture individuals' interest. Some contextual factors remain constant:

> A reader is supposed to know the healing tradition that includes monks chanting, witch doctor, foreseer, shaman, offering things to the monks. Also, a reader should know that Xieng Mieng is the king's enemy, despite the claim in some stories that he is the king's brother. . . . Regarding philosophizing and personalizing, it is common in Lao that a narrator does not mix his own opinions with the original story. Although Lao stories aim at teaching youngsters good morals, the moral is not explicitly stated. It is, in fact, the readers' responsibility to create their own moral from a story. For this reason, as I recalled my composition classes in High School, how to interpret the moral from a novel and how to integrate the moral to real life are taught at school; so when the students tell or read a story, they are supposed to infer the moral of the story at the end.

Some textual and contextual factors have changed:

> In recent publications, both in media and educational settings, the use of Pali loan words is decreasing as they are difficult to understand. Similarly, the selection of vocabulary may be influenced by the political situation. At the time [the 1968] text was written, the king still existed in Laos; therefore many respectful terms were widely used. When [the 1996] text was written, however, the monarchy had been abolished for almost three decades. As a result, many terms referring to the king had disappeared from use.

Other textual differences in the two texts, including relaxation of conventions which required regular patterns of intonation and rhyme, might be related to the general shift from an oral to a literate culture, perhaps reflecting different strategies which are needed for memorization of orally transmitted stories versus those needed for (and expected in) transmission through print. Diachronic study of other aspects of folk tales as situated events can also be very interesting from an ethnographic perspective: for example, interpreting change over time in Western classics like *Little Red Riding Hood* and *Cinderella* can be related to such cultural, social, and political factors as gender issues and notions of what content is appropriate in stories addressed to children.

Other Data Collection and Analytic Procedures

Most of the data collection and analytic procedures discussed in chapter 4 are also applicable to description and interpretation of contrasts in patterns of communication, with parallel collection and analysis conducted in multiple speech communities. A caveat that is worth repeating is that components of communication should be as similar as possible across language/culture groups in order to assure a grid within which contrasts are most likely to be salient and interpretable. The following have proved to be particularly fruitful for comparative studies.

Event retelling

A popular and productive procedure for collecting comparative narratives is use of a short wordless film/video or picture book to prompt event retelling. Use of a film/video/book as stimulus for story retelling provides maximum comparability, since subjects are performing narratives which are based on the same sensory input. Unless intended to be independent variables, controls also need to be kept on whether the retelling is oral or written, and on whether the person to whom the story is being told sees the same visual stimulus as the subjects (because the subjects' belief that they are relating new information or not may influence performance). The most commonly used film/video is *The Pear Stories* (Chafe 1980, cited in chapter 4, includes comparative analyses of retellings in English, Greek, and Japanese). The most commonly used picture book is Mayer's (1969) *Frog, Where Are You?* (Berman and Slobin 1994 includes a copy of this text and developmental analyses of retellings in English, German, Hebrew, Spanish, and Turkish).

The examples I use for this discussion are based on retellings of *The Naughty Owlet*, a wordless animated cartoon for which we have collected over 100 texts from native speakers of English and Chinese. Briefly, the plot is as follows:

A mother and father owl hatch three eggs. The third owlet to hatch has four misadventures: it disappears and is found watching television; it does not learn to fly; it does not pay attention at school and thus does not learn that foxes are dangerous; and it falls off a tree limb while playing cowboy and cannot fly back up. A fox offers to help the owlet get back up in the tree if it will climb up to his nose. The other two owlets rescue the third owlet from the fox.

Contrasts in patterns of narrative production can be examined at all levels in the resulting stories, but an ethnographic approach requires including contextual factors which are outside the usual concept of "text." Follow-up interviews may be used to explore, for instance, who is likely to relate such a story, to whom, when, where, and for what purpose. Adult retellers of *The Naughty Owlet* all consider children to be the audience because of the story's topic and the nature of its animation, but differ along a cultural dimension in considering its primary function to be to entertain (American) or to convey a moral lesson (Chinese). Potential dimensions for contrastive textual analysis include the macrostructure (global patterns of organization), including opening and closing routines, ordering of episodes, and relative proportions of attention to actions and episodes; transitions across and within events and other cohesive devices; interpretation of events (including interpretive naming and selection/omission/addition); and verbal style and structure (e.g. figurative language, formulaic sayings, backgrounding and foregrounding strategies).

For purposes of comparative analysis of narratives, an early step is to make an exhaustive list of the actions and episodes which are visible in the film/video in chronological order. This provides an etic baseline set against which to compare ordering and selective reporting in the various retellings. We have found that almost all retellings by older children and adults (regardless of language/culture) fit the same *story grammar* or narrative structure (cf. Brewer and Lichtenstein 1980; Labov 1981):

Abstract (optional)
Orientation (description of setting, introduction of participants)
Complicating episodes
Climax
Resolution or final action
Coda (optional)

This structure provides another etic set of units within which to compare proportions of attention, selective omissions, and verbal strategies (as in how transition to the climax is marked).

Dimensions where we have found language/culture-specific patterns of contrast are openings and closings; personifications of the owl "family,"

including naming and kin terms, assignments of relationships and responsibilities, and attributions of personality and motivation; omission of events
which are on the etic list and addition of events which are not; inferencing
and interpretation based on background information or experiences; symbolic
interpretation of animals, colors, and other physical elements; and formulating moral judgments or other evaluations of behavior.

  For example, contrasts in patterns of closing relate in large part to the
societal function which the tellers believe such stories serve. Representative
of American codas are:

> Naughty little owl has learned his lesson and everyone lives happily ever
> after.
> Back in the tree the three laugh about the adventures and run into the
> house to play.
> All the owls thought this was funny, so they had a big laugh and went
> home.
> Safe and sound up on the limb, her brothers explained to her about the
> bad fox and she apologized for not paying attention. They lived happily
> ever after and none of the three ever told their parents!

In contrast, the following translations are typical of endings which were
told in Chinese:

> Afterward it dared not fail to listen to lectures again.
> Afterward it knew it needed to concentrate, and couldn't fool around or
> play video games or watch television.
> Then it felt ashamed, because usually it did not study well, and it only
> loved to watch television. Then it shed tears.

Such moralizing was also integrated into the interpretation of events. For
instance, the episode of the owlet's not learning to fly was retold by one
adult in this way (translation from Chinese):

> The next day, father and mother made them do exercise and practice flying.
> In this way, when they grow up, they can live independently. Father swung
> the first baby in the air, he flew bravely over. Mother swung the second baby
> in the air, he also bravely flew over. When it was the turn of Little Red, he
> was so timid. He was very lazy too, and even did not dare to give it a try. He
> was crying in his mother's arm: "I don't want to try, I don't, I am so scared."
> His mother said this child needs more exercise later.

The same story-teller later provides this coda:

> From then, the small owlet realized that as a little child, he should study
> hard, exercise hard and not be lazy from a very young age.

Also of considerable interest in interpretation of events in these stories is the extent to which mention and amount of detail in recall is dependent on tellers' prior knowledge and on the cultural salience of the events. For example, American adults and children who retold this story gave relatively less attention to the complicating event in which the owlet did not pay attention at school than did the Chinese speakers, and only Chinese story tellers reported that the teacher was angry. On the other hand, most of the Americans mentioned that the owlets were "playing cowboy" when one fell, while few of the Chinese did. There was some misinterpretation by Chinese children who did mention that scene but said that the owlets were playing gangsters or Kung Fu. This finding is in accord with schema theory (e.g. Steffensen, Joag-Dev, and Anderson 1979), which claims that what is already known provides "ideational scaffolding" for details in recall tasks. There were two scenes which almost no one mentioned: a sequence of alternating suns and moons to represent passage of time, and the owlet's ear-tufts growing to represent embarrassment. These symbols were either not recognized or were not considered important.

In addition to showing different patterns across languages and cultures, event retelling tasks may also be highly productive for analyzing developmental factors: e.g. contrasts between children and adults in the same language, and between native speakers of a language and second language learners at different levels of competence.

Scenarios

Other popular procedures for collecting comparative texts are to devise a specific scenario and then ask members of different groups to act out or report what they would say in that situation, or to administer discourse completion tasks. The primary purpose in using these techniques is often to elicit contrasts in patterns of communication which relate to speech acts: e.g. forms which would be selected to convey specified pragmatic intent, such as requests, complaints, or responses to compliments (see Kasper and Dahl 1991; Cohen 1996 for discussions of methods and reviews of findings). Some scenarios and completion tasks allow for extended responses, but many call for only a sentence or two.

Subjects for these data collection procedures usually belong to three categories: speakers of different native languages who respond to tasks in their L1s; language learners whose responses are compared with those of native speakers of the target language; and bilinguals who respond to the same stimulus in both their L1 and L2. Analyses most frequently relate to contrasts in degrees of "directness," and/or to types of politeness strategies invoked (e.g. power versus solidarity, positive versus negative politeness, involvement versus independence; see Brown and Levinson 1987, Scollon and Scollon 2001). Notable published studies and collections include Blum-Kulka, House, and Kasper (1989), Blum-Kulka and Kasper (1993), and Hong (1998).

The scenario and discourse completion procedures provide good control across components of communication so that surface contrasts are likely to be highly salient, but serious questions can be raised concerning the validity of such findings, unless they are supported by naturalistic observation, and by interviews which explore speaker/writer intentions and their interpretation of the larger context. Minimally, self-report responses should be recognized as *ideal* rather than necessarily *real*, as discussed in chapter 4. As long as this limitation is recognized, they may yield interesting and enlightening contrasts.

The use of scenarios with extended responses is illustrated here in a study of contrastive patterns for complaints by Korean-English bilinguals which was conducted by Jihyon Park. She controlled components in her study by selecting subjects who were all Korean students enrolled in English classes in the same university in Korea, who all had the same purpose (to complain about a grade), who all used the same channel of communication (e-mail), and who all had the same addressee in the same role-relationship (a bilingual professor of theirs who was Park's collaborator). The variable component for this study is language of production, with 20 students writing e-mails of complaint in L1 Korean and 39 in L2 English. Park's primary objectives were to describe contrasts and to determine if there is pragmatic transfer in complaint strategies from L1 to L2. The following scenario was presented to subjects by the collaborating professor:

> You are taking the College English Class with me. You and three other friends studied together in a group for your final exam. After the final, you compared your answers with other friends of the study group and found that your answers were very similar to those of your friends. Later, you checked your grade and found out that you got a C while the other friends got As. Now you have to write an e-mail to me to complain about this result.

Dimensions of comparative analysis for these complaints are much the same as for the narratives discussed above. Among the most interesting of Park's findings is that many complaint strategies in the English L2 texts which a native English-speaking professor might consider "rude" are not attributable to transfer from Korean L1, but to the students' stereotypic concept that one should "be direct" in English. These L2 strategies include rhetorical questions, commands, attributions of blame, and emotional expressions (some derived from watching TV). For example:

How could this happen in the world to me? How could you give me a C
   grade?
Please read my writing carefully.
I can't accept my grade C. . . . It isn't fair.
I think that you had some mistakes grading me.
I think that it's surely your mistake to give such a grade for me.
How reasonable you are! (*intended sarcastically*)
I would say that I got a raw deal with you. Moreover, I'd tell everyone
   that there's no fair in this rat race.
Oh, my god! . . . It's so terrible!! I can't believe it.

Organizational features of the L2 complaints which probably reflect
concepts derived from English instruction and which differ from Korean
L1 are absence of an opening buffer, such as a greeting or comment about
the weather (they "get right to the point"), and explicitly marked linear
sequencing (*First of all, . . . Secondly, . . . , Finally, . . .*).

In contrast, the L1 complaints typically began with an opening buffer
(rather than getting "right to the point"), included apologies for bothering
the professor, and expressed deference. Park gives the following example to
illustrate a common sequence (translation from Korean):

Opening buffer: How are you, professor. I deeply appreciate your teaching and advice during this semester. Your class was very impressive
   and I tried my best to do well in the class.
Explanation of purpose: I'm sorry that I have to ask you about my grade
   and I'd appreciate it if you would kindly let me know your thoughts
   on this.
Discussion: I was surprised to see my grade. My teammates, who I
   studied with, all received A's while I got a C. I think I did my very
   best for the class and its requirements. Also, I was never absent from
   the class. I'm wondering why I received the grade.
Request: I apologize for my rudeness in asking you about a grade, which
   I understand as your exclusive privilege. I'd greatly appreciate it if you
   would kindly let me know why you gave me the grade.
Closing buffer: Thanks, take care.

Parallel naturalistic texts

Control of the communicative frame for comparative purposes is often
found among naturally occurring texts. This is illustrated in the situated
events described above, including Syahdan's analysis of advertisements for
the same product in Indonesia and the US. Contrasts in textual patterns

may include all of the features that were considered for event retelling and scenarios; as with all ethnographic analyses, interpretation must be situated within the social and cultural context of performance.

Genres commonly selected for analysis using parallel naturalistic texts are news accounts or editorials regarding the same or similar events which have been published in different speech communities, or by newspapers which represent differing political views in the same society (following Trew 1982).

One example is provided by Akmaral Mukanova, who compares American and Kazakh editorials addressing the US decision to break a missile defense treaty with Russia. Her focus is on patterns of figurative language in Kazakh and English. For example, the Kazakh editorial uses a metaphor which translates *The sun has set for a warm relationship*, while the English editorial uses *There is a new sheriff in town*, both to evaluate changing international relations brought about by a change in US political leadership. To interpret the Kazakh metaphor, a reader needs to understand Kazakh belief that one should not sleep during the time when the sun is going down; even a sick person should get up at that hour. The intended image is a dire one of "the end." To interpret the English metaphor, one needs to know that President Bush is from the state of Texas, part of the former "Wild, Wild West" of the US, and to understand the positive connotations which many Americans have of a sheriff bringing order to lawless situations by ignoring previous norms and establishing new rules. The metaphor of the sheriff also conveys the power of a single actor (the "Lone Ranger"), potentially opposed to processes of coalition and negotiation.

Parallel texts which are appropriate for situated comparative analysis may be found in many other genres as well. Those suggested by Kachru (1982b) which require a rich level of cultural interpretation include reviews of performances, matrimonial advertisements, obituaries, invitations, and acknowledgments (in published books).

Translation

Interlingual translation has long been recognized as an important application of comparative discourse analysis; when sensitive to differences in sociopolitical contexts, audience factors, and norms of interpretation (as well as in linguistic codes), the resulting parallel texts may also be another potentially enlightening source of information on contrasts in patterns of communication.

Some of the most reflective and best documented work has been in the domain of Bible translation. Eugene Nida (1974; 1977), for example, emphasizes the many contextual as well as textual factors which must be taken into account from the perspective of what he calls "a sociolinguistic theory of translation." These include conventions for transmission of beliefs, social considerations regarding the audience or "receptors" (e.g. level of literacy and background knowledge), culture-specific rhetorical devices, available repertoire of appropriate figurative language, and emotional and affective values communicated by style. The goal of such an approach to translation is functional equivalence through interpretation of all components of communication. Translators who commit themselves to this perspective typically spend many years in the target community in order to develop both linguistic skills and cultural understandings, and to test the validity of their textual products.

In a number of publications, Kenneth Pike discusses types of subtle misunderstandings which might easily be overlooked without adequate time and opportunity for feedback in a community. In the following example, he reports on the experience of one of his colleagues in the Summer Institute of Linguistics who was translating the Bible from Spanish to Otomí, an indigenous language of Mexico:

> They had translated the second chapter of the Gospel of Luke. When Otomí people started to read this chapter (which began the story of the birth of Jesus with a comment about the census which forced Joseph to go to Bethlehem to be enrolled in his home town) one of the listeners commented: "Well, if God wants us to take a census, we'll take a census then!" Her colleagues were flabbergasted. They saw nothing in the story to imply this, and wondered why the local people made this deduction. It turned out that in their discourse structure – radically different from that of the Spanish – an incident needed to be introduced with its principal point being mentioned at the start. Hence, since the story started with the background statement about census, they deduced that this must be the crucial point to the story, and they reacted accordingly in generalizing it and applying it to themselves. So the translators revised the Otomí version to read "The story of the birth of Jesus was like this" – and they had no further misunderstanding. (1979: 103–4)

Analysis of parallel Biblical textual patterns often also requires knowledge of social contexts of production. To illustrate these factors Huilin Chang compared Psalms in *The Holy Bible Chinese Union Version Shen Edition* with the *King James Version* (1611), from which it was translated in the years 1900–19. The Chinese Psalms are quite similar to the English in thematic content, but differ significantly (as would be expected) from the English in poetic form. The Chinese Psalms also differ radically from traditional Chinese poetry when contrasts are analyzed on that dimension, which is less expected and requires historical background for understanding. Chang explains:

> The ending year [of translation], 1919, was a crucial time in modern Chinese history. Among the developments associated with the May Fourth Movement which happened in 1919, two were notable: one was the literary revolution,

the other, the introduction of Western thought and the re-evaluation of the traditional civilization. The new reformers declared aggressively that literary Chinese was a dead language because it was no longer spoken by the people. They afterwards averred that the spoken language, being a living language, was the only fit medium for the creation of a living Chinese literature. [This translation], under a great influence of that vernacular literature trend and regarded later on as an excellent vernacular work, was a very significant milestone.

Another domain in which many parallel texts are created in translation is news reports and editorials concerning current events. A common basis for multiple translations is an international news service release from which national and regional papers select coverage. Another good source of parallel texts is newspapers which provide translations of their own texts for posting on web sites or for publication in international editions. Of particular interest for comparative analysis within this domain are what elements are retained, added, deleted, and changed from original to translation, and how these transformations relate to different sociopolitical contexts of publication and to different readerships.

Seung-Hwa Seok provides contrasts of editorials from three Korean newspapers with translations which are prepared by the newspapers to target English-speaking foreigners inside and outside Korea (typically translated in cooperation with native speakers of English who are hired by the papers for this purpose). The most salient difference between the original texts and English translations in his sample is the construction of inclusive "we" in relation to different readerships. It is also interesting to note the different amounts of information which are provided by original and translated texts when the same referent or event is described. For example, this is a literal translation from a Korean language editorial (translation and emphasis are Seok's):

> However, when [we] look at the content of the summit talk, we again realize the tremendous difference between the atmosphere of the [George W.] Bush administration and that of the Clinton administration, when *special ambassador, Cho Myong Lok, visited Washington.*

The following is the paper's translation for their English-speaking readership. It refers to the same situation, but provides much more information about the Korean envoy for that audience:

> Nevertheless, it seems that the Bush administration's stance is markedly different from that of the Clinton government, especially when we recall that North Korean armed forces chief Jo Myong-Rok visited Washington last October, in the waning days of Clinton's term of office, as special envoy for North Korean Defense Commission Chairman Kim Jong-Il.

A final example of analyzing contrasts in original and translated texts is provided by Holly Jacobson (2002), who compares the structure of and reader response to Spanish-language health brochures which originate in Spanish with those which have been translated from English. She selected brochures on matched topics of AIDS, diabetes, high blood pressure, and TB. Quantitative tests over the content show a tendency for readers to learn more about the diseases from native Spanish texts than from translations, but of more interest to us here are the qualitative measures which she incorporated: recall protocols and open-ended interviews that explored whether subjects preferred the native or translated brochures, and why.

Jacobson used essentially the same procedure for collection and analysis of recalls as was described above for contrasting story retelling. After subjects read a health brochure silently to themselves, they were asked to tell what they remembered about it. For analysis, Jacobson started with an exhaustive list of overt "idea units" in each text in order to have an etic set against which to compare what ideas were mentioned, what categories of content they belonged to (e.g. causes, symptoms, treatment), what was omitted, what was added (from inferencing and background knowledge or experience), what was changed, and how the retelling was structured. She then related different recall patterns to contrasts that she had discovered through textual analysis. One interesting finding is that use of fear strategies (e.g. referring to horrible consequences of an untreated disease) suppresses overall recall, perhaps because it has an "overshadowing" effect that keeps the reader from focusing on other relevant information. Organizational devices such as subheadings and bulleted lists are significant, with organizational features of the native language texts yielding retellings which are more cohesive and coherent than do the translations. Jacobson reports that readers who retold translations

> tended to provide listings of words and phrases, without establishing clear relationships between the idea units through the use of cohesive devices. In other words, it was not clear that they had established clear associations between the concepts and ideas during the reading of text.

As a result of this aspect of her analysis, Jacobson suggests that some of the linguistic, pragmatic, and organizational features which differed in the translated texts

> conflict with the expectations of readers. This may make it difficult for them not only to retain the information in memory, but also to synthesize and categorize idea units and establish clear relationships between them.

Responses to interviews which asked readers to rate and compare a native and translated text on the same disease (without telling them which was which) are very interesting in the extent to which subjects mention not only language factors, but evaluate and relate the content of texts to cultural values which the texts themselves do not explicitly address: family, God, and social identity. Applications of this descriptive and analytic approach to delivery of health and other social services seem to be especially promising.

Cross-Cultural Communication

The domain of cross-cultural communication is defined by interaction (spoken or written) between participants who have significantly different linguistic and cultural backgrounds. (I am not distinguishing here among *cross-cultural communication, intercultural communication*, and *interethnic communication*.) Some of the types of events mentioned above as suitable for comparative rhetorical analysis are also appropriate for cross-cultural analysis, including those which involve interaction of second language learners with native speakers of the target language, or between speakers of the same second language who are from different native language backgrounds.

As in all ethnographic studies of communication, the analysis of cross-cultural speech events requires an emphasis on the functions of communication and on the situational context within which it occurs. Participants in cross-cultural events must also still be viewed from the internal perspective of their respective speech communities, as in other comparative analyses, but the dynamic interaction between them requires additional dimensions of analysis. Multilingual speakers' or writers' production is likely to be influenced not only by the conventions of their native languages and cultures, but also by the knowledge they have of the addressees' language(s) and culture(s), by their knowledge of the resources of the linguistic code(s) selected, and by the expectations and attitudes they hold and develop in the process of interaction. There must be the same considerations of interactive construction of meaning and reciprocal negotiations as we find in an analysis which is conducted within a single community.

In extending an ethnography of communication perspective to cross-cultural communication, I am drawing heavily on the work of Gumperz (e.g. 1984, 1992) on conversational inferencing. As with contrastive rhetoric, however, most work on conversational inferencing across cultures has involved error analysis and has focused on marked instances of *mis*communication (e.g. Gumperz 1982; Michaels 1987). This is an important and revealing area of study, but we also need to consider and be able to account for the unmarked but far more common cases of skilled, artful, and *successful* cross-cultural interaction. Perhaps no other area can more readily help us identify possible universals in human communication. Multilinguals have a wider range of options for accomplishing communicative goals, including a capacity for style shifting and style creation or blending (depending on desired audience effect) which exceeds monolingual competence (Hanks 1986; Kachru 1987).

Skilled multilinguals do not necessarily merely adopt the structures and strategies used by native speakers of the linguistic code they select, any more than they necessarily merely transfer the structures and strategies of their own native language(s) and culture(s), even if they are fully conscious of the differences. When ways of speaking are transferred from native to second language contexts of use, it is often because of the affective meaning they carry, and because abandoning them might be perceived by the speaker (although perhaps not by the addressee) as a violation of values and decorum.

For example, I participated in a discussion session at an educational conference which included several Navajo teachers, all of whom were bilingual. An important goal of the session organizers had been to get those teachers' input, but none of the Navajo teachers talked. The difference that led to this breakdown was the temporal pattern of silence in turn-taking between questions and answers, which occupies a significantly longer time-space for Navajos than is generally used by non-Navajo English speakers. The non-Navajo participants in the session answered questions that had been addressed to Navajos, and the discussion leader repeated or rephrased the questions when the period of silence following them went beyond her own limit of tolerance. At the same time, the Navajo teachers were effectively kept out of the discussion because not enough time-space was ever allowed to reach an appropriate extent for them to respond. The Navajo-English bilingual teachers recognized what the problem was and I discussed it with them afterward. They had considered the non-Navajo timing pattern to be quite impolite, and the short time between questions and answers a sure sign that those who did speak had no sincere concern for the issues that were being addressed. Although all were fluent English speakers and all were aware of the differences in temporal patterning, the Navajos did not wish to add such "impolite" behavior to their communicative repertoire.

Another example of maintenance and transfer of native language patterns in the English of Alaskan Athabaskan speakers who are linguistically related to Navajo is in their resistance to writing in an "appropriate" essay style (reported by Scollon and Scollon 1979b). Producing such written text would require the Athabaskans to adopt discourse strategies which they have been socialized in their communities to consider arrogant and irrelevant – or they would be forced to acculturate in this respect and perhaps even be estranged from their home communities.

A third relevant example was provided by a graduate student in the US from Japan who persisted in bowing when she entered or left a professor's office, even though she was quite aware that her nonverbal behavior was not considered "appropriate" in an American university setting. She said that in spite of that awareness, for her to behave "like an American" (i.e. not to bow) would make her feel like a rude person, and would be disrespectful.

These examples show that factors which should be taken into account for analysis of cross–cultural communication importantly include aspects of identity and even perceptions of morality which may be involved. They illustrate ways in which multilingual speakers or writers may use patterns of communication which diverge from second language norms as a cultural identity badge, or as an indicator of personal character, even when accurately producing the surface forms of that language.

The three examples cited here have involved conscious maintenance or transfer of ways of speaking by individuals or groups in spite of fluency in a second language. Other multilingual strategies involve one interactant adopting the other's patterns when enhanced communication success or identification with that individual or group is desired, or a negotiated convergence between/among participants to a code which is native to none when identification is with the multilingual entity. For example, teachers may adopt different modes when interacting with colleagues or students from a different country to enhance communication even if they do not identify with them or their culture, and staff members of an international agency such as the World Bank may use English as a lingua franca but adopt a variety which neutralizes regional differences (discussed in chapter 3).

These are all part of the repertoire of interactional strategies which multilinguals may command for establishing and negotiating ideational or interpersonal positions or relationships, including the presentation and recognition of "face." This has been one of the most fruitful constructs for description and explanation of contrasts in patterns of communication, and it will be the focus for the following discussion.

Concepts of "Face"

"Face" is a complex construct which was probably originally embodied in the Chinese terms *lian* and *mianzi* (Hu 1944). *Lian* refers to the moral character which is publicly attributed to an individual and conferred by society (closely akin to the concept of *honor* in English), and *mianzi* refers to the prestige and reputation which results from individual achievement. Hu reports that *mianzi* had acquired its figurative meaning by the fourth century, and *lian* by the thirteenth or fourteenth. Both terms retain their literal (physical) meaning in China, referring to the physically observable visage, although there are regional differences in usage.

The concept of "face" is of import to the ethnography of communication because of its defining role in accounting for the identity and relationship of participants in a communicative event, as well as for many of the cross-cultural contrasts which are found in patterns of communication. Liu, for instance, explains contrasts in Asian students' classroom participation and silences in terms of the two meanings of "face":

> many participants stated that they were concerned about their poor English speaking abilities and so they chose to be silent in class to avoid making mistakes that, in their minds, would result in a loss of *Mianzi* since their prestige as graduate students and their perceived public images as smart students or accomplished scholars in their own fields and in their own countries would be damaged as a result of their loss of *Mianzi*. However, if they did not try to protect their *Mianzi* by keeping quiet, they might eventually suffer from the loss of *Lian* as a result of constant loss of *Mianzi*, which is an indication of their shamelessness in front of others in a given community. Growing up in such a collective culture, Asian students tend to care more about their *Mianzi* as their public image. . . . (2001: 204)

It is likely that all societies have accommodated consideration of "face" in some form in their rules for interaction, but the concept does not mean exactly the same thing nor have the same significance universally. (Discussions of cultural differences can be found in Mao 1994; Ting-Toomey 1994; Yu 2001.) Contrasts in the composition of this construct and in the highly diverse patterns of communication which relate to its realization provide an important and productive theme for investigation in cross-cultural communication.

The concept of "face" was introduced to Western sociolinguists primarily in the work of Erving Goffman, who defined it as a negotiated public image which corresponds more to the Chinese concept of *mianzi* than *lian*, but includes elements of both: a "presentation of self" in the presence of others so that "the others will in turn have to be *impressed* in some way by him" (1959: 2). It is this concept of "face" as *performance* which I adopt for the following analysis, which is meant to be illustrative of methods which might be used for cross-cultural investigation.

Constructing an Unseen Face

One communicative event which is familiar to most university students and faculty is the statement of purpose which many academic institutions require applicants to submit as part of a dossier (also typically including transcripts of grades, test scores, and letters of recommendation) used to determine eligibility and priority for admission. At institutions with which I have been affiliated in the US, these are intended to provide a faculty evaluation committee with information about prospective students beyond what can be gleaned from formal documentation. It is a cross-cultural event in many cases, when the language and cultural backgrounds of applicants are different from those of their evaluators. I use an analysis of this communicative event (conducted in collaboration with Susan Cooledge) to illustrate the application of an ethnographic perspective to this topic.

Goffman's approach to the construction of "face" as a negotiated public image appears to be an appropriate point of departure for the analysis of students' statements for several reasons. He opens his discussion of the topic with the following statements:

> When an individual enters the presence of others, they commonly seek to acquire information about him or to bring into play information about him already possessed. They will be interested in . . . his conception of self, his attitude toward them, his competence, his trustworthiness, etc. (Goffman 1967: 1)

In our sample, these are features that faculty readers and judges are clearly looking for in the statement of purpose to supplement/complement those available from course transcripts, test scores, and other "objective" evidence. Also pertinent to the event under analysis:

> If unacquainted with the individual, observers can glean clues from his conduct and appearance which allow them to apply their previous experience with individuals roughly similar to the one before them or, more important, to apply untested stereotypes to him. (Goffman 1967: 1)

In other words, the process of interpreting and acting on an image such as that which applicants present of themselves requires a high degree of inferencing. With face-to-face contact, presenters might have immediate feedback which could permit them to revise their strategies if the response to the image they were portraying was not as intended, and addressees could adjust their "frame of expectations" if the presenter did not fit stereotypes based on past experience. One immediate complication in applying Goffman's perspective to the analysis of applicants' statements of purpose is, of course, that we are not considering the physical face-to-face interaction which his approach was intended to target; the applications are in a written channel rather than oral, and the communicants are far removed in time and space. Still, applicants are clearly writing with the intent of establishing a "face" to their reviewers, although that face normally remains physically unseen.

The database for analysis of this event includes over 200 statements of purpose which were sent in applications for admission to Teaching English as a Second Language (TESL) and Second Language Acquisition MA and PhD programs in the US. Approximately two-thirds of these were from international applicants: most were from China, Taiwan, Korea, and Japan, with the remainder from elsewhere in Asia, Latin America, Europe, Sub-Saharan Africa, the Middle East, and Australia. All were written in English.

As an exercise in ethnography of communication, the primary goals of analysis were to identify and describe contrastive patterns of communication in the event, to explore "insider" perceptions, and to relate patterns to social and cultural factors attendant on the situation. The framework provided by the statements of purpose was relatively constant, including the genre, the general purpose, and the instrumentality (written English). Although the participants were all graduate student applicants addressing faculty evaluators, their perceived identity and role-relationship was one of the most salient dimensions of contrast, and the rules for interaction were heavily dependent on the social and cultural contexts of performance and interpretation.

The first step in analysis was to categorize the applicants inductively according to the theatrical "role" or multiple "roles" which they seemed to be attempting to portray, and next to match national and cultural identity with the different roles to determine correlational patterns. Cooledge gave descriptive labels to these categories: the *unique and interesting individual* (with subcategories of the *adventurer*, the *wanderer*, the *practical*, the *self-serving*); the *communal/group altruist*; the *committed altruist*; the *hopeful/ambitious*; the *accomplished/knowledgeable*; the *connected*; the *critical*; and the *not-so-perfect*.

Most US applicants presented themselves as the *unique and interesting individual*, including information which highlighted experiences on freighter trips to South America, bicycle treks across Europe, formative hardship residencies in the Andes (or on Pacific islands, or in remote European, African, and Asian villages), surviving earthquakes in Japan or Central America, and experiencing exciting Peace Corps or missionary experiences. Verbal instantiation includes such wordings as:

> In my eagerness to explore new cultures, . . .
> If accepted into the . . . program, I would bring with me a spirit of exploration and creativity.

The *wanderer* represented self as a lover of travel and exotic experiences, and only appeared at the MA (not the PhD) applicant level. A generic presentation of this face is exemplified by the statement:

> I have not decided definitely where I would like to go after getting my master's degree.

This face is not uniquely American, but also presented by some applicants from Europe, including one who wrote:

> I am applying to do an MA in TESL because I am really willing to spend some more time abroad before I begin to look for a job.

Typifying the *practical* or the *self-serving* is the US applicant who wrote quite candidly:

> Being an ESL teacher with only a Bachelor's degree makes for a very difficult employment environment.

One applicant from Europe also writes:

> Hopefully my professional growth and personal development would help me get a promotion at the English Department.

Also ambitious, but representing self as the *communal/group altruist* rather than as *self-serving* were most applicants from Russia and Latin America. Representative statements are:

> If I have an opportunity, I will apply this outstanding experience to the good of our Department as best as I can.
> I hope to return to my former job and, side by side with my fellow colleagues, be able to make substantial improvements to our English Program.

We sought to gain an insider perspective from applicants by interviewing a number of successful candidates (not necessarily writers of the statements of purpose in this sample) and asking them in retrospect to characterize what "face" they had been trying to project in their statements of purpose. For the "insider" perceptions which were elicited from successful applicants from different countries, open-ended questions to the students include:

- What image were you trying to project? Why?
- What kind of information do you think should be included? What kind of information would be inappropriate? In other words, what should you leave out?
- Is one style or organization structure more appropriate than another? Why?
- Do you recall having had any particular audience in mind when you wrote your statement?

Americans largely validated our perception that for most it was the *unique and interesting individual,* having this to say:

> The (admissions) committee would look at this as "This is who I am."
> (The purpose of the Statement is to) Make a distinction between yourself and someone else.
> (The point is to) Say how I am different.
> It's a "get to know me."

In contrast, applicants from Asia, Africa, and the Middle East in their applications almost invariably presented themselves as the *committed altruist,* dedicated to country rather than to self. Some representative statements are:

> Upon completing my graduate studies, I will return to [my country] to make some contributions to English teaching.
> I will return to [my country] to pursue my professional knowledge to use in practical situations to educate children and benefit society.
> (If admitted) I would be able to contribute to solving educational problems in [my country].
> I am determined to devote my lifetime to English education in [my country].
> (This degree) will equip me with skills necessary to improve the quality of foreign language teaching in [my country].
> (By earning this degree in ESL I would) thereby improve the methodology of its teaching in [my country's] context.
> My future plans are to make a contribution to the improvement of education in [my country].

Among the other roles, the *accomplished/knowledgeable* were almost all Americans and Europeans and the *not-so-perfect* were almost all Asian, but there were no other clear correlational patterns of role-identity with national origin.

Faculty members who had served on admission review committees were also interviewed to determine what type of "face" they were looking for in the addressees. Questions intended to elicit "insider" perceptions of faculty include:

* What traits are you looking for when you review student applications?
* What kind of information do you get from reading the statements of purpose that suggests whether that's going to be a good student for the program?
* What do you react negatively to? Why?

Americans report that they indeed value individuals who "stand out" in some respect, particularly as they perceive this as displaying "independence" and "maturity," thus showing that the American students had read their addressees accurately. The response of American faculty evaluators to self-presentation as the *committed altruist* is also generally quite positive, and often a determining factor for admission of international applicants, even as they recognize problems of truth value and sincerity. European-background faculty evaluators who were interviewed did not consider this as important, and reported valuing the *accomplished/knowledgeable* most highly. It seems noteworthy that faculty addressees do not necessarily use the same subjective criteria for evaluating domestic and international applicants, but indeed make (usually unconscious) use of expectations based on stereotypes and/or prior experience as Goffman suggests: e.g., the same degree of "individuality" and assertiveness that is considered "normal" from US applicants may be flagged as "odd" when expressed by applicants from Asia.

Another contrast in patterns of communication is in the strategies for "politeness" which applicants assume or choose to adopt between themselves and whoever they perceive their addressee to be (as outlined by Brown and Levinson 1987; see additional discussion in chapter 8 of this book and in Scollon and Scollon 2001). The two possible dimensions have been characterized as *positive, involvement*, or *solidarity* politeness versus *negative, independence*, or *deference* politeness. The former emphasizes shared experiences and values, and makes use of in-group markers such as inclusive *we*. Negative politeness makes minimal assumptions about the interests of the addressee, and makes use of deference markers such as formal names and titles. Deferential strategies consistently prevail in applications from most countries in Asia. Reasons given for application include wishing to attend "your respected university," be part of "your distinguished graduate program," and studying with "your outstanding faculty."

Non-deferential reasons for application are much more common from other parts of the world:

> *From Africa:* My choice of [institution] stems from its geographic location. Its proximity to California makes it even better.
>
> *From Israel:* The reasonable prices and good atmosphere in [state] encouraged me to apply at your University.
>
> *From Europe:* The purpose of this memo is to express my intention to become a PhD candidate, and to declare my area of specialty.
>
> *Also from Europe:* Perhaps I will be able to help improve the quality of second or foreign language instruction in the United States.
>
> *Not atypical from the US:* Given my background, experience, and interest, I do believe myself to be the ideal candidate.

Our analysis of what face and role-relationship applicants present did not in itself address questions of how writers' truthfulness or sincerity might be related to their representation of self, or to the interpretation and judgments of readers. These are clearly important factors, however, in the application and admissions processes.

Goffman gives us insights about some of the strategies that may be involved. Part of the reason for his claim that inferencing is unavoidable comes with the recognition that

> a performer tends to conceal or underplay those activities, facts, and motives which are incompatible with an idealized version of himself and his products. In addition, a performer often engenders in his audience the belief that he is related to *them* in a more ideal way than is always the case. (1959: 48)

Applicants to graduate programs often tactfully uphold a flattering personalizing solidarity effect by referring to specific faculty in the program by name, to published program ranking, or to unique characteristics of the program or locale. (This practice is encouraged by descriptive web pages which are increasingly available in all parts of the world.)

It is interesting that such strategies are at least superficially accepted at "face" value by most addressees, even when they realize that most prospective students are actually "shopping around." The illusion is seldom disrupted except for the list of other institutions to which the applicant's GRE or TOEFL scores have also been sent, which is routinely included in documents from the Educational Testing Service, or the occasional humorous slip when an applicant seals a statement of purpose in an envelope addressed to the wrong university.

Otherwise, Grice's Cooperative Principle largely reigns in Goffman's model – and in much graduate admissions screening – or at least disbelief is largely suspended barring contradictory evidence. Exaggerated claims are often excused as an understandable part of "playing the face-game":

> As members of an audience it is natural for us to feel that the impression the performer seeks to give may be true or false, genuine or spurious, valid or "phony" . . . [This is why] we often give special attention to features of the performance that cannot be readily manipulated, thus enabling ourselves to judge the reliability of the more misrepresentable cues in the performance. (Goffman 1959: 58)

Such cooperative interpretation assumes, however, that participants in communication are playing by a similar set of rules: that they hold similar values and goals, concepts of relevance and truth, and social conventions, or can bring themselves to be "in tune" with those of their interlocutor.

Otherwise, in high-stakes face-games such as admission to graduate school, serious misunderstandings can result. Recognizing and interpreting cross-cultural differences in concepts about what *can* legitimately be manipulated by applicants in their creation of face as well as understanding how and why this may be accomplished again requires an "insider" perspective.

Follow-up interviews with successful applicants to graduate programs indicate that they were quite aware of playing a "game":

> *From the US:* Give them a sense of who you are and if you're what they're looking for – their "imagined student" for this area. This differs from other parts of the application because it's more "made up." You expand and put your best foot forward.
>
> *From China:* Try to present yourself as hard-working and friendly. . . . I followed the English tradition: say I was hard-working and friendly at the beginning, then gave evidence to support it.
>
> *From Latin America:* Usually the process is to try to get what it is the people want you to say. The reality is that you don't say what you think. You learn who the professors are and what their interests are, then try to adapt.
>
> *From Great Britain:* Americans tend to sell themselves more than British people do. Therefore I tried to sell myself. If I had applied to another university, I would have undersold myself. To Americans, "I'm wonderful!" Dressing up the facts. Whole different rhetorical style going.
>
> *From Russia:* It's good to be very purposeful, persistent, show that you are a self-made man, you work hard, and are goal-oriented. I had to praise a little, to say "I want to learn from you." And it works. Americans are so predictable.

Faculty members of the US admissions committees are also aware of the "game."

Another dimension of contrastive patterns occurs in the macrostructures which the applicants construct. The vast majority of MA candidates from the US present structured narratives concerning their life experiences – often approaching "adventure stories" in temporal sequence, content, and dramatic climaxes. In contrast, very few domestic PhD applicants or international applicants at either the MA or PhD level used narrative organization for this event. Instead, most of them interpreted the writing task as calling for an essay organized quite uniformly in this sequence: (1) purpose of application, (2) supporting evidence for the viability of the application based on past experience or knowledge, (3) specific future plans for study, and then (4) ultimate objectives/goals. Indeed, several added just these headings in their texts.

Answers to this puzzle come largely from background information which applicants brought to the event from prior educational experiences and academic contacts. American undergraduates, even in academic writing classes, are encouraged to construct stories, and it is thus not surprising that they would do so on this occasion. For example, this passage is from the opening chapter of a textbook in college composition:

> we all tell stories. . . . you're selecting certain facts and details, maybe exaggerating some of them slightly and omitting others, arranging them in a particular order to make a particular point for a particular purpose. That's basically what you do when you write an academic essay. Although you may not recognize it at first, good academic writing involves good storytelling. (Colombo, Lisle, and Mano 1997)

American students with some graduate school experience evidently learn that a good story is not necessarily good academic writing in time to apply for a doctoral program. Further, they report that they consult manuals which contain advice and models for writing graduate school applications and ask professors or more advanced students for help.

Adaptations of the same manuals appear to be available worldwide, which explains the lack of cultural differences in the format of statements. Models are even being included as exercises in textbooks for teaching English as a Foreign Language, although none warn that a "native accent" in this genre may not be entirely positive from the standpoint of institutional evaluators. International students also report having asked for advice and editing from visiting American professors and friends.

Evidence for the use of models is particularly obvious in routines for opening and closing. For instance, five different applications from Korea and China in our sample begin with exactly the same sentence:

> It is a great pleasure to have an opportunity to introduce myself and my objectives of study at your school.

Multiple applications close with:

> Thank you for your kind attention to this statement. I sincerely hope that you will grant me a chance to develop my academic career at your university.
> I hope that my plans described above will meet your warm consideration.
> I here certify that the foregoing statements made by me are true, complete and correct to the best of my knowledge and belief.

In between the opening and closing routines we find contrasting patterns in style, with Asian applicants using more formal structures, literary strategies, appeals to idealistic values, and proverbs. For instance:

From China: It would be the greatest pleasure for me, a teacher of English, to see that not only the language is understood by people of different nations, but the essence of culture and human spirit is shared the world wide.

From Japan: Everlasting love for a person, dreams of contributing to our knowledge of outer space, enlightenment in Buddhism – if one could devote all one's soul to something, it would be bliss. For me, English education is that very thing.

From Korea: To those who ask how I dare to make a new start, please say that there is in my town a pear tree planted two hundred years ago, and it still bears fruit not to be distinguished from that of a young tree in flavor.

In contrast, this retrospective advice comes from an American student who was interviewed:

Use some regionalisms; don't try to maintain a highly formal tone or style through the statement. Not informal, but not so highly formal that you're coming off as an egghead. Unless the program is looking for an egghead.

Contrastive patterns were also found in content, especially in what is evidently considered relevant – what is said versus unsaid. For example, applicants from the US, Europe, and the Middle East almost never mention family or former instructors, while applicants from Asia typically do so.

From Korea: My parents have made every effort to instill in me qualities of maturity, independence and leadership, including encouraging me to go to the United States to study further in the field of TESOL.

From Taiwan: At senior high, the English teacher offered me inspiration about English.

Applicants from Europe and Africa are most likely to include names of authors that they are acquainted with, and it is probably not coincidental that the European-background faculty evaluators who were interviewed list "demonstration of knowledge of the field" as a primary criterion for admission.

Asian applicants also typically include mention of activities which are not considered particularly relevant by American evaluators, such as music and sports. Indeed, some American faculty react negatively to athletic activities as "unprofessional" references. In some cases, inclusion of extracurricular activities appears to be an excuse for perceived shortcomings.

From Taiwan: Although my heavy degree of involvement in these activities adversely affected my grades at university, . . .

From Japan: While I am aware that my background is not in language education, I believe my music training has developed in me a sensitivity to phonetics.

In contrast, American students tend not to mention shortcomings. One said in an interview:

I have bad math scores on the GREs. In the first draft I had mentioned that . . . it was just too much information.

A final step in the analysis was to seek additional information on factors which might help relate the contrastive patterns which were found to differences in cultural components of the situation such as beliefs, values, social institutions, and conventions.

One important source can be professional colleagues who share an understanding of ethnographic methods and goals, and with whom one can discuss the contrastive findings. To give one example, I mentioned that applicants from China frequently make prominent mention of participation in sports, but both American and European-background faculty say that they tend to react negatively to any focus on non-academic interests and activities because it may signal lack of serious scholarly commitment. Jun Liu, a colleague from China, explained to me that the mention of sports activities is part of a convention for constructing the face of what translates as a "Three Star Student." He says that being one requires demonstrating a balance of Correct Politics, Educational Excellence, and Physical Health. Omission of politics is considered appropriate when applications are written for US universities, but omission of sports would imply not being physically fit and thus not a "complete" honor student.

Another potential source which can enlighten interpretation is published background information, although its relevance to the topic of analysis may need to be inferred. For instance, one pattern we had noted was that all applicants from China in our sample present themselves as the *Committed Altruist*; all of their statements express commitment to return to China to teach English, even though subsequent contact with successful applicants from this group reveals that for most, that had never really been their intent. Some had not been interested in teaching English at all and switched majors soon after admission, and most had planned to remain in the US after graduation. This pattern was largely explained by an article in the *Chronicle of Higher Education* (September 24, 1999) which reported that applicants to TESL programs in the US are three or four times as likely to receive visas as are applicants in an area such as business administration.

Another pattern in statements from China is the expression of particular interest in computer-based instructional technology, and of the unavailability of an appropriate training program in China to meet this interest and need. Again, subsequent contact with successful applicants reveals that this expression of interest is not necessarily to be interpreted literally, but as a conventional expression within the social and political context of their composition. Exploration of possible reasons for contrasting patterns led us to discover yet another variable in the participant component of the event which we had not anticipated: the intended audience may include not only the admissions committee to whom the statements are addressed, but also the consular officials who have authority to grant visas and government censors.

I mentioned above that while participants in an intercultural event must (as in all ethnographic research) be viewed from the internal perspective of their respective communities, the dynamic interaction *across* communities requires additional dimensions of analysis. The writers of the Statements of Purpose we have studied are influenced not only by the conventions of their native language and culture, but also by the knowledge they have of the addressees' language and culture, by their knowledge of the resources of the lingua franca for this situation (English), and by the expectation and attitudes they hold and develop in the process of constructing a "face." Often these have been acquired from models such as those we reported which they are instructed to emulate. It bears repeating that multilinguals do not necessarily merely adopt the rhetorical structures and pragmatic interactional strategies used by native speakers of the linguistic code they select, any more than they necessarily merely transfer the structures and strategies of their own native language and culture, even if they are fully conscious and knowledgeable of the differences. Along the road to acquisition of cross-cultural communicative competence, learners develop not merely an approximative interlanguage of linguistic forms and structures, but an *interrhetoric* of transferred, transmogrified, and partially adopted pragmatic strategies for self-presentation and management of "face" in interaction.

Yamuna Kachru (1996) has written that, as producer and interpreter of texts, one must recognize "cultural meanings in rhetorical styles across language and discourse communities, especially in the broader context of the use of English as an international language" and must become more reflexively self-aware of the (usually unconscious) "imposition of one's own knowledge, experience, beliefs, and expectations" on what is heard and read. It is precisely because these cultural meanings and expectations are less visible and largely out of consciousness that they can evade detection even while distorting communication in a seemingly common linguistic form.

6

Attitudes toward Communicative Performance

Attitudes toward language and its use have been of major interest to researchers in recent years, and have been elicited and analyzed from a variety of disciplinary perspectives. Of particular relevance for ethnographers are questions of how culture-specific criteria for "speaking well" function in the definition of marking of social roles, how attitudes toward different languages and varieties of language reflect perceptions of people in different social categories, and how such perceptions influence interaction within and across the boundaries of a speech community. In addition to their value in adding to our understanding of functions and patterns of language use, answers to such questions are relevant to the explanation of language maintenance and shift, and to applied concerns in the fields of cross-cultural communication, language planning, and education. Some of these issues have been briefly addressed in the discussion of language varieties, but all warrant further attention.

Language attitude studies may be characterized as: (1) those which explore general attitudes toward language and language skills (e.g. which languages or varieties are better than others, to what extent literacy is valued); (2) those which explore stereotyped impressions toward languages and language varieties, their speakers, and their functions; and (3) those which focus on applied concerns (e.g. language choice and usage, and language learning). Underlying each focus of study are questions of the nature of language attitudes, their causes, and their effects.

One reason language attitudes are of particular interest to ethnographers is that individuals can seldom choose what attitudes to have toward a language or variety. Attitudes are acquired as a factor of group membership, as part of the process of enculturation in a particular speech community, and are thus basic to its characterization.

It is because attitudes toward communicative performance are generally culturally determined that they are so strongly influenced by the social structure of the community in question. This may be considered a Whorfian notion in its mirror image, as has been articulated by Hymes (1966b). While Whorf said that the structure of language may influence social structure, interaction, and thinking, Hymes suggests that the social structure may influence our attitudes toward particular kinds of language. In other words, the social differences are there to begin with, and we can then use concomitant linguistic differences to symbolize them. At this point, we may use language to discriminate and to control, because we may use it to categorize people, to put or keep them in their place.

Methodology

It is perhaps appropriate that this area of communication research shows the greatest division in professional attitudes toward methodology. Qualitative research is considered unreliable by many, on the one hand, because of limited samples, possible subjective biases, and lack of explanatory power. The validity of experimental research is questioned from an ethnographic perspective, on the other hand, because of the unnaturalness of the situation and means by which data are elicited and equally possible subjective biases, both in research design and interpretation of findings.

A large number of quantitative studies which relate attitudinal-motivational factors to various kinds of academic achievement have been conducted, including many of second-language proficiency. There are also a large number of studies on stereotypic attitudes which are held by one language group toward speakers of other languages or other language varieties. One common elicitation technique used is the "matched-guise" procedure, in which subjects listen to recorded samples of speech which are purported to be from different speakers. To determine attitudes toward speakers of different languages, bilingual speakers have actually been used, speaking once in one language and once in the other. Subjects rate each speaker on a series of attitudes, and an analysis is made of differential ratings of the same speaker when using different languages. These attributes often include judgments on intelligence, personality, and suitability for particular occupations. One of the most interesting findings has been the readiness of so many subjects to judge others on the basis of only limited speech samples.

A word of caution must be added about the use of quantitative measures with people from different cultural backgrounds, as it was earlier for the study of variable social markers. While the measures may be statistically reliable, the validity of such studies can be established in these situations only through qualitative research. The perceived identity of the investigator, for example, can strongly influence quantitative outcomes. Judging occupational suitability presumes a hierarchy in terms of prestige, and what this is must be determined anew for each culture being investigated. Unawareness of cultural factors can invalidate research findings. One widely accepted study of the relationship of attitudes to academic achievement among American Indians concludes Indian students have the lowest self-concept of all minority groups tested, but deduces this largely from students' feelings that they have little or no control over their environment. Many American Indian groups do not believe that actively controlling natural forces is desirable, or even reasonable, so the conclusion that they have a low self-concept based on an ethnocentric interpretation of the data is accordingly invalid.

Macaulay (1975) raises similar questions regarding the validity of many attitude studies, including Labov's (1966) tests of "linguistic insecurity" in New York City, d'Anglejan and Tucker's (1973) forced choice responses in Montreal, and Macaulay and Trevelyan's (1973) use of interviews in Glasgow.

> Probably the weakness in all three approaches lies in the attempt to investigate such a complex question as linguistic attitudes from the outside on the basis of a single hit-or-miss trial. What is missing in all three studies discussed above is corroboration from members of the speech community that the investigators' conclusions are consistent with perceptions of the situation within the community itself. (Macaulay 1975: 160)

The same questions may still be asked of recent research. On the other hand, the use of quantitative measures may allow the discovery of patterning in situations which might otherwise be seen as mere random variation. Especially in attitude research, an integration of both qualitative and quantitative procedures is clearly desirable.

Attitudes toward Language and Language Skills

Attitudes toward language in general, its nature, and its functions, may be captured by some of the expressions a speech community has that include reference to language. In many languages, for instance, the "heart" of language is perceived to be the tongue. English speakers say *She has a sharp tongue, He has a loose tongue, He speaks with two tongues* (or) *with a forked tongue*, and *She spoke tongue in cheek*. Other parts of the anatomy less often relate to language, but we also use such expressions as *Button your lip* and *He put his foot in his mouth*. The person who has a sharp tongue in English has a "hot tongue" in Dari, and "a pointed tongue" in Pashto, but "hairs on his teeth" in German.

There are abundant examples of proverbs from different speech communities which attest to the value of silence. For example: *Silence is golden*

(English), *If you talk [you'll get] a small sum of money; if you remain silent, a lot of gold* (Thai), *Because of the mouth the fish dies* (Spanish), *The way your eyes look can say more than your mouth* (Japanese), and *Man becomes wise through the ear* (Farsi). A counter-sentiment is expressed in the Serbo-Croatian proverb *(Who) asks does not wander* and the English *The squeaky wheel gets the grease.* Such admonitions are often employed in socializing children.

How language is used in various communities to categorize people according to the way they speak and what they characteristically say is also ethnographically relevant, as are perceptions of how these categories should be ranked in value. Speakers of English may be labeled *braggart, gossip, big-mouth, liar, eloquent, pedantic, loquacious, quiet,* or *tactful.* According to Albert (1972), male speakers of Rundi would value being eloquent and loquacious most highly, tactful least; being a gossip or braggart would be more highly valued in that speech community than being discrete or quiet. Speakers of Navajo would conversely value quiet and tactful, and strongly disvalue a braggart. In contrast, in the Old English poem *Beowulf,* the hero is approvingly described as "eager for praise."

Within a single speech community attitudes may vary concerning what constitutes "speaking well" for males versus females, or for members of different social classes. While eloquent and loquacious are valued categories for Burundi males, for instance, females are trained for evasiveness, careful listening, and "artful silence" (Albert 1972). Conversely, Americans traditionally value a male who is the "strong and silent" type, while a female exhibiting the same communicative behaviors is likely to be negatively valued as aloof or unfriendly.

Attitudes about the nature of language and its functions may be inferred from derogatory comments which are made about it, or restrictions placed on its use. The role of language as an agent for socialization was clearly recognized in the 1880s by the US Commissioner of Indian Affairs, as can be judged from his statement on language and educational policy:

> The first step to be taken toward civilization, toward teaching the Indian the mischief and folly of continuing in their barbarous practices, is to teach him the English language . . . we must remove the stumbling-blocks of hereditary customs and manners, and of those language is one of the most important. (Atkins 1887)

The potentially sacred nature and functions of language are illustrated in a religious edict issued in Saudi Arabia early in 1986. This edict made it an offense to discard Arabic language newspapers in trashcans, since they usually contain Mohammed's sayings and verses of the Quran (*World Press Review,* February 1987: 47).

Derogatory comments about language change, or what Roger Shuy calls "the-world-is-going-to-hell-in-a-handbasket-and-language-is-leading-the-way syndrome," may also be enlightening, in that complaints about what is changing usually reveal attitudes about what has been valued as it was. In the United States these are abundant in magazine and newspaper articles, letters to the press, and reports on the state of language and education. Comparable attitudes are also expressed elsewhere in the world. In Japan, for example, educated adults express concern about young people's declining language skills, especially in writing, blaming such media as TV, radio, and comic magazines for tempting them not to read the "good" material which would transmit such ability.

The expression of concern about writing in particular in this example also indicates greater value being placed on written versus oral language skills. While widespread, this attitude is far from universal. Oratory is highly cultivated as an art form in many speech communities, and concepts of "good" and "bad" speech are not dependent on the standardization of a language or a tradition of literacy (Bloomfield 1927), although primary valuation of oracy may accompany literacy, as shown in the following example:

> [In the Foreword to *Mein Kampf*], Hitler is most apologetic about giving his Nazi elite a *written* manual. He tells us that he knows that men are moved by the spoken, not the written, word and that every great movement owed its growth to great orators, not to great writers. (Duncan 1962: 236)

An inverted recognition of the social importance of literacy, on the other hand, may be inferred in situations where there has been denial of literacy to certain portions of the population. This practice was justified during the slavery period in the US by the belief that literacy made slaves more likely to revolt. (Related practices are discussed in chapter 8.)

Technological changes may result in changed attitudes toward speaking styles, as was illustrated during the 1980 US presidential campaign. The television camera shifted the valued political style from traditional ringing oration at a distance to the illusion of intimate encounter. John F. Kennedy's early campaign style was perceived as "bombastic" by many TV viewers, and Ronald Reagan's as "warm" and "sincere." Reagan's speech accepting the Republican nomination was very obviously and effectively directed to the camera and to the millions of people in the unseen audience rather than to the thousands actually present in the convention hall, a strategy which probably contributed to his eventual election. It was not surprising that he was called the "Great Communicator."

The most highly regarded language skill in other societies may be knowing how to use speech levels well, or the ability to use similes, metaphors, proverbs, and rhymes in appropriate contexts; the same skills are suppressed when members of such societies are studying in English-medium universities, where "directness" is the valued style and "clichés" are penalized.

Other general areas where there may be culturally based differences in general attitudes toward language include the possible consequences of speaking, and the degree to which one person may legitimately speak for another or for the group. Such information is important for the elicitation and interpretation of all data collected from members of a particular speech community.

Attitudes toward Languages and Varieties

The range of dimensions along which linguistic codes may be judged is captured by Kachru (1982a) in his listing of the dichotomous attitude-marking terms which are used to describe them. These include aesthetic/unaesthetic, correct/incorrect, cultivated/uncultivated, developed/undeveloped, educated/uneducated, effective/ineffective, proper/improper, religious/non-religious, and vigorous/non-vigorous. These dimensions refer to both formal and functional aspects of codes, and judgments apply to both multiple languages and varieties of a single language.

One interesting source of attitudinal data is the labels referring to language which may be used to characterize particular groups, whether selves or others, exemplifying the inclusive and exclusive functions of language diversity. Self-reference terms of American Indian groups are usually equivalent to "the people," and reference to other groups "the strangers" or "the enemies," but identification may make reference to language: e.g., the name of the *Popoloca* group of Oaxaca means in Nahuatl (Aztec) 'the people who babble.' Identification may also be in terms of ways of speaking: e.g., Hopkins (1977) reports that any speaker of Tzeltal or Tzotzil refers to the speech of any other Tzeltal or Tzotzil as *baȼ'il k'op* 'true (proper) speech,' and among Bambara speakers in Mali, the prestigious Segu-Kaw group refers to the Beledugu-Kaw as *nya-ni-nyele*, a phrase which includes common female names. The implication is that they look down on the Beledugu-Kaw as being women; talking "like women," whether male or female, is disvalued (Ly). Chinese speakers in Beijing give nicknames to people from other regions in accordance with how they are perceived to speak. People from Taijin are called *mie zui zi* 'Tianjin mouth' because the dialect sounds "talkative"; people from Shanxi *shanxi lao xir* 'old west people' because the dialect sounds rough, like the land in the west; and people from Henan *henan kua zi* 'Henan bumpkins' because the dialect sounds like "country folks."

Another potentially useful source of attitudinal data is the use of language features in performances and parodies (mentioned in the earlier discussion of ethnic varieties), which typically provide perceived representations of linguistic identity by highlighting stigmatized forms. Joking usually involves mimicking marked phonological and lexical features, but may be extended to more complex stylistic factors, as in the Apaches' joking imitation of "the Whiteman" as described by Basso:

> a style characterized by stock phrases, specific lexical items, recurrent sentence types, and patterned modification in pitch, volume, tempo, and voice quality – that signals to those familiar with it that a particular form of joking has begun. (1979: 9)

Jokes which make fun of syntactic differences are less common. One comes from China, where speakers of southern dialects make more extensive use of the preverbal aspect particle *you* than do northerners (including Beijing). When teasing someone or joking about the south, Beijing speakers parody this usage with constructions such as *Wo you zhi mei you dao*, roughly 'I don't know,' with *you* inserted between the elements of the fixed compound *zhi-dao* 'know' (impossible to do in Beijing dialect). This seems comparable to northern US speakers parodying southern speech by inserting the plural *you-all* in inappropriate places and producing utterances which would be ungrammatical to a southerner. Such exaggerated usage is typical (at least in English) of any effort to parody another language variety (and perhaps of parody in general as a "literary" device).

Using stereotyped features for one's own ethnic group may also be valued in joking performances, although this is even more likely to be only an in-group phenomenon: e.g. English speakers of Irish ancestry may be adept at shifting to a "brogue," and Australians may effectively use broad "Strine."

Examples abound from speech communities where personality or social characteristics are attributed to speakers of different varieties of a language. Iranian informants listed the following regional varieties of Farsi and the traits they associated with speakers of each. (NB: these attitudes were expressed prior to the 1979 revolution, or by Iranian students who had not resided in Iran since that event.)

Tehrani – industrious, sociable, pleasure-loving
Rashti – simple, stupid, dishonorable (with reference to sexual behavior)
Ishfahani – clever, skillful, witty
Shirazi – hospitable, lazy, pleasure-loving, good-sounding
Mashadi – stubborn, obstinate, closed
Yazdi – honest, industrious, stingy, religious

When speakers are from the same area in Iran, if one does not use that regional variety, he or she is perceived as not wanting to be identified with that group, and so is valued negatively. A non-group member may intentionally speak another variety for instrumental purposes: e.g., a former

Iranian resident reported that "a Tehrani in Isfahan would try to speak Isfahani rather than Tehrani so as not to be cheated."

Japan is a very complex speech community, in which the Tokyo dialect is considered standard and all others again nonstandard, and in this case there are also quite different personality traits associated with different non-standard varieties. Speakers of Zuzu Ben (in eastern Japan) are perceived as somewhat harsh and disagreeable, for instance, while speakers of the Osaka variety (in Western Japan) are perceived as friendly and gentle.

Another illustration is from the Kathmandu Valley of Nepal, where varieties of Newari are judged primarily on a standard/nonstandard dimension: the standard in Kathmandu, and the nonstandard Bhaktapur, Kirtipur, and Lalitpur (named for the four major cities). Speakers of the standard are judged educated, rich, intelligent, refined, and progressive, but also more cunning, selfish, arrogant, and dishonest than nonstandard speakers. A resident who lives in or near one of the other three cities will adopt the Standard Kathmandu variety if he or she becomes educated.

Most sociolinguistic research on regional and social varieties equates "standard" and "prestige," but the relationship of these dimensions may be much more complex. In a study of varieties of Arabic spoken in Jordan, for instance, Abdel-Jawad (1987) reports how speakers of a standard variety used in a rural community may switch to a nonstandard variety that is used in an urban area which has higher prestige. The function of such switching is to identify with the dominant urban group and avoid the stigma of the rural group membership.

Quantitative measures, including the matched guise technique, have been used to establish the reliability of such personality judgments in a variety of speech communities. An interesting question which often remains unexplored, however, is *why* speakers believe they associate such traits with varieties of language.

Reasons given by native speakers include social and physical factors, as well as historical circumstances:

In Iran, Tehrani is reportedly prestigious because it is spoken in the capital, where life is to be enjoyed "and there are opportunities for everything and everybody"; Shirazi is good-sounding because it has a great literary heritage, and has been the native dialect of many poets and musicians.

In Saudi Arabia, speakers of the Najdi variety are perceived as strong and pure because it is associated with the highly valued desert life. Additionally, it is the dialect spoken by the royal family.

In Indonesia, speakers of Hoakiau (Chinese) Malay are perceived as money-minded and hard working because of their traditional role as businessmen in the economy.

In the United States, a southern "drawl" is associated by northerners with slow movement and laziness in men, though it is often admired in women.

In Japan, speakers of Zuzu Ben are considered disagreeable because their variety of Japanese is unclear and nasalized, while the "friendly and gentle" Osaka variety makes use of a distinctive set of respectful verbs, and "the tones of these expressions are softer, and more aesthetically proper to feminine speech."

Pitch level is associated with both personality and appearance in many speech communities. In the production of Japanese females, for instance, those with higher pitch are perceived to be "cute, soft, gentle, kind, polite, quiet, young, and beautiful, and those with lower pitch to be "stubborn, self-ish, strong, and straightforward" – and less likely to attract a husband (Ohara 2001). Lower pitch in female production of American English does not carry the same negative connotations associated with gender roles (indeed, it may be considered "sexy"), but males' production with higher pitch is often considered effeminate.

In Javanese, degrees of gentleness or softness are associated with relative speed and volume perceived typical of different varieties, and with different degrees of frankness or directness. One Indonesian reports:

> As the language becomes less and less *alus* 'gentle' as we move eastward from Solo, so are the people. Generally speaking, a Javanese from Surabaya (the capital of the East Java province) is less *alus* than one from Solo or Jogjakarta, in that the former tends to talk faster and louder as well as to be more frank and straightforward than the latter.

These relationships between form and attributes may be considered a type of phonetic symbolism. A key example is provided by Fischer (1965) in his analysis of the differential development of a sandhi rule in Ponape and Truk, two Pacific islands, and the differential perceptions of personality traits in speakers of each. In Ponapean, homorganic stops dissimilate to nasal plus stop, and speakers are judged as more refined, formal, and as placing greater value on precision and quality of speech. In Trukese, a nasal assimilates to the following homorganic stop resulting in a more fortis articulation. These speakers are perceived as more aggressive, informal, and as placing greater value on fluency and quantity. The same perceptions are held by members of both speech communities toward themselves and the others, and they may shift for effect; Fischer reports that a Ponapean chief omitted sandhi to express aggression, and in Trukese there is some tendency to omit sandhi in polite speech. A completely analogous phenomenon is reported for the related dialects of Batak Toba and Batak Mandailing (Sirait).

Similarly, Navajo speakers in the western part of their reservation normally use an articulation with stronger aspiration and glottal release than do those in the eastern part, and they are judged to be "harsher" in personality; eastern Navajos may choose to use more fortis articulation to mark intensification without increasing volume. The relationship between fortis articulation and the attribution of forceful personality traits should be explored as a possible universal.

Other areas of attitude research which have received considerable attention are how speakers of one language feel about other languages as entities in themselves, and how they feel about non-native or "accented" varieties of their own. Many of these perceptions are also based on phonetic features, as the English view that German is "guttural," and the German response that "All Americans say [jæææ]." British English is perceived by German speakers to be more like their own language because final consonants are articulated, while Americans "slow down at the end." According to a Japanese saying, "One gets upset in German, romantic in French, mischievous in Spanish." The French view their own language as particularly well suited for expressing precision of thought (*Ce qui n'est pas clair n'est pas français* 'What is not clear is not French'), and Japanese see their own as excellent for literature, but ill suited to law or science.

> Japanese people do not ordinarily think of the meanings of terms in legal provisions with any precision; they are content with a general and hazy understanding. . . . In Japan lack of clarity and definition is accepted; that the meanings of terms are unclear, unlimited, and unfixed is considered natural and even desirable. (Kawashima 1979)

Foreign-accented English is generally well tolerated – even potentially prestigious, if fluent – although the native language of the speaker is a critical variable. Attitudes toward such non-native varieties as Indian English or Nigerian English, however, may be far less accepting. Kachru claims:

> such attitudes are not essentially based on linguistic value judgement but various other factors play an important role, one being a native speaker's fear of seeing *his* language disintegrate in the hands of (or shall we say, through the lips of) non-native users. (1980)

Still, speakers of English, French, German, Russian, Italian, and Spanish think it is entirely appropriate for others to learn their languages, and English speakers especially seem to operate on the assumption that they will do so. Dutch speakers, on the other hand, feel their language is very difficult for others to learn, but that it is quite appropriate for them to speak at least French, German, and English.

The Dutch seem almost irritated at having to put up with the cumbersome process of talking to a stammering "learner of Dutch". Instead, they prefer to show off their superior knowledge of foreign languages. . . . If the foreigner is to overcome this obstacle of the negative attitude toward his trying to communicate in Dutch, he must try to eradicate any signals that could be interpreted as an inability to function fully in that language. One of the clearest of these signals is an accent, and this must undoubtedly influence his efforts to lose his native accent in speaking Dutch. (Schatz)

Other negative attitudes I have heard expressed toward English speakers' trying to communicate in an incompletely learned foreign language include the response of a Turkish taxi driver who insisted "Americans are supposed to speak English" (when another American in the car gave him directions in Turkish), and that of a Chinese student who was insulted by the implication that she could not communicate adequately in English (which my attempt to use Chinese conveyed). Such attitudes present a formidable barrier for foreign language learners, but the American and British assumption that anyone will welcome another's trying to use their language is ethnocentric.

Stereotyping

Making judgments about people according to linguistic features is a common form of stereotyping; it is possible because of the highly "visible" nature of the markers in language which are correlated with extralinguistic categories in a society, such as sex, age, social class, religion, and ethnicity (discussed in chapter 3). The social categories in turn carry with them traditional attitudes and expectations which strongly influence all communication, and which govern what Goffman (1967) calls "interaction ritual."

Social "typing" or categorization is probably a necessary part of our procedures for coping with the outside world. It allows us to quickly define our orientation to other individuals, and is a basis for our cultural sense of "manners" and other conventions of interpersonal relations. It is a means for establishing preliminary relationships (Abrahams 1972). If we did not "know" how to relate appropriately to different groups of people before we were acquainted with them personally, we would be socially ineffective to say the least, and perhaps even unable to function normally in a society. "Social structure is the sum total of these typifications and of the recurrent patterns of interaction established by means of them" (Berger and Luckmann 1967: 33).

Social typing should thereby be seen as a potentially positive and in any case inevitable process. The typing may assume negative aspects, however, and then it ceases to be just a mode of socialization. It may become a means of disaffiliation or rejection, or of rationalizing prejudice, and it is this negative connotation that is usually associated with the term "stereotyping." Further, the stereotyping involves "an exaggerated belief associated with a category. Its function is to justify (rationalize) our conduct in relation to that category" (Allport 1954: 187).

Because of their negative connotations and consequences, we might like to claim that stereotypes have no basis at all in observable reality, but they often do. Tannen's (1979a) contrast of New York Jewish and Los Angeles non-Jewish conversational style, for instance, documents that New York Jewish speakers talk more, interrupt (overlap) other speakers, and use "machine-gun" questions, all of which supports common stereotypes about the way "they" talk. Stereotyping departs from observable reality, however, when such attributes as "pushy" or "rude" are inferred from these conversational strategies: i.e. judgments not about how people talk, but about what kind of people they are. From the perspective of the Jewish speakers in the study, these conversational strategies are intended as positive moves to develop rapport.

Another claim we might like to make about stereotyping is that it operates between members of different groups only at initial or superficial contact, and does not survive repeated interaction. Unfortunately, this does not necessarily lead to "better understanding."

> On the contrary, it tends to reinforce mistaken judgments of the other's intentions and tends to increase expectations that the other will behave in a certain way. . . . Misjudgment is calcified by the conviction of repeated experience. (Tannen 1979a: 161)

Stereotypic expectations may well become self-fulfilling prophesies. Our preconceptions of how a doctor "should talk," for instance, are usually met; if not, patients may be suspicious of the doctor's credentials or professional competence. I know from years of residence in the state of Texas that most Texans do not actually say *Howdy* in greeting, but the stereotype was reinforced each time I stepped up to the counter of a Texas-based airline in other parts of the country and heard *Howdy, Ma'am* (which was probably used intentionally to reinforce the corporate Texas image). The stereotype of southerners speaking more slowly than northerners, on the other hand, is generally not supported by objective observational data; it is evidently a misinterpretation of their typical "breaking" of vowels as a slower rate of speech.

Another type of stereotyping is not based on observable traits at all, but is a negation of the values held by the group which is typing. In this case, the traits which are attributed are not specific to the language of the target group, but tend to be the same for all "others" (Abrahams 1972). These are universally dehumanizing, imputing childish or animalistic behavior, immorality, and absence of manners, rules, or laws: i.e. absence of culture. The group doing this kind of stereotyping defines culture in terms of its own beliefs and practices, and then interprets all differences as deficiencies. Information about these judgments provides no insights about those being typed, but may be interesting and useful with respect to understanding the values of the source group. English speakers commonly demean speech in an unfamiliar language as "jabbering."

When groups remain at a distance from one another, stereotypes may have little effect, though this is decreasingly true in our shrinking world. Similarly, the stereotypes which a subordinate group holds toward the dominant group in a society may have little or no direct effect on that group (which is often unaware of them), although it clearly affects intergroup communication. In both cases, the stereotyping serves to strengthen group boundaries and emphasize group unity. Stereotypes which the dominant group in a society holds toward subordinate groups, on the other hand, are often adopted by those groups as part of their own self-image.

Recognition of the stereotypes which are held by and about a speech community as such are relevant for ethnographic description in at least three important respects: (1) as a dimension of the attitudes related to language which are part of the content of the description; (2) as part of the framework of sociocultural expectations within which communicative behavior must be interpreted by participants or observers; and (3) as a check on the reliability of reported data when doing research in a community other than one's own. When ethnographers are working in their own speech community, stereotypes must be recognized so that they will not bias perceptions, and so they can be brought under conscious control.

Appropriateness

Many studies of attitudes toward language use (including, but not limited to stereotypes) have not dealt with language in general, but what language or variety of language is considered more appropriate in a specific context. This is basic to all sociolinguistic survey procedures, and has included studies of Spanish and English (e.g. Fishman, Cooper, and Ma 1971), varieties of Arabic and English (El-Dash and Tucker 1975), varieties of Norwegian (Blom and Gumperz 1972), and African American English (Hoover 1975). Findings generally show that attitudes toward the appropriate use of codes in a speech community have a very high correlation with their functional distribution, and the relative social status of their speakers.

Many of the attitudes reported relate to which language or variety is considered appropriate for formal education, as opposed to informal interaction. These attitudes are particularly strong in areas where creoles are for the first time being considered viable media for instruction, at least in primary grades. The following quotation is from a letter to the editor of the Trinidad *Guardian* in response to a report on a Language Arts syllabus which includes recognition that English is not the native language of most Trinidadians:

> If the language of the barrack yard and the market is to be the accepted mode of expression in the school-room . . . there would be no need for teachers . . . We could save the high wages of those experts and set them free to go and plant peas . . . where they can give full vent to this dialect stuff. . . . What if not broken English is this dialect? . . . I feel that such discussions should be banned from our news media as a most damaging . . . exercise. (Reported by Sealey)

Conversely, Trinidadian Creole is considered the most appropriate code in events associated with local culture, conversation between intimates, joking, and "liming." According to Sealey, a person telling a joke in Standard English in her speech community will be a laughing stock, and calypsos sung in a variety of English nearer to the standard end of the creole continuum are marked as being "for export": i.e. not for the people. At the same time, many parents can be heard telling their creole-speaking children to "speak properly"; the notion that somehow the creole code is improper is instilled from early childhood in the home, and is reinforced in the schools.

Although Cape Verdean Creole has been introduced in bilingual programs in New England, there is a residual attitude among native speakers that it, too, is not appropriate for written communication. In its African context (the Republic of Cape Verde), Crioulo was the Low variety in a diglossic situation, and Portuguese the High. Even if proficiency in Standard Portuguese was not achieved, all written communication, regardless of its nature, was produced in some attempt at Standard Portuguese. This attitude is clearly reflected in Silva's recollection of an experience in Massachusetts:

> My cousin's younger sister, having come to the US before starting school and having to leave her sister a note, since the older sister did not know any English, resorted to writing the note in Crioulo. The mere fact that Crioulo was used to communicate the written message produced laughter among Crioulo speakers.

The addition of English for the immigrant speech community has resulted in a trilingual situation. The high and low functions of Standard Portuguese and Crioulo remain essentially the same as they were in Cape

Verde, with English used without a strict allocation to domain. According to Silva, rejection of Crioulo in favor of Portuguese is interpreted as more of a rejection of the cultural values and identity of the community than is symbolized by the use of English. The more recent influx of Cape Verdeans from Portugal and other former Portuguese colonies accentuated this situation.

Another reference to the High variety of a language being associated with writing is reported by an Indonesian, where *bahasa resmi* is the official/ standard language associated with education, and *bahasa sehari-hari* the daily/colloquial language associated with conversations with intimates, instructions to servants, etc. Although the High variety is more prestigious, a speaker who uses it exclusively is considered pedantic, or worse, "putting on airs." Gunarwan reports:

> I remember one occasion when, during a casual conversation, a friend made a mistake of using the literary word *semalam* 'last night' instead of the everyday word *tadi malam*. Another friend responded mockingly, saying *Si Didi belajar membaca* 'Didi learns to read', referring to a reading series formerly used in the elementary school.

There has been only minimal acceptance of native language literacy within the Navajo speech community, where Navajo generally functions for oral communication and English for written. Even in a single communicative situation, such as a meeting of tribal representatives, business is conducted in Navajo and minutes recorded in English. Unlike the cases of Cape Verde and Indonesia, relative prestige is not a factor in considering Navajo inappropriate for literacy: Navajo is currently accorded at least as much prestige as English, although that was not always so. Spolsky and Irvine suggest the reason is that "when the introduction of literacy is associated with a second language, an alien culture, and modern, technological functions, literacy in these new domains is preferred in the alien, second, or standard language" (1982: 76). Resisting native language literacy in this instance might thus be seen as a means of protecting traditional culture from the modernizing (and more public) influence of writing, or it could reflect an attitude that the native language is unworthy of being written, or that writing it would strip it of its intimacy.

The appropriateness of one language or variety in a multilingual, international context is even more complex, but rules for selection are quite distinct, and strong negative attitudes often accompany inappropriate language selection.

Speakers generally have some positive feelings about their native language, at least for expressive purposes in intimate or informal contexts with members of the same group. Attitudes toward acceptability and appropriateness for other functions can be understood only in relation to a complex of social and historical factors. Since these include the language in which questions about them are being asked, and the ethnic and linguistic identity of interviewers or observers, responses on this aspect of language attitudes are particularly susceptible to biases in elicitation and interpretation.

Language and Identity

Positive feelings about one's own language are often engendered by the role it plays as a marker of desired group identity, and negative feelings by having such identity rejected. Code alternation or shifting often signals changing feelings about group identity for an individual in different contexts, or as different emotions are aroused during a single communicative event.

One dimension of language-related attitudes which is central to the ethnographic description of a speech community is the extent to which linguistic identity is a criterion for group membership. Many American Indians who have lost their ancestral languages in the process of assimilation to English express profound regret and sense of deculturation, reporting the feeling that "We can't be Indians without an Indian language." So do many immigrants, yet many other "hyphenated" Americans who speak only English after two or more generations of residence in this country retain ethnic identity only through preservation of a little folklore, with perhaps a few traditional foods or celebrations, and express few regrets about losing ancestral languages; indeed, they are often most antagonistic toward retention of languages by others. Second-generation Americans who cannot speak the language of their grandparents or great-grandparents may have still inherited their linguistic values, with language attitudes outlasting the language itself, while still others have fully "melted."

Such diverse attitudes about language and identity are very salient in teaching or learning a second language. Most learners value their own group membership; some, however, reject their own group and wish to change; many may wish or need to function as members of more than one group and be "bicultural" as well as bilingual. Motivations may be integrative or instrumental. Any of these attitudes can be compatible with learning a second language, but they are often viewed in a negative light. Those who value their own group membership and do not wish to acculturate to the dominant group may be berated as not "well adjusted" to that society. On the other hand, those who reject their own group and wish to change may be viewed as disloyal to family and old friends. Those who try to belong to more than one group may be mistrusted by both. Other cultural factors which impact on learning and using a second language include beliefs and values about gender relations and family responsibilities (e.g. Goldstein 1997 for Portuguese-speaking immigrants in Canada; Hansen 2000 for Vietnamese-speaking immigrants in the US). A widespread belief is that females are better at second language learning than males. Whether this is universally true needs to be substantiated ethnographically, taking social and cultural variables into account.

Whatever choice is made regarding group membership, language is a key factor – an identification badge – for both self and outside perception, and this has significant implications for education. The Standard middle-class English speech patterns presented as a model in our schools are likely to be considered effeminate and thus rejected by working-class boys approaching adolescence, especially when these patterns are used by female teachers. The English of male teachers or of older boys would be much more likely to be adopted by boys wanting to establish a male identity. Studies of the acquisition of English by Puerto Rican adolescents in New York and Mexican Americans in Chicago document that the variety being learned and used is not that taught in English classes, but the non-standard variety of the dominant peer group in the communities – African American English (Wolfram 1973). The importance of peers rather than adults as models is similarly documented by Harrington in New York City:

> I was once observing an ESL [English as a Second Language] classroom in which the students were predominantly Spanish-speaking. The teacher's sole job was to try to get the children to speak English. An Egyptian child came to the school who spoke neither Spanish nor English. . . . After a month in the ESL classroom, the Egyptian child was speaking Spanish. (1978: 3)

Even very young children are aware of the function of language in establishing group identity, and use the appropriate variety to identify with friends. One six-year-old child I knew developed a lisp when a best friend lost his front teeth, and many middle-class Anglo parents found during the early years of school desegregation in the US South that their children were adding the nonstandard forms of some African American and Spanish-speaking classmates. Middle-class African American parents were often distressed in turn that their Standard-English-speaking children were being influenced by the non-standard speech of lower-class White students.

Preadolescence is the age when children in the US are most influenced by peer norms, however. This perhaps accounts for Labov et al. (1968) finding that junior high school (12- to 14-year-old) boys use more of the stigmatized features of African American English than they did when in the fifth or sixth grade (10 to 11 years old). Romaine also reports, "studies show an increase in the use of non-standard speech varieties among ethnic minority groups such as West Indians in Britain as children approach adolescence, indicating the effects of peer group allegiance" (1999: 295).

The identity function of variable pronunciation for older students is documented by Kiesling (1998), who reports that college fraternity men who associate themselves more with physical versus structural power bases differentially produce [ɪn] versus [ɪŋ] variants of *-ing*.

Temporary shifts are common in the process of intergroup communication, and research on their occurrence and effect is providing additional insight about language and identity. Giles, Taylor, and Bourhis (1973) attribute linguistic *convergence*, or the modification of language toward the variety used by other speakers in an encounter, to a desire for listeners' social approval. Linguistic *divergence*, on the other hand, occurs when speakers wish to dissociate themselves from listeners. This may be an unconscious emotional response, but can be "a deliberate tactic of ethnic dissociation and psychological distinctiveness" (Bourhis et al. 1979). Both experimental and naturalistic studies have been conducted on convergence/divergence phenomena in various languages and contexts, and include analyses of verbal codes, prosodic features such as pitch contours and rate of speech, kinesics, and other indicators of interactional synchrony (cf. Erickson 1976; Kempton 1979).

Convergence need not be perceived positively, of course, since the listeners may not want to have the speakers identify with them, or may interpret the process as mocking or condescending if their own group is lower in prestige. Also, divergence may not be negative, but merely a sign of less formality and decreased monitoring of speech. In social situations where speakers of American, British, and Australian English are represented, for instance, the dialect differences often increase as speakers become better acquainted and more relaxed.

The relationship between language and identity along this dimension is thus bidirectional: feelings of closeness or distance may trigger similarity or dissimilarity in language patterns; conversely, the feeling of being on the same linguistic "wave length" is likely to promote solidarity.

Language may also serve an important function in political or national identification. The resurgence of pride in ethnicity (and associated languages) in the United States is very threatening to many citizens of the country as a symbol of disunity and separatism; to speak a language other than English is considered un-American. Even greater intolerance may be shown toward other languages in the process of nation-building, as evidenced by the social sanctions against the use of Yiddish in Israel during its early years. The process of selecting an official language in developing multilingual countries often involves identifying which subgroup is most powerful or prestigious. Nigeria officially continues to use English in large part because to select Hausa, Igbo, or Yoruba would give preeminence to the segment of the country which identifies with that language and exclude the others. In this case English was a neutral choice, a language with which no one identified. The functions of Yoruba are expanding, however, with continuing national development. It is particularly interesting to note ways in which Yoruba is being integrated with English for ceremonial purpose. Bamgboṣe reports, for instance, that

> the wedding reception which used to be an opportunity for displaying "big grammar" is now almost invariably conducted in Yoruba with the well-educated bridegroom making an effort to speak a brand of Yoruba sprinkled with English. (1986: 30)

The relationship of language and identity is very complex, and important clues to its nature may be found in changing patterns of language distribution and use through time, as well as in synchronic phenomena.

Language Maintenance, Shift, and Spread

A basic assumption in most theories of culture change is that there are always two counterforces operating in a society: one for change and one for persistence, stability, or maintenance of the status quo. Especially in culture contact situations, the possible outcomes for the multiple languages or language varieties involved include their maintenance as separate entities, changes in one or both language systems under influence from the other, or the abandonment of one in favor of the other: i.e., one of the counterforces prevails. Of central interest is how different attitudes toward language may determine linguistic fate.

One important factor is the instrumental versus affective functions which a language is felt to serve in the community. Yiddish and Ladino are cases in point. Yiddish made it possible for Ashkenazic Jews from all over Europe to communicate with one another regardless of their national language, serving for both ethnic and religious identification. A similar function was served by Ladino (or Judeo-Spanish) for Sephardic Jews, who were widely dispersed throughout the Middle East and Latin America. With Hebrew serving religious functions, and with its selection as the national and official language of Israel, Yiddish and Ladino lost much of their *raison d'être*. Harris (1994) reported over three-quarters of her Ladino informants in New York and Israel could think of no valid reasons why the language should be passed on to the next generation, even though they themselves might feel a strong sentimental attachment to it. Not a single one of their grandchildren in either location could speak the language. Similar functional bases for shift within minority speech communities have been documented around the world, including Japanese to Portuguese in Brazil (Kanazawa and Loveday 1988), indigenous languages to Mandarin in Taiwan (Young 1988), German to English in Australia (Waas and Beach 1993), and Cantonese to English in Britain (Li 1994).

Stability of multiple languages in contact, on the other hand, occurs where each has a unique domain (cf. Fishman 1972; 1985), and is thus reserved a continuing function in society. The Armenian language has been maintained in the United States and Syria, for instance, coexisting with English and Arabic respectively. One reason for continued maintenance has been the need to know the language in order to participate in religious services, since the prevailing attitude is that Armenian is the appropriate medium for worship. Armenians who reside in the United States and have visited relatives in the former Soviet Union report that religious ties there are considerably weaker, and that use of the Armenian language there seems to be in a state of rapid decline. Similar attitudes toward the use of language in religion are also largely responsible for the survival of Assyrian in immigrant communities in the US and Europe, and at least the marginal existence of Geez in Ethiopia.

The few cases of language revival which have been documented generally involve functional redistribution. One interesting example is the resurgence of Nones, the local language of Revo' in the Italian Alps, which coexists with national Italian and regional Trentina (a process examined in detail by Fellin 2001). In the context of social, economic, and political events which is giving increasing status to Revo', the resurgence of Nones importantly includes its expanding function in the socialization of children to their local roles and responsibilities.

The surest symptom of impending language loss is, as with Ladino, when parents no longer see a reason to transmit it to their children, and may even view it as a handicap to their children's education and advancement. As summarized by Dorian (1980):

> Language loyalty persists so long as the economic and social circumstances are conducive to it; but if some other language proves to have greater value, a shift to that other language begins.

Essentially the same reason for loss is reported by Wick Miller (1971) among the Shoshoni, an American Indian group which has widespread distribution in the Western United States:

> The Shoshoni exhibit very little language loyalty. Older people are concerned that the children are not learning the language, or that they are not learning the full language, and younger speakers who do not speak it or who do not speak it well wish that they could speak it or wish that they had full control of the language. But very few do anything about it.

A second major consideration in language maintenance, shift, and spread is the social organization and ecology of the community or communities involved, and attitudes related to these factors. This may include the nature of their boundary mechanisms and political organization, as reported in Barth's (1964a) study of language shift between Pashto and Baluchi speakers in Pakistan. In this case, both groups are part of a single ecological region, with intergroup mobility and a common culture, but with two languages with differing relationships to social organization. Among the Pathan, Pashto is required for full political participation, but the structure of the Baluch tribes allows bilingual participation, and thus more easily assimilates non-Baluchi speakers. For complex historical reasons, this has contributed to the spread of Baluchi at the expense of Pashto in the region. Similar attitudes in part account for the shift from SiYeyi to SeTawana in Botswana, even though the Yeyi settled the region first and were numerically dominant. The Yeyi had a relatively flexible and egalitarian social structure which enabled them to integrate, while the Tawana had a relatively rigid and hierarchically-ordered society (Sommer 1995).

The capacity of the US economic and political structures to assimilate waves of immigrants of diverse ethnic origins is a significant factor in their concomitant assimilation to English, but the process has not applied equally to all. It is not coincidental that the more "visible" minorities, who have encountered negative attitudes toward their assimilation from the dominant groups, are most likely to have maintained separate linguistic and cultural identity.

Attempts at forced assimilation may also support language maintenance, as evidenced in Dozier's (1956) contrast of linguistic acculturation among the Yaqui Indians of Northern Mexico and Arizona and the Tewa Indians of New Mexico. The Yaqui were subject to quite tolerant early colonization by the Spanish, relatively free of friction, and the Yaqui language and culture readily adopted Hispanic traits (about 65 percent of the lexicon is Spanish-derived). But when the colonizers became less permissive a crystallization occurred, and no further assimilation took place. The Tewa language and culture remain relatively free of Spanish influence, in large part because of strong coercive attempts to repress them. The Tewa language is in more danger from English "because their attitudes toward Anglo-Americans are generally more favorable than toward Spanish-Americans" (Dozier 1956: 149).

Imperialistic expansion may also result in language spread, as evidenced in history by periods of expansion and then contraction of Turkish, Quechua, Nahuatl, and Portuguese, and more recently the spread of English and Russian. The contraction phase of Quechua and Nahuatl (languages of the former Inca and Aztec empires, respectively) is attributable to Spanish military conquest and subsequent political and economic domination. The continuing process of replacement of Nahuatl by Spanish has been analyzed by Hill and Hill (1980; 1986), who attribute the shift to a narrowing range of functions for the indigenous language. Nahuatl is still highly valued for identification and solidarity, but Spanish is highly valued for its political and economic functions as the "language of power." Unlike the case of Tewa, the functional differentiation of Nahuatl vis-à-vis Spanish is not remaining stable, for solidarity is apparently losing ground to power and prestige. The present situation, therefore, "is probably a transitory stage which will lead rapidly to language obsolescence" (Hill and Hill 1980: 345).

When the dominated area has a strong cultural tradition and feelings of cultural superiority, the indigenous language may prevail: e.g. Greek under Roman rule, and the adoption of French by speakers in Normandy. The spread of religions has also resulted in language spread. This is especially true for Arabic with the rapid spread of Islam because of the firmly rooted belief that it is impossible to translate the Quran into another language.

Patterns of marriage and kinship may also be factors in maintenance or shift. McLendon (1978), for instance, attributes much of the rapid shift among Eastern Pomo speakers (a native California language) to exogamous marriage patterns. Conversely, extended family residence and child care is a strong force for language maintenance. For example, Miller (1971) reports that for most families on the Owyhee Reservation in which children are still learning Shoshoni, there is a grandparent or some other older relative in the house. My longitudinal study of the Navajo language development of preschool children who receive primary care at home with grandparents compared with children who attend a daycare program finds extensive differences especially in lexical knowledge and morphological complexity (Saville-Troike 1996), although at least some continuing contact with elder Navajo-speaking family members is enabling the children who are enrolled in daycare to acquire a fair level of receptive competence.

Geographic or social segregation can contribute to maintenance, although settlement on reservations has obviously not "saved" most American Indian languages. Isolated communities in Central Texas which were settled by immigrant groups in the nineteenth century preserved conservative varieties of Czech, Polish, German, and Alsatian French, which have been lost for generations to those who immigrated to heterogeneous cities. A sociolinguistic survey of Texas Czech by Dutkova (1998), however, documents extensive shift to English within the last generation. This can be attributed in large measure to geographic and social integration, via better roads, convenient transportation, and mass media, increased motivation for higher education out of the immediate settlement area, and opportunities and need for more widely-dispersed employment.

Social stratification within a community is also relevant, including the degree of access that speakers of low prestige languages and varieties have to those which are more prestigious, and to jobs which require their use. The status and role of women in the community is highly significant. Where they are uneducated and remain in the home they tend to remain monolingual and contribute to maintenance of the "mother" tongue; where they are educated, bilingual, and participate in trade or other external activities, exactly the opposite has been observed. The key here is motivation and opportunity, as well as the acceptability of assimilation by the dominant group mentioned above.

A third major area of consideration is values and world view. In a broad sense, this includes attitudes toward borrowing foreign words, and the value placed on uniqueness versus homogeneity. The effect of the latter is illustrated by Hamp (1978) in his discussion of the maintenance of Albanian by settlers in Italy, where localisms are valued, versus its loss by settlers in Greece, which exclusively values all things Greek (cf. Tsitsipis 1995). The pattern persists through immigration to the United States, as Italian-Americans quickly assimilate to the local language and Greek-Americans cling tenaciously to Greek style for generations, even when they are speaking English (cf. Tannen 1981). Robert DiPietro has made the interesting observation that Albanian has been preserved within the Italian immigrant community in Wisconsin, with the Italian language (and values) probably serving as a buffer zone against English.

The social valuation of linguistic features is important to Labov's view of the "linguistic variable" as a unit of change. He analyzed the subjective attitudes of residents of Martha's Vineyard (1963) toward such matters as summer tourists, unemployment compensation, work on the mainland, and other aspects of island life, finding typical "Vineyarder attitudes" most closely associated with the occurrence of particular phonetic variables. In studies of both New York City and Martha's Vineyard, Labov finds self-identity at the root of linguistic change (1972).

Another interesting value dimension in language contact situations is how evaluation of a linguistic variable in one language is susceptible to the evaluation of variants in the dominant competing languages. Examples from Jakobson (1938) and Weinreich (1953) are the merger of /l/ and /lʲ/ in Czech, which is attributable to urban speech which was tinged with a "fashionable" German accent, and the merger of /š, tš/ with /s, ts/ in Croatian, which is attributed to the foreign accent of native speakers of Venetian Italian. Campbell (1976) adds an example from Teotepeque Pipil, Mexico, in which he explains a change from /š/ to /r̃/ as due to the negative social evaluation of a stigmatized pronunciation in Spanish.

It seems reasonable to assume that most attitudes toward language and identity also fit in this category, with positive feelings for one's own group contributing to maintenance, and negative feelings abetting loss. One somewhat surprising finding is that positive attitudes toward a language apart from pragmatic functions do not seem to enhance chances for its survival. As Fishman notes:

> in summarizing my findings concerning current language maintenance among pre-World War I arrivals in the United States coming from rural Eastern and Southern European backgrounds, I reported a long-term distinction between attitudes and use, namely, an increased esteem for non-English mother tongues concomitant with the increased relegation of these languages to few and narrower domains of language use. . . . Younger second and third generation individuals were found to view these mother tongues (almost always via translations) with less emotion but with even more positive valence. Instead of a "third generation return" there seemed to be an "attitudinal halo-ization" within large segments of all generations, albeit unaccompanied by increased usage. (1964)

Fasold (1975) offers corroboration in the finding that adolescents who are not learning Tiwa along with English still express very positive attitudes toward their language, but this has not prevented the encroachment of English into previously Tiwa domains, and is ultimately unlikely to save the language from extinction. A similar situation pertains in Ireland, where it was found that "strong sentimental attachments to Irish were not accompanied by language *use*, nor by desire to actively promote it" (Edwards 1985: 51, citing the Committee on Irish Language Attitudes Research 1975; emphasis his).

Mary Miller (1970) studied the attitudes of Pima children living on the Salt River reservation in Arizona toward which of the languages used in their community was best. The majority expressed preference for English with such practical explanations as "most people speak it," although several chose Pima because it was spoken by parents or grandparents and for ethnic identity: Pima was "best for Pimas". It is interesting to note there was an increasing preference for English with age. Miller concludes:

> . . . younger children are more influenced by the standards and language of the home and still largely unaware of attitudes of school and the outside world. With the gradual influence of the school and one's peers, the older child becomes more and more impressed with the success on the outside and the practicality of identifying with the affluent majority. (1970: 54–5)

Wick Miller (1971) also reported this phenomenon for Shoshoni children in Gosiute.

It seems quite likely that linguistic awareness and influence for conformity with the "outside world" may come at a much younger age and much less gradually if a child in a minority-language group is exposed primarily to children from the dominant language group. In the US, bilingual parents who speak other languages at home often report their children wanting to speak only English at home once they begin school; some children exacerbate this situation by insisting that their parents also speak English, or expressing feelings of shame if they cannot or will not. Children in bilingual school programs exhibit much less of this home language rejection.

School programs in themselves, however, cannot be counted on to develop or maintain minority language use among children if there is not both need for the language in the community and support among the children's peers. Evidence for this comes from study of a French-language elementary school in Canada, for instance, where it was determined that the school (St-Michel)

> has not been able to impose its goals and its conventions on its students: the experiences of children outside school, and the influence of their peer group networks evidently constrain the extent to which schools can be depended upon to be the source of language maintenance and cultural continuity in a minority community . . . (Heller nd: 13)

In a longitudinal study of over 300 children of foreign graduate students and visiting faculty in the US (Kleifgen et al. 1986), we found a dramatic shift to English dominance in spite of support for native language maintenance at both home and school. If children had arrived in this country at age five or less, they typically had difficulty communicating in their native language after two years in residence; only those who arrived at age seven or later generally maintained productive balance between their native language and English after that period of time.

Our database included children from a number of different countries, and there were some intergroup differences which illustrate some of the social factors that are involved. Japanese and Korean children experienced the least shift. Most importantly, they seldom stayed in this country for more than a year; their parents expressed concern about keeping children in the US longer for fear they would fall behind in their own school curricula, and they were less likely to bring with them older children who were at a more "critical" period of school than were parents from other countries. Also, the Japanese and Korean mothers generally spoke little or no English themselves, and the time their children were at home was frequently spent almost exclusively with other speakers of the same language background. These two groups had large and well organized support networks in the university community, including baby-sitting pools which insured consistent native language input to young children even when mothers were absent from the home. No similar network existed for the other groups in our sample.

There were also group differences in child rearing practices which must be taken into account, and in the value accorded learning English versus developing and maintaining native language skills. The faster rate of shift among Arabic children, for instance, can be attributed in part to the greater opportunity they had to play with children from other backgrounds in the community context, and in part to the value parents generally placed on their children learning English. The most notable change among children who first encountered English at age five or less was the effect it had on their pronunciation. Young Arabic speakers lost post-velar and pharyngeal articulation, for instance, and young Chinese speakers used incorrect tones. The general impression of our collaborators who speak the children's languages natively was that they spoke with a foreign (American) accent. First language attrition for older children who were in the US two or more years was limited almost entirely to loss of productive vocabulary; tests we gave (including translations of the Peabody Picture Vocabulary Test and sentence repetition tasks) indicated relatively little attrition in their receptive competence. These children expressed a feeling of awkwardness in using their native language by that time, however, and a preference for English.

Evidence of difficulty in maintenance of minority languages can also be found in the very limited success of "language recovery" programs in American Indian communities where the school has tried to develop ancestral language competence in children who have not been taught that language at home. To repeat, the surest symptom of impending language loss is when parents no longer see a reason to transmit it to their children. These same parents apparently cannot then expect the school to give it back to the children and the community, except in unusual cases and limited domains.

An interesting situation is created when a child's parents speak two different languages. In the case of different American Indian languages, Miller (1970) reports there is almost always loss of one Indian language in mixed marriages, and often both, with children speaking only English. Shift among Eastern Pomo for the same reason was reported above (McLendon 1978). Among the Tucano in the Amazon region, however, where exogamous marriage restrictions result in wives' primary languages being different from their husbands', Sorenson (1967) reports both languages are usually maintained. Most Tucano grow up at least bilingual, and often speak several languages. In the Vaupes area of Columbia and Brazil, another exogamous society, the father's language is primary, but children acquire the mother's as well (Grimes 1985). Such bilingualism can be attributed to the fact that while the parents understand each other's language, each continues to speak only his or her own.

There are individual cases where it appears that neither language is fully developed by children of linguistically mixed marriages. Plausible accounts of this fortunately rare phenomenon come from teachers in isolated villages in Alaska, for instance, where the father in a family may speak only English (but is seldom home to provide input for the child), and insists that the mother not use the Eskimo language of the community (which is her dominant tongue). Children raised in a home with the impoverished language input which results reportedly cannot function effectively either in the English-medium school or in the Eskimo community. I know of no case of this nature which has been adequately documented by a linguist or ethnographer, but I do not believe the possibility of "semilingualism" under such social conditions should be discounted in advance merely on theoretical or philosophical grounds (also discussed in chapter 2; cf. Martin-Jones and Romaine 1986).

When language loss is occurring at a community level, "there are some individuals [at lower levels of 'semispeaker' proficiency] who actually say very little yet continue to interact in a highly successful fashion with fluent speakers" (Dorian 1982: 33). This is because such individuals have receptive competence in the language and are always younger than the fluent speakers, and thus not expected to take a more active role. They participate appropriately in the interaction by using a few words when that is called for, and by following community norms for nonverbal behavior and silence. Dorian contrasts these aspects of the semispeakers' communicative competence with the foreign language learner who may have more verbal fluency, but "betrays his nonmembership in the speech community by social failures in the use of the language: speaking when he should be silent, asking 'rude' questions, failing to recognize a situation in which greetings are obligatory, and the like" (Dorian 1982: 33–4). Even when languages have been completely lost, as in some American Indian communities, indigenous "ways of speaking" may be maintained which continue to differentiate community members from the dominant English speech community whose language forms they have adopted (see Saville-Troike 1992).

Sometimes the issue is not why languages die, but why they do not. My research on the Alabama-Coushatta (Koasati) reservation in Texas in the late 1960s provided more questions than answers about why the two indigenous languages of that small community (related members of the Muskogean family) were being maintained. All of the children attended English medium schools and all monetary rewards were attached to the use of English, yet fluent Alabama and Coushatta speakers were still present in the child-generation. A survey conducted by Halmari (1998) almost 30 years later shows that although use among younger speakers is decreasing, both languages (and sometimes a combination) remain viable and vibrant media of communication for many children and young adults. Geographical and social isolation is certainly a contributing factor in maintenance of these languages, especially for older speakers, but children are integrated with native English speakers for almost all of their years of schooling. Halmari concludes that positive attitude toward maintaining linguistic competence in Alabama and Coushatta is vital for maintenance, if not sufficient in itself. Most importantly, many parents and elders in this case see a reason to transmit heritage languages to their children. In relatively simple terms, "those younger people who are fluent in Alabama or Coushatta had parents who spoke these languages to them when they were young" (Halmari 1998: 423).

Circumstances determining transmission of heritage languages are far from simple, however. Clearly the relationship between attitudes and language maintenance, shift, and spread remains a viable topic for investigation.

Taboos and Euphemisms

Attitudes toward language considered taboo in a speech community are extremely strong, and violations may be sanctioned by imputations of immorality, social ostracism, and even illness or death. No topic is universally forbidden: what cannot be said in one language can be in another and vice versa. Neither are linguistic taboos arbitrary: they relate integrally to culture-specific beliefs and practices in religion or magic, decorum, and social control.

Taboos related to religion or magic may affect a wide range of linguistic phenomena, and include animal-name avoidances in many speech communities. It may be believed that animals or spirits understand human language, and that mentioning their names would either drive them away (undesirable if one is hunting), or attract them near where they might inflict harm. Related to this belief are the restriction in the former Bangalam Upper Congo against using men's names at home while they are fishing (Frazer 1922); replacing an animal name with a semantically unrelated word which begins with the same sound (e.g., *zag^w ára* 'leopard' becomes *zamb^w ára* 'disc of wood to cut bread') in Ethiopia (Leslau 1959); and the substitution of a metaphorical expression for the animal terms (e.g. calling a wolf "uncle" or "nice little dog") by peasants in the Ukraine (Smal-Stocki 1950).

In some cases a broader scope of the linguistic system is involved, as among Faroese fishermen who use *sjómal* 'sea language' for protection from spirits and to conceal their business and destination (Lockwood 1956), or where everyday language is considered unworthy of sacred use, and in Zuñi prayers and songs in New Mexico (Newman 1955). Complimenting children is thought to be very dangerous to their health in Turkey because it may attract the evil eye, but this danger may be lessened considerably by immediately repeating the ritual expression *maşallah* 'what God hath wrought.'

Language is perhaps most awesome when words themselves are accorded power, as in speech communities where a curse is literally intended to invoke supernatural wrath, where to be in possession of individuals' names gives control over their well-being, or where to speak or write down a name will allow the soul to escape. In these cases names are concealed, or replaced, for self-protection.

All language may be banned under certain circumstances. When sacrifices are made by Igbo speakers, for instance, the officiating priest usually imposes the observance of strict silence, particularly when the purpose is diverting the attention of malevolent spirits from the carrier. If the silence is violated (a rare occurrence), the sacrifice must be repeated, and the offender has to make an additional sacrifice. Greetings were also taboo between Igbo from different villages during times when there were smallpox epidemics, because of the belief that disease can take human form. Without a greeting, no encounter has taken place (Nwoye 1985).

Taboos which relate to decorum include avoidance of terms or euphemistic reference for aesthetic or moral reasons (often for body parts or bodily functions), interlingual taboos, and respect forms. Racial and ethnic slurs can also be included in this category, especially when they are interpreted as "hate speech." Acceptability and interpretation depend on the group membership of who is using the term, who it is addressed to, and a myriad of other social circumstances. An example of the complexities which may be involved occurs in the US with use of the "n-word" (*nigger*): depending on who uses it and in what contexts, it may be highly offensive, affectionate, affiliative, or faddish (following trends in rap and other popular music).

A wide range of euphemisms in America intended to soften the verbal impact of dying, death, and burial was collected by Pound (1936). These include categories of general literary and figurative expressions (*is out of his misery, climbed the golden stair*), metaphors of sleep and rest (*laid to rest, called to the eternal sleep*), metaphors of departure (*crossed over the Great Divide, gone to the Great Beyond*), metaphors from occupations (*answered the last muster, gave up the ship*), and metaphors from sports (*ran the good race, struck out*). The material adjuncts are also renamed, as the dead (*the deceased, the late lamented*), the cemetery (*the Marble City, memorial park*), the coffin (*casket, eternity box*), the grave (*long home, deep six*), and the funeral (*planting, cold meat party*). Farghal (1995) reports that death is also the most euphemized domain in Arabic. Examples include comparable figurative expressions from Colloquial Jordanian Arabic (*xubzāt-uh xilsin* 'His bread ran out,' *'a'tā-k 'umr-uh* 'He gave you his age') and metaphors of departure in Modern Standard Arabic (*'intaqala 'ilā dār-i-l-baqā'* 'He transferred to the home of eternity').

Grimes (1977) illustrates the range of euphemistic processes used in Mexican Spanish to refer to body parts and functions, such as metaphor (e.g. *cortar flores* 'to cut flowers' = to defecate), metonomy (*el de hacer niños* 'the thing for making children' = penis), generic expressions (*hacerlo* 'to do it' = to urinate (the same phrase means 'to fornicate' in English)), infantile expressions (*hacer caca* 'to defecate'), proper names (*Doña Josefa* 'vagina'), and borrowing (*cuita* < Nahuatl *cuitlatl* 'feces'). Comparable processes reported by Farghal (1995) for Colloquial Jordanian Arabic yield such expressions as *rāh yitmašša* 'he went to take a walk' for 'urinate' and *rafa' 'ijrē-ha* for 'sexual intercourse.' The Quran also uses euphemisms for sex, frequently a term meaning "touching," and Biblical texts in English refer to *knowing* a woman.

Use of scientific or "cultured" terms, as in some of the above translations, may also be considered a euphemistic process since they create an affective distance from the informal everyday term. It was common practice for nineteenth-century scholars translating Greek and Roman tales, or record-ing the folklore of "primitive" groups, to switch to Latin for the passages which violated English language taboos.

Euphemisms are also common in the specialized jargon of many fields, including medicine. Knipple (2001) reports that the lexical socialization of resident physicians in a teaching hospital includes not only technical Latin and Greek vocabulary. The following are examples: *code brown* (bowel incontinence that can be smelled throughout the ward); *goombah* (a large unidentified mass seen on an X-ray, usually implied to be malignant); *wallet biopsy* (checking a patient's insurance status before embarking on expensive procedures).

Linguistic taboos are often related to language change: e.g., the word 'bear' probably disappeared in Slavic, Baltic, and Germanic languages be-cause of animal-name avoidance (cf. Slavic 'honeyeater,' Baltic 'one who licks,' and Germanic 'brown'), and Tonkawa (an indigenous language of Texas) underwent rapid and extensive lexical change because of the practice of changing words which sounded like the names of people who died. Scholars do not know what the original word for 'God' was in Hebrew because of the restriction against using it. Euphemisms have also caused semantic shift, as in Mexican Spanish where *huevos* 'eggs' was used for 'testicles,' and *blanquillos* 'little white ones' took over its reference function for 'eggs.'

Interlingual taboos occur in multilingual contexts, where an acceptable word in one language sounds like one which is taboo in another. Haas (1957) describes the dilemma of Thai students trying to avoid using words in their own language which they know sound like obscene words in English. In reverse, many students learning English as a foreign language refused to pronounce some words "correctly" because of phonetic similarity to obscene words in their native language (e.g., Turkish speakers do not want to say English *peach*). A useful dictionary of *Dangerous English* (Claire 1980) was published for foreign students, including words which English speakers consider "vulgar," along with their meanings (illustrated) and appropriate euphemisms; a reverse guide to English words which are obscene in other languages is still needed, and would undoubtedly explain some resistant pronunciation "problems" in English as a foreign language classes.

Personal names create one of the most common problems in this area, with English-speaking professors unwilling or embarrassed to call on any student named *Fucks*, and *Jesús* is often rechristened *Jesse* by the second week of class.

Taboos associated with respect forms include avoidance of the name of a ruler, a husband, the aged, or a mother-in-law, or silence in their presence. Total silence is observed by widows in some communities (Cohen 1956). Accidental homonymy may lead to a taboo effect. Japanese buildings often lack a numbered fourth floor since the Sino-Japanese loanword for four, *si*, is also homonymous with the verb 'to die.'

Perhaps the most stringent linguistic form of social control is social ostracism, where collective or group silence is a weapon. Among the Igbo, for instance, this is accomplished by passing a law which makes it punishable by some stipulated penalties for any member of a village to greet, accept greetings, or be aided by the person considered deviant. This extreme measure is resorted to only when all other measures adopted to bring the offender to repentance and submission to the will of the people have failed. When this happens, the entire village – men, women, and children – are forbidden to talk to him (or her) and members of his immediate family. When he re-establishes himself in the good graces of the community, the embargo on speech is lifted and he becomes a full member of the society again (Nwoye 1985).

A similar communication taboo (called "shunning") is practiced by the Amish community in the United States, and informally by anyone who is "not on speaking terms" with someone who has displeased them, or who refuses to talk to an errant spouse or child.

Knowing what *not* to do or say is obviously of great interest and importance for the ethnographer, but by their nature, taboos are difficult to elicit. Since many are sex-specific, or applicable only in cross-sex contexts, it is useful for a male and female to work as a team in collecting data. But violations may have such serious consequences for the investigator's continued acceptability in a community that sensitivity to topics about which questions should *not* be asked is often more important than finding the answers.

7

Acquisition of Communicative Competence

Child language acquisition has been an object of study for philosophers, educators, psychologists, and linguists for at least two centuries (see Bar-Adon and Leopold 1971). Observational reports and analyses over this period reflect a history of changing foci of interest within these several fields, as well as shifting theories on the nature of language itself. Such studies provide a useful background for our perspective on language learning in the inclusive sense of *the acquisition of the rules and skills which enable a member of a speech community to demonstrate and interpret appropriate communicative behavior in a wide range of social contexts.*

As in descriptive and historical linguistics generally, the study of language acquisition in the past century has in turn focused primarily on phonology, syntax, and semantics/pragmatics. As recently as the 1960s and early 1970s, theories of language acquisition were emphasizing the biological or innate factors in the process, and were relegating the social context of language learning to an amorphous sociolinguistic milieu from which children somehow constructed their language via primarily cognitive processes. Much attention has since shifted to such topics as the functions that language serves for children, what communicative strategies they use, and how these are developed and how input is structured in the processes of social interaction: in short, the acquisition of communicative competence.

Ethnographic modes of investigation are essential if such basic factors of language acquisition as these are to be adequately described and explained. We can begin to understand the total picture of how language is learned only if we examine the process within its immediate social and cultural setting, and in the context of conscious and unconscious socialization or enculturation. We must ask about the nature of linguistic input and sociolinguistic training, how and for what purposes children acquire particular communicative strategies, and how language relates to the definition of stages in the life cycle and to recognized role-relationships in the society. We must seek to identify the differential influences of family, peers, and formal education, and consider such matters as the beliefs which the community itself (including its children) holds about the nature of language origin and development. In this chapter we shall consider some of these questions.

Early Linguistic Environment

Just as some innate language development capabilities must be posited to explain the rate and sequence of children's acquisition of phonology and syntax, we must also assume that all human infants are born with the capacity to develop patterned rules for appropriate language use from whatever input is provided within their speech community. Even before a child has acquired language rules, infants evidently are able to deduce a detailed nonverbal, cognitive "script" for how events are structured or organized: e.g. "what happens when grandma visits, or how to have breakfast with father" (Kessen and Nelson 1976).

Some commonalities may be found in the sources and nature of input, although content is of course, culture-specific. Children are essentially participant-observers of communication, like small ethnographers, learning and inductively developing the rules of their speech community through processes of observation and interaction.

Sources of input for children vary depending on cultural and social factors. Mother's talk (discussed in chapter 3) is often assumed to be universally the most important source of early input, but wealthier social classes in many cultures delegate most caretaking tasks to servants, and older siblings have major childrearing responsibilities in many societies, especially where women do work which takes them away from home. The structure and relative influence of the peer group is also culturally determined, as is that of institutions for formal education. The trend to share housekeeping as well as wage-earning responsibilities as part of the "women's liberation" movement among the middle-classes in Western societies and the related concept of a shared "parenting" role for both male and female, suggests additional attention must be paid to the role of father's language as well. In early studies the father was a primary source of linguistic input in societies such as that of the Trobriand Islanders (Malinowski 1926) and the Hopi (Dennis 1940), where he had a warm and friendly relationship with his children and the mother's brother was chiefly responsible for their behavior. Among the Manus (Mead 1930), the father had the principal role in childrearing and hence might have had more linguistic influence.

In some countries family members may have a relatively minor role in child care, with primary responsibility residing in public or private day care facilities. When early care is thus institutionalized for children whose families speak the dominant language of the community, syntactic and phonological development appear to be about the same in both rate and sequence as when it is not, but the vocabulary learned may reflect differences in experience from home care. There may also be differences in communicative strategies acquired by children who attend a nursery school, as I found in my own work with kindergarten age children (particularly in the strategies used to control or manipulate other children), as well as in the domains in which vocabulary and concepts are known. For children from minority-language families, as I noted in the previous chapter, day care experiences may have a much more profound effect on language acquisition; the home language is often incompletely developed in such cases, and the rate of shift to the dominant language is often accelerated.

Among upper-classes where the primary caretaker is not a parent, but a servant who is often a speaker of a low prestige variety of the language or even another language entirely, it is interesting to note that children still acquire the more prestigious language of their family. In both Africa and Latin America the servant caring for the children is often an immigrant from rural areas in the country. Upper-class Africans and Latin Americans report that they learned to understand the language of servants, and could use it when playing with servants' children, but they were strictly reminded of their family identity and language if lower prestige forms were used in inappropriate contexts – such as with their parents or other family members. Conversely, when a caretaker is perceived to speak a prestige language, such as a French governess in an English speech community, her language is frequently acquired and maintained by children even if it is not used by their parents.

Linguistic input is also affected by family structure, and by residential patterns, including who lives in the same house and what their roles are in the caretaking process. The presence of a grandparent in the home influences the type of linguistic input to children, particularly in the degree to which traditional lore is transmitted in the form of stories, proverbs, songs, and rhymes. In minority-language families, grandparents contribute to language maintenance and multilingual development.

The quantitative aspect of language use to which children are socialized – the taciturnity/loquacity dimension – is also obviously related to their linguistic environment. Birdwhistell (1974) compared the median amount of talk per day in Pennsylvania Dutch and Philadelphia Jewish homes. He found that talk ranged from two and a half minutes a day in the former to between six and twelve hours in the latter, although the amounts of actual new information transmitted in the two types of families did not differ appreciably. Clearly the children in these contexts were being socialized to very different styles, and to some extent, functions, of speaking.

Despite statements in the linguistic literature to the contrary, when children have limited input from any source, communicative development may indeed be retarded, though this may be overcome in later childhood. Cultural and social differences sometimes are evident here. I have worked with girls from Mexican American migrant labor families who were restricted to the house (both because of their responsibility to care for younger siblings and for their own safety) until they entered school. They were found to have limited ability to express themselves in either Spanish or English upon school entry, whereas boys from the same families, who had been allowed to have a broader range of social contacts, were far more fluent in Spanish. Many deaf children of hearing parents have also been subjected to this very limited linguistic environment, particularly during the years when educational and medical authorities discouraged parents from using or teaching sign language. Adults were instructed to talk to deaf children all the time, whether the children understood or not. In these cases first language (sign) acquisition was generally delayed until children learned it from peers at school. Hearing children of deaf parents do not suffer the same communicative deprivation, since they generally learn sign at home and acquire speech as a second channel at school or from outside contacts.

Social and cultural factors affect verbal input qualitatively and functionally, as well as quantitatively, but an important caveat needs to be raised concerning the interpretation of cultural and social class differences in mother–child interaction which are reported in the literature. All such claims need to be questioned because, unless observer effect and task have been carefully controlled, they could be the result of differential responses to the investigator and the research situation (in itself a sociolinguistically and ethnographically interesting circumstance), and to the nature of the activity in which mother and child are engaged. For instance, it has been found that White, middle-class, English-speaking mothers produce twice the amount of speech when they are aware of being observed as when they are not, although the proportion of utterance types (e.g. declaratives, imperatives, questions) is similar (Graves and Glick 1978). They use far more indirect directives when aware of observation, saying such things as "Can you put the elephant on top?" rather than the direct imperative "Put the elephant on top" (1978). This indirect strategy may be the reason Laosa (1977) and others report questions being used with greater frequency by more educated groups, if the researchers are classifying utterances according to grammatical form rather than by pragmatic intent. Utterances classified according to different criteria might well contradict such findings. Some findings of structural and pragmatic differences which are reported as cultural differences (such as production of relatively more referential nouns or activity verbs) may also vary with the type of activity in which data are being collected (e.g., see

Choi 2000), further indicating that rich contextual information is required for valid interpretation and comparison.

Social Interaction

Although language acquisition is generally considered to be primarily a cognitive process, it is clearly a social process as well, and one which must take place within the context of social interaction. Furthermore, children's role in their own learning appears to be far more active than models which focused on either conditioning or innate capacity led us to believe.

All components of a communicative event are potential input to children in their construction of meaning from language, with the social identity of participants evidently the most salient (Slobin 1967). Halliday's (1975) functional-interactional approach is consonant with this view, claiming that children learn the meaning of language because of the systematic relation between what they hear and what is going on around them. Children's intent to communicate arises naturally out of the system of shared assumptions and understandings which result from the regularities and rituals of their early socialization (Cook-Gumperz 1977). Children begin to use language within this framework of presupposed knowledge, where verbalizations are only part of the message communicated by them or by adults. Halliday's treatment of acquisition considers such factors as the language which the child is reacting to and its meaning potential, the situational environment of interaction (including the roles and statuses of participants), the variety or register of language used in any specific communicative event, the linguistic system itself (both its potential and how it is constructed by the child), and the social structure within which the interaction is taking place. The salience which the identity of participants in a communicative event has for children is underscored by studies of the language selection of bilingual children in the second year (e.g. Vihman 1985; Shorrah 1986; Genesee, Boivin, and Nicoladis 1996); interlocutor is the earliest and most important contextual feature in determining language choice. Andersen (1990) finds some style-shifting for role and situation at the age of four, with appropriate variation first in family contexts, and I have recorded similar phenomena in style-shifting at a younger age even when interlocutors are not family members.

For example, the following directives/requests were all uttered by one English-speaking boy (age 3 years 7 months) during the course of a single outdoor play period in nursery school. They are categorized according to the role and status of the individual he was speaking to, and it is clear that his communicative competence already includes variability for different levels of politeness and formality.

To peers:
> *Stop that. You're gonna get a swat.*
> *Let's go fishin'.*
> *Come on you guys. Come on. Green slime.*
> *Fix my wheelers.*
> *Let me see what's that.*

To a girl he wanted to persuade to play with him:
> *You can pull me in there too. OK, Michelle?*
> *You get in the back and I'll drive, OK?*
> *You pull me now, OK?*
> *Let's go to see a show Michelle, OK?*
> *Michelle, do you wanna come with me to the show?*
> *Let's go get a . . . this time you wanna go get a ice cream cone? Wanna go to Baskin-Robbins?*

To adult caretakers:
> *Would you go get Stevie a bike?*
> *Would you put on my shoes?*

In a study of language socialization in Japan, Clancy also documents that indirection begins to be used in the third year. The mothers she observed used a wide variety of directives with their two–year–old children (including indirect questions and hints), and they provided direct translations of the indirect, polite speech of others. She concludes that "the primary means by which these children could be learning how to interpret indirection is through the pairing of indirect and direct utterances having the same communicative intent" (1986: 229).

There has been significant disagreement about how, at what age, and to what extent children use language to interact with others. Reasons for the disagreement may reflect at least in part differences in social and cultural influences on communicative behavior which relate to circumstances in observation and data collection (although the contexts are often not adequately described). Piaget (1926) claimed that children's speech is primarily ego-centric, with early conversation essentially collective monologue, and such interactional linguistic forms as commands and requests a later development. He reported that even at six and a half years of age, more than half of children's utterances are egocentric: repetition, monologue, and collective monologue. The social factors which might be involved are illustrated by Keenan's (1974) challenge to Piaget's conclusions in reporting that her twins exhibited such interactional strategies as turn-taking before the age of three, and by Dimitracopoulou's (1990) documentation of meaningful dialogue between three-year-olds who interacted regularly, but also by Garvey's (1977) lack of success in replicating Keenan's results with young children who were not acquainted. The code-switching and style-shifting in accordance with participant role-relationships which I reported above add weight to Keenan's and Dimitracopoulou's arguments that children may be sensitive to the interactional context of language use from a much earlier age than that suggested by Piaget.

While all language is learned in the process of social interaction, different linguistic forms are considered "typical" or appropriate between adults and children in different cultures. English-speaking mothers regularly use questions to stimulate interaction with children, and then react to the children's answers as if they were worthy of interest and further verbal response. In contrast, Javanese mothers often use question forms with children, but furnish the answers themselves. This is a way of teaching a child to respect an older person not only because of age, but also because of knowledge; children learn to control their behavior, to be quiet in the presence of someone who is older and respected. Blount (1972) reports a very low frequency of questions addressed to children in Samoan and Luo societies. In large part this is a cultural difference in adult–child conversational status; English speakers may give children the status of social peer, asking opinions, and allowing children to initiate conversational rounds.

Children's questions to adults are also influenced by cultural factors. In an English speech community, children are generally encouraged to use question forms to request permission or gain information, and they may legitimately use questions (especially "Why?") to prolong conversation, challenge authority, or hold the floor. Navajo children learn to use more indirect request forms at an early age, especially statements of wishing something would be so, and their questions for information are discouraged by such adult responses as "Use your eyes." English-speaking children use questions with another child as a turn-taking device, and also for competitive functions, such as an opening to display knowledge they have that the other does not. (This is similar to riddling in many societies.)

Much of the earlier research on acquisition in the process of adult–child interaction focused on the importance of children's repetition of adult speech. While this is totally inadequate to account for language learning, there are speech communities where mimicry is very common, and considered the most appropriate form of social interaction between adults and young children. Just as Tallensi children in Ghana reportedly learn other social behaviors primarily by looking and copying, for instance, the Tallensi theory of how language is learned is that "They learn little by little . . . they accompany us and listen to what we say" (Fortes 1938). This belief within the speech community influences the linguistic behavior of adults toward a child; they frequently mimic its babblings and expect repetition in return. Hogbin (1946) reports a similar prevalence of mimicry in the learning style of Wogeo children in New Guinea. With respect to language learning he reports: "I often used to hear children repeating their parent's pet phrases and characteristic intonations with remarkable accuracy. Adoption is common and the natives have a saying, 'Use your eyes to find out who begot a strange child and your ears to discover who is rearing it.'"

Mead described the use of repetition in the spontaneous native teaching of Tok Pisin to young children by older children in New Guinea:

> Young men who have been away to work for the White man return to their villages and teach the younger boys, who in turn teach the very small boys. . . . It is a common spectacle to see two or three twelve-year-old boys gathered about a three- or four-year-old little boy, "schooling him." An older boy gives the cue: "I think he can." "I think he no can." "Me like good fellow kai kai (food)." "Me like kai kai fish." "One time along taro." And the child repeats the lines in his piping little voice without any grasp of their significance. But as it fits in so well with the game of repetition for repetition's sake neither teacher nor pupil tires easily, and the result is that boys of thirteen and fourteen speak perfect pidgin although they have never been out of their isolated villages. (1930: 42)

A variety of beliefs and practices are also related to enhancing language development in children who are considered "delayed" in some respect. Among the Huli (also of New Guinea), for instance, a frog may be lightly tapped on the child's lips, teeth, and tongue (organs associated with articulation) while a chant is repeated. Goldman reports that "The rationale behind this practice involves the cultural association of frogs (*yago*) and talk" (1987: 453). What constitutes language "delay" is of course culture-specific, just as is the "remedy."

An interesting, but less common, focus in research has been on the influence which children themselves have on adult communicative behavior. Von Raffler-Engle and Rea (1978) report that much of the interaction between adults and children is nonverbal, or paralinguistic, with children often confirming understanding or triggering repetitions or paraphrase with grunts, facial expressions, or head nods, which also suggests the need to expand the scope of interaction phenomena which are to be explored and described.

The essential assumption of an interaction model is that acquisition of communicative competence is the result of interaction processes within a sociocultural context, and not just the unfolding of innate, preprogramed behavior. Descriptive data from a wide variety of speech communities clearly support this perspective, but much more ethnographically-detailed research is needed.

Language and Enculturation

Language learning for children is an integral part of their enculturation from three perspectives: (1) language is part of culture, and thus part of the body of knowledge, attitudes, and skills which is transmitted from one generation to the next; (2) language is a primary medium through which other aspects of culture are encoded and transmitted; and (3) language is a tool which children may use to explore (and sometimes manipulate) the social environment and establish their status and role-relationships within it. Partially as a result of differential social environments, language learning for a child is thus also learning to be a male, or a female, or rich, or poor, or African American, or English, or Chinese, or Muslim, or Buddhist, or dozens of other social roles and statuses into which he or she is being enculturated, and the child is learning to internalize, transform (perhaps challenge), and generalize these across situations and through time.

Another view of the central role of language in enculturation is included in the concept of *habitus* as it was formulated by Bourdieu (1991):

> habitus is assumed to take shape as an implicit aspect of habitual life experiences and to be acquired in early childhood. It constitutes an unexamined background set of assumptions about the world, as well as a set of dispositions that incline agents to act and react in certain ways. (Aukrust and Snow 1998: 222)

And yet another expression of this view by Fowler:

> The meanings of the words in a language are the community's established knowledge. A child learns the values and preoccupations of its culture largely by learning the language: language is the chief instrument of socialization, which is the process by which a person is, willy-nilly, moulded into conformity with the established systems of beliefs of the society in which s/he happens to be born. (1996: 30)

One interactional situation which has received considerable attention in relation to enculturation is conversation at family mealtime. Involved are transmission of cultural values and beliefs along with appropriate ways of speaking, as well as opportunity within many groups for children to practice and collaborate in the production of discourse. For example, Ochs and Taylor (1992) focus on problem-solving dinner talk by "mainstream American English-speaking families across diverse socio-economic backgrounds" and on how it socializes children to "scientific thinking"; Blum-Kulka (1997) focuses on how parents in three groups socialize their children to different social identities (Jewish Americans, American Israelis, and native Israelis);

and Aukrust and Snow (1998) focus on narrative and explanatory genre within Norwegian and American families and on how mealtime production relates to differential socialization for collectivism and individualism.

On a functional dimension, a number of exemplary comparative studies have related cultural transmission to how mothers structure talk to young children and to the content of their communication. In socialization for collectivism versus individualism, for instance, Aukrust and Snow cite research which finds that Japanese mothers engage babies more in social routines while American mothers do more referential naming (Fernald and Morikawa 1993); French and Japanese mothers provide more dyad-focused response while American mothers incorporate more external objects (Bornstein et al. 1992); and Estonian and Swedish mothers offer children fewer individual choices than American mothers (Junefelt and Tulviste 1997). A related finding by Blum-Kulka is that "In the discourse of Jewish American families [there is more] emphasis on individual rights and self accomplishment" (1997: 138). Structural aspects of language production may also contribute to this end. Cook (1990) claims that Japanese mothers' use of sentence-final -*no*, which indexes knowledge that is common to members of the community, helps socialize children to norms of interpersonal harmony, conformity, and affective dependence.

The relative importance of verbal explication in the socialization process is not the same in all speech communities, nor in transmitting different aspects of culture within the same community, but the whole of the transmission must be considered communication in its broadest sense. Specific modes of transmission correspond to overall patterns in culture, and to patterns of childrearing in each culture. Hall's (1959) distinction among *formal, informal,* and *technical* levels of culture and types of learning provides a useful framework for illustrating these differences.

Formal learning takes place through precept and admonition, and transmits those aspects of culture which are not to be questioned. Verbal clues that this level is involved include corrections such as "Boys don't do that" or "That's not *our* way," and, if these reproofs are challenged by children, appeals to authority may be invoked such as "Because it is" or "Because I said so." It is difficult to imagine most questions regarding the origin or meaning of words being dealt with in any other way, although attempts to do so may account for some of our folk etymologies. When a child asks "Why is that a *chair?*" the response is likely to be it is a *chair* "Because it is." At an older age, the appeal to authority becomes "Because it says so in the dictionary."

Verbalizations of formal aspects of culture often include the expression of the traditional wisdom of a community in the form of proverbs or other aphorisms. They may be contradictory (depending on the situation), but like other formal aspects of culture, their truth value is not a relevant dimension. Hopi parents also use a predominantly formal mode of enculturation in their consistent admonition to children to "Listen to the old people – they are wise," or "Our old uncles taught us that way – it is the *right* way" (Eggan 1956). Bernstein's (1972: 486) examples of positional appeals would also be considered formal in nature:

> You should be able to do that by now (age status rule).
> Little boys don't cry (sex status rule).
> People like us don't behave like that (subcultural rule).
> Daddy doesn't expect to be spoken to like that (age relation rule).

The behavior which adults expect of children may be determined at least in part by their language development, and not corrected until adults believe children can understand formal verbal directives. English-speaking adults may say "No, no" before they believe more complex directives or explanations will be understood, but this is disapproved of in speech communities where adults feel such commands are useless, or may frighten a young child.

Informal learning takes place for the most part unconsciously, primarily through nonverbal channels of communication, with the chief agent a model used for imitation. Hall estimates there are hundreds of thousands of details passed from generation to generation for which no one can give rules for what is happening, and members of the community may not even realize there are any rules involved. These are transmitted informally, and their existence often becomes consciously "visible" only if they are broken.

Much of children's verbal behavior is also learned at this level, with rules unconsciously formulated in some way on the basis of informal observation. By the age of three or four, for instance, English-speaking children have acquired the rule for giving first names and respond to foreign names as "funny," or break the rule in making up "silly" names in play. Language-specific grammatical structures are learned primarily by unconscious informal means in early childhood, since any correction usually focuses only on errors in lexical choice, or "improper" speech. Pragmatic competence is also acquired informally: English-speaking children are not told explicitly that a surface-form question such as "Wouldn't you like to put your toys away now?" is not asking for information, and that a direct "No" would be considered an inappropriate or even rude response. Appropriate indirect responses are also learned (but not taught), and these same children soon develop the competence to respond "Can I finish this first?" or "I don't feel very good" as strategies to avoid complying with such a question/directive. Much more research is needed on this area in different cultures and subcultures.

Technical learning is at an explicitly formulated, conscious level, and includes such things as what children find out in school about the grammar they have already acquired informally; rules are explained by adults, reasons are given, and deviations usually corrected without emotional and moral involvement (although instructors may adopt a moralistic attitude toward "errors" and sanctions may be imposed for violations). Written language skills are most likely to be taught in a technical mode, and more advanced oral rhetorical skills may also be developed at this level. "Etiquette" is also transmitted technically, with a number of books and even daily newspaper columns devoted to explaining rules for "proper" behavior: e.g. who should be introduced or presented to whom, appropriate forms for invitations for particular social occasions, what clothes to wear on particular occasions, etc.

All cultures make use of all three of these modes of enculturation to some degree, but formal learning tends to be prominent where authority in the family is strictly ordered in a hierarchy, in cultures where the supernatural is a pervasive control on behavior, and where there is a great respect for tradition. On the other hand, children are more likely to be taught on a technical level in an institutionally-organized society which values information and cognitive skills, and where the mental capacities of youth are accorded great respect.

Personality development is related in many respects to the acquisition of language and culture and should also be considered in the ethnography of communication, at least insofar as its association with verbal behavior or constraints on such behavior is concerned. Data on this point can sometimes provide valuable clues to norms and tolerated variability within particular speech communities. I noted earlier that children may be characterized as "good" or "bad" at least partly in terms of their language use, including not only the employment of politeness rules and "proper" vocabulary, but also features of pronunciation (cf. Fischer 1958). Even expressions of pain and stress are culturally patterned, and may be taught quite early to children. Navajos endure pain quietly, for instance, and the extent of their illness or injury may not be apparent to anyone from a different cultural background. A nurse working in a clinic on the Navajo reservation observed mothers admonishing sick infants and young children to silence their cries, and I have seen five- and six-year-old Navajo children accept vaccinations without any facial or verbal sign of discomfort.

Cultural and social information is encoded in all channels of communication, and in all dimensions of each channel. One of the most obvious carriers of differential experiences within a language group is vocabulary, especially in the relatively limited lexicon of young children. Vocabulary development (and by implication, knowledge of the domains to which the vocabulary pertains) reflects to a significant degree the ordering of priorities within a culture. In the US, for instance, schools generally do not introduce *north, east, south,* and *west* until about the forth or fifth grade level (to ten-or eleven-year-olds), but the terms and concepts have been mastered by Navajo children before they come to kindergarten because of the importance of the cardinal directions in the religious beliefs and practices of the community. It would be of interest to know at what age Eskimo children acquire differential terms for snow, Aymara (Bolivia) children different terms for potatoes, and Marshallese (Polynesian) children different terms for stages in the development of coconuts. The development of semantic categories, and indeed of all situated meaning in language, is dependent on the dictates of cultural experience (cf. Cook–Gumperz 1977). Vocabulary knowledge thus becomes a means, as well as an index, of enculturation.

From the perspective of the child within a speech community, the role of language in enculturation is both for personal growth (to communicate information, express feelings, satisfy needs, acquire knowledge, interpret the world) and for socialization (to activate, structure, and maintain social intercourse, gain acceptance, status, and identity within the group). From the perspective of the community as a whole, creating conformity and effecting transmission of the culture are the primary functions of language learning: i.e. successful socialization.

Definition of Stages and Roles

Children learn the social structure of their culture as they learn language, and learning to use appropriate forms when there is a choice is part of learning one's place in society. The set of roles learned first through family interaction, then peer group and wider community, involves age, sex, and social class. Taking a somewhat Whorfian perspective, social forces influence what is social and psychological reality for a child at various stages and in whatever roles are open to him or her in the community. To learn the complex vertical hierarchies of a society like Bali, for instance, "As [children] learn to speak, they learn that the words addressed to them by their elders and superiors are never the words in which they may answer . . ." (Mead 1955: 42). This challenges the idea that language is learned primarily through imitation.

Of particular relevance to ethnographers are questions such as how speech to or by children differs with sex or social status, what aspects of speaking might be related to concepts of the ideal or typical man, woman, or child, how speech may be instrumental in marking stages in the life cycle, and how family patterns of organization (kinship, authority, rights, responsibilities) are expressed in language.

Differences in language use by adults to boys versus girls in different cultures remain inadequately documented, although this is clearly a significant factor in sex-role differentiation. A survey of various aspects of socialization in 110 cultures (Barry, Bacon, and Child 1957) concludes there is little input differentiation by sex in infancy, but in childhood girls have more emphasis put on nurturance, obedience, and responsibility, and boys more on self-reliance and striving for achievement; we can assume this is related to differential language use to older children, but there is no explicit reference to this dimension of socialization in the survey. Blount reports (1972) that East African Luo adult males use a higher percentage of imperatives to young girls than to young boys, which would be consonant with the trend to train girls more to obedience in most cultures, and with the Luo social structure, which allows males to issue demands to females. Similar male dominance can be inferred from answers to a question asked of 126 Kamba adults in Kenya: "What is the most important thing for parents to teach a toddler?" Over 80 percent of the respondents said, "To say the word 'father'" (Edgerton 1971: 114).

Schieffelin (1990) describes how Kaluli boys are socialized by their mothers to be assertive and demanding, while girls are socialized to be independent and nurturing. Peer interaction may also be a socializing force for sex roles with young children, as Farris describes from observation in a Taiwan preschool:

> Through verbal and nonverbal interaction, boys create a childish masculine ethos that centers on action, competition, and aggression, punctuated with onomatopoeia and mild vulgarity, and that is organized and expressed discursively through loud, terse, direct forms of speech. Whereas girls create a feminine ethos that centers on the construction and maintenance of quasi-familial social relations or on authoritarian roles based on teacher models, and that is organized and expressed discursively through coy, affected, and indirect forms of speech. (1991: 198)

Some information on appropriate use of language according to sex is to be found in the folklore and traditional literature. In traditional Thai culture, female "good manners" entail gentleness, sweet words, and graceful movements, as expressed in the *Suphasit Son Ying* (Bhu ca. 1803). In addition to ways of speaking, smiling, and walking prescribed in this poetry, girls are to limit topics of conversation only to what is pleasant, and women must never argue with their husbands. In spite of some significant changes in Thai women's actual roles in the last two centuries, the ideal persists, and is still generally considered the appropriate cultural model for girls to emulate. The traditional folk tales of northern Europe similarly present females as hard working, unassertive, and soft spoken in roles like *Snow White, Sleeping Beauty*, and *Cinderella*, while males tend to be active and adventurous like *Jack and the Beanstalk* and *Robin Hood*. Males climb things, shout, leap around; females work quietly by the hearth or sleep.

In many societies differential attitudes toward the ways males and females should talk are realized in different speech training. In Burundi:

> From about the tenth year, boys in the upper social strata are given formal speech training. The "curriculum" includes . . . formulas for petitioning a superior for a gift; . . . quick-witted, self-defensive rhetoric intended to deflect an accusation or the anger of a superior. . . . Girls in the upper caste are also carefully trained, but to artful silence and evasiveness and to careful listening that will enable them to repeat nearly verbatim what has been said by visitors or neighbors. (Albert 1972)

The Abbey community (in Côte d'Ivoire) also has clearly formulated ideas of appropriate ways of speaking based on sex. "Speaking as a woman" refers to everyday informal speech spoken most of the time by anyone (male or female) while "speaking as a man" is the high variety of language, full of proverbs, symbols, and metaphors, with a loud but gentle voice, using big gestures, and avoiding hesitations. "Speaking as a child" refers to a very low variety. No normal adult would use it except to identify with children in a setting where most of the participants are quite young (Hepié). This is reminiscent of St. Paul's observation: "When I was a child I spoke as a child, but when I became a man I spoke as a man, and put away childish things."

In Farsi, children are believed to have become sociolinguistically "competent" at three years. At that time they are expected to have picked up such rules as not speaking in the presence of elders unless asked to, requesting properly, and using *shoma* (formal second person pronoun) and the correctly conjugated verb form when addressing an older person. They should also know appropriate forms of address for family members by then. In Nepal, Newar children under six are allowed the latitude of asking or saying anything for they are still considered "ignorant babies"; but once past the age of six or seven, children are strictly monitored on what they say and how they behave in social gatherings. They are not expected to use respect forms or honorifics in normal interactions until they are around twelve or fourteen, however. While even infants in Bali are thought to be fully "competent" because of belief in reincarnation, they are nevertheless expected to do nothing for themselves; words are put into their mouths and spoken on their behalf by adults, who even form the infants' hands into appropriate gestures (Mead 1955).

A number of rites of passage observed in different cultures involve receiving a new name, or new terms of address, which index change in social status. Different given names are often bestowed at christening or puberty rites, and different family names and titles with marriage. In some communities, teachers switch from using students' first names to title plus last name at about the time they begin secondary school, and in university academic circles in the US students may be invited to call professors by first name after they successfully defend their dissertation (in some departments, all graduate students are so invited). Some nicknames are considered appropriate only for children, and continued use by family may cause considerable embarrassment. Similarly, diminutive forms of names may be dropped with age, especially for males, as Johnny, Billy, and Tommy to John, Bill, and Tom. Names may also be changed because of noteworthy events or achievements by the child, or because the death of someone possessing the same name makes it taboo. Some groups believe that names are a determining factor in children's ultimate deeds in life, including Momaday (1976), a Kiowa Indian (and Pulitzer Prize winner) who reports that his own name affirmed his life. It was given to him by a storyteller who believed "a man's life proceeds from his name, in a way that a river proceeds from its source." Reviews of naming practices and their relation to cultural factors in a wide variety of speech communities have been compiled by Akinnaso (1980) and Bean (1980).

Differential naming practices have led to some problems in keeping track of informants in ethnographic research; the Navajo practice of changing names proved so confusing (perhaps the "real" one was never given an outsider) that census numbers have been the only sure means of identification for outside agencies; this number can be particularly significant in charting family relationships, since when American Indian communities were directed to choose "family" names in the early nineteenth century, brothers often chose (or were assigned) different surnames, making relationships unclear.

Naming is usually considered quite personal within a speech community, but the act clearly identifies children as belonging to the group. If a child later chooses to change group allegiance, changing names is often the most obvious sign of reaffiliation. (Cf. the English practice of a woman adopting her husband's surname upon marriage, or the Spanish practice of adding *de* plus the husband's surname after the woman's own. Surnames, of course, usually identify only relationship to the father.)

The acquisition of kinship terminology and competence in attendant interactional rights and responsibilities is also an important element of socialization from early childhood. Goldfield and Snow (1992), for instance, describe discussion of kin terms and relations with children at the age of two years. When Navajo parents and grandparents were interviewed prior to the implementation of a bilingual kindergarten program concerning what they considered most important for children to learn in the Navajo language, the invariant reply was how to ask for and give information on clan membership. This was not because the clan terms in themselves were considered so important, but because they indexed kinship relations, and that knowledge was critical for determining appropriate and moral behaviors in personal interaction.

Communicative Strategies

Children begin to learn communicative options and to select those appropriate for a given situation at a very early age, and their repertoire changes both quantitatively and qualitatively as they mature. Early stages appear to be primarily nonverbal (and very obvious to others), while those of older children are more often verbal (and may be quite subtle). For instance, aggression is often expressed physically by young children (at least among English speakers), but this behavior comes to be supplemented with verbal taunts and chants by the age of five, and may develop into one of the complex verbal dueling forms of later childhood and adolescence. The young child who may hold its breath or bang its head against the wall to gain attention later develops competence in more mature forms of nonverbal behavior (e.g. raising a hand) and appropriate verbalizations (e.g. calls, shifts in intonation, solicitation routines) for this purpose.

Children use language to create and maintain a social hierarchy in their peer group, often with routines known to all in the group which have predetermined responses and are thus controlled by the initiator. Weininger (1978) describes "knock-knock" routines started by socially subordinate children in a Texas kindergarten, which then forced higher ranking children to respond and interact with them. Directives are often used by children to establish a power position, with compliance by others interpreted as their accepting lesser status. English-speaking children use fewer imperative forms between equals than do adults, but direct more to subordinates (Mitchell-Kernan and Kernan 1977). This does not appear to represent a developmental stage in acquiring adult communicative competence, but rather a difference in linguistic strategies. There also appear to be differences in features in the social context which identify a power role for adults versus children; age and size are more salient determinants of power for children than are social or economic status (Owens 1979; for a collection of studies on communicative strategies in later childhood, see Hoyle and Adger 1998).

There is a growing body of cross-cultural information on when and how children learn to request, direct, insult, comment, and summon, and thus to what extent such acquisition may be tied to developmental factors or to cultural experiences. It seems clear that even quite young children may use language to control adult behavior, as well as that of other children, in order to get what they want, to escape punishment, to gain approval. One three-and-a-half-year-old had learned to make a request without risking refusal or negative response by giving the addressee the option, "If you want to play house with me, you can," and DiPietro (1975) reports his son acquired a verbal strategy by age four which had as its purpose putting the adult in a double bind. The child would challenge, "I bet I know what you'll say if I ask you something," and he couldn't really lose. If the adult answered "No," the child won the verbal match with, "See, I knew you'd say that"; if the adult answered "Yes," the child won by getting what he wanted.

Formulaic Expressions

While receptive competence clearly precedes production in most areas of communicative development, the reverse is often true of the acquisition of routines and polite formulas. Even infants of six or seven months are taught to wave and say *bye-bye* 'good-bye.' This, plus *please* and *thank you* are usually the first routines taught to English-speaking children. Perhaps the first sign of acquired meaning comes when a child looks sad or cries when parents say *bye-bye* before going away for a few hours, but this stage generally comes several months later than the first production.

Bauman (1976) reports a similar production-to-comprehension order in the acquisition of riddles as solicitational routines. The developmental sequence at age five begins with descriptive routines: proper form, but no misleading element as "what's red, round, and good to eat" (an apple), or "what's round and bounces" (a ball). This progresses to power and control aspects; children understand the puzzling nature of riddles, but consider answers arbitrary, and do not understand the ambiguity involved. They do understand that the poser is always right, as in "What color is blood?" "Red." "No, it's blue and Black." Competence at age seven includes recognition of the riddle as a traditional form, and routines are memorized as fixed forms, but with flaws that indicate ambiguities are still not fully comprehended. Correct performance of riddles, according to Bauman, becomes increasingly prevalent at about age eight.

The process through which children acquire ritual competence (which would include polite formulas) is "perhaps the most fundamental socialization of all since they thereby learn about the nature they are to have as actors" (Goffman 1971: 157). If a child neglects to use the proper formula, an adult may halt the sequence and prompt, "What do you say?"

What evidence there is on the acquisition of ritual forms in other speech communities suggests that mimicry and prompting of young children are both common phenomena. For instance, in Nepal, Newar children between the ages of four and six are taught to interact socially by repeating greetings or leavetakings. The parent, while greeting a visitor, turns to the child and says "Say *namaste*," and the child utters the greetings with the appropriate *wai* gesture (i.e. palms of hands together with fingers pointing upward and a slight bowing of the head).

Some routines, although common to all adults in a speech community, may not be learned until after childhood. Where greeting or leavetaking routines are complex (as in Arabic and Indonesian), competence in full forms is not expected of children, and condolence routines are also generally delayed even though the deaths of friends and family may be experienced from infancy.

At later stages of childhood, prompting in teaching ritual verbal performances may range from Boy Scout pledges, to oaths of allegiance to the flag, to recitals of religious creeds – all aspects of continued enculturation. Comparable socialization (and prompting) may continue into post-adolescence in marriage vows, legal oaths, and occupational or military domains.

Nonverbal Communication

Communicatively significant nonverbal behaviors develop along with the verbal in young children, and in some aspects precede it. Before Thai children can talk, for instance, they learn to use the *wai* gesture (described in chapter 4 and for Newar children above) when the parents or caretakers tell them to greet or say good-bye to someone. Before giving the children something to eat, the caretakers ask, "What would you do first?" and receive a *wai* in response (Ekasingh).

Unlike the culture-specific *wai*, some nonverbal behaviors appear to be "natural" to all young humans, and are perhaps even shared by higher order primates. Darwin (1872) was the first to suggest that there are facial expressions which universally convey the same emotion, and to some extent he has been supported by subsequent research (cf. Harper, Wiens, and Matarazzo 1978). Most features of nonverbal communication are language/culture-specific, however, and are learned in much the same way that language/culture-specific elements of verbal behavior are learned. In the case of the few universal behaviors (generally expressing emotion), cultural learning often takes the form of constraining gestures or facial expressions in terms of how and when they may be used: i.e., "display rules" (Ekman 1972) are language/culture-specific. Cultural constraints must also be acquired whenever nonverbal behavior appropriate for children is not considered appropriate for adults, or when different behavior is appropriate for males and females in a society.

In cross-cultural research, von Raffler-Engel (1977) describes Japanese and English children being socialized into the suppression of most hand gestures, and finds early evidence of culture-specific body movement. A Japanese girl videotaped at two years three months, for instance, bows to a pretend addressee over a toy telephone when saying good-bye, just as her mother makes a toy kangaroo bow to her on "leaving." Birdwhistell (1970) has also noted the emergence of nonverbal behaviors which are sex-specific by the age of two; American male/female differences include posture, eye behavior, and the angle of arms and legs to the body.

One of the most interesting questions in the acquisition of communicative competence is how children learn when *not* to talk, and what silence means in their speech community. In part, the relative silence of some children (e.g. Chinese, Japanese, and Hopi) over others (e.g. British and American) may be related to childrearing practices and values regarding the relative value of individual achievement and initiative; children in societies which value individual achievement generally talk more. Additionally, the cultural experience of children who will be less verbal about their needs and wishes seems to include closer physical contact with early caretakers, and expectations that adults or older siblings will care for them without need for verbalization. This also relates to attitudes even in the adult speech community that people should not, and should not have to, ask directly for what they want. In Clancy's observations of mothers interacting with two-year-olds in Japan, she noted that they would attribute speech to individuals who had actually remained silent in order to heighten children's awareness of what others' feelings might be, or provide "lessons in how to guess what others are thinking and feeling [i.e. inferencing] even when they have not spoken" (1986: 235).

Training young children to silence and heightened nonverbal perception may be considered part of the transmission of world view, as in this example reported by Locke (1980):

> A Colville Indian child from the Northwest Coast is trained to perceive with all of his senses before he learns to speak so that he may become sensitive to the world around him. A grandparent will say "Wighst" and slap his hand on a solid surface. The child who is crawling on the floor will stop playing or daydreaming or whatever he is doing and become alert at the sound of that word and will try to feel through his body and his feet the vibrations of the stream or animals walking or people walking about him. The child sharpens his peripheral vision. He listens to all the sounds about him, he focuses all his senses, including that other sense, that is sensitive to the vibrations of the earth. The training in constant. . . . Thus he is prepared to relate to other two-leggeds, four-leggeds, the winged creatures, the crawling ones, the finned ones, the rooted ones, and all of life, all of our relations.

Other potentially relevant cultural differences in childrearing practices are suggested by Wang (1977):

In order to keep the children from saying or doing something disapproved of by the authorities, Asian parents teach them to be obedient and to honor their families. Everything is arranged and decided for them. They are not given any choices; therefore, they do not have to make choices and justify their actions verbally. Silence is praised, and talkativeness is scolded. They are taught not to express their feelings.

As with other areas of sociolinguistic training, proverbs and stories may also be used to teach children to be silent. Some of these proverbs have been cited in the discussion of attitudes toward language (chapter 6). Additionally, Confucius is quoted as saying "The wise man desires to be slow to speak but quick to act," and teachers in Taiwan warn students who talk too much that "Disaster comes in through the mouth" and "One who talks too much will fail" (Wang 1977). One line from a Javanese pedagogical song-poem by W. S. Rendra reads: *Tumumgkula yen dipun dukani* 'Just look down if you are reprimanded.'

Children's learning of appropriate silence, like other communicative strategies, is not necessarily developing competence in adult norms for sociolinguistic behavior, but may involve quite different rules for adults and children. Slavey children in Canada are allowed to be relatively voluble, and yet become taciturn in old age (Christian and Gardner 1977), for instance, and in many societies it may be appropriate for children to talk freely with other children but they may be expected to be silent in the presence of adults.

Silent slots in discourse may also have different meanings for adult and child members of the same speech community. In contrast to the claim that silence is an appropriate response to inappropriate questions for adults (Lakoff 1973), English-speaking children usually consider a reply mandatory. In many cases, the same contexts which call for a formal style from adult speakers require silence of children. Formal style or verbal rituals may appropriately replace silence as they are acquired, or as the speech community feels children are old enough to use them.

Perhaps because so much of nonverbal competence is acquired during early childhood, it is learned primarily through informal and formal means and less often at a technical level. This is perhaps also the reason that appropriate nonverbal behavior is often unconscious, and why it is rarely taught and seldom completely mastered in a second language.

Peer Influence and Extended Acquisition

There has traditionally been less attention paid to continuing acquisition and refinement of language skills in later years of childhood, and into adulthood, than to early language acquisition. It has been well established that extended language acquisition must be qualitatively different because of neurological changes, such as the vastly diminished amount of uncommitted cortex (Penfield 1965), but we must also recognize that different stages of communicative development involve very different aspects of socialization, and different primary sociocultural influences. Although this basic generalization may not hold true for all cultures, young children are usually most dependent on and influenced by family, adolescents by peers, and adults by such social institutions as their workplace. We are particularly interested in knowing what verbal strategies are not learned until after childhood, how they are acquired, and what functions they have for members of a particular speech community.

As noted by Malinowski (1939):

> In many communities we find that the child passes through a period of almost complete detachment from home, running around, playing about, and engaging in early activities with his playmates and contemporaries. In such activities strict teaching in tribal law is enforced more directly and poignantly than in the parental home.

Peer group relations and influence play a very important part in the socialization of most older children and adolescents, but who or what constitutes a peer group, and the relative influence which that group has on its members, is quite culture-specific. In the mainstream, middle class of the United States, a "peer group" is defined primarily by age, and there is little latitude in this respect. A child from this group who plays with or even enjoys the company of children several years younger or older is often considered "odd." In contrast, members of the peer groups in many subcultures in the country include children in the neighborhood within a wide range of ages, particularly when older children have primary caretaking responsibilities for their younger siblings. The influence of this age-mixing is clearly seen in the language development of bilingual children; those in the care of older brothers and sisters and thus in contact with a wider range of neighborhood children usually know more English on school entry than do the oldest children of these families, or others where primary care is provided by adults at home. In other societies, such as Mexico, it is commonplace to see older children and teenagers spontaneously playing with young children in the community.

The function of language in establishing and regulating peer relations has been analyzed among Israeli children, where it includes participating appropriately in verbal exchanges which focus on sharing treats. Developing competence in the rules which govern these exchanges is related to children's moral development (Katriel 1987), and plays a role in their enculturation to the moral order of their society. A second type of peer exchange involves *brogez*, which "functions as a standardized mechanism for the regulation of conflicts among Israeli children . . . [allowing for] both the expression and the containment of aggression" (Katriel 1987: 485). An interesting aspect of events such as these which regulate interaction in peer culture is the extent to which the rules for appropriate conduct are often developed, transmitted, and maintained with little encouragement or interference from adult members of the community. Naturalistic studies of child disputing and negotiation events in other cultures include Boggs (1978), Maynard (1985), Adger (1986), Emihovich (1986), and Saville-Troike (1986). Goodwin (1990) provides an in-depth ethnographic description of how a group of African American youth construct and organize their urban community, largely through processes of verbal interaction.

In complex societies, occupational socialization (and thus the acquisition of occupation-specific communicative competence) seldom begins until well after childhood. Often a unique vocabulary (jargon) must be learned, which may be acquired through technical education, informal "on the job" observation and imitation, or a combination of both.

Prospective linguists, for instance, must learn not only a specialized vocabulary, but appropriate argumentation structures, appropriate written style to be published in professional journals, and currently appropriate examples to use in oral and written presentations. New government employees in the United States enter the bureaucratic subculture; in addition to the acquisition of new vocabulary, they must also learn to recognize and generate acronyms, and process and produce idiomatic expressions which are unique to that domain. New patterns of language use must be learned, including new forms of address, new ways to answer telephones, and often even new ways to formulate requests, invitations, jokes, and insults. Many successful corporate executives and employees learn a style of interaction called *schmoozing*, which is considered appropriate for networking and getting "the most out of an event or cocktail party" (Lewis 2001). They must also learn to master an obligatory written genre: the monthly report.

In a few societies, training in occupational rituals may begin in early childhood. Like Tibetan monks, the Cagaba (Chibchan speakers in Colombia) select their leaders through divination, and apprenticeship usually begins as soon as a chosen boy is weaned and lasts 19 years. During this time, the boy is secluded from all except the current leader (often his father) and other apprentices (Lagacé 1977). Early informal training is more common, where children who are expected to assume the role which a parent or grandparent holds are encouraged to observe, and may practice in role-playing contexts with their peers. Some Navajo boys who are expected to become medicine men have already assumed the role of storyteller among their peers by the age of five or six, and conduct play ceremonials. In these contexts the boys may exhibit skills in using voice qualities appropriate for characterizing animal voices, or intoned speech, which are generally considered far beyond the productive competence of children that age.

Part of the delay that does occur in aspects of communicative development may be attributed to the level of cognitive maturity required to acquire some concepts or functions; when this is the reason, rather than differential social requirements or experience, we should of course find little cultural variation. One area where this is a factor is the development of competence in figurative language, including the interpretation of puns, jokes, riddles, similes, metaphors, and irony (Gardner et al. 1978). While children are sensitive to some types of metaphorical language in early childhood (e.g., they may designate the *nose, mouth,* or *feet* on a picture of a mountain), speakers can really use language figuratively only after they have acquired considerable competence in its literal structure, and are at a cognitive level to process it more abstractly.

It is possible that the usual delayed acquisition of competence in a function like condoling is due to combined factors of required cognitive maturity and attitudes within a community about which events are appropriate for child participation and which not. In Saudi Arabia, for instance, condoling requires highly ritualized formulaic language including both prescribed verbal and nonverbal behavior. It is not appropriate for males to participate until they are about 14 years old, and never appropriate for females. On the other hand, in some societies it may be considered appropriate for much younger children to participate in condoling. Hogbin (1946) reports that Wogeo (New Guinea) parents at funerals instruct children of about three years to do their share of weeping, and Pukapukan (Polynesia) children commonly play burying games after the death of someone in the community in order to experience fringe-level participation in the funeral wake and burial (Beaglehole and Beaglehole 1941). Even though Abbey children in the Côte d'Ivoire do not speak at formal funeral events, they have a spectator role, and how they walk and gesture is considered very important.

English-speaking children are generally not present at wakes and funerals to learn informally by observation, but they are still expected to somehow know the "right thing to say" to the bereaved when they are old enough to participate, even for the first time. Except for priests, ministers, and funeral directors, who do learn appropriate formulas as part of their professional training, most adult English speakers remain quite insecure of their own competence in this situation, and say such things to the bereaved as "I don't know what to say," or "Words can't begin to express my feelings."

In general, then, it appears that: (1) where complex ritual forms are prescribed, children are expected to be silent, but are often allowed to observe so they have the opportunity to acquire the appropriate behaviors informally; (2) when ritual forms are used but it is considered inappropriate for children to observe them, direct instruction is required at a later stage in their enculturation; (3) where there is more flexibility in the choice of language, but still strong feelings of propriety about the choices which are made, even adult members in the community may feel linguistically insecure, or feel that language is inadequate to express emotions.

Some aspects of acquisition of communicative competence occurring in later stages of life relate to membership in new communities which are restricted by age and/or health conditions. In the US these include retirement centers, assisted living facilities, nursing homes, and hospices. For example, different routines for greeting may be appropriate (*How are you?* often has other than phatic meaning when addressed to one who is gravely ill), and different topics are considered acceptable or taboo. Relationships are also defined differently when membership in a community cycles regularly with new arrivals and deaths. Adelman and Frey (1997) provide an exemplary study of a residential facility for victims of AIDS, including how new residents are socialized, how the community is sustained through regular instances of community loss, and what bereavement rituals have evolved.

The most difficult situations for speakers probably occur when change is in progress, where old rules no longer hold but new ones have not yet codified, and where rules are not explicit or are dependent on complex contextual conditions. Speakers are generally expected to acquire such rules informally, by observing others and abstracting the appropriate patterns; boundaries for correct behavior are more likely to be clearly marked when interaction is controlled formally.

Speech Play

One of the greatest influences the peer group has on the acquisition of communicative competence in many languages comes through various kinds of speech play. Some of these contribute directly to the development of the child's control of the linguistic code (lexicon, phonology, and grammar), while others include games which provide license for children to play roles not appropriate in non-play contexts, games which allow nonviolent modes for the expression of aggression and hostility, and games which reinforce cultural knowledge and values.

Regarding development of the linguistic code, Sanches and Kirshenblatt-Gimblett see

> the foci of children's speech play – that is, whether the individual form is mainly dominated by phonological, grammatical, semantic, or sociolinguistic structure – as reflecting an exercise in whatever part of the structure the child is currently mastering. (1971: 43)

Counting rhymes such as *One, two, buckle my shoe; Three, four, shut the door* are found in many languages, generally focusing on sound, as well as serving as mnemonic devices for learning the lexical sequence. Chinese children chant numbers as they walk or play, which involves a tonal as well as lexical sequence to be learned, and Bambara children in Mali recite puns which rely on alliterations and homophones (spoken or sung by boys, usually sung by girls), such as the following:

Kelen, kerekete kelen	(one, one snail)
Fila, filanin-ko	(two, a twins' business)
Saba, afala	(three, a snake-killer)
Nani, nanògòlen	(four, dirty sauce)

Using the same phonological processes, Bambara counting puns may also be maxims which convey traditional wisdom:

Duru, dugu tè sigi masakè kò	(five, there is no town without a chief)
Wòrò, hòronya nin kadi bè ye	(six, we all like freedom)

Speech play involving counting is widely used for turn selection in children's games. Cultural diffusion is evident in the form of some of these events: e.g., children in the Philippines and Korea recite numbers in Japanese, although they are generally perceived to be nonsense routines without meaning (reported by Ablanque and Park-Mun). Another selection game which has diffused is *paper, scissors, stone*, in which children chant rhythmically for three beats and then commit to a hand shape on the fourth which represents one of the three named objects and determines the order of play (scissors cuts paper, stone breaks scissors, and paper covers stone). Children in the islands of Visayan and Mindanao in the Philippines call this event *dyangkingkoy*, which has no referential meaning for them (Ablanque).

Another form of speech play contributing to both phonology and lexicon is practiced by deaf children, who tell stories (in sign) with words in alphabetical order. The game is complicated by older children, and additional manual skill developed, by signing two different words simultaneously with the left and right hands.

Some play is designed to test verbal competence quite consciously, as in a Newar question and answer game, in which the respondent must answer quickly and in a form which rhymes with the question. A sing-song effect is created and hesitation disqualifies a participant. As in many other cases, such play is performance, and this test always has an audience. A similar pattern is found among African Americans, where the form given by the challenger must be appropriately rhymed by the person challenged.

Riddling is a common form of speech play in many communities. Among Quechua children this does not begin until near puberty, and then contributes to sexual socialization as well as language development. Isbell and Fernandez (1977) speculate such verbal play involves the exploration of ambiguous semantic categories, the development of metaphorical concepts and skills, and thus increased flexibility and creativity in language use.

Children's verbal play can yield information on a far broader scope of their socialization processes than just language development, and provides insights into the culture they are learning and the social structure of which they are a part. According to Bernstein, this is so because children's speech play influences organization of experience and behavior. It makes "the child sensitive to role and status and also to the customary relationships connecting and legitimizing the social positions within his peer group" (1960: 180). Adult ways of speaking may be practiced in make-believe roles, such as giving tea parties and offering "One lump or two," or playing school and assuming the mannerisms and speech of teacher and principal.

Insults yield particularly valuable cultural information, because a comment on cultural values is always one of their defining features. Mitchell-Kernan and Kernan (1977) reported they were able to ascertain that children had acquired particular cultural values by examining their insults. They ranked the strength of the insult, and thus the strength of the cultural value underlying it, by analyzing the nature of the response to that insult in comparison with others (a procedure that would work for adult insults as well). In a cross-cultural comparison of insults, for instance, Mitchell-Kernan and Kernan find African American children insulting primarily with comments on appearance and intellectual capacity (e.g. accusing others of being babies), while the most serious insult for Samoan children is a comment on generosity. In Korea, children's insults generally concern the honor of the family name (directed at mother first, then father); illegitimacy is often suggested, and the likelihood that the family achieved its status by cheating.

Insults are just one type of verbal contest used by children. Abrahams describes one of their general functions as "trying-on" mature roles within the safe confines of the peer group while arming the children with verbal weapons which would be useful in adult life. Among African Americans, these contests include categories labeled *rapping* (often competitive repartee between male and female), *shucking* and *jiving* (flattering and cajoling), *signifying* (goading), and *dissing* (putting down) (see Johnson 2000, especially pp. 152–5).

A verbal contest unique to young (eight- to eleven-year-old) African American females is *stepping* (organized competitive "spelling," foot stepping, and hand clapping), in which the body is used to iconically represent the shape of letters, following the spelling *M I Crooked Letter Crooked Letter I Crooked Letter Crooked Letter I Hump Back Hump Back I* for "Mississippi." Skilled performers are called *kookalaters* (< crooked letter). Gilmore (1981) reports that *stepping* was banned from the public schools in Philadelphia at one time because of its frequent sexual explicitness, but in some communities teams have been organized to put on public performances. One version given by Gilmore is as follows:

M	for the money
I	if ya give it to me
S	sock it (to me)
S	sock it
I	if I buy it from you
S	sock it
S	sock it
I	if I take it from you
P	pump it
P	push it
I	: : :

The following is an example of *playing the dozens*, another African American male verbal contest in which insults typically involve obscene reference to the addressee's mother:

I fucked your mother from house to house
she thought my dick was Mighty Mouse. (Hannerz 1969: 130)

While some may be simple one liners (e.g. "Your mother smokes a pipe," or even just "Your mother"), the more elaborate ones rhyme. Very similar is the *verbal dueling* of Turkish boys. One example reported by Dundes, Leach, and Özkök (1972: 144–5) begins with an insult:

Ananın amı.
[mother-your cunt-her]
(Your mother's cunt.)

The verbal retort must rhyme, as:

Babamın kıllı damı.
[father-my hairy roof-his]
(My father's hairy roof.)

Although it rhymes, the response is not considered a very successful one, which may warrant a further rhymed counterattack:

Uyduramadın yancığına
[Make-up-couldn't-you side-its-to-of-it]
(You didn't make a very good rhyme.)

Bin devenin kancığına
[ride camel's female-to]
(You ride a female camel.)

East Javanese children also quarrel using rhymes, although the content of theirs is seldom vulgar. This event may be between two individuals, but more often is between two groups of children. It is not uncommon for the duel to begin with:

Kambang ecèng-ecèng,	(Eceng-eceng flowers,
Kembangé suradadu,	The flowers of soldiers,
Beyèn rèntèng-rèntèng,	We used to walk hand in hand,
Saiki ngajak satru.	But now we become enemies.)

The point is to throw as many insulting rhymes as possible at the opponent, and strict turn-taking is not observed. Delays occur when one group discusses what rhyme to say next or waits for prompting from older children or relatives. When children become more and more excited, they start to use ordinary language (no rhymes), but rarely end in a physical fight.

A clear example of speech play reinforcing cultural knowledge and values is found in Saudi Arabia, where preschool boys or girls participate in competitive individual and group recitation of Quranic verses. When in a group, children raise their voices over others if they know the verse well and mumble along if they do not; each child tries to recite verses the others do not know. The event is not considered prayer because it is not accompanied by other acts required in prayer. But it is considered religious training and, additionally, practice in Classical Arabic as a kind of reading-readiness exercise. Again, the audience is an important factor in this play-performance, which in this case includes attentive and approving adults.

Another example comes from China, where traditional social roles are still transmitted to children in this mode. In the following pattern (which may be extended to great length), P1 is an older child or adult and P2 is two or three years of age. The young child is only required to repeat *li tou* 'inside sits' (prompted by P1 as needed) and provide an address term, while the older participant supplies the role function and rhyme (Jin).

P1   *Ji dan ji dan ke ke,*
       (Egg egg shell,)
P2   *Li tou zuo yige ge-ge.*
       (Inside sits a brother.)
P1   *Ge-ge chu lai mai cai.*
       (Brother comes out to buy things.)

P2   *Li tou zuo yige nai-nai.*
      (Inside sits a grandmother.)
P1   *Nai-nai chu lai shao xiang.*
      (Grandmother comes out to light incense.)
P2   *Li tou zuo yige gu-niang.*
      (Inside sits a girl.)
P1   *Gu-niang chu lai dian deng.*
      (The girl comes out to light a candle.)

One final example comes from Venezuela, where children in the preschool educational program are taught a game called *Matare*. The game begins when two children choose a name to call another child. They start by calling out an "ugly" name, which other children sing that they won't accept, and continue in this manner until a "good" name is picked and accepted by the group. Conveyed are cultural notions of the status of different occupations and appropriate sex roles: e.g., only boys can be called a name like 'shoemaker' and 'carpenter,' and only girls one like 'servant' and 'cook.'

Formal Education

In considering the place of formal education in children's acquisition of communicative competence, ethnographers are primarily concerned with what patterns of speaking are developed and used primarily as a consequence of schooling.

To begin with, some speech events are unique to the context of school. One of the first performance routines learned by kindergarten students in the United States is *Show and Tell*, which is usually considered a major step toward more complex public speaking, and has several new rules for appropriate speaking which are either learned from observing others or through explicit correction of errors (kindergarten teachers in training are given very explicit instruction in how to teach this routine to children):

1   Appropriate topics are limited by other children's interest and the teacher's sense of propriety. Part of developing competence is learning what *not* to tell, and how to leave out details of a lengthy narrative.
2   Explicit and decontextualized language is encouraged, with the teacher and other children making a conscious effort to elicit more facts with WH-questions or prompting if too much shared information is being assumed.
3   Nonverbal behavior is also prescribed, with children told to stand on both feet, face their audience, and take their hand from in front of their mouth.

Other classroom-specific communicative phenomena may be rigid turn-taking, with a raised hand to request a turn; spatial arrangement, with children seated in rows of desks or around tables; and peer interaction which is initiated and controlled by an adult.

In educational programs where the language of instruction is essentially the same code which the children have learned at home, the oral language development which takes place through formal education is primarily new vocabulary, new rules for speaking, practice in interpretation and use of a more formal style, and skills for public performance. Most emphasis is placed on acquiring a new channel of communication (writing), and on the skills and conventions involved in its interpretation and use. At the earliest stages of schooling, this includes letter or character formation, directionality, and locating what is considered the top and front of a book. (All of these conventions are of course arbitrary, and relative to which writing system is being learned.) Some pictorial conventions of nonverbal communication are also taught at this level for the interpretation of accompanying illustrations (e.g., balloons around words indicate dialogue, elongated spots on the face means that the person is crying, etc.).

In many speech communities formal education is conducted in a linguistic code quite different from the one children have acquired at home, but it is still true that the development of communicative competence in these settings emphasizes a formal style, reading and writing skills, and ways of speaking often unique to the school. Educational anthropologists have focused more on traditional education than formal schooling, but the comparative studies that do exist suggest there may be more commonality cross-nationally in ways of using language in this cultural domain than in any other, in large part because formal schooling in most of the world today stems from the same European traditions (with Quranic schools in Africa and the Middle East, or monastic schools in Tibet, being notable exceptions). This leads to differential discontinuity in ways of speaking at home versus school, and an important potential area for more ethnographic research.

Formal education is carried out largely through the medium of language, and the children who succeed are those who "learn how to learn" through abstract linguistically mediated instruction. Scribner and Cole (1973) suggest that the linguistic activities, especially the use of decontextualized language, lead to cognitive skills of abstraction and generalization which are rarely found among traditionally educated individuals. Western-type formal schooling, including the learning of reading and writing, may thus result in the development of qualitatively different cognitive abilities from those usually found in traditional societies. Ethnographers should be aware of and sensitive to this possibility in their research.

Emphasis on writing begins on school entry in most parts of the world, including the development of physical and artistic skills for producing written forms: spelling and penmanship are considered critical subjects in most Latin American schools; traditional Chinese and Japanese education values competence in calligraphy; and grading in Australian schools is normally based exclusively on written work, with frequent oral contributions often penalized. (See Michaels 1987 and Rafoth and Rubin 1988 for ethnographic studies on the development of writing, and Prior 1998 for an extensive treatment of writing in contexts of extended acquisition.)

Oral language competence is also stressed in some societies, but this often means competence in reciting what was written by others; Yugoslavian (Serbian) elementary school students reportedly must memorize great quantities of poetry, and are then graded on the fluency, smoothness, and dramatic appropriateness of their oral interpretation to the class; and traditional Chinese education based on Confucian traditions emphasized memorization and recitation of the Four Books, with the target civil service examination measuring the same competence.

Questions and answers occur in almost all classrooms of the world, in all languages, but they have quite differing functions. Teachers most commonly ask questions (sometimes called "display questions") to test student knowledge rather than to gain information on the ostensible topic, since the "right" answer is already prescribed. Former students from such diverse countries as Taiwan, Germany, and Indonesia report being highly praised if they made the expected response, but reprimanded for not being diligent enough if they did not. Learning not to volunteer answers may be learning to avoid potential reprimands, but may also be learning to be properly humble in not seeking attention or praise. That this is learned behavior is illustrated by the fact that in Japanese elementary schools children appear to be quite willing to answer questions before they are called on, but few students volunteer answers by the high school level. Teachers from the English speech community often think students from other cultures do not volunteer answers because they are "shy," but this is an ethnocentric interpretation (see Liu 2001). Asian students in classes with English speakers generally consider their classmates who do volunteer freely as being rude, inconsiderate of the teacher, and wasting class time. Latin American students frequently misinterpret the relative informality in US classrooms as lack of teacher disciplinary control, particularly at the junior high and high school levels, which accounts for teachers' return misinterpretation of their behavior as "undisciplined."

Although it is seldom listed as such, one important function of language for students in academic contexts is to convey a "proper attitude" toward school. A list of behaviors related to school success which Wallat (1981) extracted from the literature includes:

Speak positively to others.
Make positive comments to the teacher.

Speak positively about academic materials.
Answer or try to answer questions.
Initiate contacts about work assignments.

Even more indicators of "proper attitude" that she lists involve nonverbal communicative behaviors, including:

Sit up straight.
Smile at the teacher.
Use your body to show attention.
Use your body, or face, to show self-control.
Nod in agreement as the teacher speaks.

Because schools are major socializing institutions for the society in which they function, they generally transmit the values and beliefs of those who control them. The choice of language for education is a major consideration in multilingual contexts, and reflects the power structure in the country, attitudes toward group identities, and educational philosophy and priorities. Japan was forced to change its basic curricular framework after World War II to the American pattern as "progressive" educational principles were imposed along with military occupation, but with return to Japanese control, methods again changed from "learning by doing" to renewed heavy emphasis on memorization, repetition, and reading and responding in unison. Even educational practices of long standing may be changed as part of the process of social revolution, however, as evidenced by successful attempts to institute educational change in the People's Republic of China and in Turkey. The attempt in Turkey included even changing the name of the institution itself from *mektep*, which designated the traditional Quranic school, to *okul*, an invented term based on *oku-* 'to read.' However the curriculum is designed and whatever the methods of instruction, language constitutes the center of formal education, as both medium and object of instruction.

Multilingual Contexts

Children in multilingual speech communities must, in addition to learning multiple language codes, acquire skills in switching between or among them and more complex contextual rules for appropriate usage.

One of the earliest ethnographic studies of children in a bilingual community was Barker's (1947) research in Tucson, Arizona. The situation was quite typical of the southwestern United States at that time, with parents using Spanish with children at home, and children learning English at school and using it in formal relations. While Spanish continued to be used for close relationships and ceremonial relationships in the adult community, code-switching was common for informal relationships among younger bilinguals. A major shift in patterns of usage seems to have been emerging in recent years: because of bilingual education, many children have also been acquiring a formal variety of Spanish along with literacy in the process of formal instruction. (It will be interesting to see whether the legal suppression of bilingual education in Arizona and some other regions will reverse this trend.) Also, the use of code-switching in informal interaction is now common for older as well as younger speakers.

While it is usual for children to learn the official (H) language as a second language in school, in some speech communities it is actually acquired first in the home, and children learn to speak the indigenous language (L) when they are older. This phenomenon has been reported by Rensch (1977) for children in Oaxaca who first learn Spanish and then Chontal, by Tabouret-Keller (1972) for children who learn French before their patois, and by Thompson (1971) for Mexican American children who learn English before Spanish.

The age at which children can functionally differentiate codes depends to a great extent on the context of acquisition, but competence to switch appropriately according to the linguistic competence of the addressee is evident at the age of two (Genesee et al. 1996), and by situation or setting soon after. Switching by topic, or by the role-relationship between speakers other than language of the addressee, comes at a later stage in development. The degree of physical difference associated with language use, or even dress, may be a major factor. For example, Shorrab was given the following report by parents of a five-year-old Arabic-English bilingual child:

> She is capable of making a distinction between people who speak English and those who speak Arabic. In nursery school she met a girl whom she was apparently able to tell was not an Arab, so she addressed her in English, but the child, who was of Polish ancestry, did not respond. Our daughter switched to Arabic hoping that the girl would communicate with her. (1986: 81)

In Taiwan, even toddlers who knew only one word of English (*Hi*) identified me immediately as someone appropriate to say it to; on the other hand, Spanish-speaking six-year-olds in Texas refused to use Spanish with a Mexican American researcher until he took off his coat and tie.

Research on multilingual contexts typically includes consideration of language in relation to acculturation as well as enculturation phenomena, and often includes children across a range of age groups. Three books on Spanish-English speech communities in the US provide good exemplars of methods which characterize an ethnographic approach to socialization: Torres (1997) and Zentella (1997) on Puerto Ricans in the New York City area, and

Valdés (1996) on immigrants from Mexico in a border community near El Paso, Texas. All three studies involve intensive long-term investigation, collection of data through participant observation of naturally occurring situations and events, consideration of socioeconomic and political contexts for interpretation of language use, inclusion of rich detail that enables readers to hear the "voices" being represented, and relation of findings to social problems and to needs for social change. Questions addressed by Torres include what attitudes are held, how narratives relate to community ideologies, and how both are realized in patterns and content of language use; Zentella queries the nature of acquisition processes for multilingual communicative competence and the variable distribution of proficiencies across domains and time. A general research question in Valdés' research is how English language and literacy skills of children develop outside the school setting, and in her book she explores issues which provide insights into the immigrant experience.

Other potentially interesting questions include which language multilingual parents choose to use with their children, which language children use with their siblings and peers, children's attitudes toward the different codes, and the different functions assigned to each. These are particularly relevant to issues of language maintenance and shift (discussed in chapter 6).

Children's Beliefs about Language

Children themselves often have definite ideas about the nature of language, how it is learned, and how it is used, but while children have been frequent objects of observation by ethnographers, they are seldom interviewed. The probable reason for this is expressed in a quote from Jill E. Korbin, an anthropologist at Case Western Reserve University:

> Even though the anthropological emphasis has been "to grasp the native's point of view," there's been a bias against children, who are seen as less well-informed about their own cultures. (Ruark 2000)

There are exceptions, to be sure, and these have been very informative. For example, children can often be observed talking to dolls, animals, and infants, but do they believe their addressees can understand them? There are undoubtedly different beliefs underlying similar behavior depending on cultural experiences, just as there are for adults. When Miller (1970) asked Pima children "Do animals have a language?" and "Do they understand our language?" the age distribution of affirmative responses was particularly interesting. Of the children under eight, 75 percent believed animals have a language but none thought they understood ours; 90 percent of the ten-year-olds believed animals had a language and 70 percent that they understood ours; and the eleven-year-olds responded with 100 percent affirmative answers to animals understanding our language. Since much of the Pima folklore contains animal characters who possess speech, the increasing belief in this capacity probably reflects learning of the traditional stories of the tribe. (It would be very interesting to know to what extent this belief is retained in older children and among adults.)

Young children's beliefs concerning the ability of infants to talk might be particularly interesting to explore because of their intermediate status, but we cannot assume that the answers even of young children will always be truthful. Since they have already acquired some communicative strategies, they may know how to use the intermediate role as interpreters to their advantage. One three-year-old who was babbling with her baby sister was asked what the infant was saying, and she responded, "She says she wants ice cream." Of course both were rewarded. At the age of four, my own daughter carefully trained her younger brother among his first phrases to say, "I did it," whenever something was broken.

Clearly, ethnographers who study the acquisition of communicative competence should not neglect to elicit the perceptions of the children themselves. Procedures should certainly include interviews, but also role plays, playback of videotaped events to decrease the level of abstraction and aid recall, and a variety of other means. When children are informants and collaborators in research, of course, extraordinary care must be taken to obtain "informed consent" and avoid exploitation.

8

Politeness, Power, and Politics

The communicative enactment of politeness, power, and politics has been of major interest to philosophers and social scientists since long before linguistics was recognized as a field of scholarship, and as an intersection of language and other sociocultural processes it has provided a focus for theorizing and investigation within anthropological linguistics in recent years. An important conceptual development in linking the relevant phenomena came with Brown and Gilman's (1960) account of "politeness" as essentially involving two dimensions: power and solidarity. Another important concept is that of "face," including the particular positions which individuals assume and portray in a social hierarchy (e.g. Goffman 1967). We have already considered phenomena related to these constructs in our discussions of varieties of language associated with social class, with status and role, and with role-relationships (Chapter 3), and with cross-cultural communication (Chapter 5). Here we will focus primarily on the power dimension of politeness, and on how patterns of language use relate to political factors.

The politeness dimension of the "power semantic" identified by Brown and Gilman (1960) applied specifically to rules for selection of second person pronouns of address, such as *tu* versus *vous* in French, *du* versus *Sie* in German, or *tu* versus *Usted* in Spanish (symbolized as T versus V). Reciprocal use of either pronoun in the pair usually signals symmetrical power, or a relatively equal placement of the participants on a hierarchical scale of social position: mutual use of "familiar" T additionally signals closeness or solidarity, and mutual use of "polite" V signals distance or deference. Asymmetrical use of pronouns of address (one participant addressing the other as T and receiving V in return) signals unequal status, with the recipient of V recognized as being at a higher level – and thus having more power. *Unmarked* usage of reciprocal T:T would be in a conversation between friends, and of reciprocal V:V between professional colleagues who are not well acquainted, while asymmetrical T:V would be unmarked between such relatively powerful–powerless dyads as teacher–student, doctor–patient, governor–

governed, and employer–employee. The model has been extended to other linguistic structures and applied to a variety of world languages. An example is the fictive use of kinship terms in Chinese (Pan and Zhang 2001), in which the encoding of power relationships is shown by their being addressed more frequently to females than to males, and to people of lower social status (cf. the similar patterning of the use of first name versus title plus last name in English). *Marked* departures from these norms are often metaphorical, or reflective/constitutive of wider social change (as discussed in chapters 2 and 3).

The extended theory of politeness developed by Brown and Levinson (1987) also relates to power, predicting that the relative power of participants (interacting with social distance, strength of imposition, and context-dependent phenomena) will influence the nature of interaction strategies which are employed. In cases of asymmetrical exchanges, participants with more power will tend to use more politeness strategies which emphasize involvement and solidarity, while participants with less power will tend to use more strategies emphasizing distance and deference.

Acquisition of this dimension of communicative competence is in part socialization to the political structure of a society. As expressed by Mesthrie:

> The mastery of the rules of politeness, especially the ability to fine-tune one's language according to the interlocutor and other aspects of the context, presupposes a (subconscious) acknowledgement of the sociopolitical hierarchy. (2000: 345)

Mesthrie adds this quote from Pierre Bourdieu:

> the concessions of politeness are always political concessions. (1977: 95)

Language and Politics

The broad definition of "politics" which I adopt here includes not only "theory and practice of government" but also the theory and institutionalized social practice of other domains that "involve power, authority or influence, and [are] capable of manipulation" (*Encarta World English Dictionary* 1999). Relevant social domains include religion, education, commerce, medicine, and law. Some indication of the scope of issues to which this area of language study is potentially applicable can be found in the news we read every day in the newspapers or hear on radio and television. A short list ranges across ethnic warfare in Eastern Europe, Africa, and Southeast Asia; reconfiguration of political boundaries; quality of education; global environmental concerns;

international trade agreements and conflicts; impact of political rhetoric; sex discrimination; minority problems and rights; incidents of medical malpractice; and criminal investigations. While there is disagreement on the theoretical framework which should be adopted for study, and on which methods should be used for data collection and interpretation, there is general agreement that social problems need to be addressed and there is a general commitment on the part of linguists to apply scholarship to the betterment of the human condition.

Popular awareness of language differences has long had political consequences, as evidenced in the *shibboleth* versus *sibboleth* test for passage through warring lines which was recorded in the Old Testament (cited in chapter 3). Similarly, language has long played a political role in the execution of power. Although linguistics as a recognized discipline is relatively young, "the systematic study of language" has been applied to political ends throughout history. Early linguistic efforts in bilingual lexicography and grammatical description primarily served the communication needs of politically dominant or subjugated populations, such as the first bilingual texts from Ur (dating approximately 2500 BC) when Sumerians were being overwhelmed by Semitic speakers, or the grammars of Greek which served the language learning needs of Roman conquerors.

Political motivations for the application of linguistic knowledge have continued to modern times. The extensive European colonization of the sixteenth to nineteenth century brought widespread scholarly (as well as political) attention to the indigenous languages of the Americas, Africa, Asia, and the Pacific Islands. The first dictionaries and grammars of these languages were often for missionary purposes: language teaching and translation of confessor's manuals or Biblical texts for use with intended religious converts. The wordlists, grammatical patterns, and texts of American Indian languages which were collected by explorers, soldiers, and other individuals associated with US Western expansion were involved in part with the need of military personnel to communicate with scouts and captives. (Even if we disapprove of the political ends they sometimes served, this does not negate the scholarly value of these linguistic data, especially in cases where they form the only evidence for now-extinct languages.)

Many of the areas over which European colonial control was established during the sixteenth to nineteenth centuries became independent states by the end of the twentieth, and a number of indigenous tongues have taken on the status and functions of national languages. Linguists have had a direct role in the development of policies and practices related to nation-building through surveys of language distribution and use, standardization and graphization of previously unwritten languages, and language planning or modernization. In cases where indigenous languages were overrun and largely replaced by politically dominant languages, linguists have contributed to efforts for language salvage or revitalization (discussed further in Saville-Troike 2000).

Given the long history of application of linguistic knowledge to politically-charged spheres, it is somewhat surprising that "official" incorporation of social variables into at least a subset of theoretical perspectives has been so recent. Hymes (e.g. 1962) had a major leadership role in that process with his enunciation of the view that *language is first and foremost a socially situated cultural form*, and with his call for a synthesizing approach which would emphasize that recognition and understanding of much of linguistic form cannot be separated from how and why it is used. This step was followed by significant developments in variation theory (e.g. Labov 1966), systemic-functional linguistics (e.g. Halliday 1970), socially situated conversational analysis (e.g. Sacks, Schegloff, and Jefferson 1974), interactional sociolinguistics (e.g. Gumperz 1977), and critical linguistics (e.g. Kress and Hodge 1979). Each of those developments stresses the need to look at the larger sociopolitical contexts within which culturally situated language use takes place, claiming that those contexts may determine features of acquisition and use in ways that are not evident from a focus on language alone, and each stresses that without understanding *why* a language is being learned or used, it is impossible to provide a complete and valid interpretation of many significant aspects of language acquisition and performance.

Language and Social Theories

The ethnography of communication (and anthropological linguistics more generally) has been strongly influenced by three social theories: Functionalism, Interactionism, and Marxism. It is not possible to ignore any one of these and still present an adequate picture of the field, although a differing emphasis on one or another is perhaps inescapable in treating different domains. For example, in discussing basic terms and concepts, such as the interactions of language and culture, and of language and social organization, I emphasized a functionalist approach. This view holds that language is one of the integrated systems of society and culture, and that language reflects and functions in relation to social categories. I emphasized an interactional approach in discussing some of the variation in language which needs to be accounted for, such as that involved in establishing and expressing role-relationships, and in discussion of the acquisition of communicative competence. This view sees language as essentially an interactional construct, a dynamic factor in individuals' construction and realization of their social identity, and regards child language acquisition as central to socialization processes.

In discussions of power in communication, emphasis is frequently placed on critical approaches to discourse analysis and ethnography more generally, which have their roots in Marxist theory, and on the propositions that "language creates, sustains, and replicates fundamental inequalities in societies" (Mesthrie 2000: 317), that there are fundamental differences of interest between social groups, and that inequities in distribution of "linguistic capital" are related to sociopolitical exploitation and oppression. Language is viewed as "an instrument for consolidating and manipulating concepts and relationships in the area of power and control" (Fowler 1985: 61).

Philips (2000) contrasts anthropological perspectives on the relationship of language and power during the last century as differing in regard to where the locus of responsibility for the constitution of social reality is seen to lie; these perspectives correspond closely to the three social theories listed above. One view (essentially a strong version of the Sapir-Whorf Hypothesis) is that power resides in the structures of language itself, which is deterministic of perception and conceptualization. A second view is that power is created in the process of communicative interaction; within this view, there is divergence as to whether the force of agency is primarily related to social role or to discourse processes. A third view is that the locus of responsibility lies in historical processes of domination and subordination which include the nature and distribution of the political economy. Philips concludes that "All three [theoretical perspectives] are needed for a complete anthropological understanding of the relationship between language and power" (2000: 191).

Critical Discourse Analysis (CDA) differs from other approaches which are employed for socially contextualized language study in several important respects. These include the following characteristics (from Kress 1991):

1   [Critical] Discourse analysis is not an objective "value-free" science, but a socially committed activity with an acknowledged political, ideological, and ethical stance.
2   The choices which speakers and writers have in performing texts are always within structures of power and domination; "language always projects social relations and structures as wished by the participants, normally those of the more powerful participant" (p. 90).
3   [In contrast to the Saussurian notion of an arbitrary relation between linguistic signs and meanings, which most linguists accept:] Because linguistic signs are the result of social processes, "linguistic features *are never arbitrary conjuncts of form and meaning*" (p. 86; emphasis his).

Another basic difference which must be kept in mind is the definition of "discourse" itself. Within linguistics, this term usually refers to a connected unit of language beyond a single sentence. In CDA, however, discourse means "different ways of structuring areas of knowledge and social practices" or "systems of rules implicated in specific kinds of power relations" (Mesthrie 2000: 323). From this viewpoint, a *discourse community* is a group of people who share ways of thinking, believing, behaving, and using language which are embodied in particular social roles, to be compared with the more structuralist notion of *speech community* and the interactionist *community of practice* which were discussed in chapter 2.

CDA and the ethnography of communication are potentially compatible or at least complementary approaches to the study of language, but not necessarily so. From the ethnography of communication side, which generally favors bottom-up accounts of communicative phenomena (from observable performance to theoretical constructs), CDA may be "suspect" because it presupposes a particular social theory to explain communicative behavior and is too subjective in its interpretation (e.g., see critiques of CDA by Schegloff 1997 and Widdowson 1998). From a different perspective, some proponents of CDA criticize ethnographers of communication (and proponents of other approaches within sociolinguistics and anthropological linguistics) for their assumption that linguistic analysis *can* be "objective," for lack of reflexivity, and for lack of theoretical coherence (e.g., see Wetherell 1998 for a reply to Schegloff; see also Chouliaraki and Fairclough 1999). Another possible source of divergence is primary emphasis on society versus language; CDA "is primarily interested and motivated by pressing social issues, which it hopes to better understand through discourse analysis" (van Dijk 1993: 252). As stated above, my own view is that the CDA perspective on language and power, in particular, must be represented in any adequate accounts of societal functions and practices of power in language. At the same time, there is need for further understanding of the nature of language and, more broadly, human communication. Functionalist and interactionist perspectives are also fruitful to this end, and may help constrain or at least counterbalance the potential for theoretical bias. While ethnographic accounts are primarily descriptive, critical analysis can add a useful explanatory dimension which problematizes aspects of communication that might otherwise escape attention.

Linguistic Signs of Power

The most transparent linguistic signs of power are the lexical and morphological structures which are commonly employed in language to encode status and prestige, such as the use of titles and honorifics between or in reference to individuals with whom one is in an asymmetrical social relationship along an inferior-superior dimension. The social bases of power which are encoded are culture-specific, and discovering their identity and relative strength (as well as the nature of their instantiation in various aspects of communicative performance) is one of the goals of ethnographic investigation. These may include age, sex, genealogical connections, possession of material goods, social connections, physical strength, skin color, supernatural endowment, artistic talent, beauty, and spiritual or technical knowledge. A functionalist approach would hold that linguistic signs of power correlate with social values, organization, and stratification in the society that uses them, and that they influence perceptions and behaviors among individuals and groups. An interactional approach would hold that power is realized or co-constructed in such forms because some people have more control than others over the production of discourse, and that differential (and deferential) language forms help create and enact differential (and deferential) social status in the processes of communication. A critical approach would hold that the differential forms are a product of sociopolitical forces for domination and subordination, and that they function to justify and sustain inequities. Whatever the theoretical perspective, such linguistic forms are displays of power in that they index and acknowledge the capacity of some individuals, groups, and institutions in a society to control others. Failure to use such forms when they are expected can (legitimately) be interpreted as insults and/or speech acts of social resistance. Conversely, the contextually expected use of non-hierarchical forms communicates recognition of social equality or solidarity.

Other linguistic structures which encode power/powerlessness include voicing (active versus passive) and transitivity: the use of active voice in syntax typically attributes agency (and responsibility); use of passive voice or its equivalent usually does not. Similar linguistic attribution of responsibility is associated with the semantic roles for subjects and objects: for example, whether the grammatical subject of an event is an animate Agent, an inanimate Force, a Patient or Experiencer (e.g., see Fillmore 1968). Assignment of semantic role to grammatical subjects is usually a matter of voicing or verb selection, a stylistic alternative in language use which can be manipulated for ideological purposes. For example, the following statement was made by a prosecuting attorney who was accused of possible ethics violation in a murder case which resulted in a mistrial: "This case mistried because there was an accident made. It was just one of those things that happen" (*Arizona Daily Star*, July 9, 2001). His linguistic selection of Patient (*this case*) as subject of the first clause and existential (*there was*) plus underlying passive voice (*an accident was made*) in the second conveys not only lack of personal responsibility, but avoids all reference to human agency. The presiding judge in the ethics hearing ruled, "The court finds that there was no hiding of the report by Mr. Peasley," in which the power of agency is assigned ritually to the institutional *the court*, again with no personal responsibility, and the passivization and nominalization of the verb in an existential construction further remove the event from the category of intentional action.

Yet another linguistic device is expression of modality, or the speakers'/ writers' attitudes toward, or degree of confidence in, the truth of propositions they produce. In English, modality is often encoded by modal auxiliaries such as *may, shall, must,* or adverbials such as *certainly, unfortunately, obviously;* in Navajo modality is often encoded by enclitics such as -'*as* 'scornful disbelief' and -*da* 'wonderment' or discontinuous frames such as *doo xanii . . . da* 'contrariness to fact' (Young 1967); other languages have other means (e.g., see Hill and Irvine 1993). Modality has relevance to power in that "Frequent and confident judgments of validity, predictability, and (un)desirability are an important part of the practices by means of which claims to authority are articulated and legitimated authority is expressed" (Fowler 1985: 72–3). Conversely, the frequent use of "hedges" may be a mark of lack of power or control.

Linguistic signs of power are also common in other patterns of language use. These include nonverbal behavior, prosodic variables, politeness strategies related to involvement or solidarity versus independence or deference, form-function mapping in speech act production, discourse organization, and channel of transmission. Nonverbal signs of power might involve relative alignment in space, for instance: in some groups the more powerful would be literally elevated, while in others the more powerful may sit or recline while others stand, or be positioned in line according to rank; the depth of a bow or a hand-gesture (*wai*) may index the amount of power accorded to the addressee, and the relative depth in cases of reciprocity. Other nonverbal signs commonly involve eye gaze, gestures, posture, and proxemic orientation. The "body language" of powerlessness for Americans includes a deprecatory cough, giggle, head scratch, shoulder shrug, or foot shuffle.

Prosodic variables in production may contribute significantly to what is perceived as powerful or powerless speech in many communities, though this dimension of speech is often overlooked in research. A loud voice in English is often associated with power, for instance, although shift to low amplitude (especially with measured pace) is stereotypically employed in American films to heighten the portrayal of a powerful and threatening stance, and heroes are often the "strong, silent" type. Degree of aspiration following initial stops, rather than amplitude, is interpreted as forcefulness in Navajo. Another cross-cultural prosodic contrast may be found in the temporal pacing of question and answer sequences in Navajo and English. As reported in chapter 5, for Navajos (even if they are using the English language code), a time lag between question and answer demonstrates that due consideration has been given to the question. For non-Navajos, the same time lag is interpreted as indecisiveness and lack of power. One example of the political relevance of such factors comes from research by Walker (1985) on interpretation of the timing of responses in US legal proceedings: witnesses who pause before answering a lawyer's question are less likely to be believed. This is one of a growing body of findings that indicates how linguistic and paralinguistic behavior can influence the outcome of trials. Because there are differences in these variables as produced by women or members of some minority speech communities, there is a clear possibility of systematic discrimination along this dimension.

An illustration of power and solidarity differentials in politeness strategies and form-function mapping may be found in how the same English-speaking individual might request money from a friend, an elder relative, or an employer. With a friend, the borrower would probably emphasize equality and solidarity, perhaps addressing the friend as "pal" and relating the need for money to shared experience; with an older relative, the borrower would probably use strategies of deference and solidarity, using a kinship term of respect and alluding to family responsibility and dependence; and with an employer, the borrower would probably use strategies of deference and independence, including a title in address, a more formal register, and discussion of repayment.

Form-function mapping can often be examined on the dimension of the relative strength or intensity of an utterance. For example, a speech act intended to function as a directive could be enacted in the following forms by individuals who are in decreasing positions of power:

1 demand
2 request
3 suggestion
4 hint
5 entreaty

A person with less power in an asymmetrical relationship does not give orders to a person with more, and a person with more power does not beg. Other speech acts may also be strongly constrained by relative power, such as who performs apologies, who grants permission, who offers advice or excuses, and who is entitled to compliment whom about what: a student who compliments a professor, an employee who compliments an employer, or an enlisted person who compliments a military officer, for instance, may risk some embarrassment or suspicion of motives from the recipient (and the indelicate accusation from peers of "sucking up"). Similar considerations of relative power which are encoded in some speech acts operate on a global level, and they account in part for the official US government expressions of "regret" rather than "apology" when its submarine rammed a Japanese fishing vessel and its reconnaissance airplane collided with a Chinese jet fighter (two events which occurred in 2001) – and in the latter case, the nuance of official Chinese interpretation of the expression as an apology.

Also at a pragmatic level are considerations of whether a speaker has been invested with the societal power to utter some performatives at all (except in a joking key), such as "You're fired", "I hereby declare you . . . ," etc. Still other speech acts are in themselves also performances of power, including threats and acts of symbolic aggression or verbal violence. So, too, are coercive acts which force another to speak, mute expression, or compel silence.

The rights and responsibilities of individuals and groups to participate actively in certain events is tightly constrained by who has been accorded the prerequisite power by such processes as licensure, ordination, election, or birth. One example of power which is enacted in a speech event restricted by sex is the ritual wailing performed by Warao women at funerals, although they are excluded from all other forms of public discourse (Briggs 1992). The wailing entails chastisement and blame for the death of loved ones because of people who led the loved ones into bad behavior or threatened them. Potential performance of the event controls behavior of men in the community because of the threat of being the subject of chastisement in the wailing ritual, which can result in social punishment by the community and even banishment. Because of the high death rate in the group and the prominence of this event, women have an exceptionally high level of moral authority among the Warao.

Frequently described signs of power at the level of discourse organization include authority to allocate turns at talk (e.g. by teachers in classrooms, judges in courts, chairpersons of committees, or military officers), to interrupt, to determine topic continuation or switch, and to officially evaluate the contribution of others to a communicative interaction. Again looking at differences according to sex, there is a common perception that women orient more to affective topics and functions and men more to referential ones, but there is limited empirical support for this claim. Itakura (2001) develops an analytical model for investigating conversational dominance largely as a pattern of asymmetry in controlling or complying actions between participants. She relates changing patterns in male–female conversation in Japanese to the changing status of women in that society.

Also at the level of discourse organization are strategies for establishing and mitigating inclusive and oppositional relationships. For example, Johnson (1994) analyzes the occurrence of *we* in a binational conference which was convened near the US-Mexico border. From a linguistic viewpoint, *we* has the deictic function of indexing people in relation to contexts. From a political viewpoint, *we* is an involvement strategy which ranges in meaning in this instance from inclusive, as present audience and people in the border region, to oppositional (a component of *we-they*) indexing community-based action versus federal inaction, to exclusive in using only *they* in reference to *maquiladoras* (US-owned industries located in Mexico), emphasizing conflicts between "them" and "us" over environmental issues. Other discourse strategies include storytelling (e.g. personal experiences, giving plausible details), quoting credible sources or experts, and structural emphasis of "their" negative actions (van Dijk 1993: 264).

Authority is also accorded differentially to channels of communication, with writing often given more weight than speech. In most literate societies, for instance, many contracts must be in written form to be considered legally binding, ranging from transfer of property, to conditions of employment, to guarantee of product quality, to distribution of estates after death. Even traditionally oral ritual events such as taking oaths of office and exchanging marriage vows are typically validated by the presence of a religious text on which to swear and/or subsequent signatures on a written covenant. The time depth of such practices is suggested by the fact that the earliest wedding contract which has been discovered was written in cuneiform script. Weight given the written word is also evident in the sincerity that is attributed to published acknowledgment of deeds or events, as opposed to what individuals or governments say orally. For example, the Japanese government angered South Korea, China, and other Asian neighbors by refusing their demands to revise its school history texts to include information on acts of aggression committed against these countries in World War II.

The power accorded writing over speech may be due in part to its permanence and accessibility to confirmation by others, but there is also a common acceptance of some intrinsic power in the written word. Descriptive linguists vainly try to convince the laity that a word is not "right" or "wrong" because "it says so in the dictionary," and teachers who attempt to develop students' critical reading and thinking skills struggle with students' "proof" that "it says so in the book."

Acknowledgment of power in language can also be found in moves to curb it. Legal recognition of "verbal abuse" as a criminal offense in some countries highlights both the social acknowledgment that language can indeed hurt people, and the perceived limits of legitimate linguistic power in some relationships. Under most scrutiny in the US are those situations where members of a group which is culturally valued but physically weak (such as the elderly or children) are berated by caretakers.

Linguistic Performances of Power

Power is not only *displayed* through language; it is often *achieved* through language. Some of the functions of language which may be included in this category are social control, influencing feelings and shaping thought, determining access to knowledge, and otherwise institutionalizing discrimination. At a macrosocietal level, some of these functions are enacted in official or unofficial policies which privilege some languages or varieties of language over others, and thus privilege their speakers.

Social control

The realization of social control may be seen in ritual communication. In religious and magical usage, some words and speech acts are believed to have supernatural power and thus embody strong control functions in their own right, often including those which constitute blessings, curses, and charms. Such belief explains in part why sacred or archaic languages rather than vernaculars are employed in many religious rituals, and why some religious and magical texts must be recreated in exactly the same form for each performance.

When any speech event is formalized, there are fewer options open to its participants. As discussed in chapter 2, Bloch (1974) and others claim that in societies where there is more emphasis on ritual events, more direct social control is exerted than in societies where there is less emphasis on ritual. This point is relevant to the study of speech communities in their administrative domains, as well as in religious and other ceremonial areas. The functions of ritual rhetorical genres on Sumba Island, Indonesia, for instance, include creating and displaying authority as well as ratifying the power of others (Keane 1997; Kuipers 1998), and rhetorical strategies in Quechua sermons create influence for the priest and maintain social control of the congregation (Howard-Malverde 1998). The heavy patterning of ritual discourse also extends into other domains where speaker goals include construction and maintenance of system and order, such as teachers' vested authority in school classrooms to suppress student speech and control speaking rights. Prescribed rules of address and privileged efficacy ascribed to speech acts according to hierarchical rank are essential to the rigid system of control required for the operation of military organizations (where even relaxation of rules may require a speech act (e.g. "at ease") to license).

Suppression of speech as a means of social control in a larger context is illustrated by Berman (1998), where she claims it has greatly contributed to the successive ascendence of absolute rulers in Java. She further relates patterns of speech and rules for interaction which are used (and accepted) by Javanese women as contributing to their low position in the social hierarchy. These include many of the potential linguistic displays of power (or powerlessness) discussed above, such as lexical elements (adverbial time markers), nonverbal features (pauses, vocal noises, intonational contours), and discourse organization (code-switching and style-shifting, reported speech, text boundary indexicals). Berman illustrates a critical approach to language research and application in both her preface and her conclusion:

> my intention is that the people of Indonesia recognize how they have contributed to these abuses and power, and that their everyday language practices are essential sites for political and social reform. (p. v)

Language in Javanese contexts is anything but neutral, and participation and the varying degrees to which it is accomplished are socially charged, highly meaningful actions. Linguistic analyses must combine discourse processes with social processes to remove "the mask" that conceals the complex and politically charged dimensions underlying theories of person, meaning, and social action. (p. 220)

Some of the most socially important research has been conducted on events in legal and medical settings, such as that by Walker (1985) which was mentioned above. It has generally focused on the power relationships that exist in them, and on issues of justice or equity in the delivery of social services. O'Barr (1982), for instance, reports how different verbal strategies may influence jury decisions about credibility; Wodak-Engel (1984) describes how social class differences in rules for speaking lead to discrimination against working-class defendants; and Conley and O'Barr (1990) and Gibbons (1994) include documentation of how differences in narrative organization and other usage patterns create problems in courtroom communication which disadvantage particular social groups. Grimshaw summarizes the implications of similar discourse phenomena in the "powerfulness-powerlessness" domain of *control*:

> Courtroom studies show that witnesses who produce powerful speech, epitomized by assured affirmative or negative responses to questions ("yes" or "no"), are seen as more credible than those who employ hedges, hesitation forms, polite forms, question intonation, tag questions ("You know about tag questions, don't you?"), and intensifiers. Not surprisingly, control attempts by actors who speak with assertive assurance are most likely to be successful. (2000: 51)

Looking at other ways in which control is exerted in legal proceedings, research also shows how the way in which lawyers phrase questions to eyewitnesses leads them to different recollections and testimony. For instance, Shuy (1995) reports that when eyewitnesses are asked how fast a car was going when it "smashed" into another car, they estimate a speed of ten miles an hour faster than when they are asked how fast the car was going when it "ran" into the other car (Loftus 1979), and when eyewitnesses are asked if they saw "the broken glass" at the accident (with the definite article *the*), many agree that they did even though there was no broken glass present. This contrasts with their recollection when they are asked if they saw "any glass" at the accident (with the indefinite determiner *any*). Judicial control factors include determining turn-taking and speaking rights in the courtroom, giving directives about what speech and other evidence is to be included or excluded from the trial record, and wording and sequencing instructions to a jury.

Jacquemet (1996) provides analysis of judges' linguistic power in Italian courts, focusing on a set of trials which prominently featured *pentiti*, informants who typically receive immunity from prosecution in exchange for their testimony. The courtroom data include code-switching among Standard Italian, Neapolitan, and the rural Campanian variety; the judges exert control by adjusting the content of witnesses' remarks as they recast Neapolitan and Campanian utterances into Standard Italian "for the record." In these cases, multilingualism in the events gives judges more discretionary power and allows them to provide greater protection for the informants. In other multilingual contexts, the judge's power to make linguistic judgments may result in blatant discrimination. For instance, in *US v. Mendoza-Cepeda* (No. 00-3116, 8th Circuit, May 18, 2001), the judge decreed that "Since the officers did not intimidate or make any promises to the defendant, the offficers' determination that the defendant voluntarily consented to the search was reasonable even though defendant spoke no English" (example from C. Thomas Mason).

There is some danger of being overly simplistic in data collection and interpretation, of course. The power dimension is in large part a factor of the social role-relationship that participants bring with them to an encounter, but as is demonstrated in the case of medical encounters (e.g. Treichler et al. 1984; Ainsworth-Vaughn 1994, 1998), it is also a dynamic co-constructed product of interaction. In contrast to some analyses which focus only on powerful doctor questions and powerless patient answers, for instance, Ainsworth-Vaughn describes complex events which include many other conversational features in which

> patient and physician perform an intricate dance of discourse moves with multiple possible meanings, rather than filling simple questioner-questionee roles. Both participants propose to exercise power (control over information, the emerging discourse, and future actions), and both defer to one another by mitigating their attempts. (1994: 195)

Even with consideration of such complexities, however, Ainsworth-Vaughn does not deny the power asymmetries in such encounters, nor claim equality in discourse control.

Also in the domain of medicine, early sociolinguistic research on doctor–patient communication by Skopek (1975) documents miscommunication that could result in misdiagnosis or mistreatment because of differences in power, gender, ethnicity, and social class. Continued work in this area (e.g. Wodak 1996) highlights additional problems in medical communication and suggests changes in training procedures and other remediation to effect changes in discourse practices. A review of Wodak's book by Norman Fairclough from the perspective of critical social research attests to the potential political impact of sociolinguistic intervention, while adding a cautionary note:

> "Disorders of discourse" – practices that constitute "barriers to communication" – can be subjected to critique, and critique can lead to the suggestion of different practices. Such changes in discourse may contribute to changes in the "structures of organization". However, in the absence of such structural changes, changes in the discourse may actually result in more subtle, and thus more effective, forms of domination. (1999: 605)

Literacy, or lack thereof, may also be used as a powerful device for social control. Literacy tests for access to voting rights were used in the American South until the 1950s to disenfranchise the majority African American population, who had less access to good schools because of legal racial segregation.

Influencing thought

The ideological functions of language are clearly realized in such domains as news reporting, advertising, politics, and religion. Trew's (e.g. 1982) analysis of linguistic form and political ideology in news reporting, for instance, shows a clear potential for emotive vocabulary selection, sentence structure, content inclusion or exclusion, and metaphorical usage in news articles and editorials to shape public perception and sentiment. Trew presents news accounts of events at the end of the 1977 Notting Hill Carnival in London as reported by two newspapers which represent different ideologies: the *Sun*, which has no formal affiliation with a political party, and the *Morning Star*, which is a publication of the Communist Party of Great Britain. The event which both report was a clash between revelers and police. The ideological contrast is most obviously apparent in terms selected for reference to the revelers, with the *Sun* using such phrases as "the mob," "a gang of youths," "thugs," and "a rioting mob of Black youths" and the *Morning Star* referring to "groups of youngsters" and the "great gay surging carnival." Words like "mob," "gang," and "thugs" clearly connote organized lawless activity, while "youngsters" and "gay surging carnival" connote spontaneous and innocent high spirits. It is also noteworthy that the *Sun* mentioned the race of the revelers multiple times, but the *Morning Star* omitted this information entirely. Trew also analyzes who did what to whom, or the contrastive participant and thematic structures of the reports. Transitive clauses with agents are much more common in the *Sun*, with processes more frequently reported in the *Morning Star* without participants. The police are more prominent in the *Morning Star* as initiators of action, however. Verbal strategies in the two accounts project values of preserving versus contesting the status quo, and of legitimizing the actions of the establishment versus a subordinated group.

Another domain illustrating ideological force is advertising, where a major function of language use is to create needs, as well as to shape public opinion and perceptions. Which communicative symbols and strategies will be considered effective are of course (and significantly) culture specific, but they often follow conventions that are adapted from traditional visual and verbal arts. Some of the contrasts in patterns of communication which I used earlier to illustrate methods for comparative description might also be used to illustrate contrasts in strategies for influencing feelings and shaping thought. As reported in chapter 5, for instance, effective television advertisements in Japan often concentrate on setting a visual and aural mood within which an image of the product is experienced without much explicit verbalization, illustrating the potential selling power of nonverbal symbols. In contrast, effective advertisements in the US often make poetic use of alliteration, rhythm, and rhyme, as well as parallel structure, analogy, and other cohesive devices which construct "logical conclusions" for the addressees. Catchy jingles serve to cement associations and product recognition. Also recall that in his comparative analysis of advertisements for laptop computers in US and Indonesian publications, Syahdan reported much more technical information and scientific proof in English, and more appeals to prestige of ownership in Indonesian. Such comparative event analyses are of particular interest to ethnography of communication because they permit contrast within a minimally different frame of components. When interpreted within the sociocultural contexts within which they are performed, the different symbols and strategies often yield insights into differential processes for representation and construction of contrasting ideologies. Advertising, of course, generally reinforces the status quo rather than attempting to subvert it.

Many parallels with advertising may be found in the political domain, including primary reliance on nonverbal symbols in some contexts, carefully crafted verbal appeals as primary in others, and differing bases of appeals to "proof" and prestige. Slogans in politics are akin to jingles, and may also cement simplistic associations. Similar strategies are used to influence thought in the domain of religion, including power-laden nonverbal symbols, artful oratory, and differential appeals to authority, "logical" proof, and emotions such as fear of damnation and hope for salvation. Advertising jingles and political slogans share a number of cohesive and functional features with religious chants.

In addition to comparing means of influencing thought cross-culturally, ethnographers might well give more attention to intracultural analysis of how ideology is shaped verbally across institutional structures within the same societies.

Access to knowledge

Language is a major factor in inequalities of access to knowledge (and thus to power) in large part because there is differential distribution of competence across segments of society. This fact is basic to the linguistic inequalities discussed in chapter 2 and to the existence of varieties associated with activity domain or with social class, status, and role discussed in chapter 3. Distinctive varieties which exist in the communicative repertoires of complex communities are typically distributed unequally among groups of individuals, and less linguistic competence in any given domain may restrict or prevent input and participation. From a purely descriptive viewpoint, differential competence and access is seen as correlational to existing societal divisions and socialization practices; from a critical viewpoint, enabling differential access to knowledge is seen as one strategy by which some individuals, groups, and institutions establish and maintain control over others: i.e., perform power.

One such strategy is *gatekeeping*, defined by Erickson and Schultz in *The Counselor as Gatekeeper* as "brief encounters in which two persons meet, usually as strangers, with one of them having authority to make decisions that affect the other's future" (1982: xi). The concept may be extended to institutionalized tests of various kinds which have a similar function, or to prior socialization experiences as prerequisites, which are themselves only selectively available. The social implications are especially significant in education because gatekeeping encounters between students and school officials (or institutionalized extensions) often determine access to career paths, and thus to future social opportunities; they can segregate students for socialization and limit transmission of knowledge in some areas to a chosen few. I categorize them as linguistic performances of power because criteria for educational segregation or "tracking" typically include (either overtly or covertly) student display of competence in "standard" language form and "proper" usage. In multilingual societies, linguistic competence may be recognized only insofar as it is demonstrated in the official or prestigious language of the dominant group.

The nature and level of competence which students bring to such encounters may be attributed to differential linguistic experiences which are inherent in the nature of social divisions (a correlational view); it may be attributed to the general tendencies of societies to maintain the status quo; and in some cases it may be attributed to conscious engineering and deliberate discrimination. Romaine illustrates the historical occurrence of this last possibility in her account of

> how speakers of Hawai'i Creole English have been discriminated against through education in a school system which originally was set up to keep out those who could not pass an English test. In this way it was hoped to restrict the admission of non-White children into the English Standard schools set up in 1924, which were attended mainly by Caucasian children. . . . By institutionalizing what was essentially racial discrimination along linguistic lines, the schools managed to keep creole speakers in their "place" and maintain distance between them and English speakers until after World War II. (1999: 289)

In the not so distant past (1976), riots in Soweto, South Africa, were motivated in part as protests to a language policy which would not provide basic elementary education in English, a policy that was perceived as keeping the Black population in the region from acquiring the unification and international voice which English would provide, and that Afrikaans would not. Most recently, differential access to knowledge and power through a second language has been reported by Palestinians in Israel who say that limited opportunities to develop advanced English skills in their high schools block admission to better universities in the country because the entrance examinations require a knowledge of English.

An unintentional international outcome of providing advanced-level education in English, on the other hand, has been inhibiting access to knowledge in some areas. There are contemporary concerns about the power position of English as the international language for scholarly conferences and publications, since this status clearly privileges individuals in many disciplines who have received higher education in English-medium universities, and it has created discontinuities in scholarly communication within countries where not only language selection but discourse organization and bases for argumentation are mutually incompatible (e.g., see Eggington 1987 for an analysis of such academic discontinuity in Korea). The recent power of English in the field of linguistics has also resulted in native speakers of Arabic, Chinese, and other languages who return to their home countries with advanced degrees in the discipline from English-medium universities finding themselves ill-equipped to make the subject accessible to others in the national language or to relate to traditional language scholars.

Socialization which takes place in formal educational contexts is usually required for learning the language of transmission (and thus understanding the content) of fields such as law, medicine, and linguistics, but there are many other venues for socialization in other fields. Some of these are even more exclusive. In many American Indian communities, for instance, knowledge of procedures for conducting rituals (including component linguistic acts) is possessed only by those who have been selected and initiated. Other groups which strictly proscribe teaching specialized language forms to "outsiders" include some which use them for purposes of social resistance and rebellion (discussed below). Other venues for socialization, such as the workplace or sports and special interest events, also transmit language which is necessary for understanding content but do not usually impose such rigid barriers to potential access. Nevertheless, failure to learn "the cant" (cf. Philips 1982) seriously restricts participation.

A domain which warrants additional mention for maintaining power and authority by limited access to knowledge is that of religion. In instances where there are written sacred texts, they are typically encoded in language forms that are to some degree foreign or incomprehensible to the ordinary person, requiring priests or others accorded specialized knowledge for interpretation. For example, in 1525 the French Parliament banned translation of the Bible into French and in 1526 banned possession of the Bible in the vernacular; the power position of Latin as the language of scholarship in Western Europe was officially maintained, through an alliance of religious and secular authority, by an explicit attempt to keep the power of knowledge within the Catholic church and Catholic universities. On the other hand, translations of sacred texts to the vernacular have often been landmarks of social reform.

Literacy itself is a source of power, but while widespread literacy has clearly enhanced the potential for increase of access to knowledge, it has also added another dimension for inequitable distribution. In the era of slavery in the US, access to literacy was strictly controlled to prevent subversion through education; contemporary societies which deny literacy selectively to women or other groups are exerting similar discriminatory power.

Finally, choice of orthography among the literate has power. In the era of the Iron Curtain, for instance, speakers of Turkic and Iranian languages within the Soviet Union were insulated by the use of the cyrillic alphabet from information emanating from Turkey and Iran at the same time their acquisition of Russian was facilitated; political policy changes in the former Soviet empire were both enacted and symbolized by the use of the different alphabets for various non-Russian languages. Dissolution of the Soviet Union is resulting in a switch to romanization among some former political components that are now facing West. Also reported in chapter 2, many businesses in China are reflecting the powerful economic influence of

Hong Kong and Taiwan in their use of traditional (as opposed to simplified) characters, in spite of strict government directives to the contrary.

Choice of script may also be an embodiment of power quite apart from access issues. For example, the Cherokee syllabary (invented by Sequoia, an American Indian, in the nineteenth century) was deliberately designed to be unlike the Roman alphabet in a statement of Indian identity and power which was distinct from the European colonizers. Similarly, the adoption of the unique Hangul alphabet in Korea was symbolic of cultural independence. As another example of power associated with script, hiragana was considered "women's hand" in Japan and looked down upon as powerless.

Other institutional discrimination

Several examples of linguistic signs and performances which have already been discussed essentially illustrate institutionalized discrimination against some less powerful segment(s) of societies. Additional attention will be given here to discriminatory interaction patterns in institutional settings, and to discrimination which results from the privileged status which is accorded some languages and language varieties over others.

An exemplary study of interactional discrimination is provided by Placencia (2001). She presents institutional service encounters as another type of "gatekeeping," potentially limiting the access of some groups to social benefits as well as to knowledge. One such encounter is with the receptionist at a hospital or other public institution who has the power to direct individuals to an appropriate department, to delay and discourage them, or to turn them away. Placencia describes discriminatory linguistic behavior used in such contexts against indigenous (Aymara and Quechua) people in La Paz, Bolivia, as compared with usage to White-mestizos. The usage includes familiar pronominal *tú* or *vos* form in address (in contrast with polite *Usted* or *Ustedes*), and directives such as *Dígame* 'Tell me' (in contrast with indirect requests with title such as *Una preguntita señora* 'A little question Mrs./Madam'): i.e., "In recreating the ideology of the dominant classes, institutional representatives confer respectability on White-mestizo women, but withhold it from indigenous women" (p. 207). Other forms commonly used with White-mestizos but almost never with indigenous people are politeness formulas such as *por favor* 'please,' softeners in requests such as *un poco* 'a little,' and apologies such as *disculpe* 'I'm sorry.' Accompanying discriminatory nonverbal signs against indigenous people include making them wait, displays of impatience, and patronizing behavior. Follow-up interviews which Placencia conducted with the institutional representatives in her study show that the asymmetry "seems to be so ingrained" that they are unaware that they use different rules.

Another dimension of discrimination may be found in service encounters which require knowledge of specialized written conventions: e.g. those that "serve to maintain dominant social structure and class division by controlling access by consumers who must read contracts, [and] welfare recipients who must fill out forms . . ." (Rafoth 1990: 148).

Linguistic discrimination in service encounters is perhaps most obvious when the officially designated language of "service" is not one in which some of those being "served" are fluent. A lack of proficiency in the dominant language clearly contributes to discrimination against immigrants in the US and other countries where such designation has been made or where there is no provision for communication in minority languages. As a side-effect, differences in linguistic competence within immigrant families can lead to disintegration of the traditional family structure, as children who are learning the dominant language at school become translators and brokers for their parents in service encounters, inverting the power structure and undermining parental authority.

Potential language-related discrimination becomes institutionalized in the enactment of language policies, which by their very nature involve power and politics; these commonly privilege some languages or varieties of language over others, and thus privilege their speakers. Basic issues which language policies address typically concern *language choice* (designation of official language(s)) for government, legal proceedings, education, administration, news media) and *language engineering* (principles for standardization and modernization of the language(s) selected). Societal goals for these policies are often very important ones from a political viewpoint, especially at early stages of nation-building: they include strengthening national unity and identity, developing educational and economic resources, and extending networks of communication. At least partial realization of such goals is associated with language policies which have been implemented by developing nations for many centuries: for example, I noted earlier that the first emperor who unified China in the 3rd century BC imposed a standard way of writing characters "as a means to further consolidate the power of the central government" (Gao 2000: 31), and the establishment of the state of Israel in the twentieth century was furthered by the revival/modernization and imposition of the Hebrew language. The latter example also illustrates how policies may be implemented both by overt codification in laws and regulations, and by covert practices and public sentiment. Practices in the US also illustrate covert implementation of language policy at the national level, since English has never been declared the official language *de jure*, yet it clearly holds that *de facto* status and is covertly privileged in many ways.

The language policies which may contribute to nation-building and homogenization may at the same time be discriminatory when they suppress minority languages and their speakers. Where this occurs, the resulting internal societal conflict is not merely a linguistic one, but often also involves religious, economic, and cultural identity. The phenomenon is very wide-spread in the world: ethnic communities which have been thus officially suppressed include Kurdish speakers in Turkey and Iraq, Turkish speakers in Bulgaria, non-Arabic speakers in the Sudan, and speakers of American Indian languages in the US.

Some of the discrimination which results from language policy is more informal, but is none the less institutionalized in nature. For example, a social phenomenon I noted earlier that has favored learning of the dominant second language at the expense of minority languages in the US and England, and has also favored replacing nonstandard varieties with the standard in the case of bilingual or monolingual speakers, is the widespread belief that not speaking "good" English is the primary causal factor in the low economic status of large segments of minority group populations, and that learning "good" English will automatically erase class boundaries and prejudice. In other words, folk wisdom holds that the reason a group is poor or lacks economic and education opportunities – or requires support from social welfare – is that they do not learn "good" English, or they do not learn it fast enough. "Learn good English and you will be fully integrated and accepted" is a popular motto. Comparable beliefs are held in many countries about their national languages. Most linguists are convinced that the variety of a language one speaks is not an *intrinsic* barrier to educational and economic success, even as they recognize that limits on opportunities are likely to be imposed on nonstandard speakers by those who believe the mythology.

The view of this public attitude toward "nonstandard" varieties of language from a critical perspective is that it perpetuates the mythology which privileges the language of a particular group and supports the maintenance of their hegemonic status.

Critical social theory claims that a basic reason why language is such a potential force for social elevation or discrimination is that communication is part of economics, and language is a resource which forms *linguistic capital*.

> "Linguistic capital" is the power conferred upon a particular linguistic form, style or dialect associated with the legitimacy and prestige of a particular social position. . . . Differences of capital between different positions are differences of power. (Chouliaraki and Fairclough 1999: 101)

Languages may thus be assets which have value in the linguistic market-place as symbolic capital; speakers – and social institutions – may receive financial rewards, honor, or prestige (i.e. power) because of their access to these resources. Foreign languages may be of particular value. Abundant examples come with the development of a global common market which values multilingual practices. For instance, Piller (2001) reports that 60–70 percent of a corpus of German TV and newspaper advertisements are multilingual; a representative example was provided by Pastos, who noted that an advertisement for Greek wines in the flight magazine aboard Olympia Airlines was written in a combination of Greek, English, and French, clearly targeting international business people and professionals with above average incomes and education. An example of the economic benefits of knowing particular varieties of a foreign language as well comes from reports about many Western companies (e.g. General Electric, British Airways, and Amazon.com) which maintain service call centers in Bangalore, at least in part to take advantage of the low salary scale there. Because these companies do not want customers to realize that their calls have been routed to India, employment as operators requires not only excellent English skills but speech training in American or British accents, depending on the client they represent.

A very different social context is exemplified by the Shuar of Ecuador, where Hendricks (1988) reports the belief that "foreign sources of power are more potent that Shuar sources" (p. 219), and that "speaking Spanish signifies access to potential power resources other than the traditional ones" (p. 224). Knowledge of Spanish (including reading and writing skills) has become a prerequisite for election to some positions of local authority, even though the tasks to be performed do not actually require it. The power of a foreign language is also evident in television coverage of political protests around the world; placards are usually printed in English so that messages will receive the broadest range of visual media coverage.

Linguistic Resistance and Rebellion

The potential power in linguistic performances is enacted not only in the usage of individuals and groups who hold higher rank and overt prestige in the larger society, and of those who accept the conditions, but also in the codes which are developed by "alternative" groups (or counter-cultures) within the society who resist and/or attempt to subvert them. The language of these groups is "counter-language" when it arises in opposition to establishment norms.

The counter-language of three such groups is discussed by Halliday (1978) in illustration: the "pelting speech" of vagabonds in Elizabethan England (based on Harman 1567), the argot of the Calcutta underworld (based on Mallik 1972), and the "grypserka" of Polish prisons and reform schools (based on Podgórecki 1973). One common characteristic is partial relexification, so that some new vocabulary is invented, and some existing vocabulary takes on new meaning and occurs in original collocations. The process occurs primarily in specific semantic domains, "typically those that are central to the activities of the subcultures and that set it off most sharply from the established society" (Halliday 1978: 165). In some domains there is a proliferation of synonymous or nearly synonymous terms, perhaps in pursuit of either originality or secrecy (e.g., Mallik reported 21 words for "bomb" and 41 for "police"). Halliday emphasizes the range of connotations which such lexical proliferation allows, and thus the relatively greater orientation to encoding and foregrounding of social over denotational meaning. At least of equal importance to its functions in verbal art and secrecy is "the reality-generating force of the antilanguage, and especially its power to create and maintain social hierarchy" (Halliday 1978: 169). As the language of a counter-culture, counter-language is creating alternative reality, and serving the process of resocialization.

Although there are qualitative differences, some of the same features of counter-language characterize varieties of language developed within teenage cultures in many parts of the world, and to a greater extent by marginalized gangs. Vocabulary is created and transformed, exploiting double meanings and the capacity for verbal camouflage, and new written symbols are created for conveying in-group messages and "tagging." Further, establishment norms of interaction are overturned, most notably ones that signal "politeness" and "submission" in the dominant society. During the protest movement of the 1960s, for instance, Matsumoto (1988) reports that Japanese students were commonly observed using "vulgar" terms in front of professors to subvert the conventional power relationship; and rebellious adolescents in US classrooms not infrequently talk when told to keep quiet, and sulk silently when told to speak, as a challenge to teacher-power. Similarly, Simpson interprets the increasing use of "impolite pronouns" by adolescent Thai girls as "a public display of resistance to the prevailing social order," including "the accepted dictates regarding proper speech for young women" (1997: 57). These manifestations have in common the breaking of sociolinguistic rules. *Joshikousei* (female high school students in Japan) have developed a variety of speech which is unintelligible to others by blending Japanese and English words and shifting stress (Arita) for purposes of rebellion and solidarity. Functions of resistance also account in large part for increasing nonstandard usage of younger African American, Puerto Rican, and lower-class Whites in New York City: this "reflects a reversal of the value system held by the older generation, and rebellion against the middle class norms" (Labov 1964: 15). Also highly relevant is "gang graffiti as a discourse genre" (Adams and Winter 1997).

Resistance and rebellion against establishment norms of interaction are often opaque, and may not even be recognized as such outside of the suppressed community, but they take their meaning from their opposition to the dominant discourse. One example was the response to Southern segregationists' attempts to control verbal interaction between African Americans and Whites in the US prior to the 1970s (e.g. as reported by Morgan 1998). Imposed communicative rules which were intended to mark subservience included: (1) talking only when permission was granted; (2) not having direct eye contact; (3) not using educated speech (unless told to do so); and (4) determining and then saying whatever the person wanted to hear. Overt defiance of these rules could have yielded very serious negative consequences, but the antisociety (the African American subculture) undermined the dominant society with covert systems of indirectness that were interpretable only within the subjugated community; indeed, most non-African Americans are not aware that the systems existed. As a result,

> interactions, words, or phrases could have contradictory or multiple meanings beyond traditional English interpretations. Thus the *counterlanguage* functioned to signal the antisociety (e.g., Black audience) and provided a means for a speaker to reveal a social face which resisted and contested the practice of racial suppression. (Morgan 1998: 255–6)

There are many instances of passive adoption of "powerless style" by subordinate groups which could be cited; where counter-language develops, however, it characteristically gives active agency in resistance to its speakers, even when public surface behaviors may appear (to outsiders) to co-construct subservience.

Linguistic encodings of resistance cover the same range of communicative phenomena as do those of power. The work on pronouns of power and solidarity by Brown and Gilman (1960) which introduced this chapter, for instance, discusses how the usage of English *thou* and *you* was explicitly involved in the social rebellion by the Religious Society of Friends (or Quakers) beginning in the seventeenth century. They cite this explanation of the egalitarian use of *thou* from the sect's founder, George Fox:

> Moreover, when the Lord sent me forth into the world, He forbade me to put off my hat to any, high or low; and I was required to Thee and Thou all men and women, without any respect to rich or poor, great or small. (quoted in Estrich and Sperber 1952)

In addition to examples of resistance involving language structure, there are abundant examples involving different aspects of performance of speech events. For instance, Ries (1997) describes Russian construction of litanies of complaint and lament in "private talk" as genres for resisting Soviet values at a time when others were restricted, and Kuipers (1990) reports that some of the ritual speech events on Sumba, Indonesia are resistant in nature and continue to be enacted in spite of an official ban. These rituals are deemed dangerous because their power to link with traditional ancestral authority threatens the government's efforts to install its own.

Other levels of language rules which may be overturned as symbols of resistance range from those of language selection to standard spelling codes. For example, Latin continues to be used in some Roman Catholic churches as some priests and congregations resist directives to change to the use of local languages in the liturgy. Broken spelling conventions include the protest spelling of "America" as *Amerika* during the 1960s, with the *k* intended to signify facism by invoking the German spelling of the word, and the feminist spelling of "women" as *womyn* to avoid having the word appear so obviously as an inflected form of *man*.

Language Planning

Linguists have played a significant role in the development of policies and practices related to nation-building, most frequently in collecting and interpreting basic information on language resources, patterns of language use, speaker attitudes, and other input to the language planning which sometimes precedes and informs policy making.

Ethnography of communication has been applied at this stage of data collection for language planning in some developing countries, including language surveys in Africa during the 1960s which were supported in large part by the Ford Foundation; these have been reported in Fishman, Ferguson, and Das Gupta (1968), Ohannessian, Ferguson, and Polomé (1975), and elsewhere. They illustrate both the potentials and the problems of conducting such studies, as well as the possible ethical issues which may arise for scholars who participate in them. Ethnographic contributions in these surveys included direct observation of language use in diverse social contexts to supplement and validate quantitative survey instruments, and interviews with different segments of the populations to elicit feelings and beliefs about their own and other languages. Polomé provides a description of some of the procedures which were used:

> a careful survey was made of the notices posted in City Hall and in other administration buildings as a source of information for actual language use. Besides this, various enquiries were conducted on the language used in trade, particularly in the market place. In the Kenya and Ethiopia surveys, the markets in larger towns as well as smaller communities were examined as to the products being offered for sale and the ethnic background of the people selling them. A number of transactions were observed in order to register the language used for greeting, for advertising the merchandise, for the sale operation itself (including bargaining), for counting at the moment of payment,

and for the final greeting. Similarly, some observers watched a number of operations at post offices, in banks, in railway stations, in bus ticket stations, etc., carefully noting the languages used in the transactions. These data are especially valuable for checking the responses of informants in their questionnaires on the use of languages in certain social contacts. (1975: 44)

The findings from such research potentially can provide policy planners with an objective profile of language resources in the country and of their geographic and social distribution, information on the relative acceptability of different possible policy decisions to various segments of the population, and projections for language-related needs in education, communications, and economic and legal systems, and for the cost-effectiveness of options which are under consideration. In the actual implementation of these surveys, however, both daunting practical problems and serious ethical issues have been encountered. Most serious among the latter has been the lack of objectivity permitted by governments in research design and reporting within some countries because of preexisting political agendas, emotional issues, and group rivalries, including restrictions on collection and dissemination of politically unacceptable information (e.g. on level of minority language use among groups who are not officially acknowledged by governments). Results might otherwise be "subversive." Polomé included among the limitations imposed on the Tanzanian survey, for instance, that the government had already made an irreversible decision to adopt Swahili as the only commonly used national language: this meant "the status of Swahili as a national language was not to be questioned; [and] any systematic linguistic study of the local vernaculars was discouraged" (1975: 32). In Zambia, English had already been solidly established. And in Ethiopia, the researchers could only collect data which would support the government's pro-Amharic policy.

On the positive side, these surveys yielded a significant body of information on African languages and sociolinguistics which remains of significant historical interest and importance. Further, the researchers have been able to provide useful and effective recommendations about such topics as teacher training even when they were restricted to the framework which had been set by government policy. The net professional evaluation of such applied efforts will be determined as much by ideology as is the research itself.

Responsibilities and Limitations

Some might like to believe that the academic aspects of scholars' lives can and should be insulated from political vagaries, and some may even maintain that "objective" scholarship *requires* abstraction from political considerations. However, there is widespread realization among ethnographers of communication, and among others who study language in its social context, of the extent to which politics in fact *does* inescapably influence scholarship. This influence is shaped in large measure by the complex social milieu within which scholars live and work – organization structures, policies, opinions, practices, values, rewards. For research, the influence is felt in the very questions that are asked, in the collection and analysis of data, and in the interpretation and potential application of results; for teaching, the influence is found in what is considered "important" or "relevant" for students to learn and in what is included in the socialization of the next generation of researchers and teachers.

Some go even further and maintain that they have a moral, ethical, and political duty, as scholars of language, to devote some portion of their agendas to issues that are relevant to public policy and the social welfare of those whose languages they study, and to convey some portion of their results through channels that may eventually affect policy outcomes and public opinion. In other words, they believe that scholarship is not only necessarily affected by politics in various ways, but that scholars are obligated to contribute their knowledge where relevant to inform political spheres of activity. The content and processes that might constitute "influence" or "contributions" are broad in scope. It is essential for the researcher, however, to recognize that he or she is inextricably part of the very social context that is being studied, and to consciously problematize his or her role in that context.

Because the target of study in the ethnography of communication has explicitly been language in social context, and because those linguists working primarily from this perspective have needed – and generally wanted – to concern themselves with political issues, the potential applications have been obvious. These include social interests related to the value and maintenance of linguistic diversity in the world, and policies related to so-called "language rights"; particularly relevant are policies that contribute to language maintenance or shift, discussed in chapter 6, and policies that affect the language of education, access to information and civic participation, and delivery of social services.

Sometimes, however, research information can only help predict or explain the linguistic outcomes of political policies and has little chance to influence them. For example, policies of the Eisenhower administration in the US that gave individual members of American Indian groups in Oklahoma the right to sell land that had been held in common contributed to dispersal of the populations and to decline and loss of indigenous languages. Policies to open land on the vast Navajo Reservation in New Mexico and Arizona to industrial development and mining at about the same time required building roads to remote areas; Bernard Spolsky and Wayne Holm (Spolsky 1971) documented that Navajo children's proficiency in the Navajo language has a significant negative correlation with the proximity of their family's dwelling to a paved road.

In these two cases, valuation of "private property" and "economic development" by the larger society (actually, these overtly positive American values were appealed to by politically powerful interests wishing to acquire or exploit Indian land) was stronger than valuation of Indian communities' language maintenance, even though no significant material benefits ultimately accrued to the individuals or communities involved. Indeed, the predictable shift to English that resulted from those policies was likely considered a positive outcome by many policy makers.

Another case where language shift was a byproduct of other factors comes from the general demise of Yiddish in the US, as reported by Joshua Fishman (1985). Yiddish thrived in Europe prior to 1945 in large part because Yiddish speech communities were enclosed or segregated, but also because it functioned to allow Ashkenazic Jews to communicate with one another regardless of their national language. The more benevolent policies toward assimilation of minority groups in the US created a more open environment with greater access to the dominant group language, thus reducing the factors making for maintenance of the Yiddish language.

The case of Yiddish clearly illustrates the effect of social stratification on an ethnic group or community, including the degree of access that speakers of low-prestige languages and varieties have to those that are more prestigious, and to jobs that require their use. The keys here are motivation and opportunity, as well as the acceptability of assimilation by the dominant social group, factors that both create and reflect political ideology in this domain. In a converse case, the continued and even intensified segregation of African Americans in large American cities has reinforced the maintenance and even increasing differentiation of African American Vernacular English (Labov 1987). Certainly, however, no scholar would ethically recommend social repression and enforced segregation, even though research strongly suggests that such policies would contribute to/correlate positively with maintaining minority languages or social varieties of a language.

Another arena of both academic and humanitarian concern in many parts of the world has been the education of minority language students. Scholars in language-related disciplines in the US have tried for many years to use results of their research to convince policy makers that initial mother-tongue education is most viable in promoting academic achievement, but with little effect. In contradiction to the widely-held view in the US that minority language children (in particular) should "get into English as fast as possible," we have strong research evidence that minority children's educational achievement in a second language may ultimately be higher if immersion in it is postponed (e.g. see Troike 1978, 1990; González 1986; Cummins 1989), but this documented evidence has had no discernible effect on public beliefs or political policies. The trend is quite to the contrary, in fact, as legislative initiatives for the imposition of English-only policies in this country attest.

Mehan (1997) provides an illustrative critical analysis of discourse strategies used in California during a period when voters were deciding on a related initiative which intended to exclude undocumented children from public schools and health care services. The measure was overwhelmingly approved by the voters, in spite of "expert opinion" that it was not to the common good. Proponents succeeded in using emotional *us* versus *them* appeals, and countered expert testimony with images on television of furtive figures dashing across highways near the US-Mexico border and anecdotes of illegal aliens taking jobs and causing the economic woes which the state was experiencing. "Scientific evidence" to the contrary had little impact.

On the other hand, linguists in particular have been very successful in affecting educational policies and practices in the area of foreign language teaching, and have been officially encouraged to do so, because their input is perceived as furthering national interests. Archival research by Spolsky (1994) has suggested that the evidence to support so-called "linguistic approaches" as an ideological basis for teaching foreign languages (especially English) was not unequivocal, nor even well documented, but "linguistic approaches" prevailed nevertheless. The stated motivation for supporting those approaches over alternatives was sometimes political, sometimes economic, and sometimes educational. In any case, the impact of research related to foreign language pedagogy was substantial.

As recently as 1965, President Lyndon Johnson accorded overseas English teaching (English as a Foreign Language, or EFL) a high priority among the nation's world responsibilities. He proclaimed:

> The rapidly growing interest in English cuts across ideological lines. . . . An increase in the knowledge of English can contribute directly to greater understanding among nations. . . . The United States government is prepared, as a major policy, to be of active and friendly assistance to countries that desire such help in the utilization of English. (cited in Allen 1978: 60)

The noble goal asserted for the support of EFL abroad obscures the unstated political co-purposes of this policy: strengthening US ideological, commercial, and political/military ties with other countries. Language, then, became a tool for political and economic influence, and linguists were gladly welcomed to provide technical support for this goal. Official support for EFL abroad and for foreign languages domestically were thus both for strategic purposes. Since Johnson, no American president has made such a commitment to foreign language teaching.

Johnson's administration also supported the enactment of legislation that enabled bilingual education in this country, and such early childhood intervention programs as Head Start. Although members of the US academic community sometimes complain about insufficient financial support for language research, there has actually been considerable funded research activity. Allocation of money is an effective way in which the political establishment can influence what questions are addressed by researchers. I vividly recall a motivational faculty meeting I attended at the University of Texas after President Johnson proclaimed the "War on Poverty," where the Dean of the College of Education encouraged faculty to apply for research grants, declaring: "There is money in poverty." Indeed, for some time thereafter, a relative bonanza of funding became available to support sociolinguistic research related to the issue of school desegregation.

Legitimate concerns should not be focused so much on lack of politically generated economic support for research, I think, as on the lack of impact the findings of research has had, particularly in the domain of educational policy, when those findings have not supported politically favored positions. However, scholars' disappointment at this lack of impact can be attributed to some extent to political naïveté on their part. It has long been apparent, for instance, that the "bilingual education debate [is] more strongly based on political than on pedagogical considerations" (Cummins 1989: 39). Scholars need to recognize that language-related research and initiatives are necessarily going to be perceived and evaluated within the social and political climate of their day rather than on the basis of hard data.

With respect to external politics, linguists would like for their research to be accorded the same public status as medical findings, such as the discovery that DDT and smoking cause cancer, or that malaria is transmitted by mosquitos and not by night air, and to have findings lead to policies that would ban certain educational practices or at least require warning labels. But this will probably not be the case as long as discoveries are frequently in conflict with deeply held social attitudes, even when these are based on ignorance.

The ultimate caveat on this topic must be: Issues regarding language in the public sphere are always politically embedded and potentially charged, and by conducting research affecting these issues, linguists will ineluctably be supporting or challenging the interests maintaining the status quo.

9

Conclusion

Much of human existence – both individual and corporate – is mediated and constructed through communication, linguistic as well as non-linguistic. It attends the individual's entry into a society and his or her departure from it. Through it, everything from self-direction and dyadic interactions to the operation of complex nation-states is managed. Language and other aspects of communication serve many ends, from the gratification of individual desires to the organization of massive cooperative efforts. Beauty and destruction, altruism and venality, the profound and the trivial, are all accomplished within the frameworks of often unconscious bodies of social conventions which guide and constrain the possibilities of communicative action.

It is the task of the ethnography of communication to elucidate these conventions in different societies, and across their boundaries in processes of contact and intercultural dynamics, and to understand the nature and complexities of their representation and reflection in the constitutive enactment of events. Of course this task is far from complete, in spite of the wealth of relevant research and publication which has appeared in the decades since Hymes issued the call for this synthesizing approach. Indeed, the task keeps expanding as scholars from different disciplinary perspectives challenge and test basic concepts, move from relatively static descriptive models to increasingly dynamic processual accounts, explore previously uninvestigated situations and genres, and recognize new potentials for addressing social needs.

As Hymes pointed out, the traditional focus of linguistics on abstract code characteristics to the neglect of function, and the traditional focus of anthropology and sociology on the abstract patterns of cultural and social organization to the neglect of details of their enactment, left us largely ignorant of the role of language and other modes of communication in the realization of social life. While the humanistic disciplines had long dealt with such issues, often in great depth, they had usually done so within the largely unexamined context of a single cultural tradition, and so had not provided the tools required for concomitant analysis of the taken-for-granted context itself.

The recognition and definition of a new field of study, falling between existing paradigms and not fully contained within any of them, above all problematized the out-of-awareness and taken-for-granted. It required a major intellectual reorientation of perspective to see that there existed something truly new and significant to study, which could not be conveniently reduced to some existing set of concepts and methods of analysis. A significant number of scholars in recent years have achieved truly integrated accounts of language form, content, and context, and the understanding of human communication has been furthered.

Much of the work which I have cited in the preceding chapters has continued in the tradition of Franz Boas and others who focused on the study of non-Western European populations, including the indigenous languages of the Americas, Africa, and the Pacific Islands, but in a more holistic mode. Many situated descriptions of language form within ethnographic studies of communities relate language phenomena to social structure and other cultural practices, and provide in-depth analyses of ways of speaking in diverse settings and events. A major outcome of continuing this tradition has been a fuller understanding of how the social organization of a community is reflected in language use, and conversely, what role the use of language has in the process of constituting, expressing, and perpetuating society. Especially in recent years, increasing attention has been given to research on the use of European languages in urban and suburban settings, with similar holistic considerations. Several studies I have cited integrate ethnography and linguistic analyses of verbal art, also following the Boasian tradition.

Since Hymes introduced the construct of communicative competence, the ethnography of communication has also strongly influenced research on child language acquisition, with a growing emphasis on including language acquisition as part of both the means and product of socialization. Language learning has come to be viewed in a more inclusive sense as the acquisition of rules and skills which enable a member of a group to demonstrate and interpret appropriate communicative behavior in a range of social contexts. Children have essentially been recognized by many researchers as participant-observers of communication, like small ethnographers, learning and inductively developing these rules through processes of observation and interaction. Research has documented extensive cross-cultural differences in the ways considered appropriate for adults to relate to children, and in the specific sociocultural structure and content which is conveyed to children. More recent interests from this perspective have included the extended language learning of teenagers and adults as part of their socialization to peer groups, occupations, and special interests.

Another area in which the ethnography of communication has had substantial impact since its beginnings is education and delivery of other social services. Hymes voiced a strong call for such application in his Introduction to *Functions of Language in the Classroom* (1972), and in many subsequent publications. For Hymes, research and application involve a two-way sharing of knowledge – the investigator contributing scientific modes of inquiry, and participants providing the requisite knowledge and perspective of the particular community contexts. The issue is one of ethics as much as one of science.

> If linguistics and ethnography are to contribute to a democratic way of life, their knowledge and perspective must be gained and used in democratic ways. . . . Both inquiry and application are processes that involve mutuality and sharing of knowledge; neither can succeed as a one-way application. (Hymes 1972b: xiv–xv)

Some of the most notable contributions to education from an ethnographic research perspective include studies of classroom organization and participation structures, and understanding communication in schools in relation to communication in homes and communities. Contributions to medicine (e.g. analyses of doctor–patient communication) and law (e.g. research on differential effects of communication patterns in courtrooms) also date back at least three decades and continue to be highly fruitful areas of scholarship and social application. There is ever-increasing attention to the power relationships that exist in such institutional settings, and on how these relate to issues of justice and equity in the delivery of social services. Concern with language and power has also extended to analysis of communication between male–female, governor–governed, and other dyads having unequal distribution of control, as well as to how power is enacted linguistically in access to knowledge, construction of public opinion, and maintenance or change of existing social institutions.

While most attention in these studies has been given to spoken interaction, another trend is the increasing emphasis being placed on other channels of communication. Significant work is being produced in the ethnography of deaf communication, for instance, as well as on the social practices and contexts of literacy in diverse cultural settings. There is also increasing research on communication via the medium of e-mail, including the formation of "virtual" electronic speech communities. Other more recent trends include study of the nature of multilingual communicative competence, and of forms, functions, and contexts of non-native language use.

It is a very positive development that such a volume of socially relevant research within this paradigm, by scholars with similar perspectives and goals, has appeared since the first edition of this book was published in 1982. At that time I said in the concluding chapter that the effort "may barely be said to have begun." Twenty years later I am very pleased to be saying how much progress has been made, and to recognize the promise of future research.

Still, the bulk of research and publication on language and on sociocultural issues focuses on relatively narrow topics. While such focused inquiry clearly has scientific merit, it does not necessarily contribute substantially to understanding language *in* society, nor to accounting for communicative competence as a major constitutive factor in the conduct of human affairs. Pursuing these goals continues to require interdisciplinary scholarship, wherein researchers are aware and informed of findings and perceptions in other fields, and to demand more holistic ethnographic research which can provide in-depth, integrative analyses of situated communication.

A note of warning, and a continuing call for critical reflexivity of the role of the researcher, is also in order. It is necessary to recognize that the question of the use to which ethnographic research is to be put is suspect in some communities as well as an ethical issue in the profession. There are many potential applications of in-depth information on socially-constituted and constituting patterns of communication, ranging from improving education and the provision of social services to contributing to the effectiveness of advertising or propaganda and political control (or of resisting it). Even as ethnographers of language seek for a deeper understanding of the human condition, they bear a heavy responsibility to guard against the misuse of their research, and the exploitation of the communities in which they work.

References

Sources of Unpublished Examples

Students at Georgetown University in the years 1974–80, the University of Illinois in the years 1980–8, and the University of Arizona in the years 1989–2002 have provided me with many of the unpublished examples in this book. Where an example or quotation appears in the text with a name but no date, reference is made to oral information, unpublished essays or research from such sources. The students, whether specifically named in the text or not, are listed here under the language, group, or country on which they have provided information:

Abbey (Côte d'Ivoire): Marcellin Hepié
Amharic (Ethiopia): Demissie Manahlot, Mulugeta Seyoum
Arabic: Mohammed Al-Rusan, Saud Assubaiai, Atteya El-Noory, Sulaiman G. Elwedyani, Youssef Mahmoud, Ahmed Mouakket, William B. Royer, Jr.
Bambara (Mali): Issiaka Ly
Batak (Indonesia): Bistok Sirait
Belguim: Marcel Van Thillo
Berber (northwest Africa): Omar Boukella, Ghada Mardini
Bukadon (Philippines): Genoveva M. Ablanque
Cape Verdian Creole: Izione Silva
Chinese: Rey-Mei Chen, Huilin Chang, Hong-Gang Jin, Cher-Leng Lee, Hao Sun, Jun Yang
Czech: Vessna Vuchichevich
(Deaf) Sign Language: Virginia Covington, Barbara M. Kannapell, William Rudner
Dutch: Henriette Frederica Schatz
English: Carolyn T. Adger, Cheri Bridgeforth, Leonie Cottrill, Lou A. Daly, John K. Donaldson, Fr., Mary Owens, Katherine A. Spaar, Susan Van Coevern, Caroline Vickers
Farsi (Iran): Ali A. Aghbar, A. Javad Jafarpur, Ahmed A. Thabet
German: Helga Kansy, Sebine Koschorreck, Karin Steinhaus
Greek: William Alatis, Margaret Heliotis, Zara Pastos
Hebrew: Amy Aidman, Channa Seikevicz

Igbo (Nigeria): Gregory Nwoye
Indonesian/Javanese: Asim Gunarwan, Siti A. Suprapto, Syahdan
Japanese: Etsuko Arita, Midori Chiba, Tetsuo Kumatoriya, Takashi Matsunaga,
    Eri B. Shinoda, Toshiyuki Suzuki, Shoji Takano, Aoi Tsuda, Harumi Williams
Kaingáng (Brazil): Gloria Kindell
Kazakh: Akmaral Mukanova
Korean: Yong-Hwan Jo, Soon-Bok Kim, Sang Ah Ko, Hyun-Hee Kim Oh, Jihyun
    Park, Jun-Eon Park, Mae-Ran Park-Mun, Seung Hwa Seok, Rodney Tyson
Lao: Phosy Chanhming
Mixe-Zoque (Mexico): Linda Hudson O'Neill
Newari (Nepal): Jyoti Tuladhar
Quechua (Ecuador): Lucinda Hart-González
Spanish: Isabel Castellanos, María D. Clark, Annette Silverio-Borges, Carmen
    Simich-Dudgeon
Sranan/Dutch: Annemarie Jong A. Kiem, Robby Morroy
Tamil (India): Francis Britto
Tanzania: Robert Jalbert
Thai: Namtip Aksornkool, Tiraporn Bunnag, Suphatcharee Ekasingh, Penchusee
    Lerdtadsin, Premchitra Satyavanija, Pornthip Virpongse
Tongan: Michael Wimberly
Trinidadian Creole: Wendy Sealey

Books and Articles

Abdel-Jawad, Hassan R. 1987. Cross-dialectal variation in Arabic: competing
    prestigious forms. *Language in Society* 16: 359–68.
Aberle, David. 1966. *The Peyote Religion among the Navaho*. London: Aldine.
Abrahams, Roger D. 1972. Stereotyping and beyond. In Roger D. Abrahams and
    Rudolph C. Troike, eds, *Language and Cultural Diversity in American Educa-
    tion*, pp. 19–29. Englewood Cliffs, NJ: Prentice-Hall.
—— 1973. Toward a Black rhetoric: being a survey of Afro-American com-
    munication styles and role-relationships. Texas working papers in sociolinguistics
    No. 15.
—— 1983. *The Man-of-Words in the West Indies: Performance and the Emergence of
    Creole Culture*. Baltimore, MD: Johns Hopkins University Press.
Adams, Karen L. and Anne Winter. 1997. Gang graffiti as a discourse genre. *Journal
    of Sociolinguistics* 1(3): 337–60.
Adegbija, Efurosibina. 1989. A comparative study of politeness phenomena in
    Nigerian English, Yoruba and Ogori. *Multilingua* 8(1): 57–80.
Adelman, Mara B. and Lawrence R. Frey. 1997. *The Fragile Community: Living
    Together with AIDS*. Mahwah, NJ: Erlbaum.
Adger, Carolyn Temple. 1986. When difference does not conflict: successful argu-
    ments between Black and Vietnamese Classmates. *Text* 6: 223–37.
Agha, Asif. 1993. Grammatical and indexical convention in honorific discourse.
    Journal of Linguistic Anthropology 3(2): 131–63.

Aijmer, Karin. 1996. *Conversational Routines in English: Convention and Creativity.* London: Addison Wesley Longman.

Ainsworth-Vaughn, Nancy. 1994. Is that a rhetorical question? Ambiguity and power in medical discourse. *Journal of Linguistic Anthropology* 4(2): 194–214.

—— 1998. *Claiming Power in Doctor-Patient Talk.* Oxford: Oxford University Press.

Akinnaso, F. Niyi. 1980. The sociolinguistic basis of Yoruba personal names. *Anthropological Linguistics* 22(7): 275–304.

Albert, Ethel M. 1972. Culture patterning of speech behavior in Burundi. In John J. Gumperz and Dell Hymes, eds, *Directions in Sociolinguistics: The Ethnography of Communication*, pp. 72–105. New York: Holt, Rinehart & Winston.

Allen, Harold B. 1978. The teaching of English as a second language and US foreign policy. In Charles H. Blatchford and Jacquelyn Schachter, eds, *On TESOL '78: EFL Policies, Programs, Practices*, pp. 57–71. Washington, DC: TESOL.

Allport, Gordon. 1954. *The Nature of Prejudice.* Cambridge, MA: Addison-Wesley.

Andersen, Elaine Slosberg. 1990. *Speaking with Style: The Sociolinguistic Skills of Children.* New York: Routledge.

Atkins, J. D. C. 1887. Annual report of the commissioner of Indian affairs. In House Executive Document No. 1, 50th Congress, 1st session, serial 2542, pp. 19–21.

Attinasi, John, Pedro Pedraza, Shana Poplack, and Alicia Pousada. 1982. *Intergenerational Perspectives on Bilingualism: From Community to Classroom.* New York: Center for Puerto Rican Studies, City University of New York.

Aukrust, Vibeke Grøver and Catherine E. Snow. 1998. Narratives and explanations during mealtime conversations in Norway and the US. *Language in Society* 27: 221–46.

Awbery, G. M. 1984. *Cardiff Working Papers in Welsh Linguistics* 3: 1–19. (Cited in T. Arwyn Watkins. 1985. Welsh studies: language. *The Year's Work in Modern Language Studies* 46.)

Bailey, Benjamin. 2000. Switching. *Journal of Linguistic Anthropology* 9(1–2): 241–3.

Bailey, Charles-James N. 1976. The state of non-state linguistics. *Annual Review of Anthropology* 5: 93–106.

Bailey, Guy and Natalie Maynor. 1987. Decreolization? *Language in Society* 16: 449–73.

Bamgboṣe, Ayọ. 1986. *Yoruba: A Language in Transition.* Lagos: J. F. Odunjo Memorial Lectures Organizing Committee.

Bar-Adon, Aaron and Werner F. Leopold, eds 1971. *Child language: A Book of Readings.* Englewood Cliffs, NJ: Prentice-Hall.

Barker, George C. 1947. Social functions of language in a Mexican-American community. *Acta Americana* 5: 185–202.

Barry, Herbert III, Margaret K. Bacon, and Irvin L. Child. 1957. A cross-cultural survey of some sex differences in socialization. *The Journal of Abnormal and Social Psychology* 55: 327–32.

Barth, Fredrik. 1964a. Ethnic processes on the Pathan-Baluch boundary. In Georges Redard, ed., *Indo-Iranica. Mélanges présentés à Georg Morgenstierne à l'occaision de son soixantedixième anniversaire.* Wiesbaden: Otto Harrassowitz. (Reprinted in John J. Gumperz and Dell Hymes, eds (1972). *Directions in Sociolinguistics: The Ethnography of Communication*, pp. 454–64. New York: Holt, Rinehart & Winston.)

—— 1964b. *Nomads of South Persia: The Basseri Tribe of the Khamesh Confederacy*. London: Allen and Unwin.

Basso, Keith. 1970. To give up on words: silence in the Western Apache culture. *Southwestern Journal of Anthropology* 26: 213–30.

—— 1979. *Portraits of "The Whiteman": Linguistic Play and Cultural Symbols among the Western Apache*. Cambridge: Cambridge University Press.

Bateson, Gregory. 1955. A theory of play and phantasy. *Psychiatric Research Reports* 2: 39–51. American Psychiatric Association. (Reprinted in *Steps to an Ecology of Mind* (1972), pp. 177–93. New York: Ballantine.)

Baugh, John. 1983. *Black Street Speech: Its History, Structure, and Survival*. Austin, TX: University of Texas Press.

—— 2000. *Beyond Ebonics: Linguistic Pride and Racial Prejudice*. Oxford: Oxford University Press.

Bauman, Richard. 1974. Speaking in the light: the role of the Quaker minister. In Richard Bauman and Joel Sherzer, eds, *Explorations in the Ethnography of Speaking*, pp. 144–60. Cambridge: Cambridge University Press.

—— 1976. The development of competence in the use of solicitational routines: children's folklore and informal learning. Texas working papers in sociolinguistics No. 34. Austin, TX, Southwest Educational Development Laboratory.

—— 1977. Linguistics, anthropology, and verbal art: toward a unified perspective with a special discussion of children's folklore. In Muriel Saville-Troike, ed., *Linguistics and Anthropology*, pp. 13–36. Washington, DC: Georgetown University Press.

—— 1983. *Let Your Words Be Few: Symbolism of Speaking and Silence among Seventeenth-Century Quakers*. Cambridge: Cambridge University Press.

—— 2000. Genre. *Journal of Linguistic Anthropology* 9(1–2): 84–7.

Beaglehole, Ernest and Pearl Beaglehole. 1941. Personality development in Pukapukan children. In Leslie Spier, A. Irving Hallowell, and Stanley Newman, eds, *Language, Culture, and Personality*, pp. 282–98. Menasha, WI: Sapir Memorial Publication Fund.

Bean, Susan S. 1980. Ethnology and the study of proper names. *Anthropological Linguistics* 22(7): 305–16.

Bell, Michael J. 1983. *The World from Brown's Lounge: An Ethnography of Black Middle-Class Play*. Urbana: University of Illinois Press.

Benedict, Ruth. 1934. *Patterns of Culture*. Boston: Houghton Mifflin.

Bereiter, Carl and Siegfried Engelman. 1966. *Teaching Disadvantaged Children in the Preschool*. Englewood Cliffs, NJ: Prentice-Hall.

Berger, Peter and Thomas Luckmann. 1967. *The Social Construction of Reality*. New York: Doubleday.

Berman, Laine. 1998. *Speaking through the Silence: Narratives, Social Conventions, and Power in Java*. Oxford: Oxford University Press.

Berman, Ruth A. and Dan Isaac Slobin. 1994. *Relating Events in Narrative: A Crosslinguistic Study*. Hillsdale, NJ: Lawrence Erlbaum.

Bernstein, Basil. 1960. Review of *The Lore and Language of School Children*, by Iona and Peter Opie. *British Journal of Sociology* 11: 178–81.

—— 1971. *Class, Codes and Control*. London: Routledge & Kegan Paul.

—— 1972. A sociolinguistic approach to socialization; with some reference to educability. In John J. Gumperz and Dell Hymes, eds, *Directions in Sociolinguistics:*

The Ethnography of Communication, pp. 465–97. New York: Holt, Rinehart & Winston.

Bhu, Sunthorn. ca. 1803. *Suphasit Son Ying*. (Published in 1973 by Silpa Bannakarn of Bangkok; translation provided by Namtip Aksornkool.)

Biber, Douglas. 1995. *Dimensions of Register Variation: A Cross Linguistic Comparison.* Cambridge: Cambridge University Press.

Birdwhistell, Ray L. 1952. *Introduction to Kinesics: An Annotation System for Analysis of Body Motion and Gesture.* Louisville, KY: University of Louisville Press.

—— 1970. *Kinesics and Context: Essays in Body Motion Communication.* Philadelphia: University of Pennsylvania Press.

—— 1974. The language of the body: the natural environment. In Albert Silverstein, ed., *Human Communication: Theoretical Explorations*, pp. 203–20. New York: John Wiley & Sons.

Bloch, Maurice. 1974. Symbols, song, dance and features of articulation: Is relation an extreme form of traditional authority? *Archives Européennes de Sociologie* 15(1): 55–71.

—— ed. 1975. *Political Language and Oratory in Traditional Society.* New York: Academic Press.

—— 1976. The past and the present in the present. *Man* 12: 278–92.

Blom, Jan-Petter and John J. Gumperz. 1972. Social meaning in linguistic structure: code-switching in Norway. In John J. Gumperz and Dell Hymes, eds, *Directions in Sociolinguistics: The Ethnography of Communication*, pp. 407–34. New York: Holt, Rinehart & Winston.

Bloomfield, Leonard. 1927. Literate and illiterate speech. *American Speech* 10: 432–9. (Reprinted in Dell Hymes, ed. (1964), *Language in Culture and Society*, pp. 391–6. New York: Harper & Row.)

Blount, Ben G. 1972. Parental speech and language acquisition: some Luo and Samoan examples. *Anthropological Linguistics* 14(4): 119–30.

Blum-Kulka, Shoshona. 1997. *Dinner Talk: Cultural Patterns of Sociability and Socialization in Family Discourse.* Mahwah, NJ: Lawrence Erlbaum.

Blum-Kulka, Shoshona, J. House, and Gabriele Kasper, eds 1989. *Cross-Cultural Pragmatics: Requests and Apologies.* Norwood, NJ: Ablex.

Blum-Kulka, Shoshona and Gabriele Kasper, eds 1993. *Interlanguage Pragmatics.* Oxford: Oxford University Press.

Boas, Franz. 1911. Introduction. *Handbook of American Indian Languages*, pp. 1–83. Bureau of American Ethnology Bulletin 40. Washington, DC: Government Printing Office.

Boggs, Stephen T. 1978. The development of verbal disputing in part-Hawaiian children. *Language in Society* 7: 325–44.

Bornstein, Marc, et al. 1992. Maternal responsiveness to infants in three societies: the United States, France, and Japan. *Child Development* 63: 808–21.

Bourdieu, Pierre. 1977. The economics of linguistic exchanges. *Social Sciences Information* 16(6): 645–68.

—— 1991. *Language and Symbolic Power.* Cambridge, MA: Harvard University Press.

Bourhis, Richard V., Howard Giles, Jacques P. Leyens, and Henri Tajfel. 1979. Psycholinguistic distinctiveness: language divergence in Belgium. In Howard

Giles and Robert N. St. Clair, eds, *Language and Social Psychology*, pp. 158–85. Oxford: Basil Blackwell.

Brandt, Elizabeth A. 1977. The role of secrecy in Pueblo society. In Stanton Tefft, ed., *Secrecy: A Cross-Cultural Perspective*. New York: Human Sciences Press.

Brewer, William F. and Edward H. Lichtenstein. 1980. Event schemas, story schemas, and story grammar. Technical Report No. 197. Champaign, IL: Center for the Study of Reading.

Briggs, Charles L. 1984. Learning how to ask: native metacommunicative competence and the incompetence of fieldworkers. *Language in Society* 13: 1–28.

—— 1986. *Learning How to Ask: A Sociolinguistic Appraisal of the Role of the Interview in Social Science Research*. Cambridge: Cambridge University Press.

—— 1992. "Since I am a woman I will chastise my relatives": gender, reported speech and the (re)production of social relations in Warao ritual wailing. *American Ethnologist* 19(2): 337–61.

Brislin, Richard W., Walter J. Lonner, and Robert M. Thorndike. 1973. *Cross-Cultural Research Methods*. New York: John Wiley & Sons.

Brown, Bruce L., William J. Strong, and Alvin C. Rencher. 1975. Acoustic determinants of perceptions of personality from speech. *International Journal of the Sociology of Language* 6: 11–32.

Brown, Gillian and George Yule. 1983. *Discourse Analysis*. Cambridge: Cambridge University Press.

Brown, Penelope and Colin Fraser. 1979. Speech as a marker of situation. In Klaus R. Scherer and Howard Giles, eds, *Social Markers in Speech*, pp. 33–62. Cambridge: Cambridge University Press.

Brown, Penelope and Stephen Levinson. 1979. Social structure, groups and interaction. In Klaus R. Scherer and Howard Giles, eds, *Social Markers in Speech*, pp. 291–341. Cambridge: Cambridge University Press.

Brown, Penelope and Stephen Levinson 1987. *Politeness: Some Universals in Language Usage*. Cambridge: Cambridge University Press.

Brown, Roger and Albert Gilman. 1960. The pronouns of power and solidarity. In Thomas Sebeok, ed., *Style in Language*, pp. 253–76. Cambridge, MA: Massachusetts Institute of Technology.

Byram, Michael. 1997. *Teaching and Assessing Intercultural Communicative Competence*. Clevedon, Avon: Multilingual Matters.

Campbell, Lyle. 1976. Language contact and sound change. In William M. Christie, Jr., ed., *Current Progress in Historical Linguistics*. Amsterdam: North Holland.

Chafe, Wallace L., ed. 1980. *The Pear Stories: Cognitive, Cultural and Linguistic Aspects of Narrative Production*. Norwood, NJ: Ablex.

Cheshire, Jenny. 2000. The telling or the tale? Narrative and gender in adolescent friendship networks. *Journal of Sociolinguistics* 4(2): 234–62.

Choi, Soonja. 2000. Caregiver input in English and Korean: use of nouns and verbs in book-reading and toy-play contexts. *Journal of Child Language* 27: 69–96.

Chomsky, Noam. 1965. *Aspects of the Theory of Syntax*. Cambridge, MA: Massachusetts Institute of Technology.

—— 1968. *Language and Mind*. New York: Harcourt, Brace & World.

Chouliaraki, Lilie and Norman Fairclough. 1999. *Discourse in Late Modernity: Rethinking Critical Discourse Analysis*. Edinburgh: Edinburgh University Press.

Christian, Jane and Peter M. Gardner. 1977. The individual in Northern Dene thought and communication: a study in sharing and diversity. Mercury Series Canadian Ethnology Service Papers No. 35. Ottawa: National Museum of Man.

Claire, Elizabeth. 1980. *A Foreign Student's Guide to Dangerous English*. Rochelle Park, NJ: Eardley.

Clancy, Patricia M. 1986. The acquisition of communicative style in Japanese. In Bambi B. Schieffelin and Elinor Ochs, eds, *Language Socialization Across Cultures*, pp. 213–50. Cambridge: Cambridge University Press.

Clements, William M. 1995. *Native American Verbal Art: Texts and Contexts*. Tucson: University of Arizona Press.

Cohen, Andrew D. 1996. Speech Acts. In Sandra Lee McKay and Nancy H. Hornberger, eds, *Sociolinguistics and Language Teaching*, pp. 383–420. Cambridge: Cambridge University Press.

Cohen, Marcel. 1956. *Pour Une Sociologie du Language*. Paris: Paris Educations, Albin Michel.

Colombo, Gary, Bonnie Lisle, and Sandra Mano. 1997. *Frame Work: Culture, Storytelling, and College Writing*. Boston: Bedford Books.

Conley, John M. and William M. O'Barr. 1990. *Rules Versus Relationships: The Ethnography of Legal Discourse*. Chicago, IL: University of Chicago Press.

Connor, Ulla. 1996. *Contrastive Rhetoric: Cross-Cultural Aspects of Second-Language Writing*. Cambridge: Cambridge University Press.

Conrad, Susan M. 1999. The importance of corpus-based research for language teachers. *System* 27: 1–18.

Cook, Haruko Minegishi. 1990. The role of the Japanese sentence-final particle *no* in the socialization of children. *Multilingua* 9(4): 377–95.

——— 1999. Situational meanings of Japanese social deixis: the mixed use of the *masu* and plain forms. *Journal of Linguistic Anthropology* 8(1): 87–110.

Cook-Gumperz, Jenny. 1977. Situated instructions: language socialization of school age children. In Susan M. Ervin-Tripp and Claudia Mitchell-Kernan, eds, *Child Discourse*, pp. 103–21. New York: Academic Press.

Cromdal, Jakob and Karin Aronsson. 2000. Footing in bilingual play. *Journal of Sociolinguistics* 4(3): 435–57.

Cummins, Jim. 1979. Linguistic interdependence and the educational development of bilingual children. *Review of Educational Research* 49(2): 222–51.

——— 1989. Empowering minority students. Sacramento: California Association for Bilingual Education.

d'Anglejan, Alison and G. Richard Tucker. 1973. Sociolinguistic correlates of speech styles in Quebec. In Roger W. Shuy and Ralph W. Fasold, eds, *Language Attitudes: Current Trends and Prospects*, pp. 1–22. Washington, DC: Georgetown University Press.

Darwin, Charles. 1872. *The Expression of the Emotions in Man and Animals*. London: Murray.

Demisse, Teshome and M. Lionel Bender. 1983. An argot of Addis Ababa unattached girls. *Language in Society* 12: 339–47.

Dennis, Wayne. 1940. *The Hopi Child*. New York: Wiley & Sons.

Dimitracopoulou, Ionna. 1990. *Conversational Competence and Social Development*. Cambridge: Cambridge University Press.

DiPietro, Robert J. 1975. The strategies of language use. Paper presented at the second annual LACUS forum, Toronto.

Dittmar, Norbert. 1977. The acquisition of German syntax by foreign migrant workers: Heidelberger Forschungsprojekt "Pidgin-Deutsch." In David Sankoff, ed., *Linguistic Variation: Models and Methods*, pp. 1–22. New York: Academic Press.

Dorian, Nancy C. 1980. Language loss and maintenance in language contact situations. Paper presented at the Conference on the Attrition of Language Skills, University of Pennsylvania.

—— 1982. Linguistic models and language death evidence. In Loraine K. Obler and Lise Menn, eds, *Exceptional Language and Linguistics*, pp. 31–48. New York: Academic Press.

Douglas, Mary. 1970. *Natural Symbols: Explorations in Cosmology*. New York: Random House.

—— 1971. Do dogs laugh? A cross-cultural approach to body symbolism. *Journal of Psychosomatic Research* 15: 387–90.

Dozier, Edward P. 1956. Two examples of linguistic acculturation: The Yaqui of Sonora and Arizona and the Tewa of New Mexico. *Language* 32: 146–57. (Reprinted in Dell Hymes, ed. (1964), *Language in Culture and Society*, pp. 109–20. New York: Harper & Row.)

Du Bois, John W. 2000. Grammar. *Journal of Linguistic Anthropology* 91–2): 92–5.

Duncan, Hugh Dalziel. 1962. *Communication and Social Order*. Oxford: Oxford University Press.

Dundes, Alan, Jerry W. Leach, and Bora Özkök. 1972. The strategy of Turkish boys' verbal dueling. In John J. Gumperz and Dell Hymes, eds, *Directions in Sociolinguistics: The Ethnography of Communication*, pp. 139–60. New York: Holt, Rinehart & Winston.

Duranti, Allesandro. 1985. Sociocultural dimensions of discourse. In Teun A. Van Dijk, ed., *Handbook of Discourse Analysis. Volume I: Disciplines of Discourse*, pp. 193–230. New York: Academic Press.

—— 1988. Ethnography of speaking: toward a linguistics of the praxis. In Frederick J. Newmeyer, ed., *Language: The Socio-Cultural Context*, pp. 210–28. Cambridge: Cambridge University Press.

—— 1994. *From Grammar to Politics: Linguistic Anthropology in a Western Samoan Village*. Berkeley: University of California Press.

—— 1997a. *Linguistic Anthropology*. Cambridge: Cambridge University Press.

—— 1997b. Universal and culture-specific properties of greetings. *Journal of Linguistic Anthropology* 7(1): 63–97.

Duranti, Allesandro and Charles Goodwin, eds 1992. *Rethinking Context: Language as an Interactive Phenomenon*. Cambridge: Cambridge University Press.

Duranti, Allesandro and Bambi B. Schieffelin. 1987. Opening remarks: What's pragmatics? *Papers in Pragmatics* 1(1): i–ii.

Dutkova, Ludmila. 1998. Texas Czech: an ethnolinguistic study. Dissertation, University of Arizona.

Eckert, Penelope. 1999. *The Linguistic Construction of Identity in Belten High*. Oxford: Blackwell.

Eckert, Penelope and Sally McConnell-Ginet. 1999. New generalizations and explanations in language and gender research. *Language in Society* 28: 185–201.

Edgerton, Robert B. 1971. *The Individual in Cultural Adaptation: A Study of Four East African Peoples.* Berkeley: University of California Press.

Edwards, John. 1985. *Language, Society and Identity.* Oxford: Blackwell.

Eggan, Dorothy. 1956. Instruction and affect in Hopi cultural continuity. *Southwestern Journal of Anthropology* 12(4): 347–70.

Eggington, William G. 1987. Written academic discourse in Korean: implications for effective communication. In Ulla Connor and Robert B. Kaplan, eds, *Writing Across Languages*, pp. 153–67. Reading, MA: Addison-Wesley.

Ekman, Paul. 1972. Universal and cultural differences in facial expressions of emotion. In J. K. Cole, ed., *Nebraska Symposium on Motivation* (1971), pp. 207–83. Lincoln: University of Nebraska Press.

Ekman, Paul, Wallace V. Friesen, and Silvan S. Tomkins. 1971. Facial affect scoring technique: a first validity study. *Semiotica* 3: 37–58.

El-Dash, Linda and G. Richard Tucker. 1975. Subjective reactions to various speech styles in Egypt. *International Journal of the Sociology of Language* 6: 33–54.

Eliason, Marcus. 1980. "Tu" "du" or not "tu" "du." Associated Press. (Appeared in Champaign-Urbana, IL, *News-Gazette*, September).

Ellis, D. S. 1967. Speech and social status in America. *Social Forces* 45: 431–7.

Emihovich, Catherine. 1986. Argument as status assertion: contextual variations in children's disputes. *Language in Society* 15: 485–500.

Enninger, Werner and Joachim Raith. 1982. An ethnography of communication approach to ceremonial situations: a study on communication in institutionalized social contexts: the Old Order Amish church service. *Zeitschrift für Dialektologie und Linguistik Beihefte* Heft 42. Wiesbaden: Franz Steiner Verlag GMBH.

Erickson, Frederick. 1976. One function of proxemic shifts in face to face interaction. In A. Kendon, R. Harris, and M. R. Key, eds, *The Organization of Behavior in Face to Face Interaction.* The Hague: Mouton.

Erickson, Frederick and Jeffrey Shultz. 1979. When is a context? Some issues and methods in the analysis of social competence. Manuscript.

Erickson, Frederick and Jeffrey Shultz. 1982. *The Counselor as Gatekeeper: Social Interactions in Interviews.* New York: Academic Press.

Errington, J. Joseph. 1998. *Shifting Languages: Interaction and Identity in Javanese Indonesian.* Cambridge: Cambridge University Press.

Ervin-Tripp, Susan M. 1972. On sociolinguistic rules: alternation and co-occurrence. In John J. Gumperz and Dell Hymes, eds, *Directions in Sociolinguistics: The Ethnography of Communication*, pp. 213–50. New York: Holt, Rinehart & Winston.

Estrich, Robert M. and Hans Sperber. 1952. *Three Keys to Language.* New York: Rinehart.

Fairclough, Norman. 1999. Review of *Disorders of Discourse* (1996), by Ruth Wodak (London: Longman). *Language in Society* 29(4): 605–9.

Fang, Hanquan and J. H. Heng. 1983. Social changes and changing address norms in China. *Language in Society* 12(4): 495–507.

Fanshel, David and Freda Moss. 1971. *Playback: A Marriage in Jeopardy Examined*. New York: Columbia University Press.

Farghal, Mohammed. 1995. Euphemism in Arabic: a Gricean interpretation. *Anthropological Linguistics* 37(3): 366–78.

Fasold, Ralph W. 1975. How to study language maintenance and shift: the case of the Tiwa Indians. Paper presented at the Linguistic Society of America, San Francisco.

Fellin, Luciana. 2001. Language ideologies, language socialization and language revival in an Italian alpine village. Dissertation, University of Arizona.

Ferguson, Charles A. 1959. Diglossia. *Word* 15: 325–40. (Reprinted in Dell Hymes, ed. (1964), *Language in Culture and Society*, pp. 429–37. New York: Harper & Row.)

—— 1964. Baby talk in six languages. In John J. Gumperz and Dell Hymes, eds, The ethnography of communication, *American Anthropologist* 66(6): 103–14.

—— 1978. Religious factors in language spread. Paper presented for the Conference on Language Spread, Aberystwyth, Wales.

—— 1986. The study of religious discourse. In Deborah Tannen and James E. Alatis, eds, *Language and Linguistics: The Interdependence of Theory, Data, and Application*, pp. 205–13. Washington, DC: Georgetown University Press.

Fernald, Anne and Hiromi Morikawa. 1993. Common themes and cultural variation in Japanese and American mothers' speech to infants. *Child Development* 64: 637–56.

Fillmore, Charles J. 1968. The case for case. In Emmon Bach and Robert T. Harms, eds, *Universals in Linguistic Theory*, pp, 1–88. New York: Holt, Rinehart & Winston.

Fischer, John L. 1958. Social influence in the choice of a linguistic variant. *Word* 14: 47–56. (Reprinted in Dell Hymes, ed. (1964), *Language in Culture and Society*, pp. 483–8. New York: Harper & Row.)

—— 1965. The stylistic significance of consonantal sandhi in Trukese and Ponapean. *American Anthropologist* 67: 1495–1502. (Reprinted in John J. Gumperz and Dell Hymes, eds (1972), *Directions in Sociolinguistics: The Ethnography of Communication*. New York: Holt, Rinehart & Winston.)

Fishman, Joshua A. 1964. Language maintenance and language shift as fields of inquiry. *Linguistics* 9: 32–70.

—— 1966. *Language Loyalty in the United States*. The Hague: Mouton.

—— 1971. The links between micro- and macro-sociolinguistics in the study of who speaks what language to whom and when. In Joshua A. Fishman, Robert L. Cooper, and Roxana Ma, *Bilingualism in the Barrio*, pp. 583–604. Bloomington: Indiana University Press.

—— 1972. Domains and the relationship between micro and macro-sociolinguistics. In John J. Gumperz and Dell Hymes, eds, *Directions in Sociolinguistics: The Ethnography of Communication*. New York: Hold, Rinehart & Winston, pp. 435–53. (Revised version of 1971.)

—— 1980. Bilingualism and biculturalism as individual and as societal phenomena. *Journal of Multilingual and Multicultural Development* 1(1): 3–15.

—— 1985. The societal basis of the intergenerational continuity of additional languages. In Kurt R. Jankowsky, ed., *Scientific and Humanistic Dimensions of Language*, pp. 555–7. Amsterdam: John Benjamins.

Fishman, Joshua A., Robert L. Cooper, and Roxana Ma./1971. *Bilingualism in the Barrio*. Bloomington: Indiana University Press.

Fishman, Joshua A., Charles A. Ferguson, and Jyotirindra Das Gupta, eds 1968. *Language Problems of Developing Nations*. New York: John Wiley & Sons.

Folb, Edith A. 1980. *Runnin' Down Some Lines: The Language and Culture of Black Teenagers*. Cambridge, MA: Harvard University Press.

Fortes, Meyer. 1938. Social and psychological aspects of education in Taleland. *Africa* 11(4) Supplement. (Reprinted in John Middleton, ed. (1970), *From Child to Adult: Studies in the Anthropology of Education*, pp. 14–74. Austin: University of Texas Press.)

Foucalt, Michel. 1972. *The Archaeology of Knowledge*. (Translated by A. M. Sheridan Smith.) London: Routledge.

Fowler, Roger. 1985. Power. In Teun van Dijk, ed., *The Handbook of Discourse Analysis*, vol. 4: *Discourse Analysis in Society*, pp. 61–82. London: Academic Press.

—— 1996. *Linguistic Criticism*, second edition. Oxford: Oxford University Press.

Frake, Charles O. 1969. Struck by speech: the Yakan concept of litigation. In Laura Nader, ed., *Law in Culture and Society*. Chicago: Aldine. (Reprinted in John J. Gumperz and Dell Hymes, eds (1972), *Directions in Sociolinguistics: The Ethnography of Communication*, pp. 106–29. New York: Holt, Rinehart & Winston.)

Franklin, Karl J. 1977. The Kewa language in culture and society. In Stephen A. Wurm, ed., *Language, Culture, Society, and the Modern World* (Fascicle 1). Pacific Linguistics Series C, No. 40: New Guinea Area Languages and Language Study Vol. 3.

Frazer, Sir James George. 1922. *The Golden Bough: A Study in Magic and Religion*. New York: MacMillan.

Freed, Alice F. and Alice Greenwood. 1996. Women, men, and type of talk: what makes the difference? *Language in Society* 25: 1–26.

Fries, Charles C. 1945. *Teaching and Learning English as a Foreign Language*. Ann Arbor: University of Michigan Press.

Gal, Susan. 1978. Peasant men can't get wives: language change and sex roles in a bilingual community. *Language in Society* 7(1): 1–16.

—— 1979. *Language Shift: Social Determinants of Linguistic Change in Bilingual Austria*. New York: Academic Press.

Gao, Mobo C. F. 2000. *Mandarin Chinese*. Oxford: Oxford University Press.

Gardner, Howard, Ellen Winner, Robin Bechhofer, and Dennie Wolf. 1978. The development of figurative language. In Keith E. Nelson, ed., *Children's Language*, vol. 1, pp. 1–38. New York: Gardner Press.

Gardner, Peter M. 1966. Symmetric respect and memorate knowledge: the structure and ecology of individualistic culture. *Southwestern Journal of Anthropology* 22: 398–415.

Garfinkel, Harold. 1967. *Studies in Ethnomethodology*. Englewood, Cliffs, NJ: Prentice-Hall.

—— 1972. Remarks on ethnomethodology. In John J. Gumperz and Dell Hymes, eds, *Directions in Sociolinguistics: The Ethnography of Communication*, pp. 301–45. New York: Holt, Rinehart & Winston.

Garnica, Olga K. 1977. Some prosodic and paralinguistic features of speech to young children. In Catherine E. Snow and Charles A. Ferguson, eds, *Talking to Children: Language Input and Acquisition*, pp. 63–88. New York: Academic Press.

Garvey, Catherine. 1977. Play with language and speech. In Susan M. Ervin-Tripp and Claudia Mitchell-Kernan, eds, *Child Discourse*, pp. 27–47. New York: Academic Press.

Gaudart, Hyacinth. 1995. Some ways of speaking among speakers of English in Malaysia. *Journal of Asian Pacific Communication* 6(3): 193–212.

Geertz, Clifford. 1973. *The Interpretation of Cultures*. New York: Basic Books.

Genesee, Fred, Isabelle Boivin, and Elena Nicoladis. 1996. Talking with strangers: a study of bilingual children's communicative competence. *Applied Psycholinguistics* 17: 427–42.

Gibbons, John, ed. 1994. *Language and the Law*. London: Longman.

Giles, Howard. 1979. Ethnicity markers in speech. In Klaus R. Scherer and Howard Giles, eds, *Social Markers in Speech*, pp. 251–90. Cambridge: Cambridge University Press.

Giles, Howard, Klaus R. Scherer, and D. M. Taylor. 1979. Speech markers in social interaction. In Klaus R. Scherer and Howard Giles, eds, *Social Markers in Speech*, pp. 343–81. Cambridge: Cambridge University Press.

Giles, Howard, D. M. Taylor, and R. Bourhis. 1973. Towards a theory of interpersonal accommodation through language: some Canadian data. *Language in Society* 2: 177–223.

Gilmore, Perry. 1981. Spelling "Mississippi": recontextualizing a literacy-related speech event. Paper presented at the Second Annual University of Pennsylvania Ethnography in Education Research Forum, Philadelphia.

—— 1985. Silence and sulking: emotional displays in the classroom. In Deborah Tannen and Muriel Saville-Troike, eds, *Perspectives on Silence*, pp. 139–62. Norwood, NJ: Ablex.

Gleason, Jean Berko. 1975. Fathers and other strangers: men's speech to young children. In Daniel P. Dato, ed., *Developmental Psycholinguistics: Theory and Applications*, pp. 289–97. Washington, DC: Georgetown University Press.

—— 1976. Parental judgement of children's language abilities. Paper presented at the Linguistic Society of America, Philadelphia.

Gleason, Jean Berko, Ester Blank Grief, Sandra Weintraub, and Janet Fardella. 1977. Father doesn't know but: parents' awareness of their children's linguistic, cognitive, and affective development. Paper presented at the Biennial Meeting of the Society for Research in Child Development, New Orleans.

Gleason, Jean Berko and Sandra Weintraub. 1978. Input language and the acquisition of communicative competence. In Keith Nelson, ed., *Children's Language*, vol. 1, pp. 171–222. New York: Gardner Press.

Goffman, Erving. 1959. *The Presentation of Self in Everyday Life*. Garden City, NY: Doubleday.

—— 1963. *Behavior in Public Places: Notes on the Social Organization of Gatherings*. New York: The Free Press.

—— 1967. *Interaction Ritual: Essays on Face-to-Face Behavior*. Garden City, NY: Doubleday.

—— 1971. *Relations in Public: Microstudies of the Public Order*. New York: Harper & Row.

—— 1979. Footing. *Semiotica* 25(1–2): 1–29.

Goldfield, Beverly A. and Catherine E. Snow. 1992. "What's your cousin Arthur's mommy's name?": features of family talk about kin and kin terms. *First Language* 12: 187–205.

Goldman, Laurence Richard. 1987. Ethnographic interpretations of parent–child discourse in Huli. *Journal of Child Language* 14: 447–66.

—— 1993. *The Culture of Coincidence: Accident and Absolute Liability in Huli.* Oxford: Clarendon.

Goldstein, Tara. 1997. *Two Languages at Work: Bilingual Life on the Production Floor.* Berlin: Mouton de Gruyter.

González, L. Antonio. 1986. The effects of first language education on the second language and academic achievement of Mexican immigrant elementary school children in the United States. Dissertation, University of Illinois at Urbana-Champaign.

Goodman, Felicitas D. 1969. The acquisition of glossolalia behavior. Paper presented at the American Anthropological Association, New Orleans.

Goodwin, Marjorie Harness. 1990. *He-Said-She-Said: Talk as Social Organization Among Black Children.* Bloomington: Indiana University Press.

Gottschalk, Louis A. and Coldine C. Gleser. 1969. *The Measurement of Psychological States through the Content Analysis of Verbal Behavior.* Berkeley: University of California Press.

Graham, Laura R. 1995. *Performing Dreams: Discourses of Immortality Among the Xavante of Central Brazil.* Austin, TX: University of Texas Press.

Graves, Zoë R. and Joseph Glick. 1978. The effect of context on mother–child interaction: a progress report. *Institute for Comparative Human Development Newsletter* 2(3): 41–6.

Grice, H. Paul. 1975. Logic and conversation. In Peter Cole and Jerry L. Morgan, eds, *Syntax and Semantics: Speech Acts*, vol. 3, pp. 41–58. New York: Academic Press.

Grimes, Barbara F. 1985. Language attitudes: identity, distinctiveness, survival in the Vaupes. *Journal of Multicultural and Multilingual Development* 6(5): 389–401.

Grimes, Larry M. 1977. The linguistic taboo: examples from modern Mexican Spanish. *The Bilingual Review/ La Revista Bilingüe* 4(1–2): 69–80.

Grimshaw, Allen D. 2000. Control. *Journal of Linguistic Anthropology* 9(1–2): 50–3.

Grobsmith, Elizabeth S. 1979. Styles of speaking: an analysis of Lakota communication alternatives. *Anthropological Linguistics* 21(7): 355–61.

Gumperz, John J. 1970. Sociolinguistics and communication in small groups. Language-Behavior Research Laboratory, Working Paper No. 33. Berkeley: University of California.

—— 1976. The sociolinguistic significance of conversational code-switching. Language-Behavior Research Laboratory, Working Paper No. 46. Berkeley: University of California.

—— 1977. Sociocultural knowledge in conversational inference. In Muriel Saville-Troike, ed., *Linguistics and Anthropology*, pp. 191–212. Washington, DC: Georgetown University Press.

—— 1979. The retrieval and sociocultural knowledge in conversation. *Poetics Today* 1: 273–86.

—— 1982. *Discourse Strategies*. Cambridge: Cambridge University Press.

—— 1984. Communicative competence revisited. In Deborah Schiffrin, ed., *Meaning, Form, and Use in Context: Linguistic Applications*, pp. 278–89. Washington, DC: Georgetown University Press.

—— 1992. Contextualization and understanding. In Allesandro Duranti and Charles Goodwin, eds, *Rethinking Context: Language as an Interactive Phenomenon*, pp. 229–52. Cambridge: Cambridge University Press.

—— 2000. Inference. *Journal of Linguistic Anthropology* 9(1–2): 131–3.

Gumperz, John J. and Stephen C. Levinson, eds 1996. *Rethinking Linguistic Relativity*. Cambridge: Cambridge University Press.

Haas, Mary R. 1941. Tunica. In Franz Boas, ed., *Handbook of American Indian Languages*, part 4, pp. 1–143. Bureau of American Ethnology Bulletin 40. Washington, DC: Smithsonian Institution.

—— 1944. Men's and women's speech in Koasati. *Language* 20: 142–9.

—— 1957. Interlingual word taboos. *American Anthropologist* 53: 338–41.

Hall, Edward T. 1959. *The Silent Language*. Garden City, NY: Doubleday.

—— 1963. A system for the notation of proxemic behavior. *American Anthropologist* 65: 1003–26.

Halliday, Michael A. K. 1970. Functional diversity in language as seen from a consideration of modality and mood in English. *Foundations of Language* 6: 322–61.

—— 1975. *Learning How to Mean: Explorations in the Development of Language*. London: Edward Arnold.

—— 1978. *Language as Social Semiotic: The Social Interpretation of Language and Meaning*. London: Edward Arnold.

Halloran, S. Michael. 1982. Rhetoric in the American college curriculum: the decline of public discourse. *Pre/text* 3: 245–69.

Halmari, Helena. 1998. Language maintenance on the Alabama-Coushatta reservation. *Anthropological Linguistics* 40(3): 409–28.

Hamp, Eric. 1978. Problems of multilingualism in small linguistic communities. In James E. Alatis, ed., *International Dimensions of Bilingual Education*, pp. 155–64. Washington, DC: Georgetown University Press.

Hanks, William F. 1986. Authenticity and ambivalence in the text: a colonial Maya case. *American Ethnologist* 13: 721–43.

Hannerz, Ulf. 1969. *Soulside: Inquiries into Ghetto Culture and Community*. New York: Columbia University Press.

Hansen, Jette F. 2000. Social and linguistic constraints on the acquisition of an L2 phonology: a case study. Dissertation, The Ohio State University.

Harding, Susan Friend. 2000. *The Book of Jerry Falwell: Fundamentalist Language and Politics*. Princeton, NJ: Princeton University Press.

Harman, Thomas. 1567. *A Careat or Warening for Commen Cursetores Vulgarely Called Vagabones*. London: Wylliam Gryffith. Included as "A caveat for common cursitors" in Gāmini Salgādo, ed. (1972), *Cony-Catchers and Bawdy Baskets: An Anthropology of Elizabethan Low Life*. Harmondsworth: Penguin. (Cited in M. A. K. Halliday (1978), *Language as Social Semiotic*. Baltimore, MD: University Park Press.)

Harper, Robert G., Arthur N. Wiens, and Joseph D. Matarazzo. 1978. *Nonverbal Communication: The State of the Art*. New York: John Wiley & Sons.

Harrington, Charles. 1978. Bilingual education, social stratification, and cultural pluralism. *Equal Opportunity Review*, Summer. New York: ERIC Clearinghouse on Urban Education, Teachers College, Columbia University.

Harris, Tracy Kay. 1994. *Death of a Language: The History of Judeo-Spanish*. Newark, DE: University of Delaware Press.

Haviland, J. B. 1979. Guugu Yimidhirr brother-in-law language. *Language in Society* 8(3): 365–93.

Heath, Shirley Brice. 1983. *Ways with Words: Language, Life, and Work in Communities and Classrooms*. Cambridge: Cambridge University Press.

Helfrich, Hede. 1979. Age markers in speech. In Klaus R. Scherer and Howard Giles, eds, *Social Markers in Speech*, pp. 63–107. Cambridge: Cambridge University Press.

Heller, Monica. nd. *Language and Ethnic Identity in a Toronto French-Language School*. Toronto: Ontario Institute for Studies in Education.

Hendricks, Janet Wall. 1988. Power and knowledge: discourse and ideological transformation among the Shuar. *American Ethnologist* 15(2): 216–38.

Hill, Jane H. and Kenneth C. Hill. 1980. Mixed grammar, purist grammar, and language attitudes in modern Nahuatl. *Language in Society* 9: 321–48.

—— 1986. *Speaking Mexicano: Dynamics of Syncretic Language in Central Mexico*. Tucson: University of Arizona Press.

Hill, Jane H. and Judith T. Irvine, eds 1993. *Responsibility and Evidence in Oral Discourse*. Cambridge: Cambridge University Press.

Hill, Jane H. and Bruce Mannheim. 1992. Language and world view. *Annual Review of Anthropology* 21: 381–406.

Hinds, John. 1987. Reader versus writer responsibility: a new typology. In Ulla Connor and Robert B. Kaplan, eds, *Writing Across Languages: Analysis of L2 Text*, pp. 141–52. Reading, MA: Addison-Wesley.

Hobart, Mark. 1975. Orators and patrons: two types of political leader in Balinese village society. In Maurice Bloch, ed., *Political Language and Oratory in Traditional Society*, pp. 65–92. New York: Academic Press.

Hogbin, H. Ian. 1946. A New Guinea childhood: from weaning till the eighth year in Wogeo. *Oceania* 16(4): 275–96.

Holmes, Janet. 1995. *Women, Men and Politeness*. London: Longman.

Holmes, Janet and Miriam Meyerhoff. 1999. The community of practice: theories and methodologies in language and gender research. *Language in Society* 28(2): 173–83.

Hong, Wei. 1998. *Request Patterns in Chinese and German: A Cross-Cultural Study*. Munich: Lincom Europa.

Hoover, Mary Eleanor Rhodes. 1975. Appropriate use of Black English by Black children as rated by parents. Technical Report No. 46, Stanford Center for Research and Development in Teaching.

Hopkins, Nicholas A. 1977. Historical and sociocultural aspects of the distribution of linguistic variants in Highland Chiapas, Mexico. In Ben G. Blount and Mary Sanches, eds, *Sociocultural Dimensions of Language Change*, pp. 185–226. New York: Academic Press.

Howard-Malverde, Rosaleen. 1998. Words for Our Lord of Huanca: discursive strategies in a Quechua sermon from southern Peru. *Anthropological Linguistics* 40(4): 570–95.

Hoyle, Susan and Carolyn Temple Adger, eds 1998. *Kids Talk: Strategic Language Use in Later Childhood.* Oxford: Oxford University Press.

Hsu, Tung-ming. 2002. Impatience drives new discourse in China. *Taipei Times* (online edition), January 8. Translated by Perry Svensson.

Hu, Hsien Chin. 1944. The Chinese concepts of "face." *American Anthropologist* 46(1): 45–64.

Hudson, Richard A. 1980. *Sociolinguistics.* Cambridge: Cambridge University Press.

Huspek, Michael R. 1986. Linguistic variation, context and meaning: a case of -*ing*/ *in*' variation in North American workers' speech. *Language in Society* 15: 149–64.

Hymes, Dell. 1961. Functions of speech: an evolutionary approach. In Frederick C. Gruber, ed., *Anthropology and Education*, pp. 55–83. Philadelphia: University of Pennsylvania Press.

—— 1962. The ethnography of speaking. In Thomas Gladwin and William C. Sturtevant, eds, *Anthropology and Human Behavior*, pp. 13–53. Washington, DC: Anthropological Society of Washington.

—— 1966a. On communicative competence. Paper presented at the Research Planning Conference on Language Development among Disadvantaged Children, Yeshiva University.

—— 1966b. Two types of linguistic relativity. In William Bright, ed., *Sociolinguistics*, pp. 114–67. The Hague: Mouton.

—— 1967. Models of interaction of language and social setting. *Journal of Social Issues* 33(2): 8–28.

—— 1970. Linguistic aspects of comparative political research. In R. Holt and J. Turner, eds, *The Methodology of Comparative Research*, pp. 295–341. New York: The Free Press.

—— 1972a. The contribution of folklore to sociolinguistic research. In Américo Paredes and Richard Bauman, eds, *Toward New Perspectives in Folklore*, pp. 42–50. Austin: University of Texas Press.

—— 1972b. Introduction. In Courtney Cazden, Vera John, and Dell Hymes, eds, *Functions of Language in the Classroom*, pp. xi–lvii. New York: Teachers College Press.

—— 1972c. Models of interaction of language and social life. In John J. Gumperz and Dell Hymes, eds, *Directions in Sociolinguistics: Ethnography of Communication*, pp. 35–71. New York: Holt, Rinehart & Winston.

—— 1973. On the origins and foundations of inequality among speakers. *Language as a Human Problem.* Special issue of *Daedalus* 102(3): 59–85.

—— 1974. *Foundations in Sociolinguistics: An Ethnographic Approach.* Philadelphia: University of Pennsylvania Press.

—— 1979a. How to talk like a bear in Takelma. *International Journal of American Linguistics* 45(2): 101–6.

—— 1979b. Sapir, competence, voices. In Charles J. Fillmore, Daniel Kempler, and William S-Y Wang, eds, *Individual Differences in Language Ability and Language Behavior*, pp. 33–45. New York: Academic Press.

—— 1980. Tonkawa poetics: John Rush Buffalo's "Coyote and Eagle's Daughter." In Jacques Maquet, ed., *On Linguistic Anthropology: Essays in Honor of Harry Hoijer, 1979.* Malibu, CA: Undena Publications.

—— 1981. *"In Vain I Tried to Tell You"*: *Essays in Native American Ethnopoetics.* Philadelphia: University of Pennsylvania Press.

—— 1987. Communicative competence. In Ulrich Ammon, Norbert Dittmar, and Klaus J. Mattheier, eds, *Sociolinguistics: An International Handbook of the Science of Language and Society,* pp. 219–29. Berlin: Walter de Gruyter.

—— 1993. Anthropological linguistics: a retrospective. *Anthropological Linguistics* 35: 9–14.

—— 1996. *Ethnography, Linguistics, Narrative Inequality: Toward an Understanding of Voice.* London: Taylor and Francis.

—— 2000. The emergence of sociolinguistics: a response to Samarin. *Journal of Sociolinguistics* 4(2): 312–15.

Hymes, Dell, Joel Sherzer, Regna Darnell, et al. 1967. Outline guide for the ethnographic study of speech use. Manuscript. (Revised by Joel Sherzer and Regna Darnell and published in John J. Gumperz and Dell Hymes, eds (1972), *Directions in Sociolinguistics: Ethnography of Communication,* pp. 548–54. New York: Holt, Rinehart & Winston.)

Indrasuta, Chantanee. 1987. A comparison of the written compositions of American and Thai students. Dissertation, University of Illinois at Urbana-Champaign.

Irvine, Judith Temkin. 1973. Caste and communication in a Wolof village. Dissertation, University of Pennsylvania.

Isbell, Billie Jean and Fredy A. R. Fernandez. 1977. The ontogenesis of metaphor: riddle games among Quechua speakers seen as cognitive discovery procedures. *Journal of Latin American Lore* 3(1): 19–49.

Itakura, Hiroko. 2001. *Conversational Dominance and Gender: A Study of Japanese Speakers in First and Second Language Contexts.* Philadelphia, PA: John Benjamins.

Jacobson, Holly. 2002. Translation of the health brochure and impact on the target reader: a contrastive analysis of the structural and pragmatic features of texts translated into Spanish versus texts written originally in Spanish. Dissertation, University of Arizona.

Jacquemet, Marco. 1996. *Credibility in Court: Communicative Practices in the Camorra Trials.* Cambridge: Cambridge University Press.

Jakobson, Roman. 1938. On the theory of phonological associations among languages. *Proceedings of the Fourth International Congress of Linguists, Copenhagen,* pp. 45–58. (Reprinted in A. Keiler, ed., *A Reader in Historical and Comparative Linguistics* (1972), pp. 241–52. New York: Holt, Rinehart & Winston.)

—— 1960. Linguistics and poetics. In Thomas A. Sebeok, ed., *Style in Language.* Cambridge, MA: MIT Press.

Jenness, Diamond. 1929. The ancient education of a Carrier Indian. National Museum of Canada Bulletin No. 26: Annual report for 1928, pp. 22–7. Ottawa: F. A. Acland.

Johnson, Donna M. 1994. Who is we? Constructing communities in US–Mexico border discourse. *Discourse & Society* 5(2): 207–31.

Johnson, Fern L. 2000. *Speaking Culturally: Language Diversity in the United States.* Thousand Oaks, CA: Sage.

Junefelt, Karen and Tiia Tulviste. 1997. American, Estonian and Swedish mothers' regulation of their children's discourse construction. In M. D. P. de Lyra and

Joan Valsiner, eds, *Construction of Psychological Processes in Interpersonal Communication*. Hillsdale, NJ: Ablex.

Kachru, Braj B. 1976. Models of English for the third world: White man's linguistic burden or language pragmatics? *TESOL Quarterly* 10(2): 221–39.

—— 1977. Linguistic schizophrenia and language census: a note on the language situation. *Linguistics* 186: 17–32.

—— 1980. The pragmatics of non-native varieties of English. In Larry Smith, ed., *English for Cross-Cultural Communication*. London: Macmillan.

—— 1982a. The bilingual's linguistic repertoire. In Beverly Hartford, Albert Valdman, and Charles R. Foster, eds, *Issues in International Bilingual Education: The Role of the Vernacular*, pp. 25–52. New York: Plenum Press.

—— 1982b. Meaning in deviation: toward understanding non-native English texts. In Braj B. Kachru, ed., *The Other Tongue: English Across Cultures*, pp. 325–50. Urbana: University of Illinois Press.

—— 1983. *The Indianization of English: The English Language in India*. London: Oxford University Press.

—— 1986. *The Alchemy of English: The Spread, Functions and Models of Non-Native Englishes*. Oxford: Pergamon Institute of English.

Kachru, Yamuna. 1987. Cross-cultural texts: discourse strategies and discourse interpretation. In Larry E. Smith, ed., *Discourse Across Cultures*, pp. 87–100. New York: Prentice Hall.

—— 1996. Culture in rhetorical styles: contrastive rhetoric and World Englishes. In Neil Mercer and Joan Swann, eds, *Learning English: Development and Diversity*, pp. 305–14. London: The Open University.

Kanazawa, H. and L. Loveday. 1988. The Japanese immigrant community in Brazil: language contact and shift. *Journal of Multilingual and Multicultural Development* 9(5): 423–35.

Kaplan, Robert B. 1966. Cultural thought patterns in intercultural education. *Language Learning* 16: 1–20.

—— 1988. Contrastive rhetoric and second language learning: notes toward a theory of contrastive rhetoric. In Alan C. Purves, ed., *Writing Across Languages and Cultures: Issues in Contrastive Rhetoric*, pp. 275–304. Newbury Park, CA: Sage.

Kasper, Gabrielle and Merete Dahl. 1991. Research methods in interlanguage pragmatics. *Studies in Second Language Acquisition* 13(2): 215–47.

Katriel, Tamar. 1987. "Bexibùdim!": ritualized sharing among Israeli children. *Language in Society* 16: 305–20.

Kawashima, Takeyoshi. 1979. The Japanese linguistic consciousness and the law. *Japan Echo* 6(3): 105–15. (Translation from "Nihonjin no gengo ishiki to hōritsu," in *Sekai*, February 1979.)

Keane, Webb. 1997. *Signs of Recognition: Powers and Hazards of Representation in an Indonesian Society*. Berkeley: University of California Press.

Keating, Elizabeth. 1998. *Power Sharing: Language, Rank, Gender, and Social Space in Pohnpei, Micronesia*. Oxford: Oxford University Press.

Keenan, Elinor O. 1974. Conversational competence in children. *Journal of Child Language* 1: 163–83.

—— 1975. A sliding sense of obligatoriness: the polystructure of Malagasy oratory. In Maurice Bloch, ed., *Political Language and Oratory in Traditional Society*, pp. 93–112. New York: Academic Press.

—— 1976. The universality of conversational postulates. *Language in Society* 5(1): 67–80.

Kempf, Renate. 1985. Pronouns and terms of address in *Neues Deutschland*. *Language in Society* 14: 223–37.

Kempton, Willet. 1979. The rhythmic basis of interactional micro-synchrony. In Mary R. Key, ed., *Verbal and Nonverbal Communication*. The Hague: Mouton.

Kerswill, Paul. 1994. *Dialects Converging: Rural Speech in Urban Norway*. Oxford: Clarendon.

Kessen, William and Katherine Nelson. 1976. What does the child's world look like? *Carnegie Quarterly* 24(2): 1–3.

Kiesling, Scott Fabius. 1998. Men's identities in sociolinguistic variation: the case of fraternity men. *Journal of Sociolinguistics* 2(1): 69–99.

Kim, Young Yun. 1991. Intercultural communicative competence: a systems-theoretic view. In Stella Ting-Toomey and Felipe Korzenny, eds, *Cross-Cultural Interpersonal Communication*, pp. 259–75. Newbury Park, CA: Sage.

Kipers, Pamela S. 1987. Gender and topic. *Language in Society* 16: 543–57.

Kleifgen, JoAnne, Soonai Ham, Atteya El Noory, Mary Fritz, and Muriel Saville-Troike. 1986. Shifting patterns of language dominance in bilingual children. Paper presented at the American Educational Research Association, San Francisco, CA.

Knipple, Sheilendr. 2001. What's a bed plug? An L.O.L. in N.A.D. *The New York Times: Week in Review*, May 13.

Kochman, Thomas, ed. 1972. *Rappin' and Stylin' Out: Communication in Urban Black America*. Urbana: University of Illinois Press.

Kramsch, Claire. 1997. The privilege of the nonnative speaker. *PMLA* 112(3): 359–69.

Kress, Gunther. 1991. Critical discourse analysis. *Annual Review of Applied Linguistics* 11: 84–99.

Kress, Gunther and Bob Hodge. 1979. *Language as Ideology*. London: Routledge and Kegan Paul.

Kroeber, Alfred L. 1935. History and science in anthropology. *American Anthropologist* 37: 538–69.

—— 1944. *Configurations of Culture Growth*. Berkeley: University of California Press.

Kuiper, Koenraad. 1996. *Smooth Talkers: The Linguistic Performance of Auctioneers and Sportscasters*. Mahwah, NJ: Lawrence Erlbaum.

Kuipers, Joel C. 1990. *Power in Performance: The Creation of Textual Authority in Weyewa Ritual Speech*. Philadelphia: University of Pennsylvania Press.

—— 1998. *Language, Identity, and Marginality in Indonesia: The Changing Nature of Ritual Speech on the Island of Sumba*. Cambridge: Cambridge University Press.

Labov, William. 1963. The social motivation of a sound change. *Word* 19: 273–309.

—— 1964. A proposed study of Negro and Puerto Rican speech in New York City. *Project Literacy Reports*. Ithaca, NY: Cornell University.

—— 1966. *The Social Stratification of English in New York City*. Washington, DC: Center for Applied Linguistics.

—— 1970. The logic of nonstandard English. In James E. Alatis, ed., *Linguistics and the Teaching of Standard English to Speakers of Other Languages or Dialects*, pp. 1–44. Washington, DC: Georgetown University Press.

—— 1972. On the mechanism of linguistic change. In John J. Gumperz and Dell Hymes, eds, *Directions in Sociolinguistics: The Ethnography of Communication*, pp. 512–38. New York: Holt, Rinehart & Winston.

—— 1981. Speech actions and reactions in personal narrative. In Deborah Tannen, ed., *Analyzing Discourse: Text and Talk*, pp. 219–47. Washington, DC: Georgetown University Press.

—— 1987. Are Black and White vernaculars diverging? Papers from the NWAVE XIV panel discussion. *American Speech* 62: 5–12.

Labov, William, Paul Cohen, Clarence Robbins, and John Lewis. 1968. A study of the non-standard English of Negro and Puerto Rican speakers in New York City. USOE final report.

Labov, William and David Fanshel. 1977. *Therapeutic Discourse: Psychotherapy as Convention*. New York: Academic Press.

Lado, Robert. 1957. *Linguistics Across Cultures*. Ann Arbor: University of Michigan Press.

Lagacé, Robert O., ed. 1977. *Sixty Cultures: A Guide to the HRAF Probability Sample Files* (Part A). New Haven, CN: Human Relations Area Files.

Lakoff, Robin. 1973. Questionable answers and answerable questions. In Braj B. Kachru et al., eds, *Issues in Linguistics: Papers in Honor of Henry and Renée Kahane*. Urbana: University of Illinois Press.

Laosa, Luis M. 1977. Socialization, education, and continuity: the importance of the sociocultural context. *Young Children* 32(5): 21–7.

Laughlin, Robert M. 1980. *Of Shoes and Ships and Sealing Wax: Sundries from Zinacantán*. Contributions to Anthropology No. 25. Washington, DC: Smithsonian Institution.

Laver, John and Peter Trudgill. 1979. Phonetic and linguistic markers in speech. In Klaus R. Scherer and Howard Giles, eds, *Social Markers in Speech*, pp. 1–32. Cambridge: Cambridge University Press.

Leach, Edmund. 1976. *Culture and Communication*. Cambridge: Cambridge University Press.

Leap, William L. 1993. *American Indian English*. Salt Lake City: University of Utah Press.

—— ed. 1995. *Beyond the Lavender Lexicon*. Newark, NJ: Gordon and Breach.

—— 1996. *Word's Out: Gay Men's English*. Minneapolis: University of Minnesota Press.

Leap, William L. and Rajend Mesthrie. 2000. Sociolinguistics and education. In Rajend Mesthrie, Joan Swan, Andrea Deumert and William L. Leap, eds, *Introducing Sociolinguistics*, pp. 354–83. Philadelphia, PA: John Benjamins.

Lehtonen, Mikko. 2000. *Cultural Analysis of Texts*. Newbury Park, CA: Sage. (Translated by Aija-Leena Ahonen and Kris Clarke.)

Leslau. Wolf. 1959. Taboo expressions in Ethiopia. *American Anthropologist* 61: 105–7.

Lewis, Diane E. 2001. The secret to success in business: schmooze. *Arizona Daily Star*, June 25.

Li, Wei. 1994. *Three Generations, Two Languages, One Family: Language Choice and Language Shift in a Chinese Community in Britain*. Clevedon, Avon: Multilingual Matters.

Lindenfield, Jacqueline. 1990. *Speech and Sociability at French Urban Marketplaces.* Amsterdam: John Benjamins.

Lipski, John. 1982. Spanish-English language switching in speech and literature: theories and models. *Bilingual Review* 9(3): 191–212.

Liu, Jun. 2001. *Asian Students' Classroom Communication Patterns in U.S. Universities: An Emic Perspective.* Westport, CT: Ablex.

Livia, Anna and Kira Hall, eds 1997. *Queerly Phrased: Language, Gender, and Sexuality.* Oxford: Oxford University Press.

Locke, Patricia. 1980. The nature of the socio-cultural aspects of American Indian language uses. Paper presented at the Conference on Research in American Indian Education, National Institute of Education, Washington, DC.

Lockwood, W. B. 1956. Word taboo in the language of the Faroese fisherman. *Transactions of the Philological Society*, pp. 1–24. London.

Loftus, Elizabeth. 1979. *Eyewitness Testimony.* Cambridge, MA: Harvard University Press.

Lyons, John, ed. 1970. *New Horizons in Linguistics.* Harmondsworth: Penguin.

Macaulay, Ronald K. S. 1975. Negative prestige, linguistic insecurity, and linguistic self-hatred. *Lingua* 36: 147–61.

Macaulay, Ronald K. S. and G. D. Trevelyan. 1973. Language, education, and employment in Glasgow. Final report to the SSRC. Edinburgh: The Scottish Council for Research in Education.

McLendon, Sally. 1978. How languages die: a social history of unstable bilingualism among the Eastern Pomo. In Margaret Langdon, Shirley Silver, and Kathryn Klar, eds, *American Indian and Indo-European Studies*, pp. 137–50. The Hague: Mouton.

Malinowski, Bronislaw. 1926. *Crime and Custom in Savage Society.* London: K. Paul, Trench, Trubner.

—— 1935. *Coral Gardens and Their Magic: A Study of Agricultural Rites in the Trobriand Islands. Vol II: The Language of Magic and Gardening.* New York: American.

—— 1939. The group and individual in functional analysis. *American Journal of Sociology.* (Reprinted in Paul Bohanan and Mary Glazer, eds (1973), *High Points in Anthropology*, pp. 275–93. New York: Alfred A. Knopf.)

Mallik, Bhaktiprasal. 1972. *Language of the Underworld of West Bengal.* Research Search 76. Calcutta: Sanskrit College. (Cited in M. A. K. Halliday (1978), *Language as Social Semiotic.* Baltimore, MD: University Park Press.)

Mao, LuMing Robert. 1994. Beyond politeness theory: "face" revisited and renewed. *Journal of Pragmatics* 21: 451–86.

Martin-Jones, Marilyn and Suzanne Romaine. 1986. Semilingualism: a half-baked theory of communicative competence. *Applied Linguistics* 7: 26–38.

Maskarinec, Gregory G. 1995. *The Rulings of the Night: An Ethnography of Nepalese Shaman Oral Texts.* Madison: University of Wisconsin Press.

Matsumota, Yoshiko. 1988. Reexamination of the universality of the face: politeness phenomena in Japanese. *Journal of Pragmatics* 12: 403–26.

Maurer, David W. 1940. The con man and his lingo. In *The Big Con.* Indianapolis, NY: Bobbs-Merrill.

Mayer, Mercer. 1969. *Frog, Where Are You?* New York: Dial Press.

Maynard, Douglas W. 1985. How children start arguments. *Language in Society* 14: 1–30.

Mead, Margaret. 1930. *Growing Up in New Guinea: A Comparative Study of Primitive Education*. New York: William Morrow.

—— 1955. Children and ritual in Bali. In Margaret Mead and Martha Wolfenstein, eds, *Childhood in Contemporary Cultures*, pp. 40–51. Chicago: University of Chicago Press.

Mehan, Hugh. 1997. The discourse of the illegal immigration debate: a case study in the politics of representation. *Discourse and Society* 8(2): 249–70.

Mendoza-Denton, Norma. 1997. Chicana/Mexicana identity and linguistic variation: an ethnographic and sociolinguistic study of gang affiliation in an urban high school. Dissertation, Stanford University.

Mesthrie, Rajend. 2000. Critical Sociolinguistics: approaches to language and power. In Rajend Mesthrie, Joan Swann, Andrea Deumert, and William L. Leap, *Introducing Sociolinguistics*, pp. 316–53. Philadelphia, PA: John Benjamins.

Michaels, Sarah. 1987. Text and context: a new approach to the study of classroom writing. *Discourse Processes* 10: 321–46.

Miller, Mary R. 1970. The language and language beliefs of Indian children. *Anthropological Linguistics* 12(2): 51–61.

Miller, Wick R. 1971. The death of language (or) Serendipity among the Shoshoni. *Anthropological Linguistics* 13(3): 114–20.

Milroy, James. 1992. *Linguistic Variation and Change: On the Historical Sociolinguistics of English*. Oxford: Blackwell.

Milroy, James and Lesley Milroy. 1997. Varieties and variation. In Florian Coulmas, ed., *The Handbook of Sociolinguistics*, pp. 47–64. Oxford: Blackwell.

Milroy, Lesley. 1987a. *Language and Social Networks*, second edition. Oxford: Basil Blackwell.

—— 1987b. *Observing and Analysing Natural Language: A Critical Account of Sociolinguistic Method*. Oxford: Basil Blackwell.

Mitchell-Kernan, Claudia and Keith T. Kernan. 1977. Pragmatics of directive choice among children. In Susan M. Ervin-Tripp and Claudia Mitchell-Kernan, eds, *Child Discourse*, pp. 189–208. New York: Academic Press.

Momaday, Scott N. 1976. *The Names*. New York: Harper & Row.

Moonwomon-Baird, Birch. 2000. What do lesbians do in the daytime? Recover. *Journal of Sociolinguistics* 4(3): 348–78.

Morford, Janet. 1997. Social indexicality in French pronominal address. *Journal of Linguistic Anthropology* 7(1): 3–37.

Morgan, Marcyliena. 1998. More than a mood or an attitude: discourse and verbal genres in African-American culture. In Salikoko S. Mufwene, John R. Rickford, Guy Bailey, and John Baugh, eds, *African American English: Structure, History, and Use*, pp. 251–81. London: Routledge.

Mueller, Claus. 1973. *The Politics of Communication: A Study in the Political Sociology of Language, Socialization and Legitimation*. Oxford: Oxford University Press.

Muysken, Pieter. 2000. *Bilingual Speech: A Typology of Code-Switching*. Cambridge: Cambridge University Press.

Myers-Scotton, Carol. 1993. *Duelling Languages: Grammatical Structure in Codeswitching*. Oxford: Clarendon.

——, ed. 1998. *Codes and Consequences: Choosing Linguistic Varieties*. Oxford: Oxford University Press.

Newman, Stanley. 1955. Vocabulary levels: Zuñi sacred and slang usage. *Southwestern Journal of Anthropology* 11: 345–54.

Nida, Eugene A. 1974. Translation. In Thomas A. Sebeok, ed., *Current Trends in Linguistics*, vol. 12. *Linguistics and Adjacent Arts and Sciences*, pp. 1045–68. The Hague: Mouton.

—— 1977. Translating means communicating: a sociolinguistic theory of translation. In Muriel Saville-Troike, ed., *Linguistics and Anthropology*, pp. 213–29. Washington, DC: Georgetown University Press.

Nishimura, Miwa. 1986. Intrasentential code-switching: the case of language assignment. In Jyotsna Vaid, ed., *Language Processing in Bilinguals: Psycholinguistic and Neuropsychological Perspectives*, pp. 123–43. Hillsdale, NJ: Lawrence Erlbaum.

—— 1997. *Japanese/English Code-Switching: Syntax and Pragmatics*. New York: Peter Lang.

Nwoye, Gregory O. 1985. Eloquent silence among the Igbo of Nigeria. In Deborah Tannen and Muriel Saville-Troike, eds, *Perspectives on Silence*, pp. 185–91. Norwood, NJ: Ablex.

O'Barr, William M. 1982. *Linguistic Evidence: Language, Power, and Strategy in the Courtroom*. New York: Academic Press.

Ochs, Elinor and Carolyn Taylor. 1992. Science at dinner. In Claire Kramsch and Sally McConnell-Ginet, eds, *Text and Context: Cross-Disciplinary Perspectives on Language Study*, pp. 29–45. Lexington, MA: D. C. Heath.

Oh, Hyun Hee Kim. 1988. Sociolinguistic and stylistic aspects of code-switching in Korean-English bilingual children: a naturalistic, longitudinal study. Dissertation, University of Illinois at Urbana-Champaign.

Ohannessian, Sirarpi, Charles A. Ferguson, and Edgar C. Polomé, eds 1975. *Language Surveys in Developing Nations: Papers and Reports on Sociolinguistic Surveys*. Arlington, VA: Center for Applied Linguistics.

Ohara, Yumiko. 2001. Finding one's voice in Japanese: a study of the pitch levels of non-native speakers. In Aneta Pavlenko, Adrian Blackledge, Ingrid Piller, and Marya Teutsch-Dwyer, eds, *Multilingualism, Second Language Learning, and Gender*. Berlin: Mouton de Gruyter.

Opler, Morris. 1941. *An Apache Life Way*. Chicago, IL: University of Chicago Press.

Ornstein-Galicia, Jacob, ed. 1984. *Form and Function in Chicano English*. Rowley, MA: Newbury House.

Owens, Mary. 1979. Solicitation techniques among English-speaking children in the US: the use of direct and indirect request forms. Dissertation, Georgetown University.

Pan, Zhi-xin and Mai-zeng Zhang. 2001. Hanyu qinshuyu kuozhan yongfa diaocha (Fictive use of Chinese kinship terms: a sociolinguistic study). *Yuyan Jiaoxue Yu Yanjiu* 2: 10–15.

Paoletti, Isabella. 1998. *Being an Older Woman: A Study in the Social Production of Identity*. Mahwah, NJ: Lawrence Erlbaum.

Paredes, Américo and Richard Bauman, eds 1972. *Toward New Perspectives in Folklore*. Austin: University of Texas Press.

Paulston, Christina Bratt. 1976. Pronouns of address in Swedish: social class semantics and a changing system. *Language in Society* 5(3): 359–86.

Penfield, Wilder. 1965. Conditioning the uncommitted cortex for language learning. *Brain* 88(4): 787–98.

Philips, Susan U. 1976. Some sources of cultural variability in the regulation of talk. *Language in Society* 5(1): 81–95.

—— 1982. The language socialization of lawyers: acquiring the "cant." In George Spindler, ed., *Doing the Ethnography of Schooling*, pp. 176–209. New York: Holt, Rinehart & Winston.

—— 1983a. An ethnographic approach to bilingual language proficiency assessment. In Charlene Rivera, ed., *An Ethnographic/Sociolinguistic Approach to Language Proficiency Assessment*, pp. 88–106. Clevedon, Avon: Multilingual Matters.

—— 1983b. *The Invisible Culture: Communication in Classroom and Community on the Warm Springs Indian Reservation*. London: Longman.

—— 2000. Power. *Journal of Linguistic Anthropology* 9(1–2): 191–6.

Piaget, Jean. 1926. *The Language and Thought of the Child*. New York: Harcourt, Brace & World.

Pike, Kenneth L. 1979. Social linguistics and bilingual education. *System* 7: 99–109.

Piller, Ingrid. 2001. Identity construction in multilingual advertising. *Language in Society* 30: 153–86.

Placencia, María E. 2001. Inequality in address behavior at public institutions in La Paz, Bolivia. *Anthropological Linguistics* 43(2): 198–217.

Pliskin, Karen L. 1987. *Silent Boundaries: Cultural Constraints on Sickness and Diagnosis of Iranians in Israel*. New Haven, CN: Yale University Press.

Podgórecki, Adam. 1973. "Second life" and its implications. Mimeo. (Cited in M. A. K. Halliday (1978), *Language as Social Semiotic*. Baltimore, MD: University Park Press.)

Polomé, Edgar C. 1975. Problems and techniques of a sociolinguistically-oriented survey: the case of the Tanzania Survey. In Sirarpi Ohannessian, Charles A. Ferguson, and Edgar C. Polomé, eds, *Language Surveys in Developing Nations: Papers and Reports on Sociolinguistic Surveys*, pp. 31–50. Arlington, VA: Center for Applied Linguistics.

Pomerantz, Anita and B. J. Fehr. 1997. Conversation analysis: an approach to the study of social interaction as sense making practices. In Teun A. van Dijk, ed., *Discourse as Social Interaction*, pp. 64–91. Thousand Oaks, CA: Sage.

Pound, Louise. 1936. American euphemisms for dying, death, and burial. *American Speech* 11(3): 195–202.

Powell, John W. 1877. *Introduction to the Study of Indian Languages*, first edition. Washington, DC: BAE, Smithsonian Institution.

—— 1880. *Introduction to the Study of Indian Languages*, second edition. Washington, DC: BAE, Smithsonian Institution.

Prelli, Lawrence J. 1989. The rhetorical construction of scientific ethos. In Herbert W. Simons, ed., *Rhetoric in the Human Sciences*, pp. 48–68. Newbury Park, CA: Sage.

Prior, Paul. 1998. *Writing/Disciplinarity: A Sociolinguistic Account of Literate Activity in the Academy*. Mahwah, NJ: Lawrence Erlbaum.

Pye, Clifton. 1986. Quiché Mayan speech to children. *Journal of Child Language* 13: 85–100.

Pyles, Thomas. 1959. Bible belt onomastics or some curiosities of anti-pedobaptist nomenclature. *Names* 7(2): 84–100.

Rafoth, Bennett A. 1990. The concept of discourse community: descriptive and explanatory adequacy. In Gesa Kirsch and Duane Roen, eds, *A Sense of Audience in Written Communication*, pp. 140–52. Newbury Park, CA: Sage.

Rafoth, Bennett A. and Donald L. Rubin, eds 1988. *The Social Construction of Written Communication*. Norwood, NJ: Ablex.

Rensch, Calvin R. 1977. Situación actual de los estudios lingüísticos de las lenguas de Oaxaca. Paper presented at a conference on the State of Anthropology in the State of Oaxaca, Mexico.

Retmono, R. 1967. The Javanese language before and after independence: an observation of a language in a changing society. Manuscript, University of Texas at Austin.

Rickford, John R. 1999. *African American Vernacular English*. Oxford: Blackwell.

Ries, Nancy. 1997. *Russian Talk: Culture and Conversation during Perestroika*. Ithaca, NY: Cornell University Press.

Robbins, Joel. 2001. God is nothing but talk: modernity, language, and prayer in a Papua New Guinea society. *American Anthropologist* 103(4): 901–12.

Robinson, W. Peter. 1979. Speech markers, and social class. In Klaus R. Scherer and Howard Giles, eds, *Social Markers in Speech*, pp. 211–49. Cambridge: Cambridge University Press.

Romaine, Suzanne. 1999. Changing attitudes to Hawai'i Creole English. In John R. Rickford and Suzanne Romaine, eds, *Creole Genesis, Attitudes and Discourse*, pp. 287–301. Amsterdam: John Benjamins.

Ruark, Jennifer K. 2000. Seeing children and hearing them, too. *The Chronicle of Higher Education*, November 17.

Rubin, Joan. 1968. *National Bilingualism in Paraguay*. The Hague: Mouton.

Rudner, William A. and Rochelle Butowsky. 1980. Ameslan signs used by the deaf gay community. *Sign Language Studies*, December.

Sacks, Harvey. 1992. *Lectures on Conversation*. 2 vols. Oxford: Blackwell.

Sacks, Harvey, Emanuel A. Schegloff, and Gail Jefferson. 1974. A simplest systematics for the organization of turn-taking for conversation. *Language* 50(4): 696–735.

Salmond, Anne. 1975. Mama makes the man: a look at Maori oratory and politics. In Maurice Bloch, ed., *Political Language and Oratory in Traditional Society*, pp. 45–64. New York: Academic Press.

Sanches, Mary and Barbara Kirshenblatt-Gimblett. 1971. Child language and children's traditional speech play. Texas working papers in sociolinguistics No. 5. (Reprinted in Barbara Kirshenblatt-Gimblett, ed. (1976), *Speech Play: Research and Resources for the Study of Linguistic Creativity*, pp. 65–110. Philadelphia: University of Pennsylvania Press.)

Santa Ana, Otto and Claudia Parodi. 1998. Modeling the speech community: configuration and variable types in the Mexican Spanish setting. *Language in Society* 27: 23–51.

Sapir, Edward. 1915. Abnormal types of speech in Nootka. Geological Survey Memoir 62 Anthropological Series No. 5. Ottawa, Canada: Government Printing Bureau. (Reprinted in David G. Mandelbaum, ed. (1958), *Selected Writings of*

Edward Sapir in Language, Culture, Personality, pp. 179–96. Berkeley: University of California Press.)

—— 1994. *The Psychology of Culture.* (Reconstructed and edited by Judith T. Irvine.) Berlin: Mouton de Gruyter.

Saville-Troike, Muriel. 1978. *A Guide to Culture in the Classroom.* Rosslyn, VA: National Clearinghouse for Bilingual Education.

—— 1984. What *really* matters in second language learning for academic achievement. *TESOL Quarterly* 17: 199–219.

—— 1985. The place of silence in an integrated theory of communication. In Deborah Tannen and Muriel Saville-Troike, eds, *Perspectives on Silence*, pp. 3–18. Norwood, NJ: Ablex.

—— 1986. Children's dispute and negotiation strategies: a naturalistic approach. In Joshua A. Fishman et al., eds, *The Fergusonian Impact Vol. I: From Phonology to Society*, pp. 135–52. Berlin: Mouton de Gruyter.

—— 1987. Dilingual discourse: communication without a common language. *Linguistics* 25: 81–106.

—— 1988. A note on men's and women's speech in Koasati. *International Journal of American Linguistics* 54: 421–2.

—— 1992. Cultural maintenance and "vanishing" languages. In Claire Kramsch and Sally McConnell-Ginet, eds, *Text and Context: Cross-Disciplinary Perspectives on Language Study*, pp. 148–55. New York: D. C. Heath.

—— 1996. Development of the inflected verb in Navajo child language. In Eloise Jelenick, Sally Midgette, Keren Rice, and Leslie Saxon, eds, *Athapaskan Language Studies*, pp. 137–92. Albuquerque: University of New Mexico Press.

—— 2000. Linguistics and politics. *Southern Journal of Linguistics* 24(1): 1–16.

Saville-Troike, Muriel, Erica McClure, and Mary Fritz. 1984. Communicative tactics in children's second language acquisition. In Fred R. Eckman, Lawrence H. Bell, and Diane Nelson, eds, *Universals of Second Language Acquisition*, pp. 60–71. Rowley, MA: Newbury House.

Saville-Troike, Muriel, Junlin Pan, and Ludmila Dutkova. 1995. Differential effects of L2 on children's L1 development/attrition. *Southwest Journal of Linguistics* 14(1–2): 125–49.

Schegloff, Emanuel A. 1968. Sequencing in conversational openings. *American Anthropologist* 70: 1075–95.

—— 1997. Whose text? Whose context? *Discourse and Society* 9(3): 413–16.

Scherer, Klaus R. 1979. Personality markers in speech. In Klaus R. Scherer and Howard Giles, eds, *Social Markers in Speech*, pp. 147–209. Cambridge: Cambridge University Press.

Schiefflin, Bambi B. 1990. *The Give and Take of Everyday Life: Language Socialization of Kaluli Children.* Cambridge: Cambridge University Press.

Schiffrin, Deborah. 1984. Jewish argument as sociability. *Language in Society* 13: 311–35.

—— 1994. *Approaches to Discourse.* Oxford: Blackwell.

Scollon, Ronald and Suzanne B. K. Scollon. 1979a. *Linguistic Convergence: An Ethnography of Speaking at Fort Chipewyan, Alberta.* New York: Academic Press.

—— 1979b. Literacy as interethnic communication: An Athabascan case. Sociolinguistics working paper No. 59. Austin, TX: Southwest Educational Development Laboratory.

—— 2001. *Intercultural Communication: A Discourse Approach*, second edition. Oxford: Blackwell.

Scribner, Sylvia and Michael Cole. 1973. Cognitive consequences of formal and informal education. *Science* 182: 553–9.

Searle, John. 1969. *Speech Acts*. Cambridge: Cambridge University Press.

—— 1977a. A classification of illocutionary acts. In A. Rogers, R. Wall, and J. P. Murphy, eds, *Proceedings of the Texas Conference on Performatives, Presuppositions, and Implicatures*, pp. 27–45. Arlington, VA: Center for Applied Linguistics.

—— 1977b. Indirect speech acts. In Peter Cole and Jerry L. Morgan, eds, *Syntax and Semantics: Speech Acts*, vol. 3, pp. 59–82. New York: Academic Press.

Selinker, Larry. 1972. Interlanguage. *International Review of Applied Linguistics* 10: 209–31.

Shearer, Lloyd. 1988. Intelligence report. *Parade Magazine*, January 10.

Sherzer, Joel. 1974. *Namakke, sunmakke, dormakke*: three types of Cuna speech event. In Richard Bauman and Joel Sherzer, eds, *Explorations in the Ethnography of Speaking*, pp. 263–82. Cambridge: Cambridge University Press.

—— 1975. Ethnography of speaking. Manuscript, University of Texas at Austin.

—— 1983. *Kuna Ways of Speaking: An Ethnographic Perspective*. Austin: University of Texas Press.

Shimanoff, Susan B. 1980. *Communication Rules: Theory and Research*. Beverly Hills, CA: Sage.

Shorrab, Ghazi. 1986. Bilingual patterns of an Arabic-English speech Community. *International Journal of the Sociology of Language* 61: 79–88.

Shuy, Roger W. 1974. Problems of communication in the cross-cultural medical interview. Texas working papers in sociolinguistics No. 19. Austin, TX: Southwest Educational Development Laboratory.

—— 1975. Code-switching in *Lady Chatterley's Lover*. Texas working papers in sociolinguistics No. 22. Austin, TX: Southwest Educational Development Laboratory.

—— 1995. How a judge's *voir dire* can teach a jury what to say. *Discourse and Society* 6(2): 207–22.

Shuy, Roger W., Joan C. Baratz, and Walt Wolfram. 1969. Sociolinguistic forces in speech identification. NIMHR Project Report. Washington, DC: Center for Applied Linguistics.

Silverman, Philip and Robert J. Maxwell. 1978. How do I respect thee? Let me count the ways: deference towards elderly men and women. *Behavior Science Research* 13(2): 269–79.

Simpson, Rita C. 1997. Metapragmatic discourse and the ideology of impolite pronouns in Thai. *Journal of Linguistic Anthropology* 7(1): 38–62.

Sjoberg, Andrée F. 1962. Coexistent phonemic systems in Telugu: a socio-cultural perspective. *Word* 18(3): 269–79.

Skopek, Lucienne. 1975. Sociolinguistic aspects of the medical interview. Dissertation, Georgetown University.

Slobin, Dan I., ed. 1967. *A Field Manual for Cross-Cultural Study of the Acquisition of Communicative Competence* (second draft). Berkeley: University of California.

Smal-Stocki, Roman. 1950. Taboo on animal names in Ukranian. *Language* 26: 489–93.

Smith, Philip M. 1979. Sex markers in speech. In Klaus R. Scherer and Howard Giles, eds, *Social Markers in Speech*, pp. 109–46. Cambridge: Cambridge University Press.

Smith, Riley. 1973. Some phonological rules in the Negro speech of East Texas. Dissertation, University of Texas at Austin.

Snow, Catherine E. 1972. Mothers' speech to children learning language. *Child Development* 43: 549–65.

Sommer, Gabriele. 1995. *Ethnographie de Sprachwechsels: Sozialer Wandel und Sprachverhalten bei den Yeyi (Botswana)*. Küln: Rüdiger Köppe.

Sorenson, Arthur P., Jr. 1967. Multilingualism in the Northwest Amazon. *American Anthropologist* 69: 670–84.

Spolsky, Bernard. 1971. Navajo language maintenance III: accessibility of school and town as a factor in language shift. Navajo Reading Study Progress Report No. 14. Albuquerque: University of New Mexico.

—— 1994. Behind the ATSP myth. Plenary address at the American Association for Applied Linguistics Conference, Baltimore, MD.

Spolsky, Bernard and Patricia Irvine. 1982. Sociolinguistic aspects of the acceptance of literacy in the vernacular. In Florence Barkin, Elizabeth A. Brandt, and Jacob Ornstein-Galicia, eds, *Bilingualism and Language Contact*, pp. 73–9. New York: Teachers College Press.

Spradley, James P. 1979. *The Ethnographic Interview*. New York: Holt, Rinehart & Winston.

Sridhar, S. and K. Sridhar. 1980. The syntax and psycholinguistics of bilingual code-mixing. *Canadian Journal of Psychology/ Revue Canadienne de Psychologie* 34: 407–16.

Steffensen, Margaret S., Chitra Joag-Dev, and Richard C. Anderson. 1979. A cross-cultural perspective on reading comprehension. *Reading Research Quarterly* 1: 10–29.

Stoller, Paul. 1986. The reconstruction of ethnography. In Phyllis Pease Chock and June R. Wyman, eds, *Discourse and the Social Life of Meaning*, pp. 51–74. Washington, DC: Smithsonian Institution.

Strathern, Andrew. 1975. Veiled speech in Mount Hagen. In Maurice Bloch, ed., *Political Language and Oratory in Traditional Society*, pp. 185–203. New York: Academic Press.

Subrahamian, K. 1978. My Mrs. is Indian. *Anthropological Linguistics* 20(6): 295–6.

Sun, Hao. 1998. Telephone conversations in Chinese and English: a comparative study across languages and functions. Dissertation, University of Arizona.

Swedlund, Eric. 2002. $4M project at UA targets deception. *Arizona Daily Star*, January 23.

Tabouret-Keller, Andrée. 1972. A contribution to the sociological study of language maintenance and shift. In Joshua A. Fishman, ed., *Advances in the Sociology of Language*, vol. 2, pp. 364–76. The Hague: Mouton.

Talmy, Leonard. 1976. Communicative aims and means: a synopsis. In Working papers on language universals No. 20, Stanford University.

Taminian, Lucine. 2001. Playing with words: the ethnography of poetic genres in Yemen. *Anthropology News* 42(5): 50.

Tammivaara, Julie and D. Scott Enright. 1986. On eliciting information: dialogues with child informants. *Anthropology and Education Quarterly* 17: 218–38.

Tannen, Deborah. 1979a. Processes and consequences of conversational style. Dissertation, University of California at Berkeley.

—— 1979b. What's in a frame? Surface evidence for underlying expectations. In Roy Freedle, ed., *New Dimensions in Discourse Processing*, pp. 137–81. Norwood, NJ: Ablex.

—— 1980. A comparative analysis of oral narrative structures. Athenian Greek and American English. In Wallace L. Chafe, ed., *The Pear Stories: Cognitive, Cultural and Linguistic Aspects of Narrative Production*, pp. 51–87. Norwood, NJ: Ablex.

—— 1981. Indirectness in discourse: ethnicity as conversation style. *Discourse Processes* 4(3): 221–38.

—— 1993a. *Framing in Discourse*. Oxford: Oxford University Press.

——, ed. 1993b. *Gender and Conversational Interaction*. Oxford: Oxford University Press.

Tannen, Deborah and Muriel Saville-Troike. 1985. *Perspectives on Silence*. Norwood, NJ: Ablex.

Thompson, Lawrence C. 1978. Control in Salish grammar. Paper presented to the American Anthropological Association, Los Angeles.

Thompson, Roger M. 1971. Language loyalty in Austin, Texas: a study of a bilingual neighborhood. Dissertation, University of Texas at Austin.

Ting-Toomey, Stella, ed. 1994. *The Challenge of Facework: Cross-Cultural and Interpersonal Issues*. Albany, NY: State University of New York Press.

Titscher, Stefan, Michael Meyer, Ruth Wodak, and Eva Vetter. 2000. *Methods of Text and Discourse Analysis*. Thousand Oaks, CA: Sage.

Tiwary, K. M. 1975. Tuneful weeping: a mode of communication. Texas working papers in sociolinguistics No. 27. Austin, TX: Southwest Educational Development Laboratory.

Torres, Lourdes. 1997. *Puerto Rican Discourse: A Sociolinguistic Study of a New York Suburb*. Mahwah, NJ: Lawrence Erlbaum.

Treichler, Paula A., Richard M. Frankel, Cheris Kramarae, Kathleen Zoppi, and Howard B. Beckman. 1984. Problems and problems: power relationships in a medical encounter. In Cheris Kramarae, Muriel Schulz, and William M. O'Barr, eds, *Language and Power*, pp. 62–88. Beverly Hills, CA: Sage.

Trew, Tony. 1982. "What the papers say": linguistic variation and ideological difference. In Braj B. Kachru, ed., *The Other Tongue: English across Cultures*, pp. 117–56. Urbana: University of Illinois Press.

Troike, Rudolph C. 1970. Receptive competence, productive competence, and performance. In James E. Alatis, ed., *Linguistics and the Teaching of Standard English to Speakers of Other Languages or Dialects*, pp. 63–74. Washington, DC: Georgetown University Press.

—— 1978. Research evidence for the effectiveness of bilingual education. *NABE Journal* 3(1): 13–24.

—— 1990. Reconsidering bilingual education: toward a consensus in the national interest. In Gary Imhoff, ed., *Learning in Two Languages: From Conflict to*

Consensus in the Reorganization of Schools, pp. 261–83. New Brunswick, NJ: Transaction Books.

Troike, Rudolph C. and Muriel Saville-Troike. 1988. Video recording for linguistic fieldwork. *Notes on Linguistics* 37: 44–51.

Trudgill, Peter. 1974. *The Social Differentiation of English in Norwich*. Cambridge: Cambridge University Press.

—— 1975. Sex, cover prestige, and linguistic change in the urban British English of Norwich. In Barrie Thorne and Nancy Henley, eds, *Language and Sex: Difference and Dominance*, pp. 88–104. Rowley, MA: Newbury House.

—— 2000. *Sociolinguistics: An Introduction to Language and Society*, fourth edition. London: Penguin.

Tsitsipis, Luka D. 1995. The coding of linguistic ideology in Arvanítika (Albanian) language shift: congruent and contradictory discourse. *Anthropological Linguistics* 37(4): 541–77.

Tsuda, Aoi. 1984. *Sales Talk in Japan and the United States*. Washington, DC: Georgetown University Press.

Turnbull, Colin M. 1961. *The Forest People*. London: Chatto & Windus.

Tyler, Stephen A. 1972. Context and alternation in Koya kinship terminology. In John J. Gumperz and Dell Hymes, eds, *Directions in Sociolinguistics: The Ethnography of Communication*, pp. 251–69. New York: Holt, Rinehart & Winston.

Valdés, Guadalupe. 1977. The sociolinguistics of Chicano literature: toward an analysis of the role and function of language alternation in contemporary bilingual poetry. *Point of Contact* 1(4): 30–9.

—— 1996. *Con Respecto: Bridging the Distance Between Culturally Diverse Families and Schools*. New York: Teachers College Press.

van Dijk, Teun A. 1993. Principles of critical discourse analysis. *Discourse and Society* 4(2): 249–83.

Van Riper, William R. 1979. Usage preferences of men and women: *did, came*, and *saw*. *American Speech* 54(4): 279–84.

Vihman, Marilyn May. 1985. Language differentiation by the bilingual infant. *Journal of Child Language* 12: 297–324.

von Humboldt, Wilhelm. 1836. *Über die Vershiedenhiet des menschlichen Sprachbaues und ihren Einfluss auf die geistige Entwickelung des Menschengeschlects*. Royal Academy of Sciences of Berlin. (Reprinted as *Linguistic Variability and Intellectual Development* (1971), translated by George C. Buck and Frithjof A. Raben. Miami, FL: University of Miami Press.)

von Raffler-Engle, Walburga. 1977. The nonverbal adjustment of children's communicative style. In B. N. Laria and D. E. Gulstad, eds, *Papers for the 1977 Mid-America Linguistic Conference*. Columbus: University of Missouri.

von Raffler-Engle, Walburga and Catherine Rea. 1978. The influence of child's communicative style of the conversational behavior of the adult. Paper presented at the First International Congress for the Study of Child Language, Tokyo.

Waas, Margit and Bondi Beach. 1993. Loss of first language skills in the community: intermediate state. *Language Problems and Language Planning* 17(3): 225–37.

Walker, Anne Graffam. 1985. The two faces of silence: the effect of witness hesitancy on lawyers' impressions. In Deborah Tannen and Muriel Saville-Troike, eds, *Perspectives on Silence*, pp. 55–75. Norwood, NJ: Ablex.

Wallat, Cynthia. 1981. Communicative competence. Paper presented at the National Institute of Education Language Proficiency Assessment Symposium, Warrenton, VA.

Wang, Peter Chin-tang. 1977. The effect of East/West cultural differences on oral language development. Paper presented at the Chinese Languages Teacher's Association, San Francisco.

Watkins, Laurel J. 1979. Pronominal prefixes in Kiowa. Paper presented to the American Anthropological Association, Cincinnati, OH.

Watson, Graham and Robert M. Seiler, eds 1992. *Text in Context: Contributions to Ethnomethodology*. Newbury Park, CA: Sage.

Weininger, Jane C. G. 1978. Communicative strategy among children in a bilingual school environment (K-3). In James E. Redden, ed., *Proceedings of the Second International Conference on Frontiers in Language Proficiency and Dominance Testing*, Occasional Papers on Linguistics No. 3, pp. 117–25. Carbondale: Southern Illinois University.

Weinreich, Uriel. 1953. *Languages in Contact: Findings and Problems*. Publications of the Linguistic Circle of New York No. 1. (Published by Mouton in 1970.)

Wetherell, Margaret. 1998. Positioning and interpretive repertoires: conversation analysis and post-structuralism in dialogue. *Discourse and Society* 9(3): 387–412.

Whitbourne, Susan Krauss, Sarah Culgin, and Erin Cassidy. 1995. Evaluation of infantilizing intonation and content of speech directed at the aged. *International Journal of Aging and Human Development* 41(2): 109–16.

White, J. B. ca. 1870. A history of the Apache Indians of Arizona territory. Unpublished in the archives of the Smithsonian Institution. BAE ms. 179.

Whorf, Benjamin Lee. 1940. Science and linguistics. *Technological Review* 42: 229–31, 247–8. (Reprinted in John B. Carroll, ed. (1956), *Language, Thought, and Reality: Selected Writings of Benjamin Lee Whorf*, pp. 207–19. New York: Wiley.)

Widdowson, H. G. 1998. The theory and practice of Critical Discourse Analysis. *Applied Linguistics* 19(1): 136–51.

Wierzbicka, Anna. 1985. A semantic metalanguage for a crosscultural comparison of speech acts and speech genres. *Language in Society* 14: 491–514.

Wilce, James M. 1998. *Eloquence in Trouble: The Poetics and Politics of Complaint in Rural Bangladesh*. Oxford: Oxford University Press.

Witherspoon, Gary. 1977. *Language and Art in the Navajo Universe*. Ann Arbor: University of Michigan Press.

Wodak, Ruth. 1996. *Disorders of Discourse*. London: Longman.

Wodak-Engel, Ruth. 1984. Determination of guilt: discourse in the courtroom. In Cheris Kramarae, Muriel Schulz, and William M. O'Barr, eds, *Language and Power*, pp. 89–100. Beverly Hills, CA: Sage.

Wolfram, Walt. 1973. *Sociolinguistic Aspects of Assimilation: Puerto Rican English in East Harlem*. Washington, DC: Center for Applied Linguistics.

Woodward, James C., Jr. 1976. Black southern signing. *Language in Society* 5(2): 211–18.

Woolard, Kathryn A. 1987. Code-switching and comedy in Catalonia. *IPRA Papers in Pragmatics* 1: 106–22.

—— 1998. Simultaneity and bivalency as strategies in bilingualism. *Journal of Linguistic Anthropology* 8(1): 3–29.

Wright, Richard. 1975. Review of Robbins Burling (1973), *English in Black and White* (New York: Holt, Rinehart & Winston); and William Labov (1972), *Language in the Inner City: Studies in the Black English Vernacular* (Philadelphia: University of Pennsylvania Press). *Language in Society* 4(2): 185–98.

Yankah, Kwesi. 1995. *Speaking for the Chief: Okyeame and the Politics of Akan Royal Oratory*. Bloomington: Indiana University Press.

Young, R. L. 1988. Language maintenance and language shift in Taiwan. *Journal of Multilingual and Multicultural Development* 9(4): 323–38.

Young, Robert W. 1967. *English as a Second Language for Navajos*. Albuquerque, NM: Albuquerque Area Office, Bureau of Indian Affairs.

Yu, Ning. 2001. What does our face mean to us? *Pragmatics and Cognition* 9(1): 1–36.

Yurchak, Alexei. 2000. Privatize your name: symbolic work in a post-Soviet linguistic market. *Journal of Sociolinguistics* 3/4: 406–34.

Zentella, Ana Celia. 1997. *Growing up Bilingual: Puerto Rican Children in New York*. Oxford: Oxford University Press.

Zimmerman, Don H. and Candace West. 1975. Sex roles, interruptions, and silences in conversation. In Barrie Thorne and Nancy Henley, eds, *Language and Sex: Difference and Dominance*, pp. 105–29. Rowley, MA: Newbury House.

Index of Languages

General Index